Wissenschaftliche Untersuchungen zum Neuen Testament · 2. Reihe

Herausgeber/Editor

Jörg Frey (Zürich)

Mitherausgeber/Associate Editors

Markus Bockmuehl (Oxford) · James A. Kelhoffer (Uppsala)
Tobias Nicklas (Regensburg) · Janet Spittler (Charlottesville, VA)
J. Ross Wagner (Durham, NC)

609

Authorial Fictions and Attributions in the Ancient Mediterranean

Edited by

Chance E. Bonar and Julia D. Lindenlaub

Mohr Siebeck

Chance E. Bonar, born 1993; 2023 PhD in Religion at Harvard University; Postdoctoral Fellow at the Center for the Humanities at Tufts University and Lecturer in Advanced Greek at Harvard Divinity School.
orcid.org/0000-0002-3590-729X

Julia D. Lindenlaub, born 1992; 2020 PhD in New Testament and Christian Origins at the University of Edinburgh; Content Manager for Academic Journals at Cambridge University Press.
orcid.org/0000-0001-5695-8179

ISBN 978-3-16-161782-9 / eISBN 978-3-16-163561-8
DOI 10.1628/978-3-16-163561-8

ISSN 0340-9570 / eISSN 2568-7484
(Wissenschaftliche Untersuchungen zum Neuen Testament, 2. Reihe)

The Deutsche Nationalbibliothek lists this publication in the Deutsche Nationalbibliographie; detailed bibliographic data are available at *https://dnb.dnb.de.*

© 2024 Mohr Siebeck Tübingen, Germany. www.mohrsiebeck.com

This book may not be reproduced, in whole or in part, in any form (beyond that permitted by copyright law) without the publisher's written permission. This applies particularly to reproductions, translations and storage and processing in electronic systems.

The book was typeset by Martin Fischer in Tübingen using Minion typeface, printed on non-aging paper by AZ Druck und Datentechnik in Kempten.

Printed in Germany.

Table of Contents

JULIA D. LINDENLAUB and CHANCE E. BONAR
Introduction to Authorial Fictions and Attributions in the Ancient
Mediterranean 1

ROBYN FAITH WALSH
The *Epistle to the Laodiceans* and the Art of Tradition 13

CLAIRE RACHEL JACKSON
Authorial Fictions, Phoenician Paradigms, and the Reception of Achilles
Tatius' *Leucippe and Clitophon* in the *Lives* of Galaction and Episteme 39

REBECCA SCHARBACH WOLLENBERG
Outside Bible Readers as an Author Character in Rabbinic Literature:
Using Attribution to Preserve and Contain Subversive Positions 71

JULIA D. LINDENLAUB
The Fictive Author and the Reading Community in the *Apocryphon
of James* (NHC I,2) 85

NICHOLAS BAKER-BRIAN
Writing Truth and Secrets: Authorship and the Legitimising Role
of Apocalyptic in Manichaeism 105

CHANCE E. BONAR
Coauthorial Attribution and the *Teachings of Silvanus* (NHC VII,4) 127

ELENA DUGAN
Melito's Enoch: Anti-Judaism and the Transmission
of the Pseudepigrapha 151

EMILY MITCHELL
From Beyond the Grave: 'Ventriloquizing' the Enslaved and the
Emancipated in Latin Verse Epitaphs 177

VI   *Table of Contents*

JEREMIAH COOGAN
Imagining Gospel Authorship: Anonymity, Collaboration,
and Monography in a Pluriform Corpus 203

SOPHUS HELLE
Janus-Faced Authors: Production or Presentation? 225

Contributors 241

Index of Ancient Sources 243
Index of Modern Authors 251
Index of Subjects 257

Introduction to Authorial Fictions and Attributions in the Ancient Mediterranean

JULIA D. LINDENLAUB and CHANCE E. BONAR

This edited volume began as a conversation over Twitter between ourselves and Eva Mroczek, attesting to the ability of social media – when in the right hands – to connect academics over long distances and be used effectively to collaborate on shared topics of interest. That Twitter conversation became a series of four colloquia between September and December of 2021, hosted by the Bible and Religions of the Ancient Near East Collective (BRANE) and taking place over Zoom. The colloquia, also entitled "Authorial Fictions and Attributions in the Ancient Mediterranean," were an opportunity both to highlight the important contributions on attribution between our distinct academic silos and to provide a platform for new scholarship in early Judaism, early Christianity, classics, and Near Eastern studies on authorship and attribution. Some of those presentations have made their way in revised form into this collection, while others were solicited from audience members of the colloquia.

In gathering these contributions, we have made a point to prioritize the work of early career researchers across a variety of fields that study the ancient world. This was done, in large part, to give a voice to the next generation of scholars who will be teaching and producing scholarship in a landscape different than their 20th-century-trained predecessors: a landscape with shrinking and disappearing departments, fewer permanent or stable academic jobs, and further contingency whether or not one is on the tenure track. As early career researchers continue to pursue scholarship and employment in, parallel to, or outside of the professoriate, we hope that this volume can represent the type of interdisciplinary collaboration that will help us sustain each other's subdisciplines in the twenty-first century.

This volume emerged with the support of multiple scholars who helped shape the colloquia upon which it is partially based. We are particularly grateful to Karen King, Hindy Najman, Irene Peirano Garrison, Tom Geue, Eva Mroczek, and Benjamin Wright for allowing us to center much of our theoretical discussion of authorship, author-function, and attribution around their work. Additionally, we are grateful to the many scholars who responded to the colloquia's reading list and those who offered new research in ancient Mediterranean authorship: Joseph Howley, Liv Ingeborg Lied, Roberta Mazza, Hugo Méndez, Patricia Rosenmeyer, Alin Suciu, Olivia Stewart Lester, Natalie Dohrmann, James

Walters, Tim Whitmarsh, Candida Moss, Sarah Rollens, Annette Yoshiko Reed, Chance McMahon, Marieke Dohnt, and David Brakke. Tobias Nicklas and Janet Spittler have been central in shepherding this project through to publication with Mohr Siebeck.

Particularly in the fields of classics and biblical studies, there is a long history of the study of authorship and attribution that focused on determining and confirming the "real" or "historical" author. This is especially true for the concern of Christian biblical scholars and theologians over the authorship of New Testament literature, whose value to contemporary Christians partially depended on the ability to confirm that the apostles themselves (or, at least, the apostles' colleagues or successors) produced the texts and approved of their contents. For example, Samuel Tregelles's 1881 *The Historic Evidence of the Authorship and Transmission of the Books of the New Testament* was dedicated to just such a goal, arguing that he could demonstrate apostolic authorship and thus eliminate concern that anonymous texts (e.g., the gospels) or potentially pseudonymous texts (e.g., 2 Peter) were a threat to one's faith.[1] Likewise, determining the "real author" via philological and historical analysis has been important for determining whether an ancient text attributed to Vergil or Ovid, for example, should be considered part of the classical canon.[2] Such authorial attributions and our modern evaluations of them determine in what settings, how often, and in what ways ancient Mediterranean texts are read, studied, or used to inform people's lives. Such work has historically focused on delimiting a particular list of acceptable authors and texts worth reading in both biblical studies and classics. As historian of late antiquity Ellen Muehlberger put it in her examination of authorship and the "church fathers," fields like classics and early Christian studies have historically been organized around and bound by the concept of authorship and particular sets of authorial figures. Consequently, the types of knowledge we seek (and produce) are tied to authors, and "texts without a secure association to a known author stay dropped at the end of the hallway, unused."[3] Even those texts that have a secure association to a known author may be attached to the *wrong* author according to some scholars, thus making them less valuable in the eyes of some for being utilized for particular types of historical, literary, and religious work.

---

[1] Samuel Prideaux Tregelles, *The Historic Evidence of the Authorship and Transmission of the Books of the New Testament: A Lecture*, 2nd ed. (London: Samuel Bagster, 1881); cf. Joseph Agar Beet, *The New Testament: Its Authorship, Date and Worth* (London: Robert Culley, 1908).

[2] For a fuller examination, see Markus Stachon, *Tractavi monumentum aere perennius: Untersuchungen zu vergilischen und ovidischen Pseudepigraphen*, Bochumer altertumswissenschaftliches Colloquium 97 (Trier: WVT, 2014).

[3] Ellen Muehlberger, "On Authors, Fathers, and Holy Men," *Marginalia*, 20 Sept 2015, https://themarginaliareview.com/on-authors-fathers-and-holy-men-by-ellen-muehlberger/.

Introduction to Authorial Fictions and Attributions in the Ancient Mediterranean 3

Nevertheless, humanistic disciplines have shifted in recent decades in order to reexamine texts left on the outskirts (or that remain in the center of our canons) and have asked what work authorship might do beyond merely assigning otherwise-wandering texts to their "correct" authors and producing clean, orthonymous canons. As scholars have begun to read more broadly across ancient Mediterranean literature and between texts traditionally siloed into distinct academic disciplines, topics like the function of anonymity and pseudonymity have made their way to the forefront of discussions of ancient authorship.[4] In particular, the work of Roland Barthes and Michel Foucault in the 1960s and 1970s set the stage for new investigations into ancient authorship. Barthes's famous essay "The Death of the Author" questioned the centrality of the figure of the author to the meaning of a text, arguing that literary scholarship was often "tyrannically centered" on the author and their biography, often to the point of overlooking how the reader is involved where a text's meaning is created.[5] While not erasing the author altogether but rather centering them as a character worthy of analysis, Foucault's "What is an Author?" urged scholars to question the purpose that an author plays within a text: Why does it matter who the author is, and what role(s) do they play? Foucault suggests that "the author's name manifests the appearance of a certain discursive set and indicates the status of this discourse within a society and a culture" – it marks off the edges of a text, exists in relation to the text, and helps contextualize a text within a broader literary world.[6] Such an analysis of "author-function" allowed for new interpretative possibilities, moving scholarly examination away from trying to uncover the "real" author of a text and toward asking how an authorial figure does particular types of identifiable work for a text, its audience, and its writers.

Since then, much scholarship on authorship in the ancient Mediterranean has focused more on authorship as a *concept* or a *function* that has a history of its own

---

[4] Kurt Aland, "The Problem of Anonymity and Pseudonymity in Christian Literature of the First Two Centuries," in *The Authorship and Integrity of the New Testament: Some Recent Studies*, ed. Kurt Aland (London: SPCK, 1965), 1–13. Aland especially critiques New Testament scholarship of the mid-twentieth century for treating the New Testament as a distinct and separate corpus from other Mediterranean literature of the first and second centuries and calls for greater comparison across classical and near eastern corpora.

[5] Roland Barthes, "The Death of the Author," in *The Book History Reader*, ed. David Finkelstein and Alistair McCleery, 2nd ed. (London: Routledge, 2006), 277–80; cf. idem, "Theory of the Text," in *Untying the Text: A Post-Structuralist Reader*, ed. Robert Young (London: Routledge, 1981), 31–47. This is developed further by Stanley Fish (*Is There a Text in This Class: The Authority of Interpretive Communities* [Cambridge, MA: Harvard University Press, 1980]) through the concept of "interpretive communities" that shape and guide a reader's interpretative approach and the horizon of interpretative possibilities.

[6] Michel Foucault, "What is an Author?" in *The Foucault Reader*, ed. Paul Rabinow (New York: Pantheon, 1984), 107.

4   *Julia D. Lindenlaub and Chance E. Bonar*

and flexibility in how it is deployed.[7] The relationship between authorship and a text's authority has been one traditional avenue of research, since authorial attribution has been treated as a manner by which a writer can authorize or make valuable their text within a specific community.[8] The study of pseudepigraphy and forgeries especially has taken off in recent decades, with emphases both on the detection of forged literary artifacts and on reformulating traditional associations between pseudepigraphy, deceit, and creative reworking of earlier literary worlds or characters.[9] Scholars have turned their attention heavily to how attribution allows a text to be slotted into a distinct storyworld or literary tradition, often attaching a text to other texts associated with authorial names like Moses, Solomon, or John.[10] Additionally, scholarship on how theories of author-

---

[7] This overview is not meant to overlook the important work still happening across these fields that are interested in uncovering the "real author" behind a text. For example, see: Charles E. Hill, *From the Lost Teaching of Polycarp: Identifying Irenaeus's Apostolic Presbyter and the Author of* Ad Diognetum, Wissenschaftliche Untersuchungen zum Neuen Testament 186 (Tübingen: Mohr Siebeck, 2006).

[8] Egbert J. Bakker, ed., *Authorship and Greek Song: Authority, Authenticity, and Performance* (Leiden: Brill, 2017); Roberta Berardi et al., eds., *Defining Authorship, Debating Authority: Problems of Authority from Classical Antiquity to the Renaissance* (Berlin: De Gruyter, 2020). As a challenge to the relationship between authorial authenticity and authority, see Mark Letteney, "Authenticity and Authority: The Case for Dismantling a Dubious Correlation," in *Rethinking 'Authority' in Late Antiquity: Authorship, Law, and Transmission in Jewish and Christian Tradition*, ed. A. J. Berkovitz and Mark Letteney (London: Routledge, 2018), 33–56.

[9] For an example of recent detection of modern forgeries, see Kipp Davis et al., "Nine Dubious 'Dead Sea Scrolls' Fragments from the Twenty-First Century," *Dead Sea Discoveries* 24 (2017): 189–228. On rethinking pseudepigraphy, see Irene Peirano Garrison, *The Rhetoric of the Roman Fake: Latin Pseudepigrapha in Context* (Cambridge: Cambridge University Press, 2012); Tony Burke, ed., *Fakes, Forgeries, and Fictions: Writing Ancient and Modern Christian Apocrypha: Proceedings from the 2015 York Christian Apocrypha Symposium* (Eugene, OR: Cascade, 2017); Edmund P. Cueva and Javier Martínez, eds., *Splendide Mendax: Rethinking Fakes and Forgeries in Classical, Late Antique, and Early Christian Literature* (Groningen: Barkhuis, 2016); Hindy Najman and Irene Peirano Garrison, "Pseudepigraphy as an Interpretive Construct," in *The Old Testament Pseudepigraphy: Fifty Years of the Pseudepigrapha Section at the SBL*, Early Judaism and its Literature 50 (Atlanta: Society of Biblical Literature, 2019), 331–55; John North Hopkins and Scott McGill, eds., *Forgery Beyond Deceit: Fabrication, Value, and the Desire for Ancient Rome* (Oxford: Oxford University Press, 2023); Jörg Frey et al., eds., *Pseudepigraphie und Verfasserfiktion in frühchristlichen Briefen*, Wissenschaftliche Untersuchungen zum Neuen Testament 246 (Tübingen: Mohr Siebeck, 2009). On pseudepigraphy and deceit, see Bart D. Ehrman, *Forgery and Counterforgery: The Use of Literary Deceit in Early Christian Polemics* (Oxford: Oxford University Press, 2013); cf. David Brakke, "Early Christian Lies and the Lying Liars Who Wrote Them: Bart Ehrman's *Forgery and Counterforgery*," *Journal of Religion* 96 (2016): 378–90.

[10] Hindy Najman, *Seconding Sinai: The Development of Mosaic Discourse in Second Temple Judaism*, Journal for the Study of Judaism Supplements 77 (Leiden: Brill, 2003); Jed Wyrick, *The Ascension of Authorship: Attribution and Canon Formation in Jewish, Hellenistic, and Christian Traditions*, Harvard Studies in Comparative Literature 49 (Cambridge, MA: Harvard University Press, 2004); Anna Marmodoro and Jonathan Hill, eds., *The Author's Voice in Classical and Late Antiquity* (Oxford: Oxford University Press, 2013); Karen L. King, "'What is an Author?' Ancient Author-Function in the *Apocryphon of John* and the Apocalypse of John," in *Scribal*

Introduction to Authorial Fictions and Attributions in the Ancient Mediterranean 5

ship impact the ways in which biblical scholars discuss the author's "intention" have been explored in recent years.[11] Along with pseudepigraphy, research on anonymity has grown as scholars explore anonymous and untitled literature not as a deficit, but as a creative literary decision.[12] The contributions that we have gathered here intend to build upon such scholarship and continue to explore how authorial attribution functions in antiquity and modernity to contextualize texts within literary corpora, produce boundaries of acceptable knowledge, bolster key figures within a religious movement, or preserve or obscure a text's origins and potential uses.

The contributions collected in this volume are written by a variety of scholars who work on different aspects of the ancient Mediterranean and Near Eastern worlds: the Hebrew Bible, rabbinics, the New Testament, early Christianity, classics, Manichaean studies, and Near Eastern and Mesopotamian studies. In doing so, it is our hope that scholars of the ancient world will continue to collaborate in edited and co-authored volumes, journal issues, conferences, symposia, workshops, and other gatherings in order to share our resources and knowledge across traditional institutional and disciplinary boundaries.

Robyn Faith Walsh's contribution on the *Epistle to the Laodiceans*, originating in the sixth century CE, explores the pseudo-Pauline letter's complex history of interpretation and scholarly treatment: What should we make of the fact that *Laodiceans* is not written by Paul and yet its contents are cobbled together out of "authentic" Pauline letters like *Philippians*? Is this letter simultaneously Paul and not-Paul? Placing *Laodiceans* in conversation with contemporary scholarship on authorship, François Bovon's published and unpublished scholarship on *Laodiceans* and "useful books," and Andy Warhol's *S & H Green Stamps* – a piece of artwork only deemed "authentic" when *not* signed by Warhol himself – Walsh suggests that scholars turn their attention to the epistle's sixth-century

---

Practices and Social Structures Among Jesus Adherents: Essays in Honour of John S. Kloppenborg, ed. William E. Arnal et al., Bibliotheca Ephemeridum Theologicarum Lovaniensium 285 (Leuven: Peeters, 2016), 15–42; Jacqueline Vayntrub, "Before Authorship: Solomon and Prov 1:1," *Biblical Interpretation* 26 (2018): 182–206; Clarissa Breu, *Autorschaft in der Johannesoffenbarung: Eine postmoderne Lektüre*, Wissenschaftliche Untersuchungen zum Neuen Testament 541 (Tübingen: Mohr Siebeck, 2020).

[11] Clarissa Breu, ed., *Biblical Exegesis Without Authorial Intention? Interdisciplinary Approaches to Authorship and Meaning*, Biblical Interpretation Series 172 (Leiden: Brill, 2019).

[12] Tom Geue, *Juvenal and the Politics of Anonymity* (Cambridge: Cambridge University Press, 2017); idem, *Author Unknown: The Power of Anonymity in Ancient Rome* (Cambridge, MA: Harvard University Press, 2019); Robyn Faith Walsh, *The Origins of Early Christian Literature: Contextualizing the New Testament within Greco-Roman Literary Culture* (Cambridge: Cambridge University Press, 2021), esp. 134–69; Benjamin G. Wright and Eva Mroczek, "Ben Sira's Pseudo-Pseudepigraphy: Idealizations from Antiquity to the Early Middle Ages," in *Sirach and Its Contexts: The Pursuit of Wisdom and Human Flourishing*, ed. Samuel Adams, Greg Schmidt Goering, and Matthew J. Goff, Journal for the Study of Judaism Supplements 196 (Leiden: Brill, 2021), 213–39.

Latin context rather than attempt to reconstruct a hypothetical second-century Greek original. When we move away from an obsession with the "original text" and Christian origins, Walsh argues that we can better understand *Laodiceans* in light of Latin literary *imitatio* and late ancient *cento* production, in which writers patched together material from authoritative sources in order to produce a textual entity that was simultaneously new and old, Paul's and not-Paul's.

Claire Rachel Jackson's examination of the second-century Greek novel *Leucippe and Clitophon* explores the seeming absence of Achilles Tatius, its purported author, from the text as well as the novel's Byzantine reception. In the first half, Jackson explores how the paratactic opening of *Leucippe and Clitophon* places the text not in the hands of an Alexandrian convert (as the *Suda* later claimed) but rather in a Phoenician context. She posits that Cadmus haunts the novel, filling the authorial void and offering a Phoenician foundation upon which the narrative emerges. In the second half, she turns to the Byzantine *Lives of Saint Galaction and Episteme* to consider Galaction's parents: Clitophon and Gleucippe. Between the two recensions of the *Lives*, Jackson finds some authorial and thematic similarities to *Leucippe and Clitophon*, examines how Byzantine bibliographers chose to attribute hagiographical narration, and raises questions about Leucippe's narratival voice.

In her exploration of the early rabbinic tradition, Rebecca Scharbach Wollenberg offers an explanation for the construction of figures she calls "alien Bible readers" – non-Jewish characters in rabbinic literature that read biblical literature. Instead of reading alien Bible readers as Christians, as some scholarship has attempted to do in order to reconstruct the Jewish side of early Jewish-Christian relations, Wollenberg suggests that such readers are literary constructions that allow the rabbis to express dangerous, subversive, or challenging interpretations of biblical literature. Comparable to pseudepigraphic biblical characters (e.g., Moses, Enoch) becoming nodes for particular genres of Jewish literature or thought, she argues that the rabbinic character of the "alien Bible reader" gave rabbinic literature an otherized mouthpiece through which to explore non-normative hermeneutical approaches.

In her contribution on the *Apocryphon of James* (NHC I,2), Julia Lindenlaub explores how authorial fiction can be used to elevate the intellectual status of an early Christian reading community. To this end, she compares the text's epistolary framing device with a letter from Oxyrhynchus, P.Oxy. 2192, as both illustrate the textual practices of a learned reading community in the Roman Mediterranean. Positioning Christians as relevant participants in the agonistic struggles over literary expertise in this milieu, Lindenlaub reveals how the fictive letter writer, James, invokes recognizable social strategies for cultivating a reading community around shared values and practices. Turning to the manuscript context for the *Apocryphon of James*'s reception in Nag Hammadi Codex I, she shows how the vision for an intellectual community that is shaped by the text's

Introduction to Authorial Fictions and Attributions in the Ancient Mediterranean 7

authorial construct is also capitalized on in reception by the text's placement in the codex. The fictive author in the *Apocryphon of James* narratively represents a past literary circle of disciple authors, directly addresses a circle of like-minded contemporary recipients, and ultimately invites later reception among a new circle of readers.

Nicholas Baker-Brian's contribution turns to the role of apocalyptic traditions in the formation of Mani's authorial persona. After demonstrating the importance of apocalyptic literature and thought in the third-century Sasanian court and in Mani's own *Shābuhragān* (a treatise dedicated to Shapur I), he turns to a range of Manichaean literature to show how Mani's role as author of texts is shaped by his revelations and access to secret knowledge. While, as Baker-Brian demonstrates, not all were convinced by the revelatory authority on which Mani spoke and wrote, his disciples argued that Mani's apocalyptically infused authorial persona was part of a longer apostolic authorial history: Mani is an apostle of God and author much like Paul. Baker-Brian concludes by comparing Mani's approach to authorship and apocalyptic to that of Bardaisan, who rejects an apocalyptic basis for his theology and cosmology.

In his contribution on the often-overlooked *Teachings of Silvanus* (NHC VII,4), Chance Bonar explores the rationale behind attaching the name of one of Paul's associates to a text built upon Jewish wisdom and Alexandrian philosophical literary traditions. Against the arguments that attribution to Silvanus either points to an unknown third-century figure named Silvanus or is a randomly chosen name from the apostolic age, Bonar suggests that Silvanus's role as a Pauline co-author for 1–2 Thessalonians and messenger for 1 Peter may have contributed to the authorial attribution of *Silvanus*. By comparing sections of *Silvanus* to passages from these Silvanean epistles, he argues that the writer of *Silvanus* wrote the text with Silvanus's coauthorial status in mind. Bonar's contribution makes two points: (1) that *Silvanus* may be participating in and pulling from earlier Silvanean literature more than previously thought, and (2) that ancient co-authorship and its potential reception by later writers who construct narratives around coauthorial figures should not be overlooked.

In her examination of the Chester Beatty-Michigan Codex, Elena Dugan demonstrates that authorship has material, paratextual, and codicological effects on the way that early Christians arranged literature within the format provided by the codex. Dugan shows how this codex – containing the *Epistle of Enoch* alongside Melito's *On the Passover* (*Peri Pascha*) and the *Apocryphon of Ezekiel* – is a fruitful example of how the authorial figure of Enoch and his association with the antediluvian history of Israel was put to use by Christian scribes to frame an anti-Jewish literary agenda. Through a close examination of the *Epistle of Enoch*'s titular and paratextual features, as well as how its contents complement and differ from *On the Passover* and the *Apocryphon of Ezekiel*, she argues that Enoch's texts and authorial attribution are generative for early Christian manuscript culture. Building upon the growing scholarship on Jewish pseudepigrapha that wrestles with how to account for its preservation and transmission at Christian hands, Dugan offers a new avenue to explore how authorial figures associated with Israel's past and the texts attached to those figures could be (re)framed through their material inclusion in Christian codices – and how the Jewishness of such authorial figures can be used for anti-Jewish ends.

In her exploration of Latin verse epitaphs, Emily Mitchell considers the difficulty of pinning down a singular figure that might be called the "author" between the commissioner, inscriber, financier, and individuals named or purportedly speaking on the epitaph itself. This difficulty is compounded in the case of epitaphs of enslaved and freedpeople in the Roman Mediterranean. Mitchell argues that the phenomenon of "ventriloquism" takes place on the epitaphs of the enslaved, through which their enslavers make the dead speak in ways that make their still-living enslavers appear benevolent. Conversely, many epitaphs of the emancipated that ventriloquize through husbands or other familial figures minimize their former enslaver's prominence or benevolence, crafting different social and kinship ties through the inscription. Mitchell especially builds upon Orlando Patterson's famous definition of slavery as "social death" to inform her approach to ventriloquized authorial voices and the construction of enslaved and freed kinship at the moment of death.

Jeremiah Coogan's analysis of gospel authorship turns us away from traditional questions about the (in)authenticity of attributions to Matthew, Mark, Luke, and John. Instead, Coogan's contribution encourages further exploration of how early Christian writers themselves balanced their narratives of apostolic collaboration in the writing of gospel texts with their understanding of the gospel texts themselves as having a singular "monographic" agency. Through an analysis of the *Apocryphon of James* (NHC I,2), Origen of Alexandria's *Homilies on Luke*, and Epiphanius of Salamis's *Panarion*, he demonstrates that early Christian writers could distinguish collective gospel literature from personal revelation, as well as that early Christians debated how much agency individual gospel writers could have over the composition of their inspired text.

Finally, Sophus Helle rounds out the volume with a reflective afterword. He notes how the study of authorship in literary history can refer to the production of a text or the presentation of how an author figure becomes attached to a text. Through a discussion of his own research, particularly on the Babylonian epic *Gilgamesh* and Sumerian *Exaltation of Inana*, Helle argues that our fragmentary data about much of the ancient world sets certain methodological limits for our research that ought to encourage analysis of authorship-as-presentation rather than authorship-as-production. What we know best (and what is often the more interesting literary and historical information) is how later writers made sense of a text's authorial attribution. Helle points to three features of the contributions to this volume to highlight how further research on authorship-as-presentation can

Introduction to Authorial Fictions and Attributions in the Ancient Mediterranean 9

be done: (1) collaborative authorship and its disruption of traditional individualist authorial paradigms; (2) how ancient and modern aesthetic and historical value judgments influence authorial attribution; and (3) how attribution works to assign a text to a particular literary and historical context.

As this volume's editors, we hope that its readers will not only be interested in the historical, literary, and methodological insights of our contributors, but will also be inspired to continue interrogating *how* and *why* particular figures have their names attached to texts. For whom does authorial attribution matter, and what do ancient and modern writers, readers, and hearers gain from the way storyworlds are produced and circulated?

Bibliography

Aland, Kurt. "The Problem of Anonymity and Pseudonymity in Christian Literature of the First Two Centuries." Pages 1–13 in *The Authorship and Integrity of the New Testament: Some Recent Studies*. Edited by Kurt Aland. London: SPCK, 1965.

Bakker, Egbert J., ed. *Authorship and Greek Song: Authority, Authenticity, and Performance*. Leiden: Brill, 2017.

Barthes, Roland. "The Death of the Author." Pages 277–280 in *The Book History Reader*. Edited by David Finkelstein and Alistair McCleery. 2nd ed. London: Routledge, 2006.

Barthes, Roland. "Theory of the Text." Pages 31–47 in *Untying the Text: A Post-Structuralist Reader*. Edited by Robert Young. London: Routledge, 1981.

Beet, Joseph Agar. *The New Testament: Its Authorship, Date and Worth*. London: Robert Culley, 1908.

Berardi, Roberta et al., eds. *Defining Authorship, Debating Authority: Problems of Authority from Classical Antiquity to the Renaissance*. Berlin: De Gruyter, 2020.

Brakke, David. "Early Christian Lies and the Lying Liars Who Wrote Them: Bart Ehrman's *Forgery and Counterforgery*." *Journal of Religion* 96 (2016): 378–390.

Breu, Clarissa. *Autorschaft in der Johannesoffenbarung: Eine postmoderne Lektüre*. Wissenschaftliche Untersuchungen zum Neuen Testament 541. Tübingen: Mohr Siebeck, 2020.

Breu, Clarissa, ed. *Biblical Exegesis Without Authorial Intention? Interdisciplinary Approaches to Authorship and Meaning*. Biblical Interpretation Series 172. Leiden: Brill, 2019.

Burke, Tony, ed. *Fakes, Forgeries, and Fictions: Writing Ancient and Modern Christian Apocrypha: Proceedings from the 2015 York Christian Apocrypha Symposium*. Eugene, OR: Cascade, 2017.

Cueva, Edmund P. and Javier Martínez, eds. *Splendide Mendax: Rethinking Fakes and Forgeries in Classical, Late Antique, and Early Christian Literature*. Groningen: Barkhuis, 2016.

Davis, Kipp et al. "Nine Dubious 'Dead Sea Scrolls' Fragments from the Twenty-First Century." *Dead Sea Discoveries* 24 (2017): 189–228.

Ehrman, Bart D. *Forgery and Counterforgery: The Use of Literary Deceit in Early Christian Polemics*. Oxford: Oxford University Press, 2013.

Foucault, Michel. "What is an Author?" Pages 101–120 in *The Foucault Reader*. Edited by Paul Rabinow. New York: Pantheon, 1984.

Frey, Jörg et al., eds. *Pseudepigraphie und Verfasserfiktion in frühchristlichen Briefen.* Wissenschaftliche Untersuchungen zum Neuen Testament 246. Tübingen: Mohr Siebeck, 2009.

Geue, Tom. *Author Unknown: The Power of Anonymity in Ancient Rome.* Cambridge, MA: Harvard University Press, 2019.

Geue, Tom. *Juvenal and the Politics of Anonymity.* Cambridge: Cambridge University Press, 2017.

Hill, Charles E. *From the Lost Teaching of Polycarp: Identifying Irenaeus's Apostolic Presbyter and the Author of* Ad Diognetum. Wissenschaftliche Untersuchungen zum Neuen Testament 186. Tübingen: Mohr Siebeck, 2006.

Hopkins, John North and Scott McGill, eds., *Forgery Beyond Deceit: Fabrication, Value, and the Desire for Ancient Rome.* Oxford: Oxford University Press, 2023.

King, Karen L. "'What is an Author?' Ancient Author-Function in the *Apocryphon of John* and the Apocalypse of John." Pages 15–42 in *Scribal Practices and Social Structures Among Jesus Adherents: Essays in Honour of John S. Kloppenborg.* Edited by William E. Arnal et al. Bibliotheca Ephemeridum Theologicarum Lovaniensium 285. Leuven: Peeters, 2016.

Letteney, Mark. "Authenticity and Authority: The Case for Dismantling a Dubious Correlation." Pages 33–56 in *Rethinking 'Authority' in Late Antiquity: Authorship, Law, and Transmission in Jewish and Christian Tradition.* Edited by A.J. Berkovitz and Mark Letteney. London: Routledge, 2018.

Marmodoro, Anna and Jonathan Hill, eds. *The Author's Voice in Classical and Late Antiquity.* Oxford: Oxford University Press, 2013.

Muehlberger, Ellen. "On Authors, Fathers, and Holy Men." *Marginalia.* 20 Sept 2015. https://themarginaliareview.com/on-authors-fathers-and-holy-men-by-ellen-muehlberger/.

Najman, Hindy. *Seconding Sinai: The Development of Mosaic Discourse in Second Temple Judaism.* Journal for the Study of Judaism Supplements 77. Leiden: Brill, 2003.

Najman, Hindy and Irene Peirano Garrison. "Pseudepigraphy as an Interpretive Construct." Pages 331–355 in *The Old Testament Pseudepigraphy: Fifty Years of the Pseudepigrapha Section at the SBL.* Early Judaism and its Literature 50. Atlanta: Society of Biblical Literature, 2019.

Peirano Garrison, Irene. *The Rhetoric of the Roman Fake: Latin Pseudepigrapha in Context.* Cambridge: Cambridge University Press, 2012.

Stachon, Markus. *Tractavi monumentum aere perennius: Untersuchungen zu vergilischen und ovidischen Pseudepigraphen.* Bochumer altertumswissenschaftliches Colloquium 97. Trier: WVT, 2014.

Tregelles, Samuel Prideaeux. *The Historic Evidence of the Authorship and Transmission of the Books of the New Testament: A Lecture.* 2nd ed. London: Samuel Bagster, 1881.

Vayntrub, Jacqueline. "Before Authorship: Solomon and Prov 1:1." *Biblical Interpretation* 26 (2018): 182–206.

Walsh, Robyn Faith. *The Origins of Early Christian Literature: Contextualizing the New Testament within Greco-Roman Literary Culture.* Cambridge: Cambridge University Press, 2021.

Wright III, Benjamin G. and Eva Mroczek. "Ben Sira's Pseudo-Pseudepigraphy: Idealizations from Antiquity to the Early Middle Ages." Pages 213–239 in *Sirach and Its Contexts: The Pursuit of Wisdom and Human Flourishing.* Edited by Samuel Adams, Greg

Schmidt Goering, and Matthew J. Goff. Journal for the Study of Judaism Supplements 196. Leiden: Brill, 2021.

Wyrick, Jed. *The Ascension of Authorship: Attribution and Canon Formation in Jewish, Hellenistic, and Christian Traditions.* Harvard Studies in Comparative Literature 49. Cambridge, MA: Harvard University Press, 2004.

The *Epistle to the Laodiceans* and the Art of Tradition*

ROBYN FAITH WALSH

For a period in 1965, Andy Warhol refused to sign his artwork. He had applied to change his name legally to John Doe, so when curator Sam Green asked which image he should use to promote a retrospective at the Institute of Contemporary Art in Philadelphia, Warhol suggested a silkscreen of his *S & H Green Stamps*, but he delegated the task of arranging, printing, and signing the piece to Green. Green recalls:

> ... I had to sign [the *S & H Green Stamps* posters for the exhibition] all 'Andy Warhol' because he decided not to sign his work that year ... So it is actually my signature 'Andy Warhol 1965' that authenticates a Warhol as being real ... because Andy Warhol delegated the responsibility to me of making his art ...[1]

Counterintuitively, Warhol's *S & H Green Stamps* from 1965 is only "authentic" if it is signed by someone other than Warhol. It is Warhol's work with Warhol's name produced by a behind-the-scenes steward who remains, for all intents and purposes, anonymous. Only the most elite critics and insiders have the interest or knowledge to comment on the validity of the print and its signature. Outside of this elite, it is simply another Warhol – another expression of a particular aesthetic narrative in the larger corpus of Warhol's art.[2]

---

* A warm thank you to John Kirby, who read drafts of this piece with enthusiasm and a keen critical eye. Thank you, also, to Jaswinder Bolina, Nancy Evans, Christina Larson, Jessica Rosenberg, Sarah Rollens, Jennifer Eyl, Justin Ritzinger, Erin Roberts, Michael Bellofatto, and the editors of this volume – Julia Lindenlaub and Chance Bonar – for their helpful insights and feedback. All translations are my own, unless otherwise noted.

[1] Quoted from an interview with Sam Green for the BBC Documentary *Warhol: Denied* (2006). For more on the relationship between Warhol and Green, consider Guy Trebay, "A Collector of People Along With Art," *The New York Times*, 6 April 2011, http://www.nytimes.com/2011/04/07/fashion/07GREEN.html. NB: I state that Green was responsible for the production of this piece based on his own testimony; however, there are catalogue raisonné which argue that some portion of the 300 lithographs made were printed by a certain Eugene Feldman. My research for this piece certainly confirms that, when it comes to Warhol's work *writ large*, proper attribution for its physical production is often contested. I am not able to delve into that issue for this contribution, but I acknowledge the difficulties of attribution and authorship in studies of Warhol overall.

[2] As for Green, his actions were necessary to maintain cohesion in the production and promotion of Warhol as an icon of the emerging pop art movement. While members of The Factory often helped design and mass produce prints, Green's strategic intervention actively closed a gap left open by Warhol's failure to directly "name" or authorize his work in 1965. For more

14   *Robyn Faith Walsh*

A Warhol anecdote must seem like an odd place to begin a piece on the *Epistle to the Laodiceans*. But both Warhol and Paul the Apostle signal the "constructable" nature of certain authors and artists whose personae come to supersede the bounds of their individual literary or artistic output.[3] Warhol is able to allocate the responsibility of his art to a relative unknown, and that art remains "a Warhol." Christian corpora are rife with pseudepigrapha attributed to Paul, and though these texts are not written by Paul, they nevertheless remain "Pauline." In these cases, Warhol and Paul are treated as "textual entities" – open sources that are tightly associated with writings or artwork that bear their names but that may not belong to them in reality.[4]

The concept of an author as a textual entity alludes to the process of historical generalization that takes place when a cultural producer becomes "a name."[5] For some audiences, the desire to bridge perceived biographical, artistic, or literary gaps in an author's life and narrative permits the willful or even unknowing incorporation of forgeries into the canon of that author's work. This need for cohesion permits what Irene Peirano Garrison calls "retrospective fictions": new works aimed at either reinforcing, expanding, or refuting already-accepted aspects of an author's canon.[6] Analyses of retrospective fictions often focus on the relative quality of the given "fake."[7] Style and composition are useful evaluative tools, but such investigations frequently slip into speculation about the motivations of the pseudepigrapher. This study, by contrast, asks what fakes reveal about the interests of those who accept them. Considering *why* certain retrospective fictions are accepted into or rejected from an author's canon reveals a great deal about how social actors invent and inculcate new tradition(s), often at the expense of historicity.[8] Tracing a piece of pseudepigrapha on the margins of

---

on the production of Warhol silkscreens and lithographs at The Factory, see Steven Watson, *Factory Made: Warhol and the Sixties* (New York: Pantheon Books, 2003); John Richardson, *Sacred Monsters, Sacred Masters: Beaton, Capote, Dalí, Picasso, Freud, Warhol and More* (New York: Jonathan Cape, 2001).

[3] In using the term "constructable," I am borrowing language from Irene Peirano Garrison, whose work will be discussed more thoroughly in what follows: Irene Peirano, *The Rhetoric of the Roman Fake: Latin Pseudepigrapha in Context* (Cambridge: Cambridge University Press, 2012), 10–11. Hereafter, I will also use "author" to refer, at times, to both writers and other artists. In this respect, I understand "author" and "artist" to be interchangeable.

[4] Peirano, *The Rhetoric of the Roman Fake*, 10.

[5] With reference to a "cultural producer," I am borrowing language from Pierre Bourdieu (*The Field of Cultural Production: Essays on Art and Literature*, trans. Randal Johnson [New York: Columbia University Press, 1993], 115).

[6] Peirano uses the term "retrospective fiction" frequently throughout *The Rhetoric of the Roman Fake*, particularly in reference to her analysis of Vergil (*The Rhetoric of the Roman Fake*, 3).

[7] I am referring here to the title of Peirano, *The Rhetoric of the Roman Fake*.

[8] In using words like "inculcate," I am paraphrasing some of the language found in Eric Hobsbawm, "Introduction: Inventing Traditions," in *The Invention of Tradition*, ed. Eric Hobsbawm and Terence Ranger (Cambridge: Cambridge University Press, 2010), 1–2.

The Epistle to the Laodiceans and the Art of Tradition 15

acceptance also speaks to the negotiations that take place as "names" or founding figures are established and reimagined over time.

In the case of Paul, questions of historicity and historical biography are unquestionably complicated. Anachronistically understood as an early Christian figure, scholars tend to situate his writings and the pseudepigrapha associated with his name in terms of other religious writings, communities, and debates. Comparing Paul with Warhol helps to disrupt this pattern and reveal new taxonomies. For example, the 1965 *S & H Green Stamps* attributed to "Warhol" functions as a retrospective fiction because it is plausibly built on the scaffolding of Warhol's recognized work.[9] Similarly, the Latin *Epistle to the Laodiceans* (hereafter, Laodiceans) stands out as a pseudepigraphic text, but one with content taken almost verbatim (albeit, in translation) from Paul's genuine letters. We do not know whether the compiler of Laodiceans engaged in *imitatio* strategically or as an exercise; nevertheless, the sources for Laodiceans are easily discernable (Appendix 1).[10] The letter deviates from expectation with respect to its length and some of its terminology, but in using material from Paul's undisputed letters, it generates what François Bovon characterizes as a "paradoxical situation" – a text that cannot be rejected outright precisely because it is, in effect, Paul's own words.[11] As Bovon avers, Laodiceans is remarkable in that it endeavors "not to be original."[12]

By and large, critical analyses of Laodiceans are unusually consistent and concise – and vitriolic. Scholars marvel at its brevity, its lackluster content, and its lack of literary innovation. Descriptors like "worthless," "incompetent," and "uninteresting" are common.[13] At stake for these scholars is an obligation to account

---

[9] I am careful here not to overreach and suggest that 1965 *S & H Green Stamps* by Green looks precisely like what Warhol would have created personally – who is to say that Warhol would not have made significant changes to his print, had he done the work himself?

[10] I am speaking of *imitatio* in this piece in terms of its rhetorical function.

[11] François Bovon, "The Correspondence between Paul and the Corinthians and Paul's Letter to the Laodiceans," unpublished paper provided by the author (2005), 1. Several years ago, I was a research assistant for François Bovon at Harvard Divinity School, and he provided me with yet-unpublished drafts of material he had written on 1 and 2 Corinthians and Laodiceans to edit in hard copy. Sadly, he passed away in 2013 after several years of ill health. In preparing the present piece, I relocated his papers by chance. I have searched for a published version of the ideas represented in these found pages without success. It is possible that I have overlooked a publication or the version I have in hard copy represents an early draft of something that later appeared in a different form; however, it seems equally plausible that it is part of a larger project that was abandoned. After much consideration and consultation, I have elected to use this contribution as an opportunity to convey Bovon's thoughts on Laodiceans, in a limited fashion. My interests in doing so are rooted in a desire to celebrate Bovon's career while also respecting the (potentially) unfinished nature of this particular work. At the time of this writing, I am in discussions with editors of a proposed festschrift for Bovon about publishing these papers so others can consult them as well.

[12] "Original" in the sense of innovative; cited from Bovon, "Correspondence," 16.

[13] For example, n. 40–48 below.

16   *Robyn Faith Walsh*

for the existence of what they perceive to be a "stupid orthodox imitation."[14] The primary objection in such treatments is that Laodiceans is not just echoic of Paul's authentic work, but conspicuously so; as such, no new information can be obtained from the author of this forgery about the early Christians they are presumed to represent. What is principally ignored, then, is why such an obviously "insipid" forgery was accepted into any corpora in the first place.

What Bovon typifies as a "paradoxical situation" in Laodiceans may be the key. Regardless of the intentions of Laodiceans' author, this so-called hodgepodge of authentic Pauline phrases remains, in some measure, "Paul." Thus, in the face of the "openness" provided by Colossians 4:16 ("see that [this letter] is also read before the assembly at Laodicea"), the Latin Laodiceans filled a void, creating a relatively innocuous intertextual stopgap for what was otherwise a serious lacuna.[15] This Bovonian Paradox (if I may coin a phrase) articulates the sentiment of later commentators on Laodiceans, which tepidly acknowledged the letter as "bearing the name of Paul," which in itself was sufficient for it to be "venerated," if with some dubiety.[16]

Bovon was fond of speaking of "useful books" rather than viewing so-called non-canonical writings through a strict lens of orthodoxy and heresy. He sought to understand how gospel harmonies, pseudepigrapha, and so forth were valued by various Christian groups, as evidenced by their presence in antique canons. Indeed, the acceptance of retrospective fictions like pseudepigrapha requires a social group for whom the authorial name in question has some utility. Social movements, for example, often craft associations with a founding figure in order to establish a point of origin and a focal point of authority. Whether we are analyzing an artistic movement like Pop Art, or what we today call Christianity, invoking a symbol of authority is a powerful way to establish "august roots" for new movements and, in the process, evoke a sense of group solidity.[17] Laodiceans helped establish and maintain Paul's status as a founding figure and provided a narrative bridge in his development as a "textual entity." Reconsidering the history of Laodiceans and its reception offers an opportunity to reassess how, as Peirano puts it, "the ancient approach to authorship was characterized by the

---

[14] Bovon, "Correspondence," 20. In this section, Bovon is not calling Laodiceans a "stupid orthodox imitation" himself but noting that this tends to be one of the two lenses through which scholars view the letter, the other being "subtle marcionite [sic] rewriting."

[15] See Peirano (*The Rhetoric of the Roman Fake*, 10–11) for an analysis of intertextuality.

[16] Irena Backus, "Renaissance Attitudes to New Testament Apocryphal Writings: Jacques Lefevre d'Etaples and his Epigones," *Renaissance Quarterly* 51 (1998): 1175.

[17] William E. Arnal, "The Collection and Synthesis of 'Tradition' and the Second-Century Invention of Christianity," *Method and Theory in the Study of Religion* 23 (2011): 193–215, quotation on 199: "even modern groups seeking to define themselves and their identity in the *present* do so by inventing or laying claim to an ancestral identity which unifies, identifies, and gives them august (or respectable, or congenial) roots." Also consider Hobsbawm, *The Invention of Tradition*, 9.

The Epistle to the Laodiceans and the Art of Tradition   17

inability to distinguish between a real author and his literary persona."[18] It also helps us reconsider to what extent saying we have a cohesive and authentic "Paul" is part of the art of constructing tradition.

1. Laodiceans: Reception History and Scholarship

Laodiceans as we have it today is an apocryphal letter of indeterminate origin that managed to remain on the fringes of the Pauline canon from at least the sixth to roughly the sixteenth century.[19] Refuted by some as a Marcionite forgery (or, in some cases, refuted for purely stylistic reasons), it was equally accepted by others as a genuine letter of the apostle Paul, with debate about its authenticity continuing until the Council of Trent.[20] Close analysis indicates that the letter is pseudepigraphic, adapted from Paul's letter to the Philippians and augmented with lines from numerous other Pauline letters (Appendix 1). Laodiceans is, in effect, Paul's words translated, reproduced, and curated by persons other than Paul.[21]

Any discussion of "Laodiceans" must begin with clarifying *which* Laodiceans, as there are several attestations to a letter by this name among early Christian writers. As noted above, the existence of the epistle is principally tied to Paul's letter to the Colossians. Setting aside the authenticity of Colossians for a moment, Colossians 4:16 signals a compelling lacuna:

καὶ ὅταν ἀναγνωσθῇ παρ' ὑμῖν ἡ ἐπιστολή, ποιήσατε ἵνα καὶ ἐν τῇ Λαοδικέων ἐκκλησίᾳ ἀναγνωσθῇ, καὶ τὴν ἐκ Λαοδικείας ἵνα καὶ ὑμεῖς ἀναγνῶτε.

And when this letter has been read to you, see that it is also read before the assembly at Laodicea, and that you yourselves read the letter which will be forwarded from there.

This reference to an otherwise unknown Pauline letter acted as an open invitation for writers with a variety of interests to supply the would-be missing material.

---

[18] Peirano, *The Rhetoric of the Roman Fake*, 11.

[19] A letter to the Laodiceans was known in both of the so-called western and eastern churches; however, the Latin Laodiceans circulated primarily in the west. Bovon points out that the Antiochian teachers Theodore of Mopsueste and Theodoret of Cyrrhus condemned Laodiceans "probably in a polemic against western voices favorable to the letter. Epiphanius in an obscure passage seems also to have been aware of the letter and to be hostile to it. Later Timothy, presbyter of Constantinople, who became patriarch in 511 CE, says that there is a letter to the Laodiceans, but that it is a forgery of the Manicheans ([perhaps] a confusion with the Marcionites)" (Bovon, "Correspondence," 22). Overall while the western fathers looked upon Laodiceans favorably, the apocryphal third letter to the Corinthians found greater reception in the eastern church.

[20] Laodiceans was ultimately eliminated from the canon by the Council of Trent (1545–1563).

[21] Some analysts claim that Laodiceans may have additionally relied on Colossians, 1 Corinthians, and 2 Peter: Melissa Harl Sellew, "*Laodiceans* and the Philippians Fragments Hypothesis," *Harvard Theological Review* 87 (1994): 17–28, esp. 28, Appendix 1.

18   Robyn Faith Walsh

The enigmatic Muratorian Fragment (Mur. Frag.), for example, notes an epistle
to the Laodiceans existed among the Marcionites.[22] Tertullian suggests that the
Marcionites identified Ephesians under the name "Laodiceans," with Marcion
altering the title (*Adv. Marc.* 5.17.1).[23] Other murky references are found in fourth-
century sources like Filastrius of Brescia (*Diversarum haereseon liber* 89.2), who
authorizes a Laodiceans letter for private study while simultaneously cautioning
that "heretics" had interpolated some material.[24] Priscillian of Avila, known for
embracing apocrypha, cites the invitation in Colossians 4:16 in order to justify reading texts outside of the accepted canon, but it is not clear whether he
is familiar with a specific text.[25] In the fifth century, Theodore of Mopsuestia
(*Rab. Maur. Op.* 6), Theodoret, Epiphanius of Salamis (*Pan.* 42.9.4; 42.12.3), and
Jerome (*De vir. ill.* 5) all reject the letter. A century later, Timotheus curiously lists
Laodiceans among suspected Manichean forgeries.[26] It remains uncertain what
relationship, if any, these allusions have to the Laodiceans text that has survived
in the manuscript tradition.[27]

The extant letter to the Laodiceans is often referred to as the "Latin" epistle,
corresponding with the language of its earliest copies. Many scholars suggest that
the Latin text is a translation from an original Greek version, citing J. B. Lightfoot's position that "[*Laodiceans*] has not the run of a Latin original."[28] This as-

---

[22] I say "enigmatic" here because the Mur. Frag. is not without its own manuscript issues.
The codex has been dated to the seventh or eighth century, but scholars postulate a late second
century "original" given some of its internal references and a suspicion that it is a translation
from an earlier Greek text. These theories remain speculative and are routinely challenged. For
more on this issue, see Bruce Metzger, *The Canon of the New Testament* (Oxford: Clarendon
Press, 1997), 305–6.

[23] Along these lines, others have suggested that Laodiceans was confused with Hebrews or
Philemon: see for example Leon Hermann, "L'Épitre aux Laodicéens (Laodicéens et l'apologie
aux Hebreux)," *Cahiers du Cercle Ernest Renan* 58 (1968): 1–16; John Knox, *Philemon Among
the Letters of Paul: A New View of Its Place and Importance* (New York: Abingdon, 1959), 38–
47; Richard Batey, "The Destination of Ephesians," *Journal of Biblical Literature* 82 (1963): 101.

[24] For more on the attestation of Laodiceans, see Wilhelm Schneemelcher, ed. *New Testament
Apocrypha, Vol. 2: Writings Relating to the Apostles, Apocalypses, and Related Subjects*, ed. and
trans. R. McL. Wilson (Louisville: Westminster Knox Press, 1992), 42.

[25] For more on Priscillian, see Henry Chadwick, *Priscillian of Avila: The Occult and The
Charismatic Early Church* (Oxford: Clarendon Press, 1976), 81.

[26] Timotheus likely meant to indicate the Marcionites, not the Manicheans.

[27] Adolf von Harnack argues that Laodiceans is a Marcionite forgery based on its "anti-
catholic" opening. In part, he suggests that Laodiceans deviates from its otherwise close
mirroring of Philippians at the onset, borrowing from Galatians 1:1, a favorite in the Marcionite
canon. This hypothesis has largely fallen out of favor, but it is often noted in overviews of the history of scholarship: see for example Adolf von Harnack, *Marcion: das Evangelium vom fremden
Gott: Eine Monographie zur Geschichte der Grundlegung der katholischen Kirche* (Leipzig:
J. C. Hinrichs, 1921), 141.

[28] J. B. Lightfoot, *Saint Paul's Epistles to the Colossians and to Philemon: A Revised Text with
Introductions, Notes, and Dissertations* (London: Macmillan, 1892), 240. Incidentally, this claim
impresses as especially odd given that the letter itself is reputedly built upon the Greek letters
of Paul.

The Epistle to the Laodiceans and the Art of Tradition 19

sumption, however, is purely speculative and glosses the implied translation issues.[29] At present, the earliest known manuscript witness is the Codex Fuldensis from the sixth century. The same letter is found in numerous codices and translations of the Pauline corpus throughout the medieval period.[30] There is some debate that a single verse from the Latin Laodiceans is quoted in the fifth century by Ps.-Augustine, but this remains ambiguous.[31] Thus, the only secure *terminus ante quem* for the letter is the sixth century with possible references as early as the fourth century.[32]

---

[29] For more on this issue, see Philip L. Tite, *The Apocryphal Epistle to the Laodiceans* (Leiden: Brill, 2012), 1–18; Harl Sellew, "*Laodiceans*," 22; Jean-Marie Auwers and H. J. de Jonge, ed., *The Biblical Canons* (Leuven: Leuven University Press, 2003), 540; Schneemelcher, *New Testament Apocrypha*, 42.

[30] Harl Sellew, "*Laodiceans*," 22 n. 15; Schneemelcher, *New Testament Apocrypha*, 42. The manuscript tradition is largely from the western church, with only ambiguous evidence that the letter circulated in the east. There are some fifty manuscripts that relied on the Codex Fuldensis from the sixth century onward. Adolf von Harnack lists twenty-seven in his *Geschichte der altchristlichen Litteratur* (Vol. 1), and Lightfoot mentions an additional sixteen from libraries at Oxford, Cambridge, and Lambeth. Four other manuscripts were found in Spanish libraries (e. g., the Gothic Bible of Toledo). The text was translated into English and German in the fifteenth century. Among other codices in which it appears are: the Book of Armagh (Dublin, Trinity College Library, 52, ca. 807 CE); "Charlemagne's Bible" (ninth century); the two-volume "Gundulf Bible" (San Marino, California, Huntington Library, HM 62, eleventh century); the first Bohemian Bible (1488 CE); the Albigensian Bible at Lyons. See Adolf von Harnack, "Paulus, Apostel, angeblicher Brief an die Laodicener," *Geschichte der altchristlichen Litteratur bis Eusebius*, vol. 1 (Leipzig: J. C. Hinrichs, 1893), 33–37; Lightfoot, *Saint Paul's Epistles to the Colossians and to Philemon*, 281–300; Backus, "Renaissance Attitudes to New Testament Apocryphal Writings," 1169–98.

[31] Ps.-Augustine's *Speculum* quotes a single Latin verse (v. 4) that possibly corresponds to the later manuscript tradition (CSEL 12). Some have used this reference to suggest that the Latin Laodiceans circulated well before the Fulda manuscript. Given the limited nature of this evidence, not to mention the likely pastiche nature of the text, this conclusion is far from certain.

[32] As such, I will not spend time in this piece debating the existence of or the *Sitz im Leben* for a hypothetical, earlier Greek version of Laodiceans. Similarly, I will not debate the hypotheses that Laodiceans could be a Manichean or Marcionite forgery. For more on this issue, see Tite, *The Apocryphal Epistle to the* Laodiceans, 1–18. Melissa Harl Sellew argued that Laodiceans borrows the majority of its content from Philippians and, specifically, what is known in some circles as "Philippians B." "Philippians B" is part of a hypothetical partitioning of Philippians which recognizes three distinct letters within what is today the compiled canonical letter: Letter A (Phil 4:10–20); Letter B (Phil 1:1–3:1, 4:4–6, 4:20–23); and Letter C (Phil 3:2–4:3, 4:7–9). In this configuration, Letter B would have circulated before the compiled Philippians and, therefore, allows scholars to push the date for Laodiceans as early as the late first century (in a period before Letters A and C were known to Laodiceans' author). This theory has been challenged on several fronts, including the assumption that Laodiceans was unaware of anything beyond Letter B (as opposed, for instance, to the writer simply making a choice to only sample from Phil 1:1–3:1, 4:4–6, 4:20–23). For more analysis: Harl Sellew, "*Laodiceans*," 17–28; Paul A. Holloway, "The Apocryphal *Epistle to the Laodiceans* and the Partitioning of Philippians," *Harvard Theological Review* 91 (1998): 321–25; Melissa Harl Sellew, "*Laodiceans* and Philippians Revisited: A Response to Paul Holloway," *Harvard Theological Review* 91 (1998): 327–29.

20 *Robyn Faith Walsh*

Notwithstanding a puzzling reception history for this letter, the relative prevalence of Laodiceans in the manuscript tradition from the sixth century onward suggests it enjoyed some popularity.[33] Following the Fulda manuscript, it remained within the Vulgate for centuries, as Lightfoot describes: "for more than nine centuries this forged epistle hovered about the doors of the sacred Canon, without either finding admission or being peremptorily excluded."[34] Indeed, the letter was often acknowledged by church leaders and commentators while it vied for inclusion in the Pauline corpus.[35] Haimo of Auxerre excluded it from the canon while simultaneously admitting to its usefulness (*in canone non habeatur, aliquid tamen utilitatis habet*).[36] John of Salisbury deemed the piece to be the fifteenth Pauline epistle but also failed to incorporate it into the canon.[37] Jacques Lefèvre d'Étaples, in a 1512 Latin edition of Paul's letters, included it on the basis of its previous attribution to Paul and its seemingly pious content ("it breathes Christ and contains holy precepts. Wherever we read the name of Christ, wherever it is pronounced, there worship and reverence are due"), yet anticipated certain objections ("What if it is brief? There was nothing stopping the apostle from writing letters that were sometimes long and sometimes very short").[38] Lefèvre's enthusiasm was not broadly shared. By the end of the sixteenth century, letters like Laodiceans and Paul's letter to Seneca were pushed to the margins.

---

[33] For example, among the medieval manuscripts of the Vulgate that contain Laodiceans: the ninth-century Hartmut Codex, London, BL, Add. Ms. 11852 contains Laodiceans after Hebrews; the ninth-century Codex Complutensis, otherwise known as the first Bible of Alcala (held by the Madrid University Library in 1893), contains Laodiceans also after Hebrews; the tenth-century incomplete Codex Aemilianeus extant in 1893 in the Madrid Library of the Historical Academy contains Laodiceans in the margin of Colossians; the eleventh-century Codex, Paris, BNF, Ms. Lat. 309 excludes the canonical gospels but contains a summary of the Song of Songs and Laodiceans, after 1 and 2 Thessalonians; and over fifty additional medieval manuscripts in which Laodiceans appears after Colossians (twenty-one examples), after Hebrews (twenty examples), after Revelation (ten examples), after Titus (three examples), after Philemon (two examples), and after Galatians (in German only). Consult Backus, "Renaissance Attitudes to New Testament Apocryphal Writings," 1169–98.

[34] Lightfoot, *Saint Paul's Epistles to the Colossians and to Philemon*, 297.

[35] One notable rejection of Laodiceans was the Second Council of Nicea, which explicitly deemed it a forgery (*Act.* VI, *Tom.* V).

[36] Haimo, *In Epistolam ad Colossenses* iv (PL 117, col. 765A), cited from Lightfoot, *Saint Paul's Epistles to the Colossians and to Philemon*, 295.

[37] John of Salisbury, *Ep.* 209 (1165 CE): "it is the common, indeed almost universal, opinion that there are only fourteen Epistles of Paul ... But the fifteenth is that which is written to the church of the Laodiceans"; *The Letters of John of Salisbury*, ii; *The Later Letters*, ed. W.J. Millor and C.N.L. Brooke (Oxford: Clarendon Press, 1979), 323. Gregory the Great was also a supporter; *Moralia* 35.20.48; PL 76, 778C.

[38] For more on Lefèvre, see R. Ward Holder, *A Companion to Paul in the Reformation* (Boston: Brill, 2009), 61–90, quotation on 69; Backus, "Renaissance Attitudes to New Testament Apocryphal Writings," 1169. Lefèvre cited from Backus, "Renaissance Attitudes," 70.

The Epistle to the Laodiceans and the Art of Tradition 21

As noted at the onset, the overwhelming majority of scholarship on Laodiceans has focused on its source materials, quality, and composition – often in surprisingly harsh terms.[39] Lightfoot characterized the text as a collection of "Pauline phrases strung together without any definite connection or clear object"[40] that is "quite harmless, so far as falsity and stupidity combined can ever be regarded as harmless."[41] Wilhelm Schneemelcher called it a "worthless hodgepodge (*wertlose Zusammenstoppelung*)."[42] For Harnack it was "colorless and dull."[43] M. R. James found the text "wholly uninteresting" and "feebly constructed."[44] Gustav Krüger, like Schneemelcher, labeled it "worthless."[45] In more recent memory, Richard Bauckham dismissed Laodiceans as "remarkably incompetent."[46] Similarly, Régis Burnet regarded it to be tasteless or insipid (*insipide*) and "without interest (*sans intéret*)."[47] Melissa Harl Sellew, while more measured in her estimation, nonetheless uses words like "colorless" and "lackluster" to describe how Laodiceans impresses its "modern readers."[48]

Harl Sellew's passing distinction between modern sensibilities and, presumably, the ancient writing practices Laodiceans represents, encapsulates a central oversight common to this letter. While not stated outright, the "modern readers" to whom she alludes are New Testament and early Christianity scholars. This is a very particular readership, bringing a distinctive set of methods and expectations to their reading of Laodiceans. When these scholars call Laodiceans "worthless" or "insipid," what they are really saying is that it does not answer the questions traditionally asked by the field. Laodiceans resists evaluative methods like historical or redaction criticism precisely because it fails to reveal concrete

---

[39] For a fuller account of these dismissals: Tite, *The Apocryphal Epistle to the Laodiceans,* 5–6; Harl Sellew, "*Laodiceans,*" 21–22.

[40] Lightfoot, *Saint Paul's Epistles to the Colossians and to Philemon,* 289; cited from Harl Sellew, "*Laodiceans,*" 21. NB: Lightfoot does mention the possibility that *Laodiceans* is a Pauline *cento* in this passage, something that Bovon will also claim (discussed in the following).

[41] Lightfoot, *Saint Paul's Epistles to the Colossians and to Philemon,* 280.

[42] Wilhelm Schneemelcher, *Neutestamentliche Apokryphen in deutscher Übersetzung: 5. Auflage der von Edgar Hennecke begründeten Sammlung,* 2 vols. (Tübingen: Mohr Siebeck, 1987–1989) 2:42.

[43] Harnack, *Marcion,* 149.

[44] M. R. James, *The Apocryphal New Testament* (Oxford: Clarendon Press, 1924), 478; cited from Harl Sellew, "*Laodiceans,*" 21.

[45] Gustav Krüger, "Laodicenerbrief," in *Neutestamentliche Apokryphen,* 150. Also cited in Harl Sellew, "*Laodiceans,*" 21.

[46] Richard Bauckham, "Pseudo-Apostolic Letters," *Journal of Biblical Literature* 107 (1986): 469–94, cit. 485; cited in Harl Sellew, "*Laodiceans,*" 21.

[47] Régis Burnet, "Pourquoi avoir écrit l'insipide épître aux Laodicéens?" *New Testament Studies* 48 (2002): 132–41, quotation on 132.

[48] Harl Sellew, "*Laodiceans,*" 21–22: "The letter does indeed lack most signs of Paul's own passionate concern and his characteristic interest in his favorite topics; no doubt it strikes most modern readers, including myself, as a rather colorless pastiche." Tite takes a similar position: "we have ... less a sloppy plagiarist than an editor who takes on the role of author within the very arrangement at his or her disposal" (*The Apocryphal Epistle to the Laodiceans,* 102).

22 *Robyn Faith Walsh*

data about its compiler/author(s) or its so-called origins. This is a function of its rhetorical dependence and imitation of Paul and is not a failure on the part of its author. When scholars find themselves frustrated by its false attribution, its repetitive terminology, and its late appearance in the manuscript tradition, it is because they are attempting to place Laodiceans in an early Christian literary context to which it does not belong.[49] Rather than seek new approaches to this kind of writing activity or identify a more appropriate genre classification, they are quick to dismiss Laodiceans outright, to conflate the manuscript evidence, or to speculate about an earlier "Greek original" in an attempt to conform the text to their usual expectations.

Embedded in these opinions on style and composition are not only an obvious frustration with the nature of Laodiceans as a piece of *imitatio*, but also a value-judgment on the usefulness of what is generally considered heretical material.[50] Bovon recognized this tendency in his own assessment of Laodiceans, stating: "I see two reasons for such harsh judgments: a misunderstanding concerning the literary genre of the letter and a negative predisposition toward any apocryphal document." These two observations overlap in their implications. According to Bovon, if a "heretical" or apocryphal text contains close citations from canonical sources, scholars often consider the author "guilty of plagiarism" and the writing is marginalized, yet if the same text contains anything novel, these alterations are treated as "empty formul[ae]" and disregarded.[51] Laodiceans is guilty of both offenses, albeit with only minor variations to some of the lines adapted from Philippians (e. g., the word "Lord" in Philippians 3:1 is substituted with "Christ" in Laodiceans 13). Attributing concepts like plagiarism to non-canonical materials is peculiar given that the same acts of citation and allusion take place within and among accepted canonical writings. As Bovon later quips to illustrate this point: "Nobody accuses Matthew or Luke of plagiarism."[52] Furthermore, as a matter of aesthetics Bovon, like Harl Sellew, recognizes that for "modern scholars ... a document must be original and show a certain degree of creativity [to be interesting]," a threshold that, for many, Laodiceans fails to reach.[53] To deem Laodiceans or, indeed, any literary work as fundamentally *not* creative is an odd judgment on the nature of writing. Laodiceans in this respect is no different than countless other ancient texts whose compositional contexts rely on im-

---

[49] A prime example is the work of Donald N. Penny: "[*Laodiceans* is] almost completely [lacking] any statements with a meaningful theological content ... only stereotyped formulae and the most general exhortations. The result is a pious-sounding, edifying document with no particular message or theological tendency" (Donald N. Penny, "The Pseudo-Pauline Letters of the First Two Centuries" [PhD diss., Emory University, 1979], 326).

[50] Tite (*The Apocryphal Epistle to the Laodiceans*, 101–24) has also made this observation.

[51] Bovon, "Correspondence," 16.

[52] Bovon, "Correspondence," 17.

[53] Bovon, "Correspondence," 16. I have rearranged the original order of this sentence for clarity without changing any terminology.

The Epistle to the Laodiceans and the Art of Tradition   23

itation and allusion as literary practices. Laodiceans' paraphrasing of Philippians in particular is not a symptom of banality, but a strategy aimed at establishing a secure connection to the Pauline corpus, an act for which Bovon agrees "the author should not be condemned" but celebrated.[54]

Bovon was something of a vanguard in his efforts to redeem Laodiceans as an object of critical inquiry.[55] While others like Harnack or Harl Sellew are credited with bringing new perspectives to its content, their analyses largely focus on Laodiceans as a foil for rethinking broader issues of orthodoxy and heresy.[56] Bovon, by contrast, sought a concrete *raison d'être* for the letter's compositional structure. In addition to validating Laodiceans' resemblance to *imitatio*, he acknowledged that its intertextual style paralleled the practice of *cento* writing. A genre predicated on mirroring well-known lines from "highly valued literature" like Homer or Vergil, the aim of a *cento* was to create a "patchwork" of quotations culminating in "a new story consisting of familiar building-blocks."[57] If a form of prose *cento*, Laodiceans would certainly signal Paul's authority as a figure worthy of replication.[58] This kind of "intellectual activity," in Bovon's view, demonstrates how Laodiceans "defends and redraws" an interpretation of Paul as a "reliable apostle."[59] By placing Laodiceans in conversation with these ancient writing practices, Bovon expands our understanding of how this text

---

[54] Bovon, "Correspondence," 17.

[55] This is not to say, of course, that there have not been other attempts to revisit Laodiceans through new eyes. Examples include Tite as well as Gregory S. MaGee, who compares Laodiceans to the letters of Ignatius: Gregory S. MaGee, "Exalted Apostle: The Portrayal of Paul in Colossians and Ephesians" (PhD diss., Trinity Evangelical Divinity School, 2009).

[56] Harnack's work is exemplary in that he argues for the Marcionite character of Laodiceans, linking it back to the Mur. Frag. (Harnack, *Marcion*, passim). This is disputed by Tite, who states that "indeed, one would have to assume a Marcionite influence a priori in order to find anything Marcionite in the letter" (Tite, *The Apocryphal Epistle to the Laodiceans*, 7). Bart Ehrman has counter-argued that Laodiceans was written in response to the "Laodiceans" mentioned in the Mur. Frag.: Bart Ehrman, *Lost Scriptures: Books That Did Not Make It into the New Testament* (New York: Oxford University Press, 2003), 165. See also Harl Sellew, who uses Laodiceans to argue for the portioning of Philippians into two distinct letters: Harl Sellew, *Laodiceans*, passim.

[57] Karl Olav Sandnes, *The Gospel "According to Homer and Virgil": Cento and Canon* (Leiden: Brill, 2011), 107. Of note, the term "genre" is a modern designation. The ancients did not possess the same taxonomies that contemporary scholarship identifies for academic purposes. That said, ancient readers were aware that there were distinguishing features between kinds of literature (e. g., the novel, letter writing), even if they did not always use the same categories. When I use the term, I am indicating that writers conformed to certain literary conventions. While writers were perfectly capable of innovating, there are still certain rhetorical standards and training that are reflected in the works they produce; for example, consider the discussion of genre in Jennifer Eyl, "Why Thekla Does Not See Paul: Visual Perception and the Displacement of Erōs in the Acts of Paul and Thekla," in *The Ancient Novel and the Early Christian and Jewish Narrative: Fictional Intersections*, ed. Marília P. Futre Pinheiro et al. (Groningen: Barkhuis – Groningen University Library, 2012), 3–12, quotation on 3 n. 1.

[58] Bovon, "Correspondence," 17; Sandnes, *The Gospel "According to Homer and Virgil,"* 107.

[59] Bovon, "Correspondence," 18. In context Bovon is discussing an attitude, shared by Marcion, on Paul's authority contra Jerusalem.

24 Robyn Faith Walsh

may have functioned as more than a careless forgery. Compellingly, his analysis of Laodiceans' literary structure and strategic importance also augurs subsequent enquiry into pseudepigrapha.

2. Laodiceans as Pseudepigraphic Writing

The study of *pseudepigrapha* is arguably a marginalized field. Often regarded as mere "fakes," much effort is spent on disproving the imagined authenticity of such texts, with little space left over for considering these writings on their own terms. Laodiceans, too, appears to have fallen victim to this pattern. References to the letter as a piece of pseudepigrapha are usually made in passing without discussion of its broader significance.[60] Exceptions to this rule tend to analyze Laodiceans idiosyncratically, claiming that it does not conform to what is sometimes termed the "deutero-Pauline school" – a set of criteria set by the canonical deutero-Pauline and Pastoral epistles.[61] Recent research reveals that pseudepigrapha, as a class of literature, deserves reconsideration as a rich and complex kind of writing.[62] Beyond identifying the literary methods of pseudepigraphic authors, a reconsideration of the way that these texts are received, accepted, or rejected over time speaks to the work so-called fakes can do when it comes to defining an author.

Peirano's work is particularly instructive in this area. As she explains, Latin pseudepigrapha do not share the same "specific formal characteristics" that attend other genres like letter writing, *bioi*, and so forth.[63] But there are certain, identifiable characteristics of pseudepigraphic writing that demonstrate how this literature functioned in ancient corpora. The pseudonymity of a text can be an

---

[60] For example, Tite who discusses the "derivative value" of Laodiceans: "The apocryphal letters [of Paul] serve as a yardstick by which to establish criteria for identifying pseudonymous letters" (*The Apocryphal Epistle to the Laodiceans,* 10–11). Also consider his discussion of Penny: "Laodiceans is unique among the pseudepigrapha, in that Laodiceans does not directly engage debates over Paul nor does it create a fictional context within which to authenticate itself, thus rendering the letter largely harmless" (10–11 n. 253). Peirano makes little mention of early Christian pseudepigrapha, and only mentions Paul in passing in relation to the patriarchs: "while a text's false claim to authorship might be used to exclude a work from the canon, there exist several canonical books that purport to be written by one of the patriarchs, as in the case of the *Deuteronomy,* which is written in the persona of Moses, or by one of the apostles, as, for example, in the case of the letters of Paul, some of which are believed to be the work not of Paul but of one of his disciples" (*The Rhetoric of the Roman Fake,* 2).

[61] Penny in his dissertation "The Pseudo-Pauline Letters of the First Two Centuries," for example, cites eight criteria by which a reader can identify the character and function of pseudepigraphic sources (324, 334–39).

[62] I am thinking here of the work of Peirano and of Eva Mroczek (*The Literary Imagination in Jewish Antiquity* [New York: Oxford University Press, 2016]).

[63] Peirano, *The Rhetoric of the Roman Fake,* 1.

The Epistle to the Laodiceans and the Art of Tradition 25

intentional, primary aspect of its writing, or a mistaken, secondary result of its reception history; whether a carefully crafted forgery or an anonymous text that finds a later attribution, the work in question is still considered pseudepigraphic. This ambiguity is implied in the term itself, with the adjective *pseudes* meaning both "deceitful" and "wrong," the latter in a more neutral sense.[64] Peirano's work focuses on examples of pseudepigrapha that are intentionally misattributed either through explicit claims in the text itself or "through subtle allusion to and manipulation of the master-author's text."[65] In such cases, the goal is not simply to emulate or deceive but to present a creative interpretation of the "master-author's texts" that is a compelling supplement to the existing canon.

Peirano suggests that this kind of literature tends to employ a number of strategies which, in combination, contribute to its authorial pretense. First and foremost, the pseudepigrapher will attempt to emulate the language and style of the master-author, whether through borrowed terminology or phrasing or direct quotation. Often these passages or phrases are autobiographical in nature, adding to what Peirano terms the "authorial persona" being emulated.[66] Acting as a signature of sorts, these autobiographical details also aid in establishing "retrospective fictions," details that manipulate the internally expressed setting or time period of the piece in order to correspond with a specific historical era or circumstance.[67] The end result is a piece of writing that offers readers "a pseudo-autobiographical narrative centered on the persona of the master-author by forging links with his original works and autobiographical modes of understanding them."[68]

Turning back to Laodiceans, it is remarkable how well its content corresponds with Peirano's taxonomy. Paul is immediately named, and the letter proceeds to allude to familiar Pauline terminology and style ("Paul, an apostle not from mortals nor through mortals [*non ab hominibus neque per hominem*], but through Jesus Christ, to the brothers who are in Laodicea [*fratribus qui sunt Laodiciae*]"; 1). It contains specific language about perceived competitors ("And may you not be deceived by their vain insinuations [*vaniloquia insinuantium*]...";4) and cites (auto)biographical details about Paul's time in prison ("And now my bonds are for all to see [*Et nunc palam sunt vincula mea*], which I suffer in Christ ..."; 6). It ends with an internal reference to the Colossians lacuna (v. 20),

---

[64] Peirano, *The Rhetoric of the Roman Fake*, 2.

[65] This is to say, not writings subject to an "allographic phenomenon" from later editors, scribes, or the like (Peirano, *The Rhetoric of the Roman Fake*, 3).

[66] She explains: "they help readers to identify the text as a pseudo-autobiographical narrative centered on the persona of the master-author by forging links with his original works and autobiographical modes of understanding them" (Peirano, *The Rhetoric of the Roman Fake*, 3).

[67] Peirano supplies the example of pseudepigrapha addressed to Livia and Maecenas, "personalities of the Augustan period" (*The Rhetoric of the Roman Fake*, 3).

[68] Peirano, *The Rhetoric of the Roman Fake*, 3.

establishing a retrospective, fictive occasion for the letter. More than just a passing observation on its false attribution, to call Laodiceans pseudepigraphic is to recognize it as a clear and strategic piece of literature.

While we may not be able to say with confidence why Laodiceans was written,[69] the author nonetheless reveals a number of concrete interests. Not only were they (presumably) motivated to establish a clear signature for the piece through explicit and implicit references to Paul and the Pauline canon, but they also set about productively augmenting known details about Paul's life. Citing the prison correspondence, for instance, is a creative reworking of Paul's biography, providing additional narrative information about a relatively open aspect of his activities as the apostle to the Gentiles. The missing Laodiceans letter mentioned in Colossians provides an ideal pretext for this "creative supplement," and letter writing itself remains an ideal genre for communicating new biographical facts.[70] Again, we do not know the exact circumstances that motivated this author – Laodiceans may have been written with the intention to deceive – but it is equally plausible that it is an innocuous exercise designed to answer the question "What would Paul write to Laodicea?" that found its way into the canon.[71] In this respect, the study of pseudepigrapha is primarily a study of reception history. But what it achieves is an intertextual engagement with its master-author, adding to the persona of a figure whose life was already (re)constructed through texts.[72]

With all of this in mind, in reexamining scholarship on Laodiceans, one finds that the same elements of the letter which provoke criticism and are dismissed as evidence of its poor execution or relative insignificance are the same features that make it an example of good pseudepigraphic writing. Its citations from the Pauline corpus are not "feeble" attempts at imitation or "all but the most general expressions of doctrine" but intended allusions to a master-author.[73] As for the intertextual references to prison, these are not artless references back to Colossians and Philippians, but an additional signature and narrative bridge back to

---

[69] What I mean to indicate here is that we are not able to precisely identify what motivated Laodiceans' author. As Peirano points out in the cases of Vergil and Ovid, there are pseudepigrapha that came to be associated with these authors that are not suspected of being intentional forgeries. It is conceivable that Laodiceans was an exercise in pseudepigraphic writing that found its way into the Pauline canon in certain circles (*The Rhetoric of the Roman Fake*, 4).

[70] Peirano, *The Rhetoric of the Roman Fake*, 10.

[71] Peirano takes a similar position with the *Ciris* and the pseudo-Tibullan *Panegyricus Messallae* as responses to lacunae in Vergil's *Eclogues* 6.74 and poem 1.1, respectively (*The Rhetoric of the Roman Fake*, 10).

[72] Space does not permit me to treat the question of Colossians' authenticity. That said, if Colossians were also pseudepigraphic, incorporating a reference to a lacuna (in mentioning a letter to the Laodiceans) is an ingenious way to create an additional opportunity to creatively supplement Paul's body of work.

[73] Holloway, "The Apocryphal *Epistle to the Laodiceans* and the Partitioning of Philippians," 325.

The Epistle to the Laodiceans and the Art of Tradition   27

Paul's textual biography. Granted, it is possible scholars have inferred Laodiceans' connections to these pseudepigraphic techniques and judged them to be inadequate. In my view, however, the ubiquity of the "missing Greek original" thesis suggests otherwise.

Postulating an earlier, Greek version of the Latin text has divorced Laodiceans from proper consideration within the scope of Latin literature and writing practices. Naturally, this is not to imply that Greek pseudepigrapha – even Greek Pauline pseudepigrapha – do not exist. Obviously, they do. But by ignoring the manuscript evidence for Laodiceans, it follows that many of the conclusions scholars have reached about context and occasion are predicated on perceived second- or third-century concerns among early Christians, and not on sixth-century canon formation. For example, while there is clearly much to be gained from Bovon's fresh perspective on Laodiceans, like so many others, he takes for granted that there was a second-century Greek "original" for the Latin text.[74] Thus, he speculates that the author of Laodiceans intended for the letter to resolve disputes between church leaders, or perhaps help to (re)establish a "phatic code" between *ekklēsiae*.[75] He also detects in Laodiceans an interpretation of Paul that establishes his authority independent of the Jerusalem apostles, a position he associates with Ignatius of Antioch and Polycarp of Smyrna, but a proposal that shades into problematic, anachronistic debates over orthodoxy and heresy (e.g., are the adversaries in Laodiceans the same so-called Jewish Christians of Philippians 3:2, etc.).[76]

In recent years Philip Tite has taken a similar tack. While Tite helpfully argues that Laodiceans is a strategic, paraenetic letter that constructs a "fictive rhetorical situation" through the first-century figure of Paul, he nonetheless confines the letter's occasion to a general "affirmation and encouragement for a second- or third-century Christian audience."[77] Yet, the only evidence these scholars cite to

---

[74] Bovon simply cites Lightfoot on the matter and proceeds ("Correspondence," 16); cf. Lightfoot, *Saint Paul's Epistles to the Colossians and to Philemon*, 279; Harl Sellew, "*Laodiceans*," 212; Holloway, "The Apocryphal *Epistle to the Laodiceans* and the Partitioning of Philippians," 321, n. 2.

[75] Bovon, "Correspondence," 18.

[76] That said, Bovon also usefully suggests that the admonitions in Laodiceans mirror similar tropes against greed found elsewhere in ancient literature, including Acts 8:18–24 (Laodiceans 13: "praecavete sordidos in lucro") (Bovon, "Correspondence," 19). Bovon also cites Florent Heintz, *Simon 'le magician': Acts 8:5–25 et l'accusation de magie contre les prophètes thaumaturges dans l'antiquité*, Cahiers de la Revue Biblique 39 (Paris: Gabalda, 1997). Paul A. Holloway also makes this observation about invectives and associates the text with Titus 1:10–11 (Holloway, "The Apocryphal *Epistle to the Laodiceans* and the Partitioning of Philippians," 321–23). On "gnosticism," see Karen King, *What is Gnosticism?* (Cambridge, MA: Harvard University Press, 2003).

[77] Tite, *The Apocryphal Epistle to the Laodiceans*, 101. Later in his conclusion, Tite suggests some more issues that may be at play in the second century, including "the charlatan, a concern that was especially present in Christian circles in the first half of the second century" and "a

28 Robyn Faith Walsh

substantiate this claim for a "Greek version now lost" is the hypothesis of Light-foot.[78]

Abstract claims like these are a direct consequence of forcing Laodiceans into a historical context not provided by the available evidence. They are also a consequence of trying to force this document to answer questions about authorial intention that it is not able to answer, apropos of my brief discussion of New Testament methodologies above. I agree with Peirano that pseudepigrapha are best studied as "reception texts" – creative works that, through an observable process of acceptance and rejection, reveal how certain readers actively "make meaning" through the "act of reading."[79] In the case of Laodiceans, this means reconsidering its sixth-century context, its struggle to find a permanent home in the Pauline canon, and the significance of that struggle for understanding Paul's evolving persona as the founding father of early Christianity.

3. The "Transdiscursive Author" in Pseudepigrapha

Admittedly, my analysis of pseudepigrapha and reception evokes certain associations with the so-called "Death of the Author" debates.[80] When I speak of an author for whom we cannot reconstruct intentionality, or of a text for which only the reader can be observed to make meaning, you might understand me to be saying that meaning depends exclusively on the interpretation of the reader or that the true "origin" of a text is in language itself. However, it is not my intention to reinscribe this kind of theoretical framework. In the case at hand, we cannot reconstruct the author, in part, because the pseudepigraphic nature of the text deliberately obscures the identity of its creator. Moreover, with centuries of an incomplete and unreliable manuscript tradition, we have long lost the precise circumstances that gave rise to Laodiceans. From a pragmatic perspective, the only concrete activity we can observe is the reception history for this text, as evidenced by its presence (and absence) from certain canons.

That said, there emerged from these poststructuralist debates observations about the author and authorship that are useful to consider when studying the ancient world. Foucault's distinctions between an author and the "author-function" are particularly relevant to pseudepigrapha, most notably when figures

---

shift from charismatic leadership models to a sedentary leadership structure near the beginning of the second century" (123); however, these options are fairly general and do not significantly alter my overall judgment of Tite's argument.

[78] Tite, *The Apocryphal Epistle to the Laodiceans,* 3 n. 12.

[79] Peirano, *The Rhetoric of the Roman Fake,* 10–11.

[80] Robyn Faith Walsh, *The Origins of Early Christian Literature: Contextualizing the New Testament within Greco-Roman Literary Culture* (Cambridge: Cambridge University Press, 2021), 85–97.

The Epistle to the Laodiceans and the Art of Tradition 29

are tightly associated with large-scale social or cultural movements, as is the case with Paul and Christianity. In his well-known piece "What Is an Author?" Foucault explains that an author's name functions in a manner different from that of other proper names.[81] Not only does it designate the author as a historical entity, it also serves a "classificatory function" in that it has the potential to characterize other texts under that author's umbrella; he explains: "[s]uch a name permits one to group together a certain number of texts, define them, differential them from and contrast them to others."[82] The way these texts are defined, circulated, and received are the "author-function," the means by which an author's name can come to signify status and cultural value – what Foucault calls its "mode of being in discourse."[83] This "author-function" does not happen spontaneously, but is the result of an ongoing process of cultural construction that culminates in "a certain being of reason that we call 'author'."[84]

As a matter of discourse, an author's name has the ability, in certain cases, to encompass not just texts, but new theories, genres, or disciplines. Foucault termed such figures "transdiscursive"; Homer, Aristotle, Augustine, Marx, Nietzsche, and Freud are authors who not only created their own works, but also "the possibilities and the rules for the formation of other texts."[85] These "names" have significance beyond the bounds of their individual writings, generating the possibility for new discursive modalities. Furthermore, these new discursivities will always refer back to their "founder" in order to "be legislated from within the primal corpus."[86] The entire "discursive formation" depends on the core work of its individual founder.[87]

Foucault's description of the transdiscursive author representing a "primal corpus" alludes to the anxiety that can surround pseudepigrapha. The discovery of a new text by the "primal" or founding figure of a particular discourse has the potential to change its field. He illustrates this tension with reference to Freud: "the discovery of a text like Freud's 'Project for a Scientific Psychology' – *insofar*

---

[81] Michel Foucault, "What Is an Author?" *Aesthetics, Method, and Epistemology*, ed. James D. Faubion, trans. Robert Hurley et al. (New York: The New Press, 1998), 205–22, cit. 210. Of note, after finishing this piece, I was made aware of a piece by Karen King that also uses Foucault to treat pseudepigrapha: Karen L. King, "'What Is an Author?' Ancient Author-Function in the *Apocryphon of John* and the Apocalypse of John," in *Scribal Practices and Social Structures among Jesus Adherents: Essays in Honour of John S. Kloppenborg*, ed. William E. Arnal et al. (Leuven: Peeters, 2016), 15–42.

[82] Foucault, "What Is an Author?" 210.

[83] Foucault, "What Is an Author?" 211.

[84] Foucault, "What Is an Author?" 213.

[85] Foucault, "What Is an Author?" 217. For a larger critique of Freud as a historical "name": Robyn Faith Walsh, "Sigmund Freud," in *Field Notes: Revisiting the Classics in the Study of Religion*, ed. Richard Newton and Vaia Touna (New York: Bloomsbury, 2023), 69–76.

[86] Séan Burke, *The Death and Return of the Author: Criticism and Subjectivity in Barthes, Foucault and Derrida*, 3rd ed. (Edinburgh: Edinburgh University Press, 2010), 88.

[87] Burke, *The Death and Return of the Author*, 89.

30 *Robyn Faith Walsh*

as it is a text by Freud – always threatens to modify not the historical knowledge of psychoanalysis, but its theoretical field."[88] Crucially, for Foucault, the attribution of authorship is the primary factor in determining a text's significance; thus, the stakes are high if a "new" text is determined to be by *the* author. I would modify Foucault's observation slightly to say that it is not simply a matter of authenticity, but also one of acceptance: if a text purports to be by a particular author and its content fulfills some perceived lacuna in the field or in the biography of the author, it may still seep into the accepted canon regardless of true attribution. Indeed, readers are certainly capable of holding simultaneously conflicting views on the reality of an author's biography and literary production with their preferred reading or interpretation of the figure in question – for example, we may conclude through historical and stylistic analysis that Paul did not write 2 Thessalonians, or that Acts is by no means historically accurate, but they are included in the canon because they are judged to contribute to an understanding of Paul and the development of the Jesus movement.[89] In modernity, the war-era writings of Paul de Man or the controversial "black notebooks" of Martin Heidegger are only tepidly acknowledged – with some advocating to block their publication altogether (and, thereby, their canonical inclusion) – because they do not conform with previous post-war understandings of each man's respective philosophies.[90] Norman Mailer conceded that he was motivated by profit in his "novel biography" about Marilyn Monroe when he speculated that she was murdered by federal agents, yet this thesis persists in cultural imagination and discourse.[91] Warhol decided to stop personally producing and signing his art, but the entrepreneurial machine of The Factory continued to create "Warhols" in order to meet public demand. When the "name" of a transdiscursive author is established, it can be difficult to unmoor the author from their usual "mode of

---

[88] This passage appears in the version of "Qu'est-ce qu'un auteur?" presented to the Société française de Philosophie in February 1969 and translated by Josué V. Harari in his edited *Textual Strategies: Perspectives in Post-Structuralist Criticism* (Ithaca: Cornell University Press, 1979), 141–60. Passage cited from Burke, *The Death and Return of the Author*, 89 (added emphasis).

[89] On the futility of using Acts as a reliable source on the life of Paul, see Stanley K. Stowers, "The Apostle Paul," in *The History of Western Philosophy of Religion: Vol. 1 Ancient Philosophy of Religion*, ed. Graham Oppy and Nick Trakakis (New York: Oxford University Press, 2009), 145–56.

[90] For more on de Man: Burke, *The Death and Return of the Author*, 1–7; on Heidegger: Philip Oltermann, "Heidegger's 'Black Notebooks' Reveal Antisemitism at Core of His Philosophy," *The Guardian*, 12 March 2014.

[91] Norman Mailer, *Marilyn: A Biography* (New York: Grosset and Dunlap, 1973) 1, 229. On Mailer's speculation for profit: John J. O'Connor, "TV: Mailer Discusses Death of Marilyn Monroe," *The New York Times*, 13 July 1973, 71; Anonymous, "Mailer/Monroe: The Moth and the Star," *The Harvard Crimson*, 14 August 1973. Many subsequent authors and auteurs have continued to capitalize on an overtly "fictionalized" biography of Monroe that includes a variety of claims about her relationships with John F. Kennedy and Robert Kennedy – notable among them are Joyce Carol Oates' Pulitzer Prize nominated *Blonde* (New York: HarperCollins, 2000) and its film adaptation by Andrew Dominik in 2022.

The Epistle to the Laodiceans and the Art of Tradition   31

being in discourse." Therefore, the relationship between author and audience is, in some measure, reciprocal; as much as the transdiscursive author constructs discourse, they are also constructed.

Turning to our case in point, if a newly discovered Pauline letter professed a radical change in perspective or theology, it would have potential to impact how we understand both Paul and early Christianity. The manifold debates among church leaders on what constitutes orthodox and heretical writing demonstrates this concern, including contestations over the various incarnations of Laodiceans. However, these same deliberations demonstrate that acceptance of attribution is not a *fait accompli*.

It is said that concern for authenticity and attribution are thoroughly modern preoccupations; Foucault, for instance, makes this claim in "What Is an Author?" when he discusses the changing "rules of author construction" from Homer to the post-Romantic era. Ironically, he uses the criteria of the fourth- and fifth-century Jerome to make his case.[92] Historians also often invoke this paradigm. In her work on textual attribution in Second Temple Judaism, for instance, Eva Mroczek states that "tracing the origins of texts and their historical authorship is a modern scholarly preoccupation, but was not always so important for ancient writings ... appeal to ancient figures is based on the particular elements of a character's reputation and biography."[93] While there is some basis for claiming difference in the literary habits of antiquity, to claim a stark dichotomy between the "ancients" and "modern" writers is perhaps an oversimplification. There are certainly as many ancient commentators interested in determining proper attribution as there were advocates for maintaining a particular interpretation or reputation for certain figures – the same can be said for modernity.

There may be an element missing from Foucault's analysis of the author that was hinted at by Bovon when he spoke of "useful books." When an author rises to the level of being transdiscursive – when an author becomes more than just an author, but also a "name" or a persona – attribution can become fluid. If a pseudepigraphic text is useful, it may achieve acceptance, regardless of its authenticity. This does not mean that the author is "dead" or that authorial biography does not matter; however, when a figure is primarily known and defined by their writings they are, as Peirano explains, "always to some extent intertextual with their works" and, by extension, open to modification.[94] This can be a function of an author's symbolic value, particularly if the figure in question is associated with the founding of a social movement or other formation.

Eric Hobsbawm explains in his work on "invented traditions" that accepted traditions – that is, overt or tacitly accepted norms of interpretation or be-

---

[92] Foucault, "What Is an Author?" 214.
[93] Mroczek, *The Literary Imagination in Jewish Antiquity*, 53.
[94] Peirano, *The Rhetoric of the Roman Fake*, 11.

havior – must remain "sufficiently adaptable and flexible" in order to survive the changing needs of associated social groups.[95] One way to remain flexible is to reference figures and texts that represent a particular past, but are nonetheless open for continual addition, subtraction, and reinterpretation. These references to the past help to build a legitimizing foundation for present interests, whether the adaptation of a particular ritual action (e.g., the horsehair wigs of English barristers); the elevation of a relatively marginal or subversive figure to the center of an august ancestral inheritance (e.g., Vercingetorix in France); or the reclamation of a previously neglected or forgotten artist or artwork, song, or writing as a representative cultural product (e.g., the paintings of El Greco in Spain). Turning to antiquity, similar claims of status afforded by reference to the past are found in the divine genealogies of Roman emperors, the Atticisms of the Second Sophistic, the post-Aristotelian writings and biographies of Pythagoras, and later rabbinic collections of "oral Torah," to name a few.[96] Mroczek recognizes this process when discussing the numerous figures who come to be associated with otherwise anonymous texts in ancient Judaism, including Moses, David, and Solomon. She labels them "characters in search of stories" – figures who have achieved such high symbolic value that they are usefully staged as authors of texts for which they have no historical claim.[97]

Incorporating Pauline pseudepigrapha into the canon is one way to create change when a figurehead like Paul continues to foster open questions. What the reception history of the Latin Laodiceans tells us is that the text found a contested place in the canon at a time when Paul's textual biography and "character" were still "constructible."[98] The questions left open by the relatively meager information Paul supplies about himself in his genuine letters were addressed in some measure for those who included Laodiceans in the canon. Its formal elimination with the Council of Trent, however, marked an attempt at closing that particular

---

[95] Hobsbawm, *The Invention of Tradition*, 5. Hobsbawm defines "invented tradition" as: "a set of practices, normally governed by overtly or tacitly accepted rules and of a ritual of symbolic nature, which seek to inculcate certain values and norms of behavior by repetition, which automatically implies continuity with the past" (1). I am referencing Hobsbawm in a somewhat narrow sense in this section. For a critique of his larger project and Marxist influence, a useful piece is Elizabeth A. Clark, *History, Theory, Text* (Cambridge: Harvard University Press, 2009), esp. 83–85.

[96] Arnal, "The Collection and Synthesis of 'Tradition,'" 5 n. 11. On Vercingetorix: Michael Dietler, "'Our Ancestors the Gauls': Archaeology, Ethnic Nationalism, and the Manipulation of Celtic Identity in Modern Europe," *American Anthropologist* 96 (1994): 584–605. On the late influence of El Greco on the likes of Pablo Picasso: Jonathan Brown, *Picasso and the Spanish Tradition* (New Haven: Yale University Press, 1996) and John Richardson, "Picasso's Apocalyptic Whorehouse," *The New York Times Review of Books* (23 April 1987): 40–46. Some of these examples are also discussed in Walsh, *The Origins of Early Christian Literature*, 32.

[97] Mroczek, *The Literary Imagination in Jewish Antiquity*, 53.

[98] Peirano, *The Rhetoric of the Roman Fake*, 11.

The Epistle to the Laodiceans and the Art of Tradition 33

narrative – Paul was set as a transdiscursive, founding figure without the need for a fully attested and self-resonating body of work.[99]

For those dictating canon, compiling the so-called genuine Pauline letters together with select pseudepigrapha and Acts produced a sufficiently cohesive narrative for Paul. Supplements might appear in the form of iconography or critical commentary but, as a "textual entity," Paul was complete. Bill Arnal suggests that Paul's characterization in Acts had a great deal to do with this perception:

> ... presenting Paul in terms of *both* a collection of letters *and* the narrative characterization in Acts is an important innovation. The effect is to expand generously the image of Paul. The addition of the Pastorals makes Paul the letter-writer safe for Orthodoxy; while the retention of Acts incorporates the figure of Paul as an actor, a narrative player and hero of the apostolic church, appropriately unified with the twelve ... The narrative Paul of Acts – missionary, martyr, bearer of the apostolic torch to the Gentiles – becomes the model through which to read the letters ... A body of writing is *authorized* by being given an *author*, whose personality binds together the various writings as a corpus.[100]

Arnal's analysis helps illustrate that authentication and canonization are *processes*, often aimed at creating a sense of historical, aesthetic, and narrative cohesion. Laodiceans may address the omission raised by Colossians 4:16, but in the context of the counter-Reformation, it offered more questions than answers: Why was this letter so short? Why did Paul repeat himself? What else of Paul's time in prison? And, crucially, why is this letter only extant in Latin?[101] Laodiceans was not essential for accepting an orthodox understanding of Paul, but it does not follow that this means it was useless, insipid, or heretical. Returning to the "Bovonian Paradox," the letter itself remains Pauline in substance. That it rests in the Vulgate Apocrypha to this day speaks to how canon shapes interpretive communities as much as interpretive communities shape canon.

Finally, Laodiceans is not only a study in pseudepigrapha, but also in how "Paul" remains a constructible figure for scholars of the New Testament. Whether it is the illusion that we have a cohesive Pauline corpus, that Acts is historically descriptive, or reifying the notion of the early Christian "Big Bang," we must be cautious not to treat Paul like a textual entity whose biography is usefully supplemented by our own scholarship.[102] As previously discussed, the majority of scholarship on Laodiceans does not distinguish between the sixth-century

---

[99] That is, closing the lacuna set by Colossians 4:16, as I will discuss.

[100] Arnal, "The Collection and Synthesis of 'Tradition'," 205–6.

[101] Famously, Erasmus rejected any text for which a Greek original could not be found, including 1 John 5:7–8.

[102] On the concept of the early Christian "Big Bang," see Robyn Walsh, "Q and the 'Big Bang' Theory of Christian Origins," in *Redescribing The Gospel of Mark*, ed. Merrill Miller and Barry Crawford, Early Christianity and Its Literature (Atlanta: Society of Biblical Literature, 2017), 483–533; Walsh, *The Origins of Early Christian Literature*, 50–104.

34 *Robyn Faith Walsh*

Latin Laodiceans and references to letters with the same name in earlier commentary.[103] This is problematic for numerous reasons, the most obvious being that there is no extant evidence to support conflating the Latin Laodiceans with earlier references to a letter of the same name. In addition to this practical concern, there is the issue of mythologizing our subject matter. To assume the Latin Laodiceans is the same Laodiceans letter discussed in Mur. Frag. or mentioned by Tertullian, for example, infers that there is a secure tradition of known Pauline sources dating as far back as the second century.[104] Our instinct to affirm these speculative connections is yet another expression of the nature of "Paul" as a transdiscursive and constructible author.

4. Appendix: Structural and verbal dependence of *Laodiceans* on Philippians[105]

Laodiceans	Philippians	Change in Terminology (Laodiceans/Philippians)	Other NT Epistles
1	–		Gal 1:1; Col 1:2
2	1:2		Gal 1:3; Rom 1:7; 1 Cor 1:2; 2 Cor 1:2
3	1:3–4	Christ/God day of judgment/ day of Christ	Rom 2:7; see 2 Pet 2:9; 3:7
4	1:6, 10		Gal 2:5, 14; 1 Cor 1:8; 2 Pet 2:9, 3:7; Col 2:4
5	[1:12]		Gal 1:11; Rom 2:7; Eph 2:10
6	1:13		
7	1:18–20	Holy Spirit/Jesus Christ	
8	1:20–21		Gal 2:20
9	1:21; 2:2		Titus 3:5
10	2:12		Rom 2:7; 5:21; 6:22, 23; Gal 6:8
11	2:13		

---

[103] Schneemelcher is more cautious: "The dating of the Epistle to the Laodiceans is difficult for the reason that it depends on the question of the identity of this apocryphon with the one mentioned in the Muratori Canon, and this again is closely connected with the problem of its Marcionite derivation" (*New Testament Apocrypha*, 43).

[104] "There is ... also (an epistle) to the Laodiceans, another to the Alexandrians, forged in Paul's name for the sect of Marcion, and several others, which cannot be received in the catholic Church; for it will not do to mix gall with honey" (*Canon Muratori* 63–67, quoted from R. McL. Wilson translation published in Schneemelcher, *New Testament Apocrypha*, 1:36).

[105] Adapted from Harl Sellew, "*Laodiceans*," 28.

The Epistle to the Laodiceans and the Art of Tradition

Laodiceans	Philippians	Change in Terminology (Laodiceans/Philippians)	Other NT Epistles
12	[2:14]		
13	[3:1–2]		
14	4:6		1 Cor 2:16; 15:58
15	2:5; 4:7–8		1 Cor 2:16
16	1:7; 4:8–9, 22		
{17}	–		[1 Thess 5:26]
18	4:22		
19	4:23		Gal 6:18
20	–		[Col 4:16]

Bibliography

Anonymous. "Mailer/Monroe: The Moth and the Star." *The Harvard Crimson*. 14 August 1973.

Arnal, William E. "The Collection and Synthesis of 'Tradition' and the Second-Century Invention of Christianity." *Method and Theory in the Study of Religion* 23 (2011): 193–215.

Auwers, Jean-Marie and H.J. de Jonge, ed. *The Biblical Canons*. Leuven: Leuven University Press, 2003.

Backus, Irena. "Renaissance Attitudes to New Testament Apocryphal Writings: Jacques Lefevre d'Etaples and his Epigones." *Renaissance Quarterly* 51 (1998): 1169–1198.

Batey, Richard. "The Destination of Ephesians." *Journal of Biblical Literature* 82 (1963): 101.

Bauckham, Richard. "Pseudo-Apostolic Letters." *Journal of Biblical Literature* 107 (1986): 469–494.

Bourdieu, Pierre. *The Field of Cultural Production: Essays on Art and Literature*. Translated by Randal Johnson. New York: Columbia University Press, 1993.

Bovon, François. "The Correspondence between Paul and the Corinthians and Paul's Letter to the Laodiceans." Unpublished paper provided by the author, 2005.

Brown, Jonathan. *Picasso and the Spanish Tradition*. New Haven: Yale University Press, 1996.

Burke, Séan. *The Death and Return of the Author: Criticism and Subjectivity in Barthes, Foucault and Derrida*. 3rd ed. Edinburgh: Edinburgh University Press, 2010.

Chadwick, Henry. *Priscillian of Avila: The Occult and The Charismatic Early Church*. Oxford: Clarendon Press, 1976.

Dietler, Michael. "'Our Ancestors the Gauls': Archaeology, Ethnic Nationalism, and the Manipulation of Celtic Identity in Modern Europe." *American Anthropologist* 96 (1994): 584–605.

Ehrman, Bart. *Lost Scriptures: Books That Did Not Make It into the New Testament*. New York: Oxford University Press, 2003.

36   *Robyn Faith Walsh*

Eyl, Jennifer. "Why Thekla Does Not See Paul: Visual Perception and the Displacement of Erōs in the Acts of Paul and Thekla." Pages 3–12 in *The Ancient Novel and the Early Christian and Jewish Narrative. Fictional Intersections.* Edited by Marília P. Futre Pinheiro et al. Groningen: Barkhuis – Groningen University Library, 2012.

Foucault, Michel. "Qu'est-ce qu'un auteur?" Pages 141–160 *Textual Strategies: Perspectives in Post-Structuralist Criticism.* Translated by Josué V. Harari. Ithaca: Cornell University Press, 1979.

Foucault, Michel. "What Is an Author?" Pages 205–222 in *Aesthetics, Method, and Epistemology.* Edited by James D. Faubion and translated by Robert Hurley et al. New York: The New Press, 1998.

Harl Sellew, Melissa. "*Laodiceans* and the Philippians Fragments Hypothesis." *Harvard Theological Review* 87 (1994): 17–28.

Harl Sellew, Melissa. "*Laodiceans* and Philippians Revisited: A Response to Paul Holloway." *Harvard Theological Review* 91 (1998): 327–329.

Harnack, Adolf von. *Marcion: das Evangelium vom fremden Gott: Eine Monographie zur Geschichte der Grundlegung der katholischen Kirche.* Leipzig: J.C. Hinrichs, 1921.

Harnack, Adolf von. *Geschichte der altchristlichen Litteratur bis Eusebius.* Vol. 1. Leipzig: J.C. Hinrichs, 1893.

Hermann, Leon. "L'Épitre aux Laodicéens (Laodicéens et l'apologie aux Hebreux)." *Cahiers du Cercle Ernest Renan* 58 (1968): 1–16.

Hobsbawm, Eric. "Introduction: Inventing Traditions." Pages 1–14 in *The Invention of Tradition.* Edited by Eric Hobsbawm and Terence Ranger. Cambridge: Cambridge University Press, 2010.

Holder, R. Ward. *A Companion to Paul in the Reformation.* Boston: Brill, 2009.

Holloway, Paul A. "The Apocryphal *Epistle to the Laodiceans* and the Partitioning of Philippians." *Harvard Theological Review* 91 (1998): 321–325.

James, M.R. *The Apocryphal New Testament.* Oxford: Clarendon Press, 1924.

John of Salisbury. *The Later Letters.* Edited by W.J. Millor and C.N.L. Brooke. Oxford: Clarendon Press, 1979.

King, Karen L. *What is Gnosticism?* Cambridge, MA: Harvard University Press, 2003.

King, Karen L. "'What Is an Author?' Ancient Author-Function in the Apocryphon of John and the Apocalypse of John." Pages 15–42 in *Scribal Practices and Social Structures among Jesus Adherents: Essays in Honour of John S. Kloppenborg.* Edited by William E. Arnal et al. Leuven: Peeters, 2016.

Knox, John. *Philemon Among the Letters of Paul: A New View of Its Place and Importance.* New York: Abingdon, 1959.

Lightfoot, J.B. *Saint Paul's Epistles to the Colossians and to Philemon: A Revised Text with Introductions, Notes, and Dissertations.* London: Macmillan, 1892.

MaGee, Gregory S. "Exalted Apostle: The Portrayal of Paul in Colossians and Ephesians." PhD diss., Trinity Evangelical Divinity School, 2009.

Mailer, Norman. *Marilyn: A Biography.* New York: Grosset and Dunlap, 1973.

Metzger, Bruce. *The Canon of the New Testament.* Oxford: Clarendon Press, 1997.

Mroczek, Eva. *The Literary Imagination in Jewish Antiquity.* New York: Oxford University Press, 2016.

O'Connor, John J. "TV: Mailer Discusses Death of Marilyn Monroe." *The New York Times.* 13 July 1973.

Oltermann, Philip. "Heidegger's 'Black Notebooks' Reveal Antisemitism at Core of His Philosophy." *The Guardian*, 12 March 2014.

The Epistle to the Laodiceans and the Art of Tradition   37

Peirano, Irene. *The Rhetoric of the Roman Fake: Latin Pseudepigrapha in Context*. Cambridge: Cambridge University Press, 2012.

Penny, Donald N. "The Pseudo-Pauline Letters of the First Two Centuries." PhD diss., Emory University, 1979.

Richardson, John. "Picasso's Apocalyptic Whorehouse." *The New York Times Review of Books* (23 April 1987): 40–46.

Richardson, John. *Sacred Monsters, Sacred Masters: Beaton, Capote, Dalí, Picasso, Freud, Warhol and More*. New York: Jonathan Cape, 2001.

Sandnes, Karl Olav. *The Gospel "According to Homer and Virgil": Cento and Canon*. Leiden: Brill, 2011.

Schneemelcher, Wilhelm. *Neutestamentliche Apokryphen in deutscher Übersetzung: 5. Auflage der von Edgar Hennecke begründeten Sammlung*. 2 vols. Tübingen: Mohr Siebeck, 1987–1989.

Schneemelcher, Wilhelm, ed. *New Testament Apocrypha, Vol. 2: Writings Relating to the Apostles, Apocalypses, and Related Subjects*. Edited and translated by R. McL. Wilson. Louisville: Westminster Knox Press, 1992.

Stowers, Stanley K. "The Apostle Paul." Pages 145–156 in *The History of Western Philosophy of Religion: Vol. 1 Ancient Philosophy of Religion*. Edited by Graham Oppy and Nick Trakakis. New York: Oxford University Press, 2009.

Tite, Philip L. *The Apocryphal Epistle to the Laodiceans*. Leiden: Brill, 2012.

Trebay, Guy. "A Collector of People Along With Art." *The New York Times*. 6 April 2011. http://www.nytimes.com/2011/04/07/fashion/07GREEN.html.

Walsh, Robyn. "Q and the 'Big Bang' Theory of Christian Origins." Pages 483–533 in *Redescribing The Gospel of Mark*. Edited by Merrill Miller and Barry Crawford. Early Christianity and Its Literature. Atlanta: Society of Biblical Literature, 2017.

Walsh, Robyn Faith. *The Origins of Early Christian Literature: Contextualizing the New Testament within Greco-Roman Literary Culture*. Cambridge: Cambridge University Press, 2021.

Walsh, Robyn Faith. "Sigmund Freud." Pages 69–76 *Field Notes: Revisiting the Classics in the Study of Religion*. Edited by Richard Newton and Vaia Touna. New York: Bloomsbury, 2023.

Watson, Steven. *Factory Made: Warhol and the Sixties*. New York: Pantheon Books, 2003.

Authorial Fictions, Phoenician Paradigms, and the Reception of Achilles Tatius' *Leucippe and Clitophon* in the *Lives* of Galaction and Episteme[*]

CLAIRE RACHEL JACKSON

Rumours of the death of the author have been greatly exaggerated. Despite the persistent debates over their life, demise, and resurrection throughout the twentieth century,[1] the author, as Margaret Mullett has put it, has proved decidedly harder to bury than to kill.[2] For classical scholarship in particular, the fragmentary state of the evidence has often facilitated an over-reliance on authorial biography as a means of fixing texts within literary ancestries, historical contexts, and teleological frameworks of tradition and dependency.[3] Seen through this lens, not only can the author's intentions be recovered, but any textual inconsistencies can be neutralised by the right combination of historical analysis, literary genealogical inquiry, and philological acumen. Recent scholarship, however, has challenged these neat fictions by drawing attention

---

[*] I am very grateful to the editors for the invitation to contribute to this volume and for their advice and support throughout. Many thanks to Talitha Kearey for our discussions on authorship, and to all the members of the *Novel Echoes* research group in Ghent for our thought-provoking dialogue about the *Lives*. I am particularly grateful to Julie Van Pelt for advice on bibliography, and to Benedek Kruchió for sharing forthcoming work ahead of publication. Special thanks are due to Koen De Temmerman for his insightful feedback and enthusiasm for this contribution. This project has received funding from the European Research Council (ERC) under the European Union's Horizon 2020 research and innovation programme (grant agreement No. 819459 – NovelEchoes).

[1] The most prominent touchstones are Roland Barthes, "The Death of the Author," in *The Book History Reader*, ed. David Finkelstein and Alistair McCleery, 2nd ed. (London: Routledge, 2006), 277–80; Michel Foucault, "Qu'est-ce qu'un auteur?" *Bulletin de la société française de philosophie* (1969): 75–104. See also Seán Burke, *Authorship: From Plato to the Postmodern. A Reader* (Edinburgh: Edinburgh University Press, 1995); idem, *The Death and Return of the Author: Criticism and Subjectivity in Barthes, Foucault and Derrida*, 3rd ed. (Edinburgh: Edinburgh University Press, 2008); the essays in Maurice Biriotti and Nicole Miller, eds., *What Is an Author?* (Manchester: Manchester University Press, 1993), all with further bibliography.

[2] Margaret Mullett, "In Search of the Monastic Author: Story-telling, Anonymity, and Innovation in the 12th Century," in *The Author in Middle Byzantine Literature: Modes, Functions, Identities*, ed. Aglae Pizzone (Berlin: De Gruyter, 2014), 171.

[3] Acutely discussed by Tom Geue, *Author Unknown: The Power of Anonymity in Ancient Rome* (Cambridge, MA: Harvard University Press, 2019), 1–25; Marco Formisano and Cristiana Sogno, "Origins and Original Moments in Late Greek and Latin Texts," *Arethusa* 54 (2021): 269–73.

40 *Claire Rachel Jackson*

to the way ancient texts themselves exploit the interpretative possibilities of anonymity, authorial absence, and pseudepigraphic authority.[4] In particular, ancient biography has increasingly been reconfigured as a site of reception, where the narratives put forward about an author's life function as a critical response to the works attributed to them.[5] As a result of this shift, authorship can be seen not simply as a historical construct surrounding the creation of a text, but also as a posthumous fiction generated both by and for later audiences.[6] Authors, therefore, are as much a function of reception as composition, and the spectrum of fictions surrounding their role and identity can be continuously resurrected and reinterpreted as the work circulates.

This relationship between author, fiction, and reception is both epitomised and problematised by the second-century novel *Leucippe and Clitophon*, attributed to Achilles Tatius. Although this well-attested appellation means that the work is not technically anonymous, essentially nothing is known about the named author. The tenth-century *Suda*, the earliest source of any detailed information, describes the author of *Leucippe and Clitophon* as an Alexandrian who converted to Christianity, eventually becoming a bishop, and also wrote several scientific treatises (α 4695).[7] All of this information is at very best shrouded in doubt, if not outright scepticism, since there is no other external evidence to support any of the *Suda*'s claims.[8] The *Suda* in fact names the novelist as Achilles

---

[4] Irene Peirano, "Ille ego qui quondam: On Authorial (An)onymity," in *The Author's Voice in Classical and Late Antiquity*, ed. Anna Marmodoro and Jonathan Hill (Oxford: Oxford University Press, 2013), 251–85; Geue, *Author Unknown*; Irene Peirano Garrison and Hindy Najman, "Pseudepigrapha and Pseudepigraphy," in *The Old Testament Pseudepigrapha: Fifty Years of the Pseudepigrapha at the SBL*, ed. Matthias Henze and Liv Ingeborg Lied (Atlanta: Society of Biblical Literature, 2019), 331–54.

[5] Among others, see Barbara Graziosi, *Inventing Homer: The Early Reception of Ancient Epic* (Cambridge: Cambridge University Press, 2002); Koen De Temmerman and Kristoffel Demoen, eds., *Writing Biography in Greece and Rome: Narrative Technique and Fictionalization* (Cambridge: Cambridge University Press, 2016); Richard Fletcher and Johanna Hanink, eds., *Creative Lives in Classical Antiquity: Poets, Artists, and Biography* (Cambridge: Cambridge University Press, 2016).

[6] This can be seen in feminist responses to Barthes, "The Death of the Author." For example, Nancy K. Miller (*Subject to Change: Reading Feminist Writing* [New York: Columbia University Press, 1988], 102–22) argues that the death of the author denies authority to writers traditionally marginalised from the canon by virtue of their gender identity, sexuality, or race, and recognition of a female literary tradition necessitates at least some kind of engagement with the historical author's identity. On the other hand, Toril Moi argues that Barthes' theories must be embraced in order to unravel the patriarchal framework of authorial authority (*Sexual/Textual Politics: Feminist Literary Theory* [London: Routledge, 1985]). For an overview of such responses, see Andrew Bennett, *The Author* (Abingdon and New York: Routledge, 2005), 83–89.

[7] Tim Whitmarsh (*Achilles Tatius: Leucippe and Clitophon. Books I–II* [Cambridge: Cambridge University Press, 2020], 1–4) and Karl Plepelits ("Achilles Tatios," in *The Novel in the Ancient World*, ed. Gareth Schmeling, 2nd ed. [Leiden: Brill, 2003], 387–416, esp. 387–88) survey this evidence more fully.

[8] The most tenacious feature is the identification of the author as Alexandrian, which recurs throughout the testimonia to and manuscripts of the novel and which has often been accepted as

Authorial Fictions, Phoenician Paradigms 41

Statius, a variant spelling which has provoked questions about the reliability of this entry.[9] Not only is the novel attributed to an unknown author with an unreliable tradition, but this is paralleled by the lack of authorial intrusion into the narrative itself. In contrast to other novelists, the author of *Leucippe and Clitophon* never gives their own name or hints at their presence within the narrative.[10] Instead, the novel is narrated in the first-person, initially by a nameless character, and then by the eponymous Clitophon, and offers a narrative of the text's creation through oral storytelling in contrast to the scripted materiality of the novel itself. Whether or not this authorial anonymity was intentional, the lack of explicit authorial intervention into this embedded network of ego-narrators draws attention to this absence and invites awareness of the relationship between the author as the source of the novel and its own fictions of creation.

The late antique and Byzantine reception of *Leucippe and Clitophon*, moreover, explicitly resurrects these authorial fictions. The *Life* of Saint Galaction and Episteme, two Christian saints who live in a celibate marriage before their mutual martyrdom, circulates in two versions. An earlier, unattributed text has been dated to anywhere between the third and ninth centuries (*BHG* 665), while a later version reworks this narrative for inclusion in Symeon Metaphrastes' *Menologion*, a tenth-century compilation of saints' lives arranged according to the liturgical calendar (*BHG* 666).[11] Although the two texts differ from each other stylistically, in both versions Galaction's father is named Clitophon and his mother is named either Gleucippe or Leucippe, in what has long been recognised as an allusion to the novel.[12] While the novel is well-cited in

---

plausible due to the detailed description of the city in the novel itself (*L&C* 5.1). This, however, is a circular argument, in which the text serves as evidence of the author's circumstances and these circumstances then reify the value of the novel.

[9] *Suda* α 4695: Ἀχιλλεὺς Στάτιος, Ἀλεξανδρεύς, ὁ γράψας τὰ κατὰ Λευκίππην καὶ Κλειτοφῶντα ... The ninth-century writer Photius names him Achilles Tatius (*Bibliotheca* codex 87, 66a14–15), followed by the majority of manuscripts and other testimonia. On this see Whitmarsh, *Achilles Tatius*, 2.

[10] By contrast, Chariton is named in the first-person preface to *Callirhoe* (1.1.1), whereas Heliodorus' *Aithiopika* ends with a biographical *sphragis* (10.41.4). Xenophon of Ephesus and Longus are less explicit but still offer points of connection between paratextual authorial information and the openings of their respective novels, as in the case of Xenophon, which opens in the titular Ephesus (1.1.1). Longus' prologue is discussed further below.

[11] On the dating of the earlier text, see A. P. Alwis, *Celibate Marriages in Late Antique and Byzantine Hagiography: The Lives of Saints Julian and Basilissa, Andronikos and Athanasia, and Galaktion and Episteme* (London: Bloomsbury, 2011), 8–10; Nikoletta Kanavou, "Reflections on the Relationship between the Life and Passion of Saints Galaktion and Episteme and the Ancient Greek Novel," *Jahrbuch der Österreichischen Byzantinistik* 70 (2021): 209 n. 4; Benedek Kruchió, "Galaction and Episteme: Converting Erotic Fiction," forthcoming. Simon Ford is preparing a reassessment of the dating of *BHG* 665 due to its presentation of Christian persecution and religious practice. On the dating of the *Menologion*, see Christian Høgel, *Symeon Metaphrastes: Rewriting and Canonization* (Copenhagen: Museum Tusculanum Press, 2002), 62–80.

[12] Noted as early as Hippolyte Delehaye, *Les Passions des Martyrs et les Genres Littéraires*

42 *Claire Rachel Jackson*

the centuries after its composition,[13] the incorporation of its protagonists into a Christian hagiographical genealogy is not only unparalleled, but also raises questions about exactly what kind of intertextual relationship is evoked by this reference. Given the wide range of dating possibilities, most scholarship on the *Lives'* relationship with Achilles Tatius has prioritised the earlier text, especially as a representative of an early tradition, in order to minimise the chronological and cultural distance between the two.[14] Yet when considered holistically, it becomes clear that each *Life* responds to the issues of authorial authority and narratorial reliability raised in the prologue to *Leucippe and Clitophon* and reworks them in accordance with contemporary Christianised concepts of authorship. Despite this gulf in chronology and religion, the *Lives* interrogate the fictions of authorship explored in the prologue of Achilles Tatius' novel and testify to how these authorial models are reshaped by later readers across the novel's early reception history.

This contribution argues that Achilles Tatius' *Leucippe and Clitophon* programmatically explores questions of authorship and authority in ways which shape its later reception in Late Antiquity and Byzantium. I suggest that the novel's famous prologue repeatedly thematises origins, narrators, and authority in ways that draw attention to the author's absence from this framing narrative. The second half of this contribution then explores how each *Life* of Galaction and Episteme respectively responds to these tensions and how they resonate within the contexts of Christian hagiographical literature. In particular, Achilles Tatius' novel marks its intricate architecture of inset narrators with Phoenician symbolism, which not only carries associations of contested mythologies, legendary origins, and foundational authority, but also thematises the significance of the author's absence from the prologue. For the *Lives*, however, this Phoenician framing becomes a key site of negotiation with the novel as a source of textual authority. In this way, the goal of this contribution is not to identify biographical information about the authors of any of these texts or to shed light on the circumstances of their composition. Instead, it explores how *Leucippe and Clitophon* itself invites and problematises these neat fictions of authorship, and how they are reflected and refracted in its Christian hagiographical reception.

(Brussels: Société des Bollandistes, 1921), 319; Heinrich Dörrie, "Die griechischen Romane und das Christentum," *Philologus* 93 (1938): 274–75.

[13] See the overviews of Suzanne Macalister, *Dreams and Suicides: The Greek Novel from Antiquity to the Byzantine Empire* (London and New York: Routledge, 1996), 108–10; Whitmarsh, *Achilles Tatius*, 13–17; *contra* Plepelits, "Achilles Tatios," 411.

[14] For example, Kanavou, "Reflections," 209–10; Kruchió, "Galaction and Episteme." This disregard for the later *Life* corresponds to the traditional disdain for Metaphrastes' *Menologion*, on which see Høgel, *Symeon Metaphrastes*, 9–10.

Authorial Fictions, Phoenician Paradigms   43

1. Authors and Authority

Despite the absence of any reference to the named author of *Leucippe and Clitophon* within the novel itself, the opening of the text repeatedly raises questions about origins and creators, perspective and authority.[15] The novel begins with an unnamed narrator recounting his arrival in Sidon following a shipwreck, which leads him to a beautiful painting of Europa. After describing the image in detail, his praise of the painting sparks a conversation with a stranger, the eponymous Clitophon, whom he coaxes into telling his own romantic adventures (1.1.1–1.3.1). Once Clitophon takes over the first-person narration of the novel, however, the unnamed narrator and the Sidonian framing are never mentioned again.[16] Instead, the novel ends with Leucippe and Clitophon's marriage and subsequent voyage to Byzantium (8.19.3), and the dissonance between this conclusion and Clitophon retroactively telling this story to a stranger in Sidon in the absence of Leucippe is never explained. There is no evidence to suggest that this disparity is anything other than deliberate,[17] which further emphasises the anonymity of the unnamed narrator, about whom no identifying information is given,[18] and instead frames Clitophon as the principal narrator of the novel. Clitophon's ego-narration throughout the novel has attracted much attention for

---

[15] This is not confined to the introduction, as the various aetiological digressions in the work, such as the source of Tyrian purple (2.11.4–8), return to this theme of origins and authority. See J. R. Morgan, "Achilles Tatius," in *Narrators, Narratees, and Narratives in Ancient Greek Literature*, ed. Rene Nünlist, Angus M. Bowie, and Irene de Jong (Leiden: Brill, 2004), 502–3; Whitmarsh, *Achilles Tatius*, 208–11. On the relationship between authorship and authority in classical literature, see Simon Goldhill, "The Sirens' Song: Authorship, Authority, and Citation," in *What Is an Author?* 137–54.

[16] One possible exception is the textual problem at 1.4.3, where Clitophon compares Leucippe to an image of either Selene or Europa on a bull. While historically scholars have favoured reading Europa to more closely connect the opening ekphrasis with the rest of the novel, contemporary scholarship now prioritises Selene as better attested in the manuscripts and for better sense of the Greek sentence. On this see Helen Morales, *Vision and Narrative in Achilles Tatius' Leucippe and Clitophon* (Cambridge: Cambridge University Press, 2004), 37–48, with further bibliography. This ambiguity nonetheless teases the disconnect between the unnamed narrator and Clitophon's narration, noted by Whitmarsh, *Achilles Tatius*, 138. See also De Temmerman on another metaleptic slippage between the prologue and the rest of the novel: Koen De Temmerman, "A Flowery Meadow and a Hidden Metalepsis in Achilles Tatius," *Classical Quarterly* 59 (2009): 667–70.

[17] On this see I. D. Repath, "Achilles Tatius' *Leucippe and Cleitophon*: What Happened Next?" *Classical Quarterly* 55 (2005): 250–65; Saiichiro Nakatani, "A Re-Examination of Some Structural Problems in Achilles Tatius' *Leucippe and Clitophon*," *Ancient Narrative* 3 (2003): 74–79; Morgan, "Achilles Tatius," 494; Morales, *Vision and Narrative*, 143–51.

[18] Apart from the functional explanation of how he came to Sidon, his only identifying feature is that he is erotically inclined (1.2.1). The comment that the Sidonians call the Phoenician goddess Astarte (1.1.2) implies that the narrator is unfamiliar with the region; see Morgan, "Achilles Tatius," 494; Morales, *Vision and Narrative*; Whitmarsh, *Achilles Tatius*, 71–74.

44 Claire Rachel Jackson

how it characterises and problematises him as a character within the narrative.[19] Against this, the unnamed narrator's brief, undistinguished appearance might seem to mediate between author and narrator, and as such to validate Clitophon's ego-narration according to generic convention.[20]

Yet the unnamed narrator's appearance is more unsettling than it might seem at first glance, especially by comparison to Longus' roughly contemporary novel *Daphnis and Chloe*.[21] While this novel similarly begins with an anonymous narrator's description of a painting, a framing which is also not revisited at the end of the text,[22] the prologue nonetheless makes explicit a relationship between prefatory image and written book.[23] The unnamed narrator, inspired by the painting, constructs a story of four books (τέτταρας βίβλους ἐξεπονησάμην; *praef.* 3), mirroring the four books of the novel. In addition, Longus' anonymous narrator is linguistically distanced from the story they tell, as the rest of the novel is narrated in the third-person, and also at the level of characterisation, since the narrator is implied to be an elite tourist in contrast to the rustic protagonists.[24] This is not to downplay the complexity of Longus' intricate play between narrator, author, and characters,[25] but rather to point out how *Daphnis and Chloe* facilitates the identification of the unnamed narrator with the work's author. Despite the undeniable artifice of this narrative of creation, as the writer

---

[19] The bibliography on Clitophon's narration is vast; see B.P. Reardon, "Achilles Tatius and Ego-Narrative," in *Greek Fiction: The Greek Novel in Context*, ed. John Robert Morgan and Richard Stoneman (London: Routledge, 1994), 80–96; Tim Whitmarsh, "Reading for Pleasure: Narrative, Irony and Erotics in Achilles Tatius," in *Ancient Novel and Beyond*, ed. Stelios Panayotakis, Maaike Zimmerman, and Wytse Hette Keulen (Leiden: Brill, 2003), 195–205; Marko Marinčič, "Advertising One's Own Story: Text and Speech in Achilles Tatius' *Leucippe and Clitophon*," in *Seeing Tongues, Hearing Scripts: Orality and Representation in the Ancient Novel*, ed. Victoria Rimell, Ancient Narrative Supplementum 7 (Groningen: Barkhuis & Groningen University Library, 2007), 168–200. See also the overview of Morgan, "Achilles Tatius," with further citations. Compare with Winkler on the embedded first-person narration of Kalasiris in Heliodorus' *Aithiopika*: J.J. Winkler, "The Mendacity of Kalasiris and the Narrative Strategy of Heliodoros' *Aithiopika*," *Yale Classical Studies* 27 (1982): 93–158.

[20] Suggested by G.W. Most, "The Stranger's Stratagem: Self-Disclosure and Self-Sufficiency in Greek Culture," *Journal of Hellenic Studies* 109 (1989): 114–33. For critique of this point. see Morales, *Vision and Narrative*, 146–47.

[21] On the relative dating of these novels see Whitmarsh, *Achilles Tatius*, 30.

[22] This perhaps derives from Plato's *Symposium*; on the importance of this text for *Leucippe and Clitophon*, see Karen ní Mheallaigh, "Philosophical Framing: The Phaedran Setting of *Leucippe and Clitophon*," in *Philosophical Presences in the Ancient Novel*, ed. J.R. Morgan and Meriel Jones, Ancient Narrative Supplementum 10 (Groningen: Barkhuis & Groningen University Library, 2007), 239–40.

[23] Marinčič, "Advertising One's Own Story," 171–72.

[24] The third word of the novel, θηρῶν (*praef.* 1) establishes the narrator's elite status in contrast to the work's rustic protagonists, and his need for an interpreter of the painting (*praef.* 3) suggests that he is not local to the area.

[25] Morgan ("Nymphs, Neighbours, and Narrators") has argued for a distinction between the author and narrator of Longus; this is critiqued in more detail by Calum Maciver, "Longus' Narrator: A Reassessment," *Classical Quarterly* 70 (2020): 827–45.

Authorial Fictions, Phoenician Paradigms 45

of a book much like if not the novel itself, Longus' narrator is analogous to the work's author, and both are kept at a level of distance from the novelistic protagonists. This space of contact between author and narrator is crucial to Dorrit Cohn's influential definitions of narrative, with the possibility of divergence between the two exemplifying her titular "distinction of fiction."[26]

Leucippe and Clitophon, however, establishes no such distance. While the anonymous first-person narrator might be synonymous with the novel's author, there are no clues in the text to encourage or discourage this identification.[27] And yet this question of who is speaking resonates throughout the prologue. The detailed description of the painting of Europa repeatedly raises questions of mediation and perspective, and the protracted dramatisation of the transition between the unnamed narrator's and Clitophon's narration makes visible the interplay between different voices and viewpoints.[28] In contrast to Longus' prologue, however, where despite his anonymity the narrator's presence is instantly felt, *Leucippe and Clitophon* does not make clear who is speaking at the outset of the text (1.1.1–2):[29]

Σιδὼν ἐπὶ θαλάττῃ πόλις· Ἀσσυρίων ἡ θάλασσα· μήτηρ Φοινίκων ἡ πόλις· Θηβαίων ὁ δῆμος πατήρ. δίδυμος λιμὴν ἐν κόλπῳ πλατύς, ἠρέμα κλείων τὸ πέλαγος· ᾗ γὰρ ὁ κόλπος κατὰ πλευρὰν ἐπὶ δεξιὰ κοιλαίνεται, στόμα δεύτερον ὀρώρυκται, καὶ τὸ ὕδωρ αὖθις εἰσρεῖ, καὶ γίνεται τοῦ λιμένος ἄλλος λιμήν, ὡς χειμάζειν μὲν ταύτῃ τὰς ὁλκάδας ἐν γαλήνῃ, θερίζειν δὲ τοῦ λιμένος εἰς τὸ προκόλπιον. ἐνταῦθα ἥκων ἐκ πολλοῦ χειμῶνος σῶστρα ἔθυον ἐμαυτοῦ τῇ τῶν Φοινίκων· Ἀστάρτην αὐτὴν καλοῦσιν οἱ Σιδώνιοι.

Sidon is a city on the sea. The sea is the one of the Assyrians. The city is the mother of the Phoenicians. The people are the father of the Thebans. There is a broad double harbour in the bay, gently enclosing the sea. Where the bay is hollowed out along its right-hand side, a second opening has been dug out. The water flows in again and becomes a second harbour from the first, with the result that the lighter ships can spend the winter there in the calm waters, but pass the summer in the forecourt of the bay. When I came there after a severe storm, I sacrificed thanks-offerings for my own safety to the goddess of the Phoenicians: the Sidonians call her Astarte.

This paratactic opening occludes the presence of the narrator, which is only felt with the delayed introduction of first-person verbs after the initial, verbless description of Sidon (ἥκων ... ἔθυον).[30] At this moment of transition between the novel as a textual composition attributable to a named author and the various

---

[26] Dorrit Cohn, *The Distinction of Fiction* (Baltimore: Johns Hopkins University Press, 2000), especially 58–78, 132–49.

[27] Marinčič, "Advertising One's Own Story," 174–75.

[28] Tim Whitmarsh, *Narrative and Identity in the Ancient Greek Novel: Returning Romance* (Cambridge: Cambridge University Press, 2011), 78. This may be exacerbated by the textual problem at 1.4.3: on this see n. 16 above.

[29] Text taken from Jean-Philippe Garnaud, *Achille Tatius: Le Roman de Leucippé et Clitophon* (Paris: Les Belles Lettres, 1991), translations my own.

[30] Noted by Morgan, "Achilles Tatius," 493.

46   *Claire Rachel Jackson*

narrators who structure its fictional narrative, *Leucippe and Clitophon* locates it-self instead by reference to geography. But this geography is symbolic as much as literal. The description of the city as the mother of the Phoenicians refers to its status as one of the most prominent cities of the ancient civilisation, with the juxtaposition of μήτηρ ... ἡ πόλις suggesting a colonial metropolis which sustains further settlements.[31] While the following mention of the Thebans might seem to recentre Greek geography and literary history, they are here framed as the children of the Phoenicians and as a colonial settlement of Sidon.[32] These references obliquely invoke the mythic traditions surrounding Cadmus, who founds Thebes after leaving his Phoenician homeland while searching for his abducted sister Europa.[33] This framing foreshadows the following ekphrasis of the painting of Europa, which is introduced with a repetition of the opening's distinctive syntax (1.1.2):

Εὐρώπης ἡ γραφή· Φοινίκων ἡ θάλασσα· Σιδῶνος ἡ γῆ.

The painting was of Europa. The sea was the Phoenicians'. The land was Sidon.

This pattern repeats a third time with Clitophon's first words as the novel's ego-narrator, which prominently proclaim his Phoenician identity (1.3.1):

ὁ δὲ ἄρχεται λέγειν ὧδε· ἐμοὶ Φοινίκη γένος, Τύρος ἡ πατρίς, ὄνομα Κλειτοφῶν, πατὴρ Ἱππίας ...

He began to speak like this. "My family is Phoenician, my fatherland is Tyre, my name is Clitophon, my father is Hippias ..."

These repeated echoes of the novel's opening both invoke programmatic mentions of Phoenician geography, myth, and identities and also mark key transition points in the work's narratorial architecture. From the novel's anonymous opening to the embedded description of the Europa painting to the beginning of Clitophon's ego-narration, these syntactical parallels mark the faultlines in the different levels of narration in the prologue through a recurrent thread of emblematic Phoenician references.

---

[31] Whitmarsh, *Achilles Tatius*, 118. According to Strabo 16.2.22, Sidon competed with Tyre for the title of μητρόπολις of the Phoenicians.

[32] Whitmarsh, *Narrative and Identity*, 76. This more dependent relationship stands in contrast to earlier sources, where Phoenician and Greek ties are often framed as mutually beneficial, such as Eur. *Phoen.* 208–19. On this see Erich Gruen, *Rethinking the Other in Antiquity* (Princeton: Princeton University Press, 2011), 236; Josephine Crawley Quinn, "Phoenicians and Carthaginians in Greco-Roman Literature," in *The Oxford Handbook of The Phoenician and Punic Mediterranean*, ed. Carolina Lope-Ruiz and Brian R. Doak (New York: Oxford University Press, 2019), 672–74.

[33] Noted without further elaboration by Ebbe Vilborg, *Achilles Tatius: Leucippe and Clitophon. A Commentary* (Gothenburg: Almqvist & Wiksell, 1962), 18; Whitmarsh, *Achilles Tatius*, 118. Cadmus is mentioned explicitly at 2.2.1, which is also possibly foregrounded here. Exactly how these myths relate to the history of the region is long debated; see Gruen (*Rethinking the Other*, 233–34) for a brief overview with further references.

Authorial Fictions, Phoenician Paradigms 47

But why are these narrative junctures marked specifically with Phoenician references? The significance of Clitophon's self-professed Phoenician identity has prompted much discussion in scholarship, especially in light of the homonymic allusions to the different meanings of φοῖνιξ which recur throughout the novel.[34] Less attention, however, has been paid to the intersection of the novel's narrative architecture with these Phoenician symbols, especially in light of the prologue's thematisation of narratorial voices and authorial absence. Against this, I want to argue that these allusions implicitly invoke Cadmus as a paradigm of authority and foundation who exposes and exploits this question of authorial and narratorial identity within *Leucippe and Clitophon*.[35] As mentioned above, the myth of Cadmus is alluded to implicitly due to the novel's opening references to the colonisation of Thebes and the painting of Europa, which trace the central plot of Cadmus' journeys from Phoenicia to Boeotia in search of his abducted sister.[36] Although a well-circulated myth, certain aspects of the narrative, such as Cadmus' reign as ruler of Thebes, remain underdeveloped in the ancient sources.[37] Instead, Cadmus' story is programmatically framed as one of origins and foundation. In Ovid's *Metamorphoses*, for example, Cadmus' search for Europa initiates both the foundation of the city and the Theban cycle that structures the third book of the poem. Nonnus' fifth-century epic the *Dionysiaca* opens its central narrative with a traditional epic invocation asking the Muse to tell of the wanderings of Cadmus, the titular deity's grandfather (*Dion.* 1.45).[38] Even where the myth is rationalised, as in *Narrations* of Conon, preserved in Photius' ninth-century *Bibliotheca*, it remains a story with a strong foundational, even aetiological slant. Likely composed in the Augustan period, Conon, ac-

---

[34] For example, the discussions of the date-palm at 1.17.3–5 and 2.14.2 and the mythical bird at 3.25.1; Françoise Briquel-Chatonnet, "L'image des Phéniciens dans le roman grec," in *Le monde du roman grec*, ed. Marie-Françoise Baslez, Philippe Hoffmann, and Monique Trédé (Paris: Presses de l'École Normale Supérieur, 1992), 189–97; Morales, *Vision and Narrative*, 48–50; Koen De Temmerman, *Crafting Characters: Heroes and Heroines in the Ancient Greek Novel* (Oxford: Oxford University Press, 2014), 155; Whitmarsh, *Achilles Tatius*, 71–74.

[35] The importance of Cadmus in the novels is noted by Briquel-Chatonnet ("L'image des Phéniciens dans le roman grec," 190), albeit without much elaboration. An interesting parallel here is the role of Moses as a paradigm of authorship as a way of claiming authority and establishing traditions in later Mosaic discourse; on this, see Hindy Najman, *Seconding Sinai: The Development of Mosaic Discourse in Second Temple Judaism* (Leiden: Brill, 2003).

[36] See the surveys of Ruth B. Edwards, *Kadmos the Phoenician: A Study in Greek Legends and Their Mycenaean Age* (Amsterdam: Hakkert, 1979); Angela Kühr, *Als Kadmos nach Boiotien kam* (Stuttgart: Franz Steiner, 2006); Gruen, *Rethinking the Other*, 233–36.

[37] Noted by Edwards, *Kadmos the Phoenician*, 23.

[38] Fotini Hadjittofi, "Nonnus' Europa and Cadmus: Re-configuring Masculinity in the *Dionysiaca*," in *Nonnus of Panopolis in Context III: Old Questions and New Perspectives*, ed. Filip Doroszewski and Katarzyna Jażdżewska (Leiden: Brill, 2021), 263–81, esp. 264. On Cadmus in the *Dionysiaca*, see Nina Aringer, "Kadmos und Typhon als vorausdeutende Figuren in den *Dionysiaka*: Bemerkungen zur Kompositionskunst des Nonnos von Panopolis," *Wiener Studien* 125 (2012): 85–105.

48 *Claire Rachel Jackson*

cording to Photius, used the abduction of his sister as a pretext to conquer the continent of Europe (*Narr.* 37, *Bibl.* 137b27–138a15). By marking the seams of the prologue's narrative layers with references to Phoenician myth, *Leucippe and Clitophon* invokes the spectre of Cadmus as a figure of foundation and beginnings who acts as a foil to the vacuum of authorial authority that characterises the opening of the novel.

These oblique allusions in practice reinforce the questions about who speaks and from what perspective that are thematised throughout the novel's prologue. The opening of Herodotus' *Histories* describes a rationalised story of the abduction of Europa in which unknown Greeks kidnap her from Tyre in retaliation for the Phoenician's earlier assault on Io, and links this chain of mythical abductions to the origins of conflict between East and West (1.2.1–5.3).[39] Yet, as Herodotus notes, this series of events is highly contested, with Phoenicians and Greeks offering different accounts of the events, Io's agency, and the blame apportioned to both sides (1.4.1–5.3). While Cadmus' foreign origins and foundation of Thebes are consistently asserted, his exact homeland is debated in later sources, and the legend shifts in tandem with the political and historical circumstances of ancient sources.[40] Achilles Tatius' novel alludes to this disputed history right from the outset with the association of Sidon with the foundation of Thebes, since Cadmus elsewhere is said to come from Tyre.[41] As a founder of cities and a catalyst for mythic narrative, the implicit paradigm of Cadmus might seem in *Leucippe and Clitophon* to embody a source of authority at the opening of the novel, yet in practice it undercuts the possibility of such authoritative control. Although rarely accepted in full, Dan Selden's influential proposal that the novel's prologue invites different interpretations based on whether it is viewed through Greek or Phoenician lenses rightly foregrounds this contested framing.[42] Rather than just offering contrasting readings, however, the prologue thematises throughout issues of perspective and authority that draw attention to the origins and mediation of the narrative. As Tim Whitmarsh puts it, the novel "opens with a culturally disorientating move, a reminder that there is more than one way to tell a story."[43] Cadmus' implicit presence through these Phoenician mythic

---

[39] Herodotus does not mention Cadmus in this opening but cites his travels to Boeotia at 2.49 and mentions his search for Europa at 4.147, suggesting that these various narrative elements were already linked.

[40] Gruen, *Rethinking the Other*, 235; Quinn, "Phoenicians and Carthaginians."

[41] As at *L&C* 2.2.1, where Cadmus is invoked specifically as a Tyrian deity. Lucian's roughly contemporary *de Dea Syria* also plays with these disputed affiliations by identifying a Sidonian temple as belonging variously to Astarte, Selene, and Cadmus' sister Europa (4). See Morales, *Vision and Narrative*, 45.

[42] Daniel L. Selden, "Genre of Genre," in *The Search for the Ancient Novel*, ed. James Tatum (Baltimore: Johns Hopkins University Press, 1994), 39–64; with the critique of Morales, *Vision and Narrative*, 43–45.

[43] Whitmarsh, *Achilles Tatius*, 74.

Authorial Fictions, Phoenician Paradigms 49

symbols, therefore, seemingly offers a paradigm of authority amongst the prologue's authorial absence and narratorial anonymity, but in practice it demonstrates just how disputed this authority is.

While traditionally the abduction of Europa is the impetus for Cadmus' wanderings, *Leucippe and Clitophon* inverts this lens. The implicit reference to the foundation of Thebes in the opening lines of the novel not only foreshadows the subject of the painting which dominates the prologue, but also compounds these issues of perspective and authority. Although lacking personal asides or explicit value-judgements, the eroticised description of the painting is mediated through the narrator's viewpoint, emphasised by his comment that while he admired the rest of the painting, he was particularly taken with the image of Eros leading the bull due to his own erotic inclinations (ἅτε δὲ ὢν ἐρωτικὸς; 1.2.1). The narrator's verbalised admiration of the painting sparks a response from a bystander, later revealed to be Clitophon, which positions this inset ekphrasis as the connecting point between their narratives. Given its prominence, the painting has long been mined for proleptic references to the rest of the narrative.[44] Again, however, *Leucippe and Clitophon* teases the importance of the painting as a source of narrative authority only to undercut it. While the painting is said from the outset to be of Europa (1.1.2), after a brief reference to a girl sitting on a bull (ἐν τῇ θαλάττῃ ταῦρος ἐπενήχετο, καὶ τοῖς νώτοις καλὴ παρθένος ἐπεκάθητο, ἐπὶ Κρήτην τῷ ταύρῳ πλέουσα; 1.1.3), she is not mentioned again until the voyeuristic description of her body towards the end of the ekphrasis (1.1.10–12). Instead, the narrator focuses on the natural beauty of the landscape (1.1.3–4).

ἐκόμα πολλοῖς ἄνθεσιν ὁ λειμών· δένδρων αὐτοῖς ἀνεμέμικτο φάλαγξ καὶ φυτῶν. συνεχῆ τὰ δένδρα· συνηρεφῆ τὰ πέταλα· συνῆπτον οἱ πτόρθοι τὰ φύλλα, καὶ ἐγίνετο τοῖς ἄνθεσιν ὄροφος ἡ τῶν φύλλων συμπλοκή. ἔγραψεν ὁ τεχνίτης ὑπὸ τὰ πέταλα καὶ τὴν σκιάν, καὶ ὁ ἥλιος ἠρέμα τοῦ λειμῶνος κάτω σποράδην διέρρει, ὅσον τὸ συνηρεφὲς τῆς τῶν φύλλων κόμης ἀνέῳξεν ὁ γραφεύς.

The meadow bloomed with many flowers, and a phalanx of trees and plants mingled with them. The trees were dense, the leaves thick-shaded, the branches joined with the leaves, and the interweaving of the plants became a thatched roof for the flowers. The artist had painted even the shadow under the leaves, and the sun gently flowed down through the meadow here and there, inasmuch as the painter had opened the thick canopy of the plants' foliage.

---

[44] Shadi Bartsch, *Decoding the Ancient Novel: The Reader and the Role of Description in Heliodorus and Achilles Tatius* (Princeton: Princeton University Press, 1989), 48–55; Morales, *Vision and Narrative*, 37–48; Lena Behemenberg, "Le mythe comme signe: *Ekphrasis* et le jeu de la préfiguration dans *Le Roman de Leucippé et Clitophon* d'Achille Tatius," in *Mythe et Fiction*, ed. Danièle Auger and Charles Delattre (Paris: Presses Universitaires de Paris Ouest, 2010), 239–55; *contra* Peter von Möllendorf, "Bild-Störung: Das Gemälde von Europas Entführung in Achilleus Tatios' Roman *Leukippe und Kleitophon*," in *Europa – Stier nd Sternenkranz: Von der Union mit Zeus zum Staatenverbund*, ed. Almut-Barbara Renger and Roland Issler (Bond: Vandenhoeck & Ruprecht, 2009), 145–64, all with further bibliography.

50 Claire Rachel Jackson

The plants of the meadow are not only described in eroticised language, pre-figuring the voyeuristic depiction of Europa which follows, but are also presented as untouched by human interference, with the plants framed as the autonomous agents of their interactions.[45] Increasingly, however, the seemingly natural, self-directed foliage is encroached upon by reminders of the artist as the figure responsible for shaping the scene (ἔγραψεν ὁ τεχνίτης ... ὁ γραφεύς). These reminders of the artist as the creative authority behind the image not only act as a foil to the artifice of this ekphrastic description and the narrator's mediation of it, but also tease the image of a fictional architect within the narrative in contrast to the thematised silence of the novel's named author. The increasing intrusion of creative control into the seemingly untouched meadow continues with the sudden appearance of a ditch-digger (ὀχετηγός; 1.1.6) within the painting's garden. This irrigator again reinforces the artifice of the meadow in contrast to its seemingly uncontrived appearance, but also recalls the recently invoked artist of the painting and reflects outwards onto the creator of the novel itself.[46] In particular, the ditch-digger has long been recognised as an echo of the ὀχετηγός in the *Iliad* (21.257–62),[47] which adds to the literary allusivity of this reference. Within the prologue's repeated thematisation of authority figures and authorial paradigms, this figure again draws attention to the construction of the novel as a literary artwork. Even as the painting invites audiences to look for proleptic connections with the rest of *Leucippe and Clitophon*, the embedded images of and references to the painting's artist again emphasise the absence of the author as the text's creator from the prologue of the novel.

In contrast to the unnamed narrator's awe at the painting, Clitophon bemoans his erotic sufferings. In order to coax the reluctant stranger to tell his story, the narrator leads him away from the painting to a nearby grove (1.2.3):

καὶ ταῦτα δὴ λέγων δεξιοῦμαί τε αὐτὸν καὶ ἐπί τινος ἄλσους ἄγω γείτονος, ἔνθα πλάτανοι μὲν ἐπεφύκεσαν πολλαὶ καὶ πυκναί, παρέρρει δὲ ὕδωρ ψυχρόν τε καὶ διαυγές, οἷον ἀπὸ χιόνος ἄρτι λυθείσης ἔρχεται. καθίσας οὖν αὐτὸν ἐπί τινος θώκου χαμαιζήλου καὶ αὐτὸς παρακαθισάμενος, "ὥρα σοι," ἔφην, "τῆς τῶν λόγων ἀκροάσεως· πάντως δὲ ὁ τοιοῦτος τόπος ἡδὺς καὶ μύθων ἄξιος ἐρωτικῶν."

---

[45] As R. P. Martin notes, the repetition of συν- compounds parallels both the interweaving of the plants and converts artefacts of the human world, such as the phalanx (φάλαγξ) and the roof (ὄροφος), into emblems of this natural, unstructured foliage ("A Good Place to Talk: Discourse and Topos in Achilles Tatius and Achilles Tatius and Philostratus," in *Space in the Ancient Novel*, ed. Michael Paschalis and Stavros A. Frangoulidis, Ancient Narrative Supplements 1 [Groningen: Barkhuis & Groningen University Library, 2002], 146). Whitmarsh (*Achilles Tatius*, 124) points out the eroticised implications of the repeated compounds (συνεχῆ ... συνηρεφῆ ... συνῆπτον ... συμπλοκή).

[46] Martin ("A Good Place to Talk") goes further to describe the ὀχετηγός as a representation of the novelist.

[47] See Whitmarsh, *Achilles Tatius*, 125.

Authorial Fictions, Phoenician Paradigms 51

As I said these things I took him by the hand and led him to a certain neighbouring grove, where many plane trees grew densely and cold clear water flowed, just like that which comes from freshly melted snow. After having sat him down on some seat low to the ground and then sitting myself down beside him, I said, "now is the time to hear your stories. This kind of place is entirely pleasant and worthy of erotic narratives."

This description clearly recalls the famous description of the grove in Plato's *Phaedrus* (229a1–230c5), a popular point of reference in imperial Greek literature,[48] and the iconic plane trees (πλάτανοι) perhaps sharpen the allusion by closely echoing the name of the philosopher (Πλάτων).[49] This reference, however, is not simply aesthetic. As Karen ní Mheallaigh has shown, the invocation of the *Phaedrus* is fitting within Achilles Tatius' novel not only as a dialogue about love, but also as a work which questions the truth of mythic narratives and the authority of written texts.[50] The Platonic dialogue famously characterises writing as illegitimate speech that can escape its creator's control, an argument validated by Phaedrus' failed attempt to pass off another person's text as his own spontaneous speech.[51] The novelistic narrator describes the Platonic scene as not simply appropriate for erotic stories (μύθων ἄξιος ἐρωτικῶν), but also for their performance (ἀκρόασις), a term which foregrounds speech, listening, and recitation.[52] This conceit of the novel originating from a chance conversation stands in contrast to the novel itself, not just as a written text but as a work of crafted literary allusion to texts such as the *Phaedrus*, which may thematise orality but which are preserved, paradoxically, through writing. As such, the novel's conceit of oral performance within this Platonic framework implicitly activates the paradox of writing laid out in the *Phaedrus* and reinforces the themes of authorial authority and narratorial control evoked throughout the novel's prologue.[53]

But this paradox becomes explicit when framed through the Phoenician paradigms that have characterised the opening of *Leucippe and Clitophon*. Seen

---

[48] M. B. Trapp, "Plato's *Phaedrus* in Second-Century Greek Literature," in *Antonine Literature*, ed. D. A. Russell (Oxford: Oxford University Press, 1990), 141–73.

[49] Whitmarsh (*Achilles Tatius*, 125) describes the plane trees as "the most formulaic element of such Phaedran scenes."

[50] ní Mheallaigh, "Philosophical Framing"; see also De Temmerman, *Crafting Characters*, 156–57.

[51] Harvey Yunis, *Plato: Phaedrus* (Cambridge: Cambridge University Press, 2011), 223–25, with further bibliography. As noted by Bennett (*The Author*, 10–11), this anxiety in many ways anticipates Barthes' death of the author.

[52] Whitmarsh, *Achilles Tatius*, 133. The description of erotic stories also recalls Clitophon's initial refusal to recount his own adventures due to their similarity to myth in wording, which suggestively questions the truth or falsehood of these stories (μύθοις ἔοικε; 1.2.2) (Morales, *Vision and Narrative*, 50–56).

[53] Marinčič ("Advertising One's Own Story," 172–75), building on Danielle van Mal-Maeder ("Au Seuil des Romans Grecs: Effets de réel et effets de creation," *Groningen Colloquia on the Novel* 4 [1991]: 13–14), argues that this paradox is only implicit in the prologue, a position rightly critiqued by ní Mheallaigh ("Philosophical Framing," 233 n. 7).

52   *Claire Rachel Jackson*

through this lens, the prologue's disjunction between script and speech, especially framed through Platonic anxieties about writing, also evokes the mythic tradition crediting Cadmus as the inventor of Greek writing. According to Herodotus, Cadmus and his companions taught the Phoenician alphabet to the Greeks, which became the basis for Greek writing and which he refers to at one point as Cadmeian letters (Καδμήια γράμματα; 5.59.1).[54] This is a highly contested mythology, not least of all in the *Phaedrus*, where Socrates describes the origin of writing in Egypt, to which Phaedrus tartly comments that Socrates invents whatever stories he pleases (275b3–4).[55] Nonetheless, given the repeated references to Phoenician markers throughout the prologue, this connotation not only reinforces the prominence of Cadmus as an implicit paradigm, but also fortifies his association with authorial authority given his role as the inventor of writing.[56] While the Platonic framing of this scene broaches this disjunction between the novel's conceit of originating in an oral conversation and its materiality as a written work, the wider connection with Cadmus and Phoenician myth in the prologue makes these tensions between authorial text and narratorial speech explicit.

Immediately afterwards, Clitophon begins his ego-narration with the statement that he is a Phoenician (ἐμοὶ Φοινίκη γένος; 1.3.1), after which the unnamed narrator fades from view. This initial claim of identity, modelled after the distinctive rhythm of the novel's opening, has often been interpreted programmatically as a statement about his narratorial reliability. As Helen Morales has demonstrated, this may play into traditional stereotypes of Phoenicians as liars and Phoenician narrative as gruesome and sexually lurid, both of which can be seen to resonate with the ensuing events of Clitophon's narrative.[57] But as the climax of the prologue, it also marks the transition to a point of view emphatically distinct from any kind of implied author at the start of the work. By aligning Clitophon within these Phoenician narratorial fictions and highlighting the absence of the work's creator, the prologue to the novel teases the importance of the author as a source of narrative and hermeneutic authority

---

[54] Hdt. 5.58.1–59.1 is a paradigmatic point of reference for later sources: see also Pomponius Mela 1.65. Edwards (*Kadmos the Phoenician*, 23 n. 32) offers a fuller list of references. The *Journal* of the Trojan War attributed to Dictys, for example, claims to be translated from the Phoenician letters which Cadmus brought to the Greeks; see ní Mheallaigh ("The 'Phoenician Letters'") on the wider implications of this claim within imperial literary culture.

[55] Yunis, *Plato, ad loc.* Edwards (*Kadmos the Phoenician*, 22–23) notes some of these competing traditions.

[56] Maria Rocchi stresses the connection between these Phoenician letters and Cadmus' mythic connections with artistic song and writing ("Kadmos e i *Phoinikeia Grammata*," in *Atti del II Congresso Internazionale di Studi Fenici e Punici, Roma, 9–14 Novembre 1987*, Volume Secundo [Rome: Consiglio nazionale delle ricerche, 1991], 529–33).

[57] Morales, *Vision and Narrative*, 48–56; see also De Temmerman, *Crafting Characters*, 156–58.

Authorial Fictions, Phoenician Paradigms 53

while simultaneously undercutting it. Despite its early date, *Leucippe and Clitophon* exploits the interpretative possibilities of authorial anonymity and first-person narrations in ways that both anticipate the author's death in twentieth-century criticism and also testify to their enduring survival.

2. Holy Fictions

The reception history of *Leucippe and Clitophon* offers fertile ground for the resurrection of these authorial fictions. Although Achilles Tatius' novel has perhaps the best-attested late antique and Byzantine reception among the extant examples of the genre, the reference to it in the hagiographical *Lives of Saint Galaction and Episteme* stands out for its overtness. This narrative of the chaste marriage and eventual martyrdom of the eponymous saints exists in two versions: an earlier text (*BHG* 665), which was later reworked for inclusion in the tenth-century *Menologion* attributed to Symeon Metaphrastes, a collection of saints' lives arranged according to the liturgical calendar (*BHG* 666). Although nominally the story of the eponymous saints, both texts devote a large proportion of their narrative to the story of Galaction's parents, named as Clitophon and Gleucippe in the earlier text, which the Metaphrastic version corrects to Leucippe.[58] This onomastic overlap evokes Achilles Tatius' protagonists in such an overt way that it cannot be coincidental, corresponding to Metaphrastes' apparent knowledge of Achilles Tatius displayed elsewhere in the *Menologion*.[59] Seen through this lens, the hagiographical narratives become the spiritual and literary descendants of the earlier novel and epitomise the broader conclusion that "the heirs of the novels' heroes are Christian saints."[60]

The wider implications of this neat teleology, however, have not yet been considered. One strand of scholarship has argued that the *Lives* are a sequel to *Leucippe and Clitophon*, a framing which collapses the cultural and chronological distances between the texts in order to emphasise their narrative continuity.[61]

---

[58] One manuscript of the earlier text alone names her Leucippe; on this see Alwis, *Celibate Marriages*, 39. While the *Menologion* was clearly popular after its composition, with nearly two hundred manuscripts dating from the eleventh century alone (Stratis Papaioannou, "Authors [With an Excursus on Symeon Metaphrastes]," in *The Oxford Handbook of Byzantine Literature*, ed. Stratis Papaioannou [Oxford: Oxford University Press, 2021], 482–524, xxi with n. 17), the correction to Leucippe seems consistent across the tradition.

[59] As S. M. Trzaskoma demonstrates in "The Storms in Theodoros Daphnopates (Ep. 36), Symeon Metaphrastes (*BHG* 1878) and Achilles Tatius (3.1.1–5.6)," *Byzantion* 87 (2017): 375–86.

[60] Charis Messis, "Fiction and/or Novelization in Byzantine Hagiography," in *A Companion to Byzantine Hagiography, Vol. II: Genres and Contexts*, ed. Stephanos Efthymiadis (Farnham and Burlington, VT: Ashgate, 2014), 326.

[61] The *Lives* "may be read as a continuation of the late antique story, a novel sequel with a proper Christian ending" (Ingela Nilsson, "Desire and God Have Always Been Around, in Life and Romance Alike," in *Plotting with Eros: Essays on the Poetics of Love and the Erotics of Read-*

54   Claire Rachel Jackson

Others, however, have contested this claim due to the lack of sustained reference to the novel beyond this onomastic overlap.[62] Ironically this might be seen to validate this label since, as Terry Castle puts it, "a sequel can never satisfy its readers' desire for repetition ... its tragedy is that it cannot literally reconstitute its charismatic original."[63] By contrast, another strand has argued that the *Lives* serve to legitimise or deliberately rework the pagan novel for Christian audiences in order to emphasise new priorities of chastity, faith, and martyrdom.[64] These strands are neither discrete nor exclusionary, but taken collectively they allow for the fiction of an orderly relationship between the *Lives* and the novel, with the hagiographies acting as either the continuation or the inversion of *Leucippe and Clitophon*.

But such framings risk obscuring the questions about authority and appropriation at stake in this claim of genealogical descent. As Simon Goldhill has argued, textual citation, especially of texts from the past, is never an uncomplicated action, as it opens up possibilities for irony and subversion which threatens the authority such references attempt to actualise.[65] More precisely, although claims of familial affiliation are not unprecedented in classical antiquity or Christian literature,[66] the *Lives*' presentation of the titular saint as the child of the novelistic protagonists is complicated by with the specific circumstances of Achilles Tatius' novel. In the *Sibylline Oracles*, for example, one of the Sibyls is said to be the daughter-in-law of Noah (3.809–29), which writes Christian literature into

---

ing, ed. Ingela Nilsson [Copenhagen: Museum Tusculanum Press, 2009], 256). *Galaction and Episteme* "provides its audience with a Christian sequel to the 'happily-ever-after' ending to the pagan novel" (MacAlister, *Dreams and Suicides*, 110). See also Margaret Mullett, "Novelisation and/or Fiction in Byzantium: Narrative After the Revival of Fiction," in *Byzantine Narrative: Papers in Honour of Roger Scott*, ed. John Burke et al. (Melbourne: Australian Association for Byzantine Studies, 2006), 1–28, 4; Kruchió, "Galaction and Episteme."

[62] Alwis, *Celibate Marriage*, 39–40; Kanavou, "Reflections on the Relationship," 216–19. Giorges Giatromanolakes offers the most sustained exploration of the thematic and linguistic parallels between the texts (Ἀχιλλέως Ἀλεξανδρέως Τατίου: Λευκίππη καὶ Κλειτοφῶν. Εἰσαγωγή – μεφάφραση – σχόλια [Athens: Hidryma Goulandrē-Chorn, 1990], 745–47).

[63] Terry Castle, *Masquerade and Civilization: The Carnivalesque in Eighteenth-Century English Culture and Fiction* (Stanford: Stanford University Press, 1986), 134.

[64] Patrick Robiano, "Pour en finir avec le christianisme d'Achille Tatius et d'Héliodor d'Émèse: la lecture des *Passions de Galaction et d'Épistèmè*," *L'Antiquité Classique* 78 (2009): 145–60; see also Kruchió, "Galaction and Episteme." MacAlister (*Dreams and Suicides*, 111) offers the most balanced critique by claiming that Christian readers "incorporated [the novels] into their own belief system. Whether this was a judicious move ... or whether the novels were taken for granted as spiritual allegories in the earlier period for which we have no evidence for their allegorical treatment, can only be a matter for speculation."

[65] Goldhill, "The Sirens' Song," most forcefully articulated at 150–52.

[66] See Hafner on claims of genealogical descent in classical biographical traditions: Markus Hafner, "Fathers and Sons – and Daughters: Genealogical Co-Authorship, Offspring Metaphors, and the Language of Legitimacy," in *Ut Pictura Poeta: Autorbilder und die Lektüre antiker Literatur*, ed. Ute Tischer, Ursula Gärtner, and Alexandra Forst (Turnhout: Brepols, 2022), 341–65.

Authorial Fictions, Phoenician Paradigms   55

the classical canon even as the poem explicitly critiques Homeric authority.[67] These contradictory impulses are exacerbated within the *Lives* by the novel's own issues with authority, closure, and anonymity. The text's unknown narrator and notoriously open ending facilitate a seemingly harmonious continuation of Leucippe and Clitophon's story, while as the anecdote found in the *Suda* demonstrates, the lack of biographical detail about Achilles Tatius allows for both the author and, by extension, their text to be converted to Christianity.[68] If authors function to unify texts, as Foucault suggests, however, continuations by other writers disrupt this by making visible the appropriation of their authority in accordance with the priorities and desires of later readers.[69] Although the language of sequels and legitimisation offers a straightforward narrative of the relationship between the novel and the hagiographies, they therefore fail to appreciate the more dissonant repercussions of this appropriation. By making Galaction the son of Leucippe and Clitophon, the *Lives* challenge the novel's authority even as they claim it for themselves by exploiting the anonymity of the text, its narrator, and its author.

Such frameworks also risk ignoring the *Lives'* own contexts of composition and attribution. Although a universal phenomenon visible throughout literary history, authorship is nonetheless deeply inflected by the generic, cultural, and publishing frameworks within which texts are composed and received. While the ambiguity over the dating of the earlier text precludes any definitive assertions about the exact temporal gulf between the *Lives* and the novel, both hagiographies reflect specifically Christian conventions of authorship. Neither text is attributed to a named author, as is common in late antique hagiography,[70] but this is not due simply to a lack of literary sophistication or a failure of transmission. Instead, as various scholars have argued, the anonymity of early hagiographers can be a deliberate choice, albeit one with a variety of effects. In some cases the effacement of the author as an individual emphasises the saint as

---

[67] The relationship is made clear at *Sib. Or.* 1.287–90, in what Buitenwerf suggests is an expansion of this point: Rieuwerd Buitenwerf, *Book III of the Sibylline Oracles and its Social Setting* (Leiden: Brill, 2003), 299–300. On this claim and its relationship with Homeric paradigms within the text, see Emma Greensmith, "The Wrath of the Sibyl: Homeric Reception and Contested Identities in the Sibylline Oracles 3," in *Late Hellenistic Greek Literature in Dialogue*, ed. Jason Konig and Nicolas Wiater (Cambridge: Cambridge University Press, 2022), 207–209. See also *Jewish Ant.* 1.15.1. I am extremely grateful to Chance Bonar for these references.

[68] The anecdote from the *Suda* that Achilles Tatius became Christian has been cited in support of the *Lives'* legitimising function, as in Dörrie, "Die griechischen Romane," 273–76; Robiano, "Pour en finir avec le christianisme d'Achille Tatius et d'Héliodor d'Émèse," 146.

[69] Foucault, "Qu'est-ce qu'un auteur?" On the terminology of sequels and continuation, see Gerard Genette, *Palimpsests: Literature in the Second Degree*, trans. Channa Newman and Claude Doubinsky (London: University of Nebraska Press, 1997), 161–65.

[70] Derek Krueger, *Writing and Holiness* (Philadelphia: University of Pennsylvania Press, 2004), 95–109; Papaioannou, "Authors," 496–98.

56 *Claire Rachel Jackson*

a collective archetype of virtue,[71] in others it authenticates the narrative through the adoption of an eyewitness narrator,[72] or sublimates the author's agency and instead asserts God as the true authority responsible for the text.[73] Rather than simply reflecting the exploration of anonymity found within *Leucippe and Clitophon*, therefore, the *Lives'* suppression of any authorial intrusion within the narrative adds a specifically Christian resonance to these questions of authority, agency, and authorial identity.

While the later version of the *Life* found in the tenth-century *Menologion* is also not attributed to any author, it is nonetheless intrinsically connected to the work's compiler Symeon Metaphrastes, whose very name attests to his editorial role. The exact nature of *metaphrasis* is at the very least broad, if not impossible to define, as it covers a spectrum of engagement with earlier texts running from literal translation, to paraphrase, to creative rewriting.[74] The majority of the nearly 150 saints' lives collected in the *Menologion* can be traced back to earlier narratives, but only eight are attributed to a named author, even if the prior version is not anonymous in other sources.[75] In an encomium for the compiler written a century or so after the publication of the *Menologion*, however, Michael Psellus claims that Metaphrastes changed the style but not the substance of source texts and praises his work in contrast to the simplicity and artlessness of earlier hagiographers. While Metaphrastes' interventions seem to have imposed a certain amount of uniformity on the disparately sourced texts,[76] the *Menologion* lacks a singular authorial voice.[77] Despite Psellus' suggestions that he worked with a group of creative collaborators to produce the collection, the work is attributed to Metaphrastes alone, who in the centuries after its pub-

---

[71] P. Cox Miller, "Strategies of Representation in Collective Biography: Constructing the Subject as Holy," in *Greek Biography and Panegyric in Late Antiquity*, ed. Tomas Hägg and Philip Rousseau (Berkeley: University of California Press, 2000), 221–22; Simon Goldhill, "Why Don't Jews Write Biography?" in *Being Christian in Late Antiquity: A Festschrift for Gillian Clark*, ed. Carol Harrison, Caroline Humfress, and Isabella Sandwell (Oxford: Oxford University Press, 2014), 22.

[72] Claudia Rapp, "Storytelling as Spiritual Communication in Early Greek Hagiography: The Use of *Diegesis*," *Journal of Early Christian Studies* 6 (1998): 431–48; Martin Hinterberger, "Autobiography and Hagiography in Byzantium," *Symbolae Osloenses* 75 (2000): 149.

[73] Krueger, *Writing and Holiness*, 103–4, citing the example of Athanasius' *Life of Anthony*; Alwis, *Celibate Marriages*, 293–94. On Byzantine authorship more generally, see the survey of Papaioannou ("Authors") and the essays in Aglae Pizzone, ed., *The Author in Middle Byzantine Literature: Modes, Functions, Identities* (Berlin: De Gruyter, 2014).

[74] For an overview of this concept, see the essays in Stavroula Constantinou and Christian Høgel, eds., *Metaphrasis: A Byzantine Concept of Rewriting and Its Hagiographical Products* (Leiden: Brill, 2021).

[75] On this, see Papaioannou, "Authors," 504–5. See also the catalogue in Høgel (*Symeon Metaphrastes*, 172–204), which lists the source texts for the Metaphrastic material.

[76] Høgel, *Symeon Metaphrastes*, 135–49.

[77] Papaioannou, "Authors," 504.

Authorial Fictions, Phoenician Paradigms 57

lication is even sanctified for his religious and stylistic achievements.[78] These blurred boundaries between author and editor not only offer a particularly knotty paradigm for Byzantine conceptions of authorship,[79] but also complicate the later *Life*'s relationship with Achilles Tatius' novel as a source text. How, then, do the *Lives* respond to and tackle the questions of narratorial and authorial authority raised by *Leucippe and Clitophon*? Beyond adopting the names of its protagonists, the influence of the novel's prologue is visible from the outset of both *Lives*, albeit in different ways. The earlier hagiography opens with a first-person prologue from an initially unnamed narrator in what might appear to be an echo of Achilles Tatius' novel. Yet, a closer look at this preface reveals the extent to which it reworks the framing of the novel (*BHG* 665, 1).[80]

διήγησιν ξένην καὶ παράδοξον ἀκούσατε σήμερον παρ' ἐμοῦ, ἀγαπητοί, ἥτις ἐστὶ χρήσιμος ταῖς ὑμετέραις ψυχαῖς· καὶ γὰρ ὑπάρχει λίαν ὠφέλιμος, ἐάν τις οὐ μόνον ἀκροατὴς γένηται ἀλλὰ καὶ ποιητής ... τούτου χάριν παραινῶ ὑμᾶς, πεποθημένοι μου ἀδελφοί, ἵνα μὴ ἐν παρέργῳ δέξησθε ἥνπερ ὑμῖν μέλλω διηγήσασθαι πολιτείαν καὶ μαρτυρίαν, ἀλλὰ ταύτην ἐν ταῖς ὑμετέραις ψυχαῖς ἀκριβῶς ἱστορήσαντες καὶ ἀληθινῷ πόθῳ ἐγγράψαντες σπεύσητε τῷ ταύτης ζήλῳ ποιηταὶ γενέσθαι καὶ οὐκ ἀκροαταί. κἀγὼ γὰρ ὁ ταπεινὸς καὶ ἐλάχιστος Εὐτόλμιος, ὁ ταύτην ὑμῖν τὴν ψυχωφελῆ ἱστορίαν προθέμενος, εἰ καὶ αὐτόπτης γέγονα καὶ ὑπηρέτης τῶν τῶν ἐμῶν δεσποτῶν ἀγωνισμάτων καὶ ἀθλημάτων, ἀλλ' οὐκ ἐζήλωσα τούτων τὸν ἀγγελικὸν καὶ ἀσώματον βίον ... παρακαλῶ οὖν ὑμᾶς, ἀγαπητοί, ὅπως μὴ εἰς τὴν τοῦ λόγου μου βλέψητε βεβηλότητα καὶ εὐτέλειαν· ἀμαθὴς γάρ εἰμι καὶ εἰκότως οὐκ ἰσχύσω τὴν διήγησιν ὑμῖν ἐν πείρᾳ ποιήσασθαι· ἀλλ' οἶδα ὑμᾶς ὅτι οὐ πρὸς τὸ ἀκριβὲς τοῦ λόγου βλέποντες ἀναβάλλεσθε τὴν διήγησιν, ἀλλὰ πρὸς τὸ τῆς πίστεως ταπεινόν μου ἀπόφθεγμα εὐπειθήσαντες τὸν παρ' ἐμοῦ ἱστορεῖσθαι μέλλοντα ἀκούσετε βίον σὺν μαρτυρίῳ.

Listen, today, beloved, to a strange and wondrous narrative by me, that is useful for your souls. For it is very beneficial for someone if they should become not only one who hears, but one who acts ... for this reason, in order that you should not receive the life and testimony which I am about to narrate to you as a marginal work, I advise you, my dearly beloved brothers, to hasten with zeal for this – to become those who act and not those who hear, by recording it accurately and inscribing it with true desire in your souls. For I, Eutolmius, the unworthy and the least, who sets this soul-edifying narrative before you, although an eyewitness and servant of the struggles and contests of my masters, did not imitate their angelic and incorporeal life ... Therefore, I beg you, beloved, do not look at the coarseness and shabbiness of my language; for I am unlearned and shall probably not have the capacity to convey the story to you easily in one attempt. But I know that you will not look at the precision of the language and reject the story, but trusting the humble apophthegm of my faith, will listen to the life and martyrdom, which will be narrated by me.

---

[78] Papaioannou, "Authors," 509–11; Laura Franco, "Le *Vite* di Simeone Metafrasta: osservazioni sulla tecnica compositive," in *Bisanzio nell'età dei Macedoni: Forme della produzione etteraria e artistica*, ed. Fabrizio Conca and Gianfranco Fiaccadori (Milan: Cisalpino, 2007), 97. On the composition of the *Menologion*, see Høgel, *Symeon Metaphrastes*, 89–126.

[79] As explored in Papaioannou, "Authors," 504–11.

[80] Text and translation lightly adapted from Alwis, *Celibate Marriages*, 279–93.

58   *Claire Rachel Jackson*

Although lacking the complex interweaving of narrators and artistic ekphrasis that characterise the novel, the earlier *Life*'s prologue resonates especially with the introduction of Clitophon in Achilles Tatius' novel. The *Life* is marked by reminders of orality, with its opening (ἀκούσατε) and closing (ἀκούσετε) injunctions to listen recalling *Leucippe and Clitophon*'s conceit of arising from a chance conversation with strangers.[81] Similarly, the emphasis upon the narrative as strange and extraordinary (ξένην καὶ παράδοξον) perhaps echoes Clitophon's characterisation of his adventures as resembling myth (τὰ γὰρ ἐμὰ μύθοις ἔοικε; 1.2.2). While not uncommon in hagiographical texts, these features of the prologue, by comparison with Achilles Tatius' novel, frame the *Life* as an act of faith rather than fiction. The very first word of the text characterises it as a διήγησις, a programmatic term in late antique hagiography which carries with it connotations of simplicity and truthfulness,[82] in contrast to the novel's elaborate self-presentation which teases the question of its reliability. The prologue, however, repeatedly insists upon its utility to its audiences (χρήσιμος ταῖς ὑμετέραις ψυχαῖς), not just as an oral story but as an impetus to action, with the religious value of the narrative reinforced by the Biblical references scattered throughout.[83] This clear articulation of the *Life*'s religious authority through direct, unfiltered communication between speaker and audience implicitly rebukes the crafted artifice of Achilles Tatius' novel and its conceit of originating from an oral story.

Most strikingly, in contrast to the thematised anonymity of the speaker at the opening of *Leucippe and Clitophon*, the narrator of the *Life* is not only identified by name, but his personal knowledge of the hagiographical protagonists is stressed. The narrator names himself as Eutolmius and describes himself as a witness to the events of the narrative, but frames this concessively, since he was not able to imitate the ascetic perfection of the titular saints (εἰ καὶ αὐτόπτης γέγονα καὶ ὑπηρέτης τῶν τῶν ἐμῶν δεσποτῶν ἀγωνισμάτων καὶ ἀθλημάτων).[84] First-place narration is by no means atypical in hagiography, and Eutolmius' insistence upon his own unworthiness to narrate such a virtuous story is so conventional that, as Derek Krueger puts it, "rather than a rhetoric of false modesty, it might be more accurate to speak of a rhetoric of longed-for humility."[85] In

---

[81] Most strikingly marked at 1.2.3, with the mention of ἀκρόασις (ὥρα σοι ... τῆς τῶν λόγων ἀκροάσεως), on which see previous discussion.

[82] Rapp, "Storytelling as Spiritual Communication." See also Messis and Papaioannou, "Orality and Textuality," 247–48.

[83] The prologue's insistence upon action rather than just listening recalls James 1:22 and Romans 2:13. See Alwis, *Celibate Marriages*, 279, with notes.

[84] Eutolmius' statement that this failure was due to his desire for the flesh over the spirit (τὴν σάρκα μᾶλλον ποθήσας ὑπὲρ τὸ πνεῦμα; 1) perhaps foreshadows the central theme of the saints' celibate marriage. On this see Alwis, *Celibate Marriages*, 62–63.

[85] Krueger, *Writing and Holiness*, 98. See also Thomas Pratsch, *Der hagiographische topos: Griechische Heiligenviten in mittelbyzantinischer Zeit* (Berlin: De Gruyter, 2005), 22–26.

Authorial Fictions, Phoenician Paradigms	59

contrast to the enigmatic anonymity of Achilles Tatius' opening narrator, the earlier *Life* seems to have superficially solved these issues by naming the narrator, clarifying his relationship to the events narrated, and aligning him within generic conventions. But Eutolmius also raises issues of authority and authenticity by thematising his own reliability (ἀκρίβεια) as a narrator. At one point he links the accuracy of his account to the work's value as a religious text (ἀλλὰ ταύτην ἐν ταῖς ὑμετέραις ψυχαῖς ἀκριβῶς ἱστορήσαντες …), while at the end of the prologue he contrasts the precision of the text's language with the sincerity of its faith (οὐ πρὸς τὸ ἀκριβὲς τοῦ λόγου βλέποντες ἀναβάλλεσθε τὴν διήγησιν, ἀλλὰ πρὸς τὸ τῆς πίστεως ταπεινόν). The insistence upon the authority of eyewitness testimony and the authenticity of its religious value, despite its simple style, might be seen as an attempt to solve the novel's sly subversions of narratorial and authorial authority by rooting its account in faith, veracity, and reliability.[86] Yet, the laboured and shifting insistence upon the accuracy of Eutolmius' account demonstrates the difficulty of neutralising the problems of authority and reliability inherent to first-person narration, epitomised and exacerbated by the *Life*'s relationship with Achilles Tatius' novel.

By contrast, the Metaphrastic version removes these issues by casting the narrative in a third-person narration (*BHG* 666, 1).[87]

τῆς πρὸς τῷ Λιβάνῳ ὄρει Φοινίκης, πολλαὶ μὲν πόλεις καὶ ἕτεραι, νοτιώτεραι καὶ προσάρκτιοι · ταύτης δὲ καὶ ἡ τῶν ἄλλων πασῶν διαφέρουσα καὶ τοῖς ἀρκτίοις κειμένη μέρεσιν, Ἔμεσα. ἣν ἐνεγκοῦσαν ἔσχε καὶ θρεψαμένην ἀνήρ, ὄνομα Κλειτοφῶν, γένος ἐπίσημος, πλοῦτον οὐδενὸς τῶν πολιτῶν δεύτερος, τὴν σύνεσιν πολλῷ τῶν ἄλλων ὀξύτερος. τούτῳ τοίνυν συνῆπτο γυνὴ Λευκίππη τοὔνομα …

In Phoenicia, by Mount Lebanon, there are many cities, some of them in the south and some in the north; to this region, in its northern parts, belongs also that city which surpasses all others: Emesa. This was the fatherland that bore and raised a man of noble lineage by the name of Clitophon, who was second to none among the citizens in wealth, and much sharper than all others in sagacity. A woman named Leucippe was married to him …

This opening is striking not only by contrast to *Leucippe and Clitophon* and the earlier *Life*, but also within the *Menologion* as a whole. Michael Psellos praises Metaphrastes for his prologues, which he claims were often included alongside the prefaces of the source texts,[88] and Høgel has shown that throughout the *Menologion* Metaphrastes tends to retain the first-person narrators and pro-

---

[86] Kanavou ("Reflections on the Relationship," 210 n. 11) classifies Eutolmius as "not a wholly reliable narrator" due to the limitations of his perspective in the story itself, but this ignores the wider significance of these prefatory claims of ἀκρίβεια.

[87] Text and translation from Stratis Papaioannou, *Christian Novels from the Menologion of Symeon Metaphrastes* (Cambridge, MA: Harvard University Press, 2017).

[88] Høgel, *Symeon Metaphrastes*, 141–42.

60 *Claire Rachel Jackson*

logues of the earlier hagiographies he adapts.[89] Yet the Metaphrastic text betrays awareness of the earlier *Life*'s prologue, since Eutolmius is mentioned by name as a witness to the events who buries the saints' bodies after their martyrdom (24, 41). Assuming the integrity of the transmitted text,[90] the choice to remove the earlier *Life*'s prologue and omit the first-person narration is not just deliberate, but marked. If the earlier *Life* responds to the authority issues found in the opening of Achilles Tatius' novel by naming the work's first-person narrator and authenticating his knowledge of the events of the narrative, the Metaphrastic version, by contrast, tackles these problems by removing the narrator entirely.

The Metaphrastic prologue, moreover, makes visible a key tension in the *Lives*' respective relationships with *Leucippe and Clitophon*. In contrast to the mythic geography that characterises the opening of the novel, the earlier *Life* baldly situates the narrative in Emesa, which is not mentioned in Achilles Tatius' work (2):

ἦν τις ἀνὴρ ἐν τῇ πόλει Ἐμέσῃ εὐγενὴς καὶ ἔνδοξος ὡς οὐκ ἄλλος τις ἦν κατοικῶν ἐν αὐτῇ, ὃς ἐκόμα πλούτῳ πολλῷ καὶ περιφανὴς ἦν εἰς τὰς πέριξ πόλεις καὶ χώρας, ὀνόματι Κλειτοφῶν· ἐκέκτητο δὲ γυναῖκα ὡραιοτάτην, θυγατέρα γεγονυῖαν Μέμνονος τοῦ τοπάρχου, ὀνόματι Γλευκίππην.

There was a certain man in the city of Emesa, of noble birth and of high repute such as no other man who lived in the city enjoyed. He abounded in great wealth, was famous in the neighbouring cities and countryside, and was called Clitophon. He possessed a very beautiful wife, the daughter of the toparch Memnon, and she was called Gleucippe.

The relocation of the work to Emesa has often been interpreted as an intrusion from another ancient novel, Heliodorus' *Aithiopika*, which ends by identifying the author by name as a Phoenician from Emesa.[91] This overlap between novelistic fiction and authorial biography is especially significant given the fantastical geography of the *Life*, where many of the narrative landmarks are inconsistent or unverifiable.[92] Given that Psellus argues that Achilles Tatius imitates Heliodorus' work, contrary to modern assessments of chronology,[93] this land-

---

[89] See Høgel (*Symeon Metaphrastes*, 146–48) on first-person narrators, with the additional discussion of Franco, "Le *Vite* di Simeone Metafrasta." As Papaioannou (*Christian Novels*, xix) points out, a parallel example of narrative reframing can be found in the *Life* of Pelagia of Antioch (*BHG* 1479).

[90] This becomes increasingly plausible given that, as Papaioannou (*Christian Novels*, xxi) notes, the texts of the *Menologion* were largely fixed by the eleventh century, as seen in the large number of manuscripts from that date.

[91] *Aith.* 10.41.4; Kanavou, "Reflections on the Relationship," 214; Kruchió, "Galaction and Episteme." The reference to Gleucippe's father also raises the spectre of Heliodorus' novel, since an ancestor of Heliodorus' heroine is called Memnon 4.8.3 whereas Leucippe's is called Sostratus (1.3.1–4.3). Alwis (*Celibate Marriages*, 295) sees this as "a subtle way of creating distance from Tatios."

[92] Alwis, *Celibate Marriages*, 294–97, 302–303.

[93] *de Heliodoro et Achille Tatio iudicium*, 66 (Dyck). This is also implied in Photius' ninth-century *Bibliotheca*, where he notes Achilles Tatius' resemblance to Heliodorus' novel (codex 87, 66a24–8).

Authorial Fictions, Phoenician Paradigms   61

scape may have a symbolic function of returning Achilles Tatius' protagonists to the source of their perceived archetype. Yet, regardless of the reasons behind this move, the Metaphrastic text frames this setting in such a way as to bring the later *Life* into closer dialogue with *Leucippe and Clitophon*. While the *Menologion*'s version maintains the Emesan setting, it is prefaced in the very first words of the text with a reference to Phoenicia (τῆς πρὸς τῷ Λιβάνῳ ὄρει Φοινίκης ...; 1). By foregrounding this geographical marker, Metaphrastes' text mirrors the novel's opening insistence upon its Phoenician setting and brings the later *Life* linguistically closer to Achilles Tatius' text. Metaphrastes' closer knowledge of the novel can also be seen in the introduction of Clitophon, where the description of his name and status (ὄνομα Κλειτοφῶν, γένος ἐπίσημος πλοῦτον, οὐδενὸς τῶν πολιτῶν δεύτερος ...) echoes the novel's distinctive staccato syntax (ἐμοὶ Φοινίκη γένος, Τύρος ἡ πατρίς, ὄνομα Κλειτοφῶν, πατὴρ Ἱππίας ...; 1.3.1).[94] Rather than marking the novel's narrative architecture, therefore, Phoenicia in the *Lives* is converted into a site of negotiation with their literary parentage.

The *Lives* return most explicitly to questions of authorship, authority, and literary genealogies through the character of Leucippe. Although the Metaphrastic text sanitises the earlier descriptions of physical violence, both *Lives* make clear the abuse Leucippe faces from her husband due to their childlessness.[95] After Leucippe converts to Christianity, however, she not only prompts her husband to become a Christian, but conceives her child Galaction as a result of her newfound faith.[96] As such, Leucippe is not just the literal mother of the saint, but also the source of the hagiography, as she facilitates the continuation of her story through the figure of her son and ensures its Christian character through her conversion.[97] The *Lives*, moreover, also give Leucippe a key narratorial role within the narrative. After meeting the monk Onouphrios, Leucippe narrates her troubles with infertility and spousal abuse to him, which leads to her baptism and pregnancy. Although both versions of the *Lives* transmit the content of Leucippe's speech, the earlier hagiography ascribes her words to divine influence (ἡ δὲ πρὸς αὐτὸν ὡς θεόθεν κινουμένη ἀντέφησεν; 3), whereas the Metaphrastic text gives Leucippe more agency over her narration (6):

---

[94] Noted by Giatromanolakes, Ἀχιλλέως Ἀλεξανδρέως Τατίου, 745.

[95] For example, *BHG* 665, 2 stresses that Leucippe has been beaten violently (ἦν δὲ τυφθεῖσα ἡ κυρία μου τῇ ἡμέρᾳ ἐκείνῃ σφοδρῶς παρὰ τοῦ ἀνδρὸς αὐτῆς), which the Metaphrastic text omits.

[96] *BHG* 665, 5; *BHG* 666, 11–12. As Alwis (*Celibate Marriage*, 296) notes, this narrative arc has its origins in the biblical narratives of Sarah and Elizabeth, who are unable to bear children until divine intervention. See also Pratsch, *Der hagiographische topos*, 72–74.

[97] In both texts, moreover, Leucippe's death marks the transition between the first half of the story about the novelistic protagonists and the second, involving Galaction and Episteme's marriage and martyrdom (*BHG* 665, 6; *BHG* 666, 18).

62 Claire Rachel Jackson

λόγων οὖν κινηθέντων, καὶ τῆς ὁμιλίας οὕτω παραταθείσης, διηγεῖτο μὲν ἡ Λευκίππη τὰ καθ᾽ ἑαυτήν· καὶ ὡς πεπήρωται αὐτῇ τὰ τῆς μήτρας, καὶ ὡς οὐδεὶς εὑρεθείη θεῶν ἄχρι καὶ τήμερον, τῶν δεσμῶν τούτων ἀνεῖναι αὐτὴν καὶ τοῦ τῆς ἀτεκνίας αἴσχους ἀπαλλάξαι δυνάμενος.

They started talking, and their conversation became prolonged. Leucippe told her story: how her womb was defective, and how, until that day, no one among the gods was to be found who could free her from these bonds and release her from the shame of childlessness.

Leucippe's verbal agency here stands in stark contrast to her novelistic predecessor. Despite being rewritten in the third person and being transmitted in indirect speech, Leucippe's ability to control her own words here has no parallel in *Leucippe and Clitophon*, where her voice is entirely filtered through Clitophon's ego-narration. As Helen Morales has pointed out, in Clitophon's account Leucippe only speaks to express her love for him or to verify her chastity, both of which align with his erotic and narratorial priorities.[98] After being enslaved and showing Clitophon the suffering literally inscribed upon her body (τὰ νῶτα διαγεγραμμένα; 5.17.6), Clitophon, who believes Leucippe to be dead, either cannot or does not read this corporeal text, and does not recognise her.[99] In the *Lives*, however, Leucippe is able to not only verbalise her sufferings, but also to have them acknowledged by a sympathetic listener. As such, Leucippe's narration not only shapes the text decisively as both a Christian hagiography and a continuation of the novel, but positions her as an authorial figure with agency over her own words. In addition, Leucippe's actions also allude more closely to the source text of the novel. While there are few linguistic parallels with the novel in either hagiography, one of the closest examples comes in the Metaphrastic text, where Leucippe feigns illness (ἡ Λευκίππη δὲ καὶ νοσεῖν σκηψαμένη; 11) in a near echo of Achilles Tatius' work (σκηψαμένη δὲ καὶ ἡ Λευκίππη νοσεῖν; 2.16.1).[100] In the novel, however, Leucippe pretends to be ill in order to sneak Clitophon into her bedroom, whereas in the hagiography her fake sickness allows her to display her piety and conceive her son through immaculate conception. Leucippe's words and actions, therefore, both align the hagiography with the novel and subvert the source text by converting its erotic implications into a specifically Christian form.

Leucippe's speech, moreover, is framed in suggestive language. Not only does she narrate her situation (διηγεῖτο), a cognate term to the διήγησις that

---

[98] Morales, *Vision and Narrative*, 200–1.

[99] On the relationship between body and text in novelistic heroines see John R. Morgan, "The Erotics of Reading Fiction: Text and Body in Heliodorus," in *Théories et Pratiques de la Fiction à la Époque Impériale*. ed. Christophe Brechet, Anne Videau, and Ruth Webb. (Paris: Picard, 2013) 225–38.

[100] This parallel is not mentioned in the list of Giatromanolakes (Ἀχιλλέως Ἀλεξανδρέως Τατίου, 746–47), not all of which are equally convincing.

Authorial Fictions, Phoenician Paradigms 63

characterised the earlier *Life*, but she is said to tell her own story (τὰ καθ' ἑαυτήν) in an echo of ancient novelistic titling conventions.[101] In narrating her own experiences through this marked terminology, therefore, Leucippe is not just given unprecedented agency as a novelistic heroine, but is also positioned as a kind of novelist herself. This is particularly marked given that the novel is referred to in various Byzantine testimonia simply by the name of its female protagonist, eliding the distance between Leucippe the character and *Leucippe* the novel.[102] By having Leucippe tell her own story using the formula of a novelistic title, Metaphrastes not only brings to the forefront the hagiographical narrative's connections with its novelistic predecessor, but also appropriates its authority through converting its embodiment to Christianity and making her the mother of a saint.[103] While readings of the *Life* have often focused on how to interpret Galaction's novelistic ancestry, less attention has been paid to Leucippe as the parent of a saint and the lynchpin between hagiography and novel. Rather than simply promulgating or converting the source text, Leucippe the character as representative of *Leucippe* the novel epitomises what is stake in this appropriation of authorship, narrative authority, and closure within the Christianised context of late antique hagiography.

As Andrew Bennett argues, while the author may function as an indeterminate gesture at a spectrum of meaning ranging from historical writer to fictional persona to author-function, that empty reference paradoxically constructs the author.[104] Authorship exposes the boundaries between literary history and narrative fiction and encroaches upon any neat distinctions that can be made between creators, narrators, and characters, and it makes uncomfortably visible issues of authority and interpretation. *Leucippe and Clitophon* actively engages with these issues not just through the indeterminacy between its occluded author and unknown narrator, but also through its continual invocations and rejections of paradigms of authority. In other words, despite the absence of the author, the opening of the novel nonetheless abounds with questions of where this narrative has come from, making visible the slippage between textual origins and authorial

---

[101] On Achilles Tatius, see Tim Whitmarsh, "The Greek Novels: Title and Genre," *American Journal of Philology* 126 (2005): 591–92. While *Leucippe and Clitophon*'s title is not specifically attested with κατά, as the article points out, both are possible across the broader tradition of novelistic titles.

[102] Most famously by Michael Psellus (*de Heliodoro et Achille Tatio iudicium*, 4–5 and *passim*), but also in the *Corpus Parisinum* 3.276 and Iohannes Georgides, *Sententiae* 240, both from the ninth to tenth-centuries. I am grateful to Nicolò D'Alconzo for help with these references. See also Whitmarsh, "The Greek Novels," 292.

[103] This is also especially striking given the invocation of Plato's *Phaedrus* at the opening of the novel, which frames anxieties about the authority of writing through metaphors of parenthood and illegitimacy (275d9–e5). See Hafner ("Fathers and Sons," 351–54) on this imagery in genealogies found in classical biographical traditions.

[104] Bennett, *The Author*, 120–21.

64   *Claire Rachel Jackson*

authority. While the *Lives* implicitly raise the spectre of the authorial paradigms and narratorial concerns which characterise *Leucippe and Clitophon*, they respond to them in divergent ways. Although the earlier text tackles the question of authorial authority by framing the work through a first-person eyewitness, the Metaphrastic version demonstrates a closer knowledge of the novel and subtly corrects features of its predecessor. By foregrounding the novel as a specifically Phoenician text and framing Leucippe as an authorial figure, the later *Life* engages with the issues of authorship not only raised in the novel itself, but also compounded by the earlier hagiography's reworking of these paradigms.

This hagiographic engagement with the novel is undoubtedly facilitated by the authorial silence within *Leucippe and Clitophon*, just as Symeon Metaphrastes' reworking of the martyrdom of Galaction and Episteme is by the anonymity of the earlier *Life*. As Papaiannou puts it when discussing Byzantine authorship more generally: "anonymity and apocryphal attribution ... allowed for and, in a sense, invited alteration, adaptation, and transformation."[105] Both *Lives*, however, exploit these issues not as a consequence of *Leucippe and Clitophon*'s circumstances of composition, but as they are raised and explored within the novel itself, and as they resonate with the wider contexts of Christian literature, Byzantine conventions of authorship, and hagiographic precedents. Instead of seeing the *Lives* as a sequel to or conversion of the novel, this contribution has aimed to show the extent to which these later hagiographies grapple with what is at stake in these claims of literary descent and authority. By tracing *Leucippe and Clitophon*'s reception from the imperial era into Byzantium, therefore, we can see how these authorial fictions are suppressed, evoked, rejected, and even resurrected.

Bibliography

Alwis, A. P. *Celibate Marriages in Late Antique and Byzantine Hagiography: The Lives of Saints Julian and Basilissa, Andronikos and Athanasia, and Galaktion and Episteme.* London: Bloomsbury, 2011.

Aringer, Nina. "Kadmos und Typhon als vorausdeutende Figuren in den *Dionysiaka*: Bemerkungen zur Kompositionskunst des Nonnos von Panopolis." *Wiener Studien* 125 (2012): 85–105.

Barthes, Roland. "The Death of the Author." Pages 277–280 in *The Book History Reader.* Edited by David Finkelstein and Alistair McCleery. 2nd ed. London: Routledge, 2006.

Bartsch, Shadi. *Decoding the Ancient Novel: The Reader and the Role of Description in Heliodorus and Achilles Tatius.* Princeton: Princeton University Press, 1989.

Behemenberg, Lena. "Le mythe comme signe. *Ekphrasis* et le jeu de la préfiguration dans *Le Roman de Leucippé et Clitophon* d'Achille Tatius." Pages 239–255 in *Mythe et Fiction.*

---

[105] Papaioannou, "Authors," 500–1.

Authorial Fictions, Phoenician Paradigms 65

Edited by Danièle Auger and Charles Delattre. Paris: Presses Universitaires de Paris Ouest, 2010.

Bennett, Andrew. *The Author.* Abingdon and New York: Routledge, 2005.

Biriotti, Maurice and Nicole Miller, eds. *What Is an Author?* Manchester: Manchester University Press, 1993.

Briquel-Chatonnet, Françoise. "L'image des Phéniciens dans le roman grec." Pages 189–197 in *Le monde du roman grec.* Edited by Marie-Françoise Baslez, Philippe Hoffmann, and Monique Trédé. Paris: Presses de l'École Normale Supérieur, 1992.

Buitenwerf, Rieuwerd. *Book III of the Sibylline Oracles and its Social Setting.* Leiden: Brill, 2003.

Burke, Séan. *Authorship: From Plato to the Postmodern. A Reader.* Edinburgh: Edinburgh University Press, 1995.

Burke, Séan. *The Death and Return of the Author: Criticism and Subjectivity in Barthes, Foucault and Derrida.* 3rd ed. Edinburgh: Edinburgh University Press, 2008.

Castle, Terry. *Masquerade and Civilization: The Carnivalesque in Eighteenth-Century English Culture and Fiction.* Stanford: Stanford University Press, 1986.

Cohn, Dorrit. *The Distinction of Fiction.* Baltimore: Johns Hopkins University Press, 2000.

Constantinou, Stavroula and Christian Høgel, eds. *Metaphrasis: A Byzantine Concept of Rewriting and Its Hagiographical Products.* Leiden: Brill, 2021.

Delehaye, Hippolyte. *Les Passions des Martyrs et les Genres Littéraires.* Brussels: Société des Bollandistes, 1921.

De Temmerman, Koen. *Crafting Characters: Heroes and Heroines in the Ancient Greek Novel.* Oxford: Oxford University Press, 2014.

De Temmerman, Koen. "A Flowery Meadow and a Hidden Metalepsis in Achilles Tatius." *Classical Quarterly* 59 (2009): 667–670.

De Temmerman, Koen and Kristoffel Demoen, eds. *Writing Biography in Greece and Rome: Narrative Technique and Fictionalization.* Cambridge: Cambridge University Press, 2016.

Dörrie, Heinrich. "Die griechischen Romane und das Christentum." *Philologus* 93 (1938): 273–276.

Edwards, Ruth B. *Kadmos the Phoenician: A Study in Greek Legends and Their Mycenaean Age.* Amsterdam: Hakkert, 1979.

Fletcher, Richard and Johanna Hanink, eds. *Creative Lives in Classical Antiquity: Poets, Artists, and Biography.* Cambridge: Cambridge University Press, 2016.

Formisano, Marco and Cristiana Sogno. "Origins and Original Moments in Late Greek and Latin Texts." *Arethusa* 54 (2021): 269–273.

Foucault, Michel. "Qu'est-ce qu'un auteur?" *Bulletin de la société française de philosophie* (1969): 75–104.

Franco, Laura. "Le *Vite* di Simeone Metafrasta: osservazioni sulla tecnica compositive." Pages 95–117 in *Bisanzio nell'età dei Macedoni: Forme della produzione etteraria e artistica.* Edited by Fabrizio Conca and Gianfranco Fiaccadori. Milan: Cisalpino, 2007.

Garnaud, Jean-Philippe. *Achille Tatius: Le Roman de Leucippé et Clitophon.* Paris: Les Belles Lettres, 1991.

Genette, Gerard. *Palimpsests: Literature in the Second Degree.* Translated by Channa Newman and Claude Doubinsky. London: University of Nebraska Press, 1997.

Geue, Tom. *Author Unknown: The Power of Anonymity in Ancient Rome.* Cambridge, MA: Harvard University Press, 2019.

66   *Claire Rachel Jackson*

Giatromanolakes, Giorges. Ἀχιλλέως Ἀλεξανδρέως Τατιου: Λευκίππη καὶ Κλειτοφῶν. Εἰσαγωγή – μεφάφραση – σχόλια. Athens: Hidryma Goulandrē-Chorn, 1990.

Goldhill, Simon. "The Sirens' Song: Authorship, Authority, and Citation." Pages 137–154 in *What Is an Author?* Edited by Maurice Biriotti and Nicole Miller. Manchester: Manchester University Press, 1993.

Goldhill, Simon. "Why Don't Jews Write Biography?" Pages 13–38 in *Being Christian in Late Antiquity: A Festschrift for Gillian Clark*. Edited by Carol Harrison, Caroline Humfress, and Isabella Sandwell. Oxford: Oxford University Press, 2014.

Graziosi, Barbara. *Inventing Homer: The Early Reception of Ancient Epic*. Cambridge: Cambridge University Press, 2002.

Greensmith, Emma. "The Wrath of the Sibyl: Homeric Reception and Contested Identities in the Sibylline Oracles 3." Pages 178–2130 in *Late Hellenistic Greek Literature in Dialogue*. Edited by Jason Konig and Nicolas Wiater. Cambridge: Cambridge University Press, 2022.

Gruen, Erich. *Rethinking the Other in Antiquity*. Princeton: Princeton University Press, 2011.

Hadjittofi, Fotini. "Nonnus' Europa and Cadmus: Re-configuring Masculinity in the *Dionysiaca*." Pages 262–281 in *Nonnus of Panopolis in Context III: Old Questions and New Perspectives*. Edited by Filip Doroszewski and Katarzyna Jażdżewska. Leiden: Brill, 2021.

Hafner, Markus. "Fathers and Sons – and Daughters: Genealogical Co-Authorship, Offspring Metaphors, and the Language of Legitimacy." Pages 341–365 in *Ut Pictura Poeta: Autorbilder und die Lektüre antiker Literatur*. Edited by Ute Tischer, Ursula Gärtner, and Alexandra Forst. Turnhout: Brepols, 2022.

Hinterberger, Martin. "Autobiography and Hagiography in Byzantium." *Symbolae Osloenses* 75 (2000): 139–164.

Høgel, Christian. *Symeon Metaphrastes: Rewriting and Canonization*. Copenhagen: Museum Tusculanum Press, 2002.

Kanavou, Nikoletta. "Reflections on the Relationship between the Life and Passion of Saints Galaktion and Episteme and the Ancient Greek Novel." *Jahrbuch der Österreichischen Byzantinistik* 70 (2021): 209–220.

Kruchió, Benedek. "Galaction and Episteme: Converting Erotic Fiction." Forthcoming.

Krueger, Derek. *Writing and Holiness*. Philadelphia: University of Pennsylvania Press, 2004.

Kühr, Angela. *Als Kadmos nach Boiotien kam*. Stuttgart: Franz Steiner, 2006.

Macalister, Suzanne. *Dreams and Suicides: The Greek Novel from Antiquity to the Byzantine Empire*. London and New York: Routledge, 1996.

Maciver, Calum. "Longus' Narrator: A Reassessment." *Classical Quarterly* 70 (2020): 827–845.

Mal-Maeder, Danielle van. "Au Seuil des Romans Grecs: Effets de réel et effets de creation." *Groningen Colloquia on the Novel* 4 (1991): 1–33.

Marinčič, Marko. "Advertising One's Own Story: Text and Speech in Achilles Tatius' *Leucippe and Clitophon*." Pages 168–200 in *Seeing Tongues, Hearing Scripts: Orality and Representation in the Ancient Novel*. Edited by Victoria Rimell. Ancient Narrative Supplementum 7. Groningen: Barkhuis & Groningen University Library, 2007.

Martin, R. P. "A Good Place to Talk: Discourse and Topos in Achilles Tatius and Achilles Tatius and Philostratus." Pages 143–160 in *Space in the Ancient Novel*. Edited by Michael

Paschalis and Stavros A. Frangoulidis. Ancient Narrative Supplements 1. Groningen: Barkhuis & Groningen University Library, 2002.

Messis, Charis. "Fiction and/or Novelization in Byzantine Hagiography." Pages 313–341 in *A Companion to Byzantine Hagiography, Vol. II: Genres and Contexts*. Edited by Stephanos Efthymiadis. Farnham and Burlington, VT: Ashgate, 2014.

ní Mheallaigh, Karen. "Philosophical Framing: The Phaedran Setting of *Leucippe and Clitophon*." Pages 231–244 in *Philosophical Presences in the Ancient Novel*. Edited by J. R. Morgan and Meriel Jones. Ancient Narrative Supplementum 10. Groningen: Barkhuis & Groningen University Library, 2007.

ní Mheallaigh, Karen. "The 'Phoenician Letters' of Dictys of Crete and Dionysius Scytobrachion." Cambridge Classical Journal 58 (2012): 181–93.

Miller, Nancy K. *Subject to Change: Reading Feminist Writing*. New York: Columbia University Press, 1988.

Miller, P. Cox. "Strategies of Representation in Collective Biography: Constructing the Subject as Holy." Pages 209–254 in *Greek Biography and Panegyric in Late Antiquity*. Edited by Tomas Hägg and Philip Rousseau. Berkeley: University of California Press, 2000.

Moi, Toril. *Sexual/Textual Politics: Feminist Literary Theory*. London: Routledge, 1985.

Möllendorf, Peter von. "Bild-Störung: Das Gemälde von Europas Entführung in Achilleus Tatios' Roman *Leukippe und Kleitophon*." Pages 145–164 in *Europa – Stier und Sternenkranz: Von der Union mit Zeus zum Staatenverbund*. Edited by Almut-Barbara Renger and Roland Issler. Bond: Vandenhoeck & Ruprecht, 2009.

Morales, Helen. *Vision and Narrative in Achilles Tatius' Leucippe and Clitophon*. Cambridge: Cambridge University Press, 2004.

Morgan, J. R. "Achilles Tatius." Pages 493–506 in *Narrators, Narratees, and Narratives in Ancient Greek Literature*. Edited by Rene Nünlist, Angus M. Bowie, and Irene de Jong. Leiden: Brill, 2004.

Morgan, J. R. "The Erotics of Reading Fiction: Text and Body in Heliodorus." Pages 225–38 in *Théories et Pratiques de la Fiction à la Époque Impériale*. Edited by Christophe Brechet, Anne Videau, and Ruth Webb. Paris: Picard, 2013.

Most, G. W. "The Stranger's Stratagem: Self-Disclosure and Self-Sufficiency in Greek Culture." *Journal of Hellenic Studies* 109 (1989): 114–133.

Mullett, Margaret. "In Search of the Monastic Author: Story-telling, Anonymity, and Innovation in the 12th Century." Pages 171–198 in *The Author in Middle Byzantine Literature: Modes, Functions, Identities*. Edited by Aglae Pizzone. Berlin: De Gruyter, 2014.

Mullett, Margaret. "Novelisation and/or Fiction in Byzantium: Narrative After the Revival of Fiction." Pages 1–28 in *Byzantine Narrative: Papers in Honour of Roger Scott*. Edited by John Burke et al. Melbourne: Australian Association for Byzantine Studies, 2006.

Najman, Hindy. *Seconding Sinai: The Development of Mosaic Discourse in Second Temple Judaism*. Leiden: Brill, 2003.

Nakatani, Saiichiro. "A Re-Examination of Some Structural Problems in Achilles Tatius' *Leucippe and Clitophon*." *Ancient Narrative* 3 (2003): 63–81.

Nilsson, Ingela. "Desire and God Have Always Been Around, in Life and Romance Alike." Pages 235–260 in *Plotting with Eros: Essays on the Poetics of Love and the Erotics of Reading*. Edited by Ingela Nilsson. Copenhagen: Museum Tusculanum Press, 2009.

Papaioannou, Stratis. "Authors [With an Excursus on Symeon Metaphrastes]." Pages 482–524 in *The Oxford Handbook of Byzantine Literature*. Edited by Stratis Papaioannou. Oxford: Oxford University Press, 2021.

68   *Claire Rachel Jackson*

Papaioannou, Stratis. *Christian Novels from the Menologion of Symeon Metaphrastes.* Cambridge, MA: Harvard University Press, 2017.

Peirano, Irene. "Ille ego qui quondam: On Authorial (An)onymity." Pages 251–285 in *The Author's Voice in Classical and Late Antiquity.* Edited by Anna Marmodoro and Jonathan Hill. Oxford: Oxford University Press, 2013.

Peirano Garrison, Irene and Hindy Najman. "Pseudepigrapha and Pseudepigraphy." Pages 331–354 in *The Old Testament Pseudepigrapha: Fifty Years of the Pseudepigrapha at the SBL.* Edited by Matthias Henze and Liv Ingeborg Lied. Atlanta: Society of Biblical Literature, 2019.

Pizzone, Aglae, ed. *The Author in Middle Byzantine Literature: Modes, Functions, Identities.* Berlin: De Gruyter, 2014.

Plepelits, Karl. "Achilles Tatios." Pages 387–416 in *The Novel in the Ancient World.* Edited by Gareth Schmeling. 2nd ed. Leiden: Brill, 2003.

Pratsch, Thomas. *Der hagiographische topos: Griechische Heiligenviten in mittelbyzantinischer Zeit.* Berlin: De Gruyter, 2005.

Quinn, Josephine Crawley. "Phoenicians and Carthaginians in Greco-Roman Literature." Pages 671–683 in *The Oxford Handbook of The Phoenician and Punic Mediterranean.* Edited by Carolina Lope-Ruiz and Brian R. Doak. New York: Oxford University Press, 2019.

Rapp, Claudia. "Storytelling as Spiritual Communication in Early Greek Hagiography: The Use of *Diegesis.*" *Journal of Early Christian Studies* 6 (1998): 431–448.

Reardon, B. P. "Achilles Tatius and Ego-Narrative." Pages 80–96 in *Greek Fiction: The Greek Novel in Context.* Edited by John Robert Morgan and Richard Stoneman. London: Routledge, 1994.

Repath, I. D. "Achilles Tatius' *Leucippe and Cleitophon*: What Happened Next?" *Classical Quarterly* 55 (2005): 250–265.

Robiano, Patrick. "Pour en finir avec le christianisme d'Achille Tatius et d'Héliodor d'Émèse: la lecture des *Passions de Galaction et d'Épistèmè.*" *L'Antiquité Classique* 78 (2009): 145–60.

Rocchi, Maria. "Kadmos e i *Phoinikeia Grammata.*" Pages 529–533 in *Atti del II Congresso Internazionale di Studi Fenici e Punici, Roma, 9–14 Novembre 1987.* Volume Secundo. Rome: Consiglio nazionale delle ricerche, 1991.

Selden, Daniel L. "Genre of Genre." Pages 39–64 in *The Search for the Ancient Novel.* Edited by James Tatum. Baltimore: Johns Hopkins University Press, 1994.

Trapp, M. B. "Plato's *Phaedrus* in Second-Century Greek Literature." Pages 141–173 in *Antonine Literature.* Edited by D. A. Russell. Oxford: Oxford University Press, 1990.

Trzaskoma, S. M. "The Storms in Theodoros Daphnopates (Ep. 36), Symeon Metaphrastes (*BHG* 1878) and Achilles Tatius (3.1.1–5.6)." *Byzantion* 87 (2017): 375–386.

Vilborg, Ebbe. *Achilles Tatius: Leucippe and Clitophon. A Commentary.* Gothenburg: Almqvist & Wiksell, 1962.

Whitmarsh, Tim. *Achilles Tatius: Leucippe and Clitophon. Books I–II.* Cambridge: Cambridge University Press, 2020.

Whitmarsh, Tim. "The Greek Novels: Title and Genre." *American Journal of Philology* 126 (2005): 587–611.

Whitmarsh, Tim. *Narrative and Identity in the Ancient Greek Novel: Returning Romance.* Cambridge: Cambridge University Press, 2011.

Whitmarsh, Tim. "Reading for Pleasure: Narrative, Irony and Erotics in Achilles Tatius." Pages 195–205 in *Ancient Novel and Beyond*. Edited by Stelios Panayotakis, Maaike Zimmerman, and Wytse Hette Keulen. Leiden: Brill, 2003.

Winkler, J.J. "The Mendacity of Kalasiris and the Narrative Strategy of Heliodoros' *Aithiopika*." *Yale Classical Studies* 27 (1982): 93–158.

Yunis, Harvey. *Plato: Phaedrus*. Cambridge: Cambridge University Press, 2011.

Outside Bible Readers as an Author Character in Rabbinic Literature

Using Attribution to Preserve and Contain Subversive Positions

REBECCA SCHARBACH WOLLENBERG

In the past twenty years, we have come to a growing consensus that ancient and late antique Mediterranean pseudepigraphy represents a "generative mechanism that enables the growth of a tradition" by allowing the ongoing creative generation of discourses, traditions, and genres "tied to a founder."[1] Drawing on Michel Foucault's notion that the author-function can be transdiscursive (establishing a constellation of characteristic motifs, figures, structures, and discourses that can be reused by others),[2] scholars of this school have refigured late antique pseudepigraphy as a participatory "multi-faceted phenomenon, the methods and motives of which prove far more complex than modern notions of literary frauds and forgeries"[3] that have historically clung to the scholarly categorization of pseudepigraphy.[4]

This insight has served a particularly important function by bringing pseudepigraphic texts in from the cold within the field of biblical studies. By demonstrating that pseudepigraphic authorship represents "not precritical religious dogma about literal authorship but a poetic and honorific association of a body of texts with a [biblical] character" who has become linked to certain types of genres and traditions,[5] researchers have been able to short-circuit a mode of

---

[1] Hindy Najman and Irene Peirano Garrison, "Pseudepigraphy as an Interpretive Construct," in *Old Testament Pseudepigrapha: Fifty Years of the Pseudepigrapha Section at the SBL*, ed. Matthias Henze and Liv Ingeborg Lied (Atlanta: Society of Biblical Literature, 2019), 351. For more extended accounts of this position, see Hindy Najman, *Seconding Sinai: The Development of Mosaic Discourse in Second Temple Judaism* (Leiden: Brill, 2003), especially 1–40 and eadem, *Past Renewals: Interpretative Authority, Renewed Revelation, and the Quest for Perfection in Jewish Antiquity* (Leiden: Brill, 2010), especially 73–86.

[2] Michel Foucault, "What Is an Author?" *The Foucault Reader*, ed. and trans. Paul Rabinow (New York: Pantheon Books, 1984), 114. For a more expansive exploration of this theme, see Robyn Faith Walsh's essay in this volume.

[3] Annette Yoshiko Reed, "Pseudepigraphy, Authorship, and the Reception of 'the Bible' in Late Antiquity," in *The Reception and Interpretation of the Bible in Late Antiquity*, ed. Lorenzo DiTomasso and Lucian Turcescu (Leiden: Brill, 2008), 479–80.

[4] Annette Yoshiko Reed, "The Modern Invention of 'Old Testament Pseudepigrapha'," *Journal of Theological Studies* 60 (2009): 403–36.

[5] Eva Mroczek, *The Literary Imagination in Jewish Antiquity* (Oxford: Oxford University Press, 2016), 84.

scholarly evaluation in which pseudepigraphic texts were evaluated primarily for authenticity and the subsequent "value that they had for the study of biblical books" – a practice that had served to artificially divide sacred traditions from the same period into a hierarchy of "scriptural" texts and marginalized works.[6] By destabilizing the "hegemony of the biblical,"[7] the work of the past twenty years has done much to refigure our conception of late antique sacred writing as a scriptural universe[8] in which the "biblical exists only in assemblage with other entities"[9] – "scripture" existing simultaneously nowhere and in diffusion throughout a textual network.

In this essay, I would invite the reader to examine a specific granular detail within this broader picture and consider the ways in which the practice of pseudepigraphy sometimes functioned to variegate a sacred reading culture[10] or scriptural network[11] by leveraging marginalized or outside author characters to preserve traditions of dissent or difference within a reading culture or scriptural assemblage. We are familiar with the ways in which this sort of variegation functioned in the networks of late antique Greek and Latin authors from the work of classicist William Johnson, who has demonstrated how the reading culture of the high Roman elite is seen best in the triangulation between two divergent lenses to give the image depth and richness. On the one hand, he introduces us to the unironic self-portraits of elite Roman readers who saw themselves as participating in a reading culture in which membership was defined by possessing the length and "depth of education" necessary to transform unmarked *scriptio continua* into "sensible statements with meaningful phrasing," and to "perceive the underlying structural disposition, generic features, and allusive

---

[6] Benjamin Wright, "Pseudepigrapha Within and Without Biblical Studies," in *Old Testament Pseudepigrapha: Fifty Years of the Pseudepigrapha Section at the SBL*, ed. Matthias Henze and Liv Ingeborg Lied (Atlanta: Society of Biblical Literature, 2019), 133–56.

[7] Eva Mroczek, "The Hegemony of the Biblical in the Study of Second Temple Literature," *Journal of Ancient Judaism* 6 (2015): 2–35.

[8] On this concept, see Guy Stroumsa, *The Scriptural Universe of Ancient Christianity* (Cambridge: Harvard University Press, 2016).

[9] On which, see the theoretical reflection in David Lambert, "Is Bible 'Scripture'?" *Metatron* 1 (2022): 315–29. For an elaboration on Deleuze's theory of assemblage in relation to the Bible, see Stephen D. Moore, *The Bible after Deleuze: Affects, Assemblages, Bodies Without Organs* (Oxford: Oxford University Press, 2022).

[10] That is, the "observation that reading is not the cognitive processing of an individual of the technology of writing but *rather the negotiated construction of meaning within a particular sociocultural context*" (William A. Johnson, *Readers and Reading Culture in the High Roman Empire: A Study of Elite Communities* [Oxford: Oxford University Press, 2010], 12).

[11] By which I mean something closer to David Brakke's (in many ways analogous) concept of varied communal "scriptural practices": David Brakke, "Scriptural Practices in Early Christianity: Towards a New History of the New Testament Canon," in *Invention, Rewriting, Usurpation: Discursive Fights over Religions Traditions in Antiquity*, ed. David Brakke, Anders-Christian Jacobsen, and Jörg Ulrich (Bern: Peter Lang, 2012), 263–80.

Outside Bible Readers as an Author Character in Rabbinic Literature   73

contacts within the classical traditions and contemporary [literary] trends"[12] in minimally processed textual transcripts – ideally, on first sight.[13] On the other hand, in the contemporaneous works of Lucian, a marginalized cultural insider who poses as an outsider in his literary works, we are given a glimpse of an alternate vision of this elite Roman reading culture characterized by a satirist's "dig[s] against scholars' unreasonable expectations (or indeed pretensions) to knowledge" about the intricacies of this textual system.[14] Through the triangulations of these two opposing perspectives on the same object, a portrait emerged that was not only rich but plausible – made sharper by the intersection of self-evaluation and critique.

I would invite us to consider the ways in which the practice of pseudepigraphy produced a similar triangulation within the authorless assemblages of other late antique Mediterranean traditions, such as early rabbinic tradition. That is, I propose that a similar result was achieved in these very different bodies of thought by triangulating a sacred reading culture's official vision of itself with the portrait it paints of other sacred reading cultures. As a case study, we will analyze early rabbinic portraits of alien Bible readers – Christian, gnostic, and other outside Bible readers[15] – as representing a form of collective author character.

In the past twenty years, Jewish studies seems to have explored every possible avenue for thinking about the early centuries of Jewish-Christian relations – without reaching any discernable consensus about how early rabbinic authorities thought about and related to their Christian compatriots – even in a single region or period.[16] In this essay, I would like to propose that solutions to this problem have eluded us, in part, because many narratives about Christian(-like)[17] characters in early rabbinic traditions were not really stories about Christians at all. In saying this, I do not mean to reopen the question of just how

---

[12] Johnson, *Reading Culture*, 200.

[13] As we see in the "man of letters" who is able to detect a forgery of Galen after merely glancing at the text at a book stall (Johnson, *Reading Culture*, 85).

[14] Johnson, *Reading Culture*, 159.

[15] I use the terminology of "outside" or "alien" Bible readers to capture the category of the *min*, that ever elusive Bible-reading opponent of the rabbinic position who is frequently identified with historical Christians but sometimes less clearly identified with a particular historical movement.

[16] The literature on these questions has become far too broad to cite here. Diverse framings of the secondary literature can be found in the recent work of Ra'anan Boustan and Joseph E. Sanzo, "Christian Magicians, Jewish Magical Idioms, and the Shared Magical Culture of Late Antiquity," *Harvard Theological Review* 110 (2017): 219–20; Reuven Kiperwasser, "What Is Hidden in the Small Box? Narratives of Late Antique Roman Palestine in Dialogue," *Association for Jewish Studies Review* 45 (2021): 78–79; Michal Bar Asher Siegel, *Jewish-Christian Dialogues on Scripture in Late Antiquity: Heretic Narratives of the Babylonian Talmud* (Cambridge: Cambridge University Press, 2019), 2–5.

[17] For the purposes of this article, this category will encompass a variety of competing readers of scriptural text – but particularly those who valorize scripture as the only source of religious authority and who speak the language of supersessionism.

74 Rebecca Scharbach Wollenberg

many Christian characters we can actually find in early rabbinic tradition.[18] Nor do I intend to relitigate the problem of how one knows a(n imaginary rabbinic) Christian when one sees one.[19] I would suggest instead that many early rabbinic stories featuring Christian(-like) scriptural readers are not fundamentally about communal competition or the boundaries of acceptable religious thought in any form.

I would argue instead that these early rabbinic portraits of outside Bible readers represent an unusual form of the pseudepigraphic founder tradition – each individual portrait participating in the tradition of a collective author character with its own transdiscursive structures, thematics, and attributes within rabbinic literature. For it quickly emerges that many (if not most) of the statements and narratives attributed to this collective author character are traditions that reflect on the problem of scriptural reading – particularly the dangers of different scriptural reading practices and the affordances that written text possesses (or lacks) as a medium for covenantal transmission. While it may seem counterintuitive to employ vivid narratives on one topic (sectarian debate) to think through an apparently unrelated problem (the nature of scripture), Christine Hayes first drew our attention to this rabbinic rhetorical technique in an essay that noted a displacement on precisely this juncture between portraits of intercommunal debate and the uses of scripture, in which she argued that "rabbinic authors introduce or exploit the presence of *minim* (i.e., heretics or sectarians) and Romans (in bSanhedrin 90b–91a) in order to voice and thus grapple with their own ambivalence and radical doubt concerning non-contextual methods of exegesis."[20] As a collective author character, the outside Bible reader came to be utilized as a conventional mouthpiece that simultaneously preserved and contained rabbinic doubts about the nature of written scripture and its affordances. Just as pseud-

---

[18] On which, see Adiel Schremer, *Brothers Estranged: Heresy, Christianity, and Jewish Identity in Late Antiquity* (Oxford: Oxford University Press, 2010).

[19] On which, see Michal Bar Asher Siegal, "Heresy and the *Minim* of the Babylonian Talmud," *Jewish Thought* 1 (2019): 9–31 and the secondary literature analyzed there.

[20] Christine Hayes, "Displaced Self-Perceptions: The Deployment of *Minim* and Romans in *B. Sanhedrin* 90b–91a," in *Religious and Ethnic Communities in Later Roman Palestine*, ed. Hayim Lapin (Lanham, MD: University Press of Maryland, 1999), 250. Since that essay, this phenomenon has been increasingly well-documented in other facets of the literature on late antiquity in recent years. We know, for instance, that early rabbinic thinkers leveraged vivid images of fictional women to tell stories about changes in rabbinic honor culture, evolving scholarly episteme, and other concerns of the rabbinic male elite. On which, see Rebecca Scharbach Wollenberg, "The Bad Wife Who Was Good: Women as a Way of Life in Genesis Rabbah 17:3," *Prooftexts* 37 (2018): 56–85 and the literature cited there. Similarly, early Christian authors appear to have employed Jewish characters to dramatize questions such as the appropriate role of rational skepticism in the faith community (Serge Ruzer, "Reasonable Doubt and the 'Other': Jewish Scepticism in Early Christian Sources," in *Expressions of Sceptical Topoi in (Late) Antique Judaism*, ed. Reuven Kiperwasser and Geoffrey Herman [Berlin: De Gruyter, 2021], 69–84 and the literature cited there).

epigraphic biblical characters came to be associated with their own distinctive discourses and genres, so the rabbinic "character" of the alien Bible reader came to be associated with a distinctive discourse that gave voice to rabbinic anxieties about the dangers of written scripture and its affordances. By allowing fictional outsiders to ruminate on the darker side of written scripture, this pseudepigraphic discourse of the alien Bible reader held space for such doubts within the rabbinic tradition while blunting their subversive normative implications.

As was true for pseudepigraphic author characters drawn from the Bible, rabbinic traditions attributed particular interests and practices to the collective character of the outside Bible reader as an anchor for the "revelations" that this character would voice. First and foremost, these fictional religious rivals are frequently portrayed in rabbinic sources as avid consumers of written text as a source of religious and cultural information. Indeed, interest in the written text of the Hebrew Bible is often cited as the defining and consuming interest of this religious rival, in distinction from their rabbinic peers. As bAvodah Zarah 4a, for instance, puts this contrast in narrative form:

R. Abahu praised Rav Safra to the heretics as a great man. They exempted him from taxes for thirteen years. One day they encountered him [Rav Safra] and said to him "It is written, 'Only you have I known from all the families of the earth, therefore I will hold you accountable for all of your sins' (Amos 3:2)." [The heretics asked] "One who is angry, does he take it out on the object of his affections?" He was silent and did not say anything to that. They snuck a cloth around his throat and were hurting him. Then R. Abahu encountered them and he said to them "Why are you hurting him?" They said to him, "Did you not tell us that he was a great man? But he did not know how to tell to us the exegesis of this verse." R. Abahu said to them "I spoke to you in regards Tannaitic traditions. Did I say anything about biblical traditions to you?" They said to him, "Why is there a difference in your learning [since you do know scripture and he doesn't]?" He said to them "We that live among you, we put it upon ourselves to study [scripture] closely and they [who come from Babylonia] don't study it closely." They said to him "Then you tell us [the exegesis of this verse]!" He said to him "I will give you a parable: what is the matter like? Like a man who is collecting money from two men – one a friend and another, an enemy. From his friend, it is collected little by little. From his enemy it is collected all at once."

In this portrait of our collective author character, Christian[21] *minim* are not only well-versed in the Hebrew Bible but hold it up as the primary (perhaps

---

[21] On which identification, see Daniel Boyarin, *Borderlines: The Partition of Judeo-Christianity* (Philadelphia: University of Pennsylvania Press, 2004), 223; idem, "Hellenism in Jewish Babylonia," in *The Cambridge Companion to Talmud and Rabbinic Literature,* ed. Charlotte E. Fonrobert and Martin S. Jaffee (Cambridge: Cambridge University Press, 2007), 357–58; William Horbury, *Jews and Christians: In Contact and Controversy* (Edinburgh: T&T Clark, 1998), 200–26, especially 204; Richard Kalmin, "Christians and Heretics in Rabbinic Literature of Late Antiquity," *Harvard Theological Review* 87 (1994): 155–69. As Yaakov Teppler points out, moreover, "Rabbi Abbahu is known from other sources as a disputant against minim whose identity as Christians is already indubitable" (Yaakov Teppler, *Birkat HaMinim: Jews and Christians in Conflict in the Ancient World* [Tübingen: Mohr Siebeck, 2007], 125–26). On this last

76   *Rebecca Scharbach Wollenberg*

exclusive) standard by which a "great man" of religion may be measured. In this tale, knowing the scriptural writings is portrayed as a matter of literal life or death – in which lack of knowledge will quickly produce a strangling scarf around the ignorant's neck. Moreover, this concern with written scripture is portrayed as limited to Christian readers. Indeed, the Christian emphasis on scriptural interpretation is explicitly contrasted to the rabbinic valuation of scripture voiced by the Jewish players in this interaction, who profess a surprisingly dismissive attitude towards the text of the Bible. R. Abahu speaks of reading the Bible as if it is not entirely a welcome task. As he puts it, "We *impose it upon ourselves* to reflect upon it." Nor, it appears, does R. Abahu think it is at all necessary for a rabbinic Jew to concern himself with the biblical text. He seems untroubled by the fact that the Babylonian rabbinic authorities "do not reflect upon it," and indeed he implies that the Palestinian sages themselves would not study the Bible if not for the historical accident that they find themselves living among Christians (as he explains, "*since we find ourselves among you*, we impose it upon ourselves to reflect upon it").[22]

In other portraits of outside Bible readers, this collective author character is not only ascribed a general interest in the biblical text but demonstrates a persistent, almost obsessive, focus on a certain type of rigid textual close reading – a practice that the frame narrative characterizes as a particularly ineffective mode of engaging with the scriptural tradition. For while Christian Bible readers are generally portrayed as enthusiastic and widely read[23] consumers of sacred text, early rabbinic narratives often express great impatience with the tendentiousness and superficiality they attribute to the textual reading practices of their imaginary Christian interlocutors. In yBerakhot 9:1, for instance, R. Simlai complains, "every time the heretics start breaking up a verse" to prove a point, "their answer is right there beside them!" At the very moment when he is bemoaning this tendency to take snippets of textual evidence out of context, a group of Christians suddenly appears. They say, "what about this place in Genesis where it is written 'let us make man in *our* image and likeness? [Doesn't that imply a plural Godhead?]'." Rabbi Simali replies: "But it isn't then written they made man in *their* image but 'God created man in *his* image' [Gen 1:27] with a singular verb [which shows that it is a royal we]." They were apparently satisfied with this and went away. But no sooner had they gone than they came back saying, "What about that place [in Joshua 22:22] where it is written, 'Lord Divine God, Lord

---

point, compare Adiel Schremer, "Stammaitic Historiography," in *Creation and Composition: The Contributions of the Bavli Redactors (Stammaim) to the Aggada*, ed. Jeffrey Rubenstein (Tübingen: Mohr Siebeck, 2005), 223–24.

[22] For more on the theme of Palestinian scriptural expertise as a reaction to Christian use of the Bible in Palestine, see Richard Kalmin, "Patterns and Developments in Rabbinic Midrash of Late Antiquity," in *Hebrew Bible/Old Testament: The History of Its Interpretation*, ed. Magnes Saebo (Goettingen: Vandehoeck and Ruprecht, 1996), 1:288–89.

[23] These readers are widely read as their prooftexts are taken from multiple biblical books.

Divine God he knows' [with three divine names just like the trinity]?" He said to them, "But here, too, *they* know isn't written [with a plural verb] but *he knows* in the singular." The passage goes on and on like this, as these outside Bible readers leave and come back repeatedly to bring verse after verse of apparently plural nouns attached to singular verbs. As a matter of fact, many of these verses would make excellent prooftexts for trinitarian theology – a plural divine noun attached to a singular verb is a perfect jumping off point for thinking about a godhead that is simultaneously plural and unified. The rabbis may even have gathered these particular prooftexts from such a source.[24] But that does not matter for our purposes. As this passage leverages these verses, they serve to demonstrate that the outside Bible reading characters portrayed here are perpetually (perhaps permanently) dedicated to a detail-oriented textual reading technique that does not serve them, but which they cannot change. For Rabbi Simlay's interrogators do not even bother to adapt their exegetical tactics from one failed foray to another – but repeatedly cite plural nouns attached to singular verbs immediately after being (successfully) reprimanded for that very mistake. In other words, passages such as these serve primarily to convey this author character's keenness to "dismantle" (פרק) the written text of scripture with their close reading – detaching verse from verse and phrase from phrase – so that they can verbally throw the shards at their rabbinic rivals.

Given that the outsider biblical reader character was assigned an almost obsessive interest in scriptural text, it is not surprising that this author character often functions in early rabbinic tradition as a vehicle to explore the theoretical critiques of writing as a medium for sacred revelation. We find such critiques, for instance, in well-known early rabbinic narratives about the role of scriptural writings in the jostling between late antique Jews and Christians over who could more authentically claim the status of Israel. First and foremost among the disturbing traits attributed to written communication in these stories is the tendency of written text to open its heart indiscriminately to anyone who can decipher it. This quality is treated as particularly troublesome with regards to the biblical text since the Hebrew Bible tradition so often addressed its audience in an all-embracing second person plural, with the result that anyone who engaged directly with biblical literature found themselves addressed as "Israel" (that is, as a part of God's chosen people and one of his beloved children). As one well-known[25] rabbinic tradition develops this theme:[26]

---

[24] For more on this, see Burton Visotzsky, "Trinitarian Testimonies," in *Fathers of the World: Essays in Rabbinic and Patristic Literature* (Tübingen: Mohr Siebeck, 1995), 61–74.

[25] Marc Bregman, "Mishnah and LXX as Mystery: An Example of Jewish-Christian Polemic in the Byzantine Period," in *Continuity and Renewal: Judaism in Eretz Israel during the Byzantine-Christian Era*, ed. Lee Levine (Jerusalem: Yad Ben Zvi, 2004), 333. Compare Martin S. Jaffee, "Rabbinic Oral Tradition in Late Byzantine Galilee: Christian Empire and Rabbinic Ideological Resistance," in *Orality, Literacy, and Colonialism in Antiquity*, ed. Jonathan A. Draper (Atlanta:

78   *Rebecca Scharbach Wollenberg*

Moses requested that the Mishnah [that is, the rabbinic legal tradition] be given in writing but the Holy One, blessed be he, foresaw that, in the future, the gentile nations would translate the Bible and read it in Greek and would say "they are not Israel." The Holy One, blessed be he, said to him, "Lo, Moses, in the future, the nations will say 'we are Israel, we are the children of God' and Israel will say 'we are the children of God' and thus far the scales are balanced. The Holy One, blessed be he, said to the nations of the world, 'what do you mean, you are my sons? I don't recognize any but he who has my *mysterion* in his hand. That one is my son." They said to him, "And what is your *mysterion?*" He said to them, "It is the [oral tradition of the] Mishnah."

This passage expresses relief that the use of writing to convey religious knowledge was highly circumscribed in the late antique Judaism because the few sacred writings they did possess had proven treacherously promiscuous – making it possible for strange new readers not only to consume the Biblical text and re-spond to its call but to effectively make it their own, reinscribing it in their own language and claiming the title of Israel for themselves.

Worse yet, the passage complains, the success of the outside Bible readers demonstrates how vulnerable written text is because it is socially anchorless – unless carefully guarded, it quickly passes beyond the control of both its author and its original recipient. Since written text can speak for itself – and need not pass directly from one speaking person to another – it has no demonstrable prov-enance and there is no way to prove to whom it is addressed. As this passage puts it, when outside Bible readers lay claim to the privileges bestowed on Israel by a written text, the "scales are balanced" – there is no way of deciding between the claims. According to this passage, even God himself cannot distinguish between them. This interaction thus reveals that written text represents a problematic medium for communicating important cultural and religious capital because it does not possess the social protections that adhere to an oral tradition passed from person to person in a careful chain of custody. Or as the passage puts it using the Greek idiom, written scripture lacks the security of a *mysterion* (a

---

Society of Biblbical Literature, 2004), 186–91; Steven D. Fraade, "Concepts of Scripture in Rabbinic Judaism: Oral Torah and Written Torah," in *Jewish Concepts of Scripture*, ed. Ben-jamin Sommer (New York: New York University Press, 2012), 39–40; Samuel Isaac Thomas, *The "Mysteries" of Qumran: Mystery, Secrecy, and Esotericism in the Dead Sea Scrolls* (Leiden: Brill, 2009); Hagith Sivan, *Palestine in Late Antiquity* (Oxford: Oxford University Press, 2008), 389–92. No reader familiar with the rhetoric of early Christianity will fail to hear the echoes of Chris-tian supersessionism in this imagined dialogue. However, Marc Bregman has been able to trace the imagined interlocutor of the rabbinic author of this tale to a very specific historical period. He argues that this passage was formulated in reaction to claims such as those preserved in the work of the fourth-century bishop, Hilary of Poitier, according to whom Christian editions of the Septuagint represented a perfect translation of the Hebrew revelation, which was composed in keeping with the knowledge of an ancient "mystery" (that is, a secret oral tradition concerning the true unequivocal meaning of the Hebrew text).

[26] Cited here in its final iteration in the classical rabbinic period: Pesikta Rabbati, Chapter 5 (Vienna, 1880), 14b.

carefully guarded and controlled oral tradition). In such passages, outside Bible readers pose questions and make claims that are alarmingly difficult to dispute – leaving the air heavy with doubt and critique about the nature of written revelation even as the official rabbinic position formally triumphs.

Early iterations of such rabbinic charges against the medium of written text were frequently attributed to outside Bible readers associated with Mediterranean Christianity – referring to an ethnically Gentile community that reads the Bible in Greek, alluding to New Testament tropes, and echoing recognizable early Christian literary motifs. Yet later additions to this tradition would increasingly abstract the author character of the outside Bible reader beyond these Christian(-like) portrayals – ascribing a wider and more diverse array of communal backgrounds to its pseudepigraphic authors. In bSanhedrin 91a, for instance, a surprisingly wide variety of outside Bible readers use strikingly similar reading techniques in their attempts to disenfranchise and impoverish the Jews on the basis of the written text of the Hebrew Bible:

When the sons of Africa came to dispute with the people of Israel before Alexander the Macedonian, they said to him, "The Land of Canaan is ours, as it is written, 'The Land of Canaan [according] to its border' (Num 34:2). And Canaan was the forefather of these people." Geviha ben Pesisa said to the sages, "Give me permission and I will go and dispute with them before Alexander the Macedonian. If they are victorious over me, say, 'You have conquered a layman.' But if I triumph over them, say to them 'The Torah of Moses has conquered you'." They gave him permission and he went and disputed with them. He said to them, "From where do you bring proof?" They said to him, "From the Torah." He said to them, "Then I, too, will not bring any evidence except from the Torah: as it is said, 'Cursed is Canaan, a slave of slaves he will be to his brothers' (Gen 9:25) A slave who bought pieces of property, to whom does the slave [belong] and to whom does the property [belong]? Moreover, how many years it has been that you have not served us!" King Alexander said to them, "Give him an answer." They said to him, "Give us three days' time." He gave them time. They checked and did not find an answer. They immediately fled and left their fields still seeded and their vineyard still planted ...

Then again another time, the sons of Egypt came to dispute with the people of Israel before Alexander the Macedonian. They said to him, "Behold it is said, 'God gave the people a pleasant aura in the eyes of the Egyptians and they lent them' (Exod 12:36). Give us the silver and gold that you took from us." Geviha ben Pesisa said to the sages, "Give me permission and I will go and dispute with them before Alexander the Macedonian. If they are victorious over me, say 'You have conquered a layman.' But if I triumph over them, say to them 'The Torah of Moses our teacher has conquered you'." They gave him permission and he went and disputed with them. He said to them, "From where do you bring proof?" They said to him, "From the Torah." He said to them, "Then I, too, will not bring any evidence except from the Torah: as it is said, 'The sojourning of the children of Israel which they sojourned in Egypt was four hundred and thirty years' (Exod 12:40). Give us the wages of the six hundred thousand that slaved in Egypt four hundred and thirty years." Alexander Macedonia said to them, "Give him an answer." They said to him, "Give us three days' time." He gave them time. They checked and did not find an answer. They immediately fled and left their fields still seeded and their vineyard still planted ...

80   *Rebecca Scharbach Wollenberg*

> Then again another time, the sons of Yishmael and the sons of Keturah came to dispute with the people of Israel before Alexander the Macedonian. They said to him, "The Land of Canaan is ours and theirs, as it is written 'And these are the generation of Yishmael son of Abraham' (Gen 25:12) and it is written 'These are the generations of Isaac son of Abraham' (Gen 25:19)." Geviha ben Pesisa said to the sages, "Give me permission and I will go and dispute with them before Alexander the Macedonian. If they are victorious over me, say 'You have conquered a layman.' But if I triumph over them, say to them 'The Torah of Moses our teacher has conquered you'." They gave him permission and he went and disputed with them. He said to them, "From where do you bring proof?" They said to him, "From the Torah." He said to them, "Then I, too, will not bring any evidence except from the Torah, as it is said 'Abraham gave all that was his to Isaac and to the sons of Abraham's concubines' (25:6). A father who gave legacies to his children during his lifetime and sent this one away from that one, then this one has nothing at all coming to him from that one."

These narrative encounters amplify the concerns expressed in previous passages regarding the transferrable nature of written documents when they represent the biblical text as a literal deed to the land of Israel and suggest that anyone who can lay hands on that deed may theoretically bring it before a court as effective evidence of ownership. Through the legal machinations of a series of outside Bible readers, this passage expresses concern that a tangible representation of the covenant between God and Israel in the written text of the Bible represents not only a theological message but a physical object which, like all material goods, may be alienated from its owners by a savvy thief. Through the dangerously plausible misinterpretations of these outsider readers, the passage exemplifies the rabbinic charge that written text, as a fixed and limited message, cannot provide its own exegesis and is thus worrisomely vulnerable to misinterpretation. Indeed, the drama of this narrative rests on the fact that each of the exegetical claims that these outsider Bible readers make against Israel on the basis of the biblical text are seductively plausible. The charges brought pose a very real danger to the rights of the Jewish people precisely because they are so difficult to discredit conclusively.

This narrative also adds new charges to the rabbinic list of objections to using writing as a medium to communicate important communal knowledge. The passage draws our attention, for instance, to a potentially problematic quality that may adhere to written text. That is, the aura of authority, self-evidence, and completeness that black letters on white parchment take on in some cultural contexts. For once the outside Bible readers in this story have taken up the written text as a source of authoritative knowledge, one becomes constrained to argue from the fixed and limited formula of the "written text alone." In other words, this dialogue with outside Bible readers vividly demonstrates the dangers posed by the elevation of sacred text as a source of religious authority when we see how quickly written text can be turned into the *only* source from which one can bring

Outside Bible Readers as an Author Character in Rabbinic Literature 81

proof – the written text becomes a closed system in which other ways of knowing (such as tradition or reason) no longer have evidentiary power.

In stories such as these, a series of strikingly similar characters in rabbinic literature offer a collection of interlocking critiques and reflections on the dangers posed by written scripture. In these almost pseudepigraphic narrative capsules, a disconcerting (even subversive) facet of rabbinic thought is preserved and given voice by the practice of attributing it to an author character identified as an opponent. There is no question that *some* early rabbinic thinkers could, and did, read for information.[27] And yet, a series of recent studies has demonstrated that early rabbinic sources were often suspicious (sometimes even denigrating) concerning the affordances offered by written text as a means of transmitting important religious[28] and cultural information[29] – not only regarding the rabbinic tradition but even in connection with scripture itself.[30] While it has been a relatively straightforward task to document that many classical rabbinic traditions cultivated a certain lack of reliance on written text as a source of religious or cultural information, rabbinic portraits of their own reading practices do not always shed much light on the *motivations* that underpinned the early rabbinic distrust of written text. It is only in these highly dramatized narrative portraits of an alien reading culture that we begin to see clearly the outlines of the media theory that structured the rabbi's own approach to sacred text. In attributing these reflections to a series of outside Bible readers – author characters purported to be rivals but included in rabbinic literature always as interlocutors – the rabbinic tradition was able to host a rich trove of subtle but specific critiques of sacred writing and its affordances.

---

[27] On which, see Daniel Picus, "Ink Sea, Parchment Sky: Rabbinic Reading Practices in Late Antiquity" (PhD diss., Brown University, 2017).

[28] On the provisional revival of the terminology "religion" in late ancient studies, see Duncan McRae, *Legible Religion: Books, Gods, and Ritual in Roman Culture* (Cambridge, MA: Harvard University Press: 2016), 6–8.

[29] See, for instance, Rebecca Scharbach Wollenberg, "The Dangers of Reading as We Know It: Sight Reading as a Source of Heresy in Classical Rabbinic Literature," *Journal of the American Academy of Religion* 85 (2017): 709–45; eadem, "The Book that Changed: Tales of Ezran Authorship as a Form of Late Antique Biblical Criticism," *Journal of Biblical Literature* 138 (2019): 143–60; Eva Mroczek, "Without Torah and Without Scripture: Biblical Absence and the History of Revelation," *Hebrew Studies* 61 (2020): 97–122; Eva Mroczek, "Hezekiah the Censor and Ancient Theories of Canon Formation," *Journal of Biblical Literature* 140 (2021): 481–502.

[30] Rebecca Scharbach Wollenberg, *The Closed Book: How the Rabbis Taught the Jews (Not) to Read the Bible* (Princeton: Princeton University Press, 2023).

Bibliography

Boustan, Ra'anan and Joseph E. Sanzo. "Christian Magicians, Jewish Magical Idioms, and the Shared Magical Culture of Late Antiquity." *Harvard Theological Review* 110 (2017): 217–240.

Boyarin, Daniel. *Borderlines: The Partition of Judeo-Christianity.* Philadelphia: University of Pennsylvania Press, 2004.

Boyarin, Daniel. "Hellenism in Jewish Babylonia." Pages 336–364 in *The Cambridge Companion to Talmud and Rabbinic Literature.* Edited by Charlotte E. Fonrobert and Martin S. Jaffee. Cambridge: Cambridge University Press, 2007.

Brakke, David. "Scriptural Practices in Early Christianity: Towards a New History of the New Testament Canon." Pages 263–280 in *Invention, Rewriting, Usurpation: Discursive Fights over Religions Traditions in Antiquity.* Edited by David Brakke, Anders-Christian Jacobsen, and Jörg Ulrich. Bern: Peter Lang, 2012.

Bregman, Marc. "Mishnah and LXX as Mystery: An Example of Jewish-Christian Polemic in the Byzantine Period." Pages 333–342 in *Continuity and Renewal: Judaism in Eretz Israel during the Byzantine-Christian Era.* Edited by Lee Levine. Jerusalem: Yad Ben Zvi, 2004.

Fraade, Steven D. "Concepts of Scripture in Rabbinic Judaism: Oral Torah and Written Torah." Pages 31–46 in *Jewish Concepts of Scripture.* Edited by Benjamin Sommer. New York: New York University Press, 2012.

Hayes, Christine. "Displaced Self-Perceptions: The Deployment of *Minim* and Romans in *B. Sanhedrin* 90b–91a." Pages 249–289 in *Religious and Ethnic Communities in Later Roman Palestine.* Edited by Hayim Lapin. Lanham, MD: University Press of Maryland, 1999.

Horbury, William. *Jews and Christians: In Contact and Controversy.* Edinburgh: T&T Clark, 1998.

Foucault, Michel. "What Is an Author?" Pages 101–120 in *The Foucault Reader.* Edited and translated by Paul Rabinow. New York: Pantheon Books, 1984.

Jaffee, Martin S. "Rabbinic Oral Tradition in Late Byzantine Galilee: Christian Empire and Rabbinic Ideological Resistance." Pages 171–191 in *Orality, Literacy, and Colonialism in Antiquity.* Edited by Jonathan A. Draper. Atlanta: Society of Biblical Literature, 2004.

Kalmin, Richard. "Christians and Heretics in Rabbinic Literature of Late Antiquity." *Harvard Theological Review* 87 (1994): 155–169.

Kalmin, Richard. "Patterns and Developments in Rabbinic Midrash of Late Antiquity." Pages 285–302 in *Hebrew Bible/Old Testament: The History of Its Interpretation.* Vol. 1. Edited by Magnes Saebo. Göttingen: Vandehoeck and Ruprecht, 1996.

Kiperwasser, Reuven. "What Is Hidden in the Small Box? Narratives of Late Antique Roman Palestine in Dialogue." *Association for Jewish Studies Review* 45 (2021): 76–94.

Johnson, William A. *Readers and Reading Culture in the High Roman Empire: A Study of Elite Communities.* Oxford: Oxford University Press, 2010.

Lambert, David. "Is Bible 'Scripture?'" *Metatron* 1 (2022): 315–329.

McRae, Duncan. *Legible Religion: Books, Gods, and Ritual in Roman Culture.* Cambridge, MA: Harvard University Press, 2016.

Moore, Stephen D. *The Bible after Deleuze: Affects, Assemblages, Bodies Without Organs.* Oxford: Oxford University Press, 2022.

Mroczek, Eva. "The Hegemony of the Biblical in the Study of Second Temple Literature." *Journal of Ancient Judaism* 6 (2015): 2–35.

Mroczek, Eva. "Hezekiah the Censor and Ancient Theories of Canon Formation." *Journal of Biblical Literature* 140 (2021): 481–502.

Mroczek, Eva. *The Literary Imagination in Jewish Antiquity.* Oxford: Oxford University Press, 2016.

Mroczek, Eva. "Without Torah and Without Scripture: Biblical Absence and the History of Revelation." *Hebrew Studies* 61 (2020): 97–122.

Najman, Hindy. *Past Renewals: Interpretative Authority, Renewed Revelation, and the Quest for Perfection in Jewish Antiquity.* Leiden: Brill, 2010.

Najman, Hindy. *Seconding Sinai: The Development of Mosaic Discourse in Second Temple Judaism.* Leiden: Brill, 2003.

Najman, Hindy and Irene Peirano Garrison. "Pseudepigraphy as an Interpretive Construct." Pages 331–355 in *Old Testament Pseudepigrapha: Fifty Years of the Pseudepigrapha Section at the SBL.* Edited by Matthias Henze and Liv Ingeborg Lied. Atlanta: Society of Biblical Literature, 2019.

Picus, Daniel. "Ink Sea, Parchment Sky: Rabbinic Reading Practices in Late Antiquity." PhD diss., Brown University, 2017.

Reed, Annette Yoshiko. "The Modern Invention of 'Old Testament Pseudepigrapha.'" *Journal of Theological Studies* 60 (2009): 403–436.

Reed, Annette Yoshiko. "Pseudepigraphy, Authorship, and the Reception of 'the Bible' in Late Antiquity." Pages 467–490 in *The Reception and Interpretation of the Bible in Late Antiquity.* Edited by Lorenzo DiTomasso and Lucian Turcescu. Leiden: Brill, 2008.

Ruzer, Serge. "Reasonable Doubt and the 'Other': Jewish Scepticism in Early Christian Sources." Pages 69–84 in *Expressions of Sceptical Topoi in (Late) Antique Judaism.* Edited by Reuven Kiperwasser and Geoffrey Herman. Berlin: De Gruyter, 2021.

Schremer, Adiel. *Brothers Estranged: Heresy, Christianity, and Jewish Identity in Late Antiquity.* Oxford: Oxford University Press, 2010.

Schremer, Adiel. "Stammaitic Historiography." Pages 219–236 in *Creation and Composition: The Contributions of the Bavli Redactors (Stammaim) to the Aggada.* Edited by Jeffrey Rubenstein. Tübingen: Mohr Siebeck, 2005.

Siegal, Michal Bar Asher. "Heresy and the *Minim* of the Babylonian Talmud." *Jewish Thought* 1 (2019): 9–31.

Siegel, Michal Bar Asher. *Jewish-Christian Dialogues on Scripture in Late Antiquity: Heretic Narratives of the Babylonian Talmud.* Cambridge: Cambridge University Press, 2019.

Sivan, Hagith. *Palestine in Late Antiquity.* Oxford: Oxford University Press, 2008.

Stroumsa, Guy. *The Scriptural Universe of Ancient Christianity.* Cambridge: Harvard University Press, 2016.

Teppler, Yaakov. *Birkat HaMinim: Jews and Christians in Conflict in the Ancient World.* Tübingen: Mohr Siebeck, 2007.

Thomas, Samuel Isaac. *The "Mysteries" of Qumran: Mystery, Secrecy, and Esotericism in the Dead Sea Scrolls.* Leiden: Brill, 2009.

Visotzsky, Burton. "Trinitarian Testimonies." Pages 61–74 in *Fathers of the World: Essays in Rabbinic and Patristic Literature.* Tübingen: Mohr Siebeck, 1995.

Wollenberg, Rebecca Scharbach. "The Bad Wife Who Was Good: Women as a Way of Life in Genesis Rabbah 17:3." *Prooftexts* 37 (2018): 56–85.

Wollenberg, Rebecca Scharbach. "The Book that Changed: Tales of Ezran Authorship as a Form of Late Antique Biblical Criticism." *Journal of Biblical Literature* 138 (2019): 143–160.

Wollenberg, Rebecca Scharbach. *The Closed Book: How the Rabbis Taught the Jews (Not) to Read the Bible*. Princeton: Princeton University Press, 2023.

Wollenberg, Rebecca Scharbach. "The Dangers of Reading as We Know It: Sight Reading as a Source of Heresy in Classical Rabbinic Literature." *Journal of the American Academy of Religion* 85 (2017): 709–745.

Wright, Benjamin. "Pseudepigrapha Within and Without Biblical Studies." Pages 133–156 in *Old Testament Pseudepigrapha: Fifty Years of the Pseudepigrapha Section at the SBL*. Edited by Matthias Henze and Liv Ingeborg Lied. Atlanta: Society of Biblical Literature: 2019.

The Fictive Author and the Reading Community
in the *Apocryphon of James* (NHC I,2)*

JULIA D. LINDENLAUB

As the essays in this collection illustrate, authorship could be leveraged to perform all sorts of rhetorical work in the ancient Mediterranean world. My contribution to this mosaic posits an authorial fiction crafted to elevate the intellectual status of an early Christian reading community. A striking letter found at Oxyrhynchus and dated to the second century, P.Oxy. 2192, attests senders and recipients engaged as a social group in scholarly pursuits. These associates navigate the book collections of both individual and bookseller, select specialist texts for sending and copying, and acknowledge another literary circle seemingly engaged in the same enterprise. This reading community coheres around shared intellectual values and literary expertise. In the *Apocryphon of James* (NHC I,2), the text's sender and recipients are similarly depicted as a reading community set apart by their specialised literary interests and attendant textual practices. Deployed through epistolary literary features, this text's authorial fiction sets the tone for a reading community of educated intellectuals. The *Apocryphon of James* (*Ap. Jas.*) begins with an epistolary address from its fictive author, the disciple James, to a lacunose recipient and details composing and sending the present book as well as another book previously circulated. James furthermore admonishes his recipient to ensure that only a privileged readership is entrusted with such texts. Comparing the epistolary authorial fiction of the *Apocryphon of James* with the Oxyrhynchus letter, I identify parallels between their social circles demarcated by a sophisticated reading culture. James' – and his readers' – imagined participation in social activities like those found in P.Oxy. 2192 can thus be understood as recognisable and even desirable in the text's prospective second-century Egyptian provenance. The authorial fiction of James and his reading community validates the shared values and practices of a social group defined as experts in specialist literature. In light of this papyrological evidence from Oxyrhynchus, the *Apocryphon of James'* authorial fiction evokes a privileged social circle of educated readers invested in the possession, circulation, and interpretation of prized literature.

86   *Julia D. Lindenlaub*

1. Intellectual Authors and Readers in Early Christianity

The reading cultures evoked in both P.Oxy. 2192 and the *Apocryphon of James* are helpfully contextualised by scholarship placing Christians within the intellectual culture of the Roman empire in the first three centuries CE.[1] This backdrop more-over foregrounds literary authorship as a site of power for advertising intellectual ideals. It is widely acknowledged that the emergence of Christian identity was intimately bound up with the interpretation and production of texts, but textual practices in antiquity were also generative for the identity formation of many intellectually minded social groups. Early Christians in this imperial world were not immune to aspirations toward the elite social status of the literate and literary.

There is a fine line to walk when situating early Christian texts within the intellectual culture of the imperial milieu, balancing modern assumptions regarding the "intellectual" with the standards we find in antiquity.[2] Yet, scholar-ship on early Christianity and the classical world has increasingly enriched our understanding of how Christians and their peers navigated the social agonism of elite intellectual culture. Beginning as early as Christian literature of the late first century, Robyn Faith Walsh has argued that Christians were more sophisti-cated cultural contributors than often supposed in New Testament scholarship.[3]

---

* This essay benefitted from a wealth of expertise provided by participants in the Early Chris-tianity seminar of the British New Testament Society and the Nag Hammadi and Gnosticism unit of the Society of Biblical Literature. I am especially grateful to my co-editor Chance Bonar and to our contributor Jeremiah Coogan for their incisive feedback and bibliography recommendations as generous and thoughtful readers of this piece.

[1] Walsh, Eshleman, and Secord each exemplify this trend and will be discussed further in what follows: Robyn Faith Walsh, *The Origins of Early Christian Literature: Contextualizing the New Testament within Greco-Roman Literary Culture* (Cambridge: Cambridge University Press, 2021); Kendra Eshleman, *The Social World of Intellectuals in the Roman Empire: Sophists, Philosophers, and Christians* (Cambridge: Cambridge University Press, 2012); Jared Secord, *Christian Intellectuals and the Roman Empire: From Justin Martyr to Origen*, Inventing Chris-tianity (University Park, PA: Pennsylvania State University Press, 2020).

[2] On scholarly approaches to this topic in early Christian studies and the use of the term "intellectual," see: Lewis Ayres and H. Clifton Ward III, "Introduction and Acknowledgments," in *The Rise of the Christian Intellectual*, ed. Lewis Ayres and H. Clifton Ward III, Arbeiten zur Kirchengeschichte 139 (Berlin: De Gruyter, 2020), 1–6; Christoph Markschies, "Intellectuals and Church Fathers in the Third and Fourth Centuries," in *Christians and Christianity in the Holy Land: From the Origins to the Latin Kingdoms*, ed. Ora Limor and Guy G. Stroumsa (Turnhout: Brepols, 2006), 239–56; idem, "Preface," in *Rise of the Christian Intellectual*, vii–xii.

[3] Walsh, *Origins of Early Christian Literature*. See also Walsh's contribution to this volume for further context on her approach to authorship. I am here interested in Walsh's compar-ison of Christian writers with the *pepaidoumenoi*, rather than with cultic expertise in antiquity (on which see: Heidi Wendt, *At the Temple Gates: The Religion of Freelance Experts in the Roman Empire* [Oxford: Oxford University Press, 2016]; idem, "Christians as and among Writ-er-Intellectuals in Second-Century Rome," in *Christian Teachers in Second-Century Rome: Schools and Students in the Ancient City*, Supplements to Vigiliae Christianae 159 [Leiden: Brill, 2020], 84–108). Religious expertise and educated expertise were distinct categories in the social world of the ancient Mediterranean.

The Fictive Author and the Reading Community in the Apocryphon of James   87

By thinking of authors in antiquity as "literate specialists,"[4] Walsh emphasises the common social context in which the literary work of Christians and non-Christians alike took place: "a writer's most immediate and formative social network was his circle of fellow writers and literary critics – an interconnected network of authors and literate consumers with particular kinds of intellectual knowledge and skill."[5] As part of the network of readers and writers in the ancient world, Christians were relevant participants in the social spheres of intellectual authority and literary accomplishment. Focusing primarily on the second century, Kendra Eshleman advances a related position, examining the self-fashioned expertise of the individual together with the social construction of group identity.[6] Early Christians as well as representatives of the Second Sophistic exhibit similar social tendencies toward the promotion of educated experts to define hierarchies or wield authority.[7] Though their education and expertise were applied in different fields, "Christian intellectuals were closer in background and *habitus* to Second Sophistic *pepaideumenoi* than either would have liked to admit."[8] The concept of the expert in antiquity also guides Jared Secord's study on Christian intellectuals through the third century.[9] Secord has a capacious view of the ancient intellectual, applied across various fields of knowledge and expressed through diverse competencies, dependent on opportunities for education and socio-economic status. Christians in the imperial milieu are thus not excluded from this world of intellectuals defined as "people who presented themselves as authority figures because of what they knew or claimed to know, especially if this knowledge was based on the possession of high-level literacy."[10] Christians and pagans

---

[4] Walsh, *Origins of Early Christian Literature*, 112–13. For other treatments of literate specialists in the second century, see also: Joseph A. Howley, *Aulus Gellius and Roman Reading Culture: Text, Presence, and Imperial Knowledge in the* Noctes Atticae (Cambridge: Cambridge University Press, 2018); David Braund, John Wilkins, and Glen Bowersock, eds., *Athenaeus and His World: Reading Greek Culture in the Roman Empire* (Oxford: Oxford University Press, 2000).

[5] Walsh, *Origins of Early Christian Literature*, 109–10. Compare Last's interest in the social bonds based on *paideia* bridging those of religious association: Richard Last, "Communities That Write: Christ-Groups, Associations, and Gospel Communities," *New Testament Studies* 58 (2012): 173–98; idem, "The Social Relationship of Gospel Writers: New Insights from Inscriptions Commending Greek Historiographers," *Journal for the Study of the New Testament* 37 (2015): 223–52.

[6] Eshleman, *Social World of Intellectuals*. On the Second Sophistic and Christian intellectuals, see further: Laura Salah Nasrallah, "Mapping the World: Justin, Tatian, Lucian, and the Second Sophistic," *Harvard Theological Review* 98 (2005): 283–314.

[7] On the reading cultures corresponding to such social dynamics, see: William A. Johnson, *Readers and Reading Culture in the High Roman Empire: A Study of Elite Communities* (Oxford: Oxford University Press, 2010), 180–81.

[8] Eshleman, *Social World of Intellectuals*, 14.

[9] Secord, *Christian Intellectuals and the Roman Empire*.

[10] Secord, *Christian Intellectuals and the Roman Empire*, 2. This definition is reliant neither upon recognition in ancient sources as a "successful" intellectual nor upon biographical evidence for education or social class.

88 *Julia D. Lindenlaub*

alike participated in the very same sociological norms for reading and writing, and representatives on either side would "draw on the authorizing power of education" and the "rhetoric of paideia" in order to "position themselves as authoritative arbiters of text and truth."[11] While the "usual suspects" for which we have biographical knowledge, such as Clement or Tatian, may be the more obvious candidates for study in this area, we shall see that an authorial fiction can reflect this context just as well.

In an influential essay featured in multiple contributions to this volume, Karen King illustrates how author-function maps onto the wider world of the ancient intellectual.[12] As King writes, author-function may serve to claim "elite status, quality of education, [and] learned literary style."[13] The case studies in her essay are *Revelation* and the *Apocryphon of John*, both of which exhibit multiple points of contact with my observations on the *Apocryphon of James* in what follows. Tobias Nicklas also chooses *Revelation* as his example for seeking the Christian intellectual in an authorial construct.[14] Nicklas gleans from the literary features of this text – not least the epistolary – signs of the ascribed author's textual expertise, including appeals to fictive "books" and sophisticated literary source use of the Jewish scriptures. Moreover, as the status of the author and the text are elevated, so also is the status of that text's readership, such that the recipients are even "blessed" for their knowledge of the apocalypse.[15] Both of these essays are methodologically instructive for my approach to the *Apocryphon of James*. Narrowing to research on *Ap. Jas.* itself, David Brakke argues for an elite intellectual provenance based on internal evidence. Brakke posits that in the *Apocryphon of James*, those who are limited by their understanding only of "plain speech" are excluded from the privileged circle of "an educated elite" textual community equipped to study and understand Jesus' words in the text.[16]

---

[11] Jeremiah Coogan, "Meddling with the Gospel: Celsus, Early Christian Textuality, and the Politics of Reading," *Novum Testamentum* 65 (2023): 420. Coogan's essay spotlights Celsus' criticisms of Christians as a case study. On Celsus and Tatian as participants in the same intellectual culture, see further: Matthew R. Crawford, "Tatian, Celsus, and Christianity as 'Barbarian Philosophy' in the Late Second Century," in *The Rise of the Christian Intellectual*, 45–80.

[12] Karen L. King, "'What Is an Author?': Ancient Author-Function in the *Apocryphon of John* and the Apocalypse of John," in *Scribal Practices and Social Structures among Jesus Adherents: Essays in Honour of John S. Kloppenborg*, ed. William E. Arnal et al. (Leuven: Peeters, 2016), 15–42. King develops her approach from: Michel Foucault, "What Is an Author?" in *Aesthetics, Method, and Epistemology*, ed. James D. Faubion, trans. Robert Hurley et al. (New York: The New Press, 1998), 205–22. I am likewise informed by how authorial fictions – or "fakes" – are situated within elite education by literary imitation: Irene Peirano Garrison, *The Rhetoric of the Roman Fake: Latin Pseudepigrapha in Context* (Cambridge: Cambridge University Press, 2012).

[13] King, "'What Is an Author?'" 35.

[14] Tobias Nicklas, "Crazy Guy or Intellectual Leader? The Seer of Revelation and his Role for the Communities of Asia Minor," in *Rise of the Christian Intellectual*, 7–24.

[15] Nicklas, "Crazy Guy or Intellectual Leader?" 12–13.

[16] David Brakke, "Parables and Plain Speech in the Fourth Gospel and the Apocryphon of James," *Journal of Early Christian Studies* 7 (1999): 187–218. Brakke's approach develops the theo-

The Fictive Author and the Reading Community in the Apocryphon of James   89

In adapting its compositional sources from a specialist corpus of recognised gospel literature, the *Apocryphon of James* enables "a textually oriented mode of Christian socialization based on an educational model of salvation."[17] The *Apocryphon of James'* mixture of plain speech and cryptic parable thus invites scholarly engagement, and in this way mirrors prevalent Christian intellectualism in Roman Egypt of the period – particularly represented by Clement and Origen.[18] Brakke's case for the text's provenance in such a sophisticated cultural milieu serves as the final touchstone for my own analysis. The present essay provides another vantage point from which to compare Christian intellectual aspirations in the *Apocryphon of James* with the intellectual elite of the imperial world – that of authorial fiction. In *Ap. Jas.*, authorial fiction is used to control the parameters of the reading community and to elevate the intellectual values of this learned readership.

---

ry of "textual communities" from: Brian Stock, *The Implications of Literacy: Written Language and Models of Interpretation in the Eleventh and Twelfth Centuries* (Princeton: Princeton University Press, 1983); idem, *Listening for the Text: On the Uses of the Past* (Philadelphia: University of Pennsylvania Press, 1990); cf. Heath's critique of Stock's work applied to early Christianity: Jane M. F. Heath, "'Textual Communities': Brian Stock's Concept and Recent Scholarship on Antiquity," in *Scriptural Interpretation at the Interface between Education and Religion: In Memory of Hans Conzelmann*, ed. Florian Wilk, Themes in Biblical Narrative 22 (Leiden: Brill, 2018), 5–35. See also Brakke's own further development of "scriptural practices": "Scriptural Practices in Early Christianity: Towards a New History of the New Testament Canon," in *Invention, Rewriting, Usurpation: Discursive Fights over Religious Traditions in Antiquity*, ed. David Brakke, Anders-Christian Jacobsen, and Jörg Ulrich, Early Christianity in the Context of Antiquity 11 (Frankfurt: Peter Lang, 2012), 263–80.

[17] Brakke, "Parables and Plain Speech," 203. Compare Yadin-Israel's inclusion of the *Apocryphon of James* as an example of the decline of prophecy as a "non-intellectual" authority in early Christianity: Azzan Yadin-Israel, "Christian, Jewish, and Pagan Authority and the Rise of the Christian Intellectual," in *The Rise of the Christian Intellectual*, 174 n. 38, 175 n. 40.

[18] In addition to Brakke's examples from Clement and Origen, see also Heath's work on Clement as a Christian intellectual: Jane M. F. Heath, *Clement of Alexandria and the Shaping of Christian Literary Practice: Miscellany and the Transformation of Greco-Roman Writing* (Cambridge: Cambridge University Press, 2020). Consider also the example of Basilides as another Alexandrian Christian intellectual: Winrich A. Löhr, *Basilides und seine Schule: Eine Studie zur Theologie- und Kirchengeschichte des zweiten Jahrhunderts* (Tübingen: Mohr Siebeck, 1996). I find Brakke's ("Parables and Plain Speech") appeal to Clement and Origen as case studies for parallels with Alexandrian Christianity persuasive evidence for the *Apocryphon of James'* Egyptian provenance and aim to advance this position through my own parallels with the Oxyrhynchus context. On the education, textual practices, and reading culture of Christians at Oxyrhynchus, see especially: Lincoln H. Blumell, *Lettered Christians: Christians, Letters, and Late Antique Oxyrhynchus*, New Testament Tools, Studies and Documents 39 (Leiden: Brill, 2012); Harry Y. Gamble, *Books and Readers in the Early Church: A History of Early Christian Texts* (New Haven, CT: Yale University Press, 1995); AnneMarie Luijendijk, "Books and Private Readers in Early Christian Oxyrhynchus: 'A Spiritual Meadow and a Garden of Delight,'" in *Books and Readers in the Premodern World: Essays in Honour of Harry Gamble*, ed. Karl Shuve, Writings from the Greco-Roman World Supplements 12 (Atlanta: Society of Biblical Literature, 2018), 101–36; eadem, *Greetings in the Lord: Early Christians and the Oxyrhynchus Papyri*, Harvard Theological Studies 60 (Cambridge, MA: Harvard University Press, 2008).

90 *Julia D. Lindenlaub*

2. P.Oxy. 2192

The textual practices of elite reading communities in Roman Egypt are vividly portrayed in the example of P.Oxy. 2192. Dated by its Greek script to the second century, P.Oxy. 2192 has at least three different hands distinguished within it.[19] Despite a regrettably incomplete condition, the body of the text appears to have been written by an experienced scribe, followed by the sender's own subscription with postscript. A second postscript follows in a third hand, which may be that of a recipient or of a sender. Following this, yet another postscript appears to add a further hand, but the text here is not clearly preserved. In the sender's initial postscript, the writer instructs:

Have a copy made of books six and seven of Hypsicrates' *Men Who Appear in Comedies* and send it to me. Harpocration says that Pollio has them among his books, and probably others have them too. And he also has prose epitomes of Thersagorus's *Myths of Tragedy*.

Following this, the second postscript adds:

Demetrius the bookseller has them [that is, the two books of the *Men Who Appear in Comedies*], according to Harpocration. I have ordered Apollonides to send to me some of my own books – which ones you'll find out from him. And if you find any volumes of Seleucus's work on *Tenses/Metrics/Rhythms* that I don't own, have copies made and send them to me. Diodorus's circle also has some that I don't own.

As William Johnson describes in his work on reading culture in the high empire, the social relationships and textual practices attested by this fragment reflect an elite reading community. This group of associates well versed in Greek literature is bound together "on the basis of their knowledge of, and facility with, literary texts."[20] The details in this letter demonstrate these individuals' expert knowledge and the literate education characteristic of imperial intellectuals. The books named therein suggest this social stratum, as does the facility these figures have with individual libraries, local booksellers, and procedures for copying and circulating literature.[21] Considering the inevitable costs of such pursuits, these individuals and their associates appear deeply invested – both intellectually and financially – in the pursuit of knowledge. Access to books presented a practical

---

[19] The translation and delineation of scribal hands here follows Johnson, *Readers and Reading Culture*, 180–81.

[20] Johnson, *Readers and Reading Culture*, 203.

[21] For further context on booksellers in Roman antiquity, and particularly Christian participation in the book trade, see representatively: Harry Y. Gamble, "The Book Trade in the Roman Empire," in *The Early Text of the New Testament*, ed. Charles E. Hill and Michael J. Kruger (New York: Oxford University Press, 2012), 23–36; Jan Heilmann, *Lesen in Antike und frühem Christentum: Kulturgeschichtliche, philologische sowie kognitionswissenschaftliche Perspektiven und deren Bedeutung für die neutestamentliche Exegese*, Texte und Arbeiten zum Neutestamentlichen Zeitalter (Tübingen: Narr Francke Attempto, 2021), 271–89; Peter White, "Bookshops in the Literary Culture of Rome," in *Ancient Literacies: The Culture of Reading in Greece and Rome*, ed. William A. Johnson and Holt N. Parker (Oxford: Oxford University Press, 2009), 268–78.

The Fictive Author and the Reading Community in the Apocryphon of James 91

concern for any reading community in the ancient Mediterranean, and the assembly of written resources for specialised disciplines cultivated reliance on exclusive networks of readers and writers.[22] The texts named in this fragment are just such sources – reference materials for the study of classical drama and sophisticated commentary on tragedy and comedy.[23] The papyrus' discerning readers understood both how to adjudicate texts appropriate to their discipline and where to find them: "expertise in a discipline, such as law or medicine, demanded access to an even more rarified network of other readers with the right specialist texts."[24] To this end, the sender and recipient in this quest for copies rely upon a mutual network of learned experts. Moreover, there appear to be two distinct yet acquainted social circles engaged in a related project. The mention of "Diodorus' circle" seems to reference another reading community centred around the figure of Diodorus, but more importantly around an interest in the same expert literature the sender and recipient seek. Hence, we may refer in turn to "Harpocration's circle" as a distinct but related reading community.[25] With these features, P.Oxy. 2192 reveals much about educated elites in Roman Egypt socially engaged in an intellectual endeavour: the study of literature among a group of like-minded peers. This precedent for epistolary correspondence in literate, educated social networks completes our introduction to the epistolary features soon to be seen in the *Apocryphon of James*. In *Ap. Jas.*, an authorial fiction is used to invoke the values and practices of a comparable reading community.

3. *Apocryphon of James* (NHC I,2)

This essay began by surveying the context for Christian literary endeavours steeped in an imperial context of intellectual social identity construction. With this milieu in view, aspirations of status achieved through education and knowledge can be seen to cross the barriers of religious identity and shape the reading cultures of Christian and non-Christian alike. The example of P.Oxy. 2192 from second-century Roman Egypt furthermore narrowed this backdrop to the practical concerns of a particular reading community connected by shared interests and expertise in learned pursuits. I now turn to a different kind of "letter" – but one that bears remarkable resemblance to P.Oxy. 2192. The *Apocryphon of James* significantly resembles early Christian gospel writings but remains

---

[22] Jeremiah Coogan, "Failed Gospels and Disciplinary Knowledge in Origen's *Hom. Luc.* 1," in *Unruly Books: Rethinking Ancient and Academic Imaginations of Religious Texts*, ed. Esther Brownsmith, Marianne B. Kartzow, and Liv Ingeborg Lied (London: Bloomsbury T&T Clark, 2024), forthcoming.

[23] Johnson, *Readers and Reading Culture*, 183.

[24] Coogan, "Failed Gospels and Disciplinary Knowledge."

[25] Johnson, *Readers and Reading Culture*, 182.

92   *Julia D. Lindenlaub*

distinguished by its blending of generic features. Composed in Greek, likely in the later part of the second century,[26] this text reconfigures narratives of Jesus' life into its dialogue format with an epistolary framing device.[27] This "secret book" begins in epistolary fashion introducing the text's authorial fiction: a "James" resembling both the brother of Jesus and the member of the twelve.[28] This purported author goes on from epistolary address (1.1–2.7) to relate a curious scene in which the twelve disciples are producing other written accounts of Jesus (2.8–15). The dialogue is then introduced properly when the authorial character James is taken aside by Jesus together with Peter so that they may receive exclusive revelation (2.33–15.33). James and Peter follow Jesus in an ascension scene that is ultimately hindered by the reintroduction of the other disciples to the narrative (15.34–16.2). The epistolary framing device then resumes to close the text, as James again addresses his readers directly after sending away the other disciples, including Peter (16.12–30). Other parts of the text will reappear in subsequent discussion, but with the comparative example of P.Oxy. 2192 in mind, I begin with the recognisable features of the text's epistolary opening.

Though the start of this text is riddled with lacunae, some reconstruction produces the following epistolary greeting and address:

1.1 [James] writes to | [...] those: Peace | [be with you from] Peace, | [love from] Love, 5 [grace from] Grace, | [faith] from Faith, | life from Holy Life! |

Since you asked | that I send 10 you a secret book | which was revealed to me | and Peter by the Lord, | I could not turn you away | or gainsay (?) you; 15 but [I have written] it in | the Hebrew alphabet and | sent it to you, and you | alone. But since you are | a minister of the salvation 20 of the saints, endeavour earnestly | and take care not to rehearse | this text to many – this | that the Savior did not wish | to tell to all of us, his 25 twelve disciples. | But blessed will they be | who will be saved through | the faith of this discourse.

I | also sent you, 30 ten months ago, another secret | book which the Savior | had revealed to me. Under the circumstances, however, | regard that one | as revealed 35 to me, James; but this one ...[29]

---

[26] This date follows Hartenstein and Plisch, among others, in this trend: Judith Hartenstein and Uwe-Karsten Plisch, "'Der Brief des Jakobus' (NHC I,2)," in *Nag Hammadi Deutsch* 1: *NHC I,1–V,1*, ed. Hans-Martin Schenke et al. (Berlin: De Gruyter, 2001), 10–17.

[27] The text's epistolary features rather than its dialogue features are of present interest; for thorough discussion of the *Apocryphon of James* in the context of dialogue gospels or "gnostic dialogues," I am informed by Sarah Parkhouse, *Eschatology and the Saviour: The 'Gospel of Mary' among Early Christian Dialogue Gospels*, Society for New Testament Studies Monograph Series 176 (Cambridge: Cambridge University Press, 2019), 13–68.

[28] It remains ultimately unclear whether one or the other (or both) is specifically invoked, but my interest in the author-function of this figure does not necessitate identifying "James" beyond his self-presentation in the *Apocryphon of James*. Myllykoski provides an overview of this issue: Matti Myllykoski, "James the Just in History and Tradition: Perspectives of Past and Present Scholarship (Part II)," *Currents in Biblical Research* 5 (2007): 73–122.

[29] The epistolary frame is here cut off by a substantial lacuna (2.1–7). I follow Williams' critical edition for the translation throughout, including Williams' tentative reconstructions

The Fictive Author and the Reading Community in the Apocryphon of James   93

James' authorship is easily determined by self-reference despite its absence due to a lacuna; the name of the recipient is not so easily recoverable. The writer responsible for composing this text adopts the literary persona of one of Jesus' earliest followers – not an uncommon strategy in Christian literature rife with accounts of James, Peter, John, Paul, and others. Yet we find this authorial figure engaged in the act of composition, demonstrating and even valorising his literacy.[30] Moreover, James claims to be the author of not just one book but two: *Ap. Jas.* itself and a text sent "ten months ago, another secret book" (1.30–31). Though nothing is known about the unnamed and otherwise unattested prior book, in apocryphal texts like this one, references to additional books, even if entirely fictional, can be used to signal that the implied author "is well-read and highly knowledgeable."[31] The deliberate mention of James' bilingual competencies in Hebrew and Greek reinforces this image. Though the *Apocryphon of James'* Coptic manuscript clearly renders a Greek original, this detail has a rhetorical impact beyond connotations of esoteric mystery or early Jesus tradition.[32] The fiction of an author apparently well equipped to compose literature in both Hebrew and Greek presents an educated person of some learned ability – not unlike a figure such as Origen.[33] This James is scribally adept and is depicted as an educated writer well-versed in linguistic translation, specifically the language of the earliest Christian tradition.[34] The fictive author James thus functions in the

---

in brackets: Francis E. Williams, "The Apocryphon of James," in *Nag Hammadi Codex I (The Jung Codex): Introductions, Texts, Translations, Indices*, ed. Harold W. Attridge (Leiden: Brill, 1985): 13–53.

[30] On "valorising" the literate James, see: John S. Kloppenborg, "Literate Media in Early Christ Groups: The Creation of a Christian Book Culture," *Journal of Early Christian Studies* 22 (2014): 21–59; Gregory P. Fewster, "Ancient Book Culture and the Literacy of James: On the Production and Consumption of a Pseudepigraphal Letter," *Zeitschrift für Antikes Christentum* 20 (2016): 387–417.

[31] Hugo Lundhaug, "Fictional Books in Coptic Apocrypha," *Journal for the Study of the Pseudepigrapha* 32 (2023): 333. The *Apocryphon of James* features as a notable example in Lundhaug's discussion.

[32] Brakke's ("Parables and Plain Speech," 205–6) interest in an intellectual background for this text allows room for both implications.

[33] Hebrew is included as a component of Origen's status as a Christian intellectual by Secord (*Christian Intellectuals and the Roman* Empire, 134–38). On linguistic ability among Christians in the imperial world, including Origen, I am further informed by: James Clackson, *Language and Society in the Greek and Roman Worlds*, Key Themes in Ancient History (Cambridge: Cambridge University Press, 2015), 143–70.

[34] As educated elites in the imperial world could be distinguished by proficiency in Greek and Latin (cf. Clackson, *Language and Society*, 88), we may consider Hebrew functioning analogously while invoking greater affinity with the language of early Jesus tradition and the Jewish scriptures (cf. Nicklas' ["Crazy Guy or Intellectual Leader?" 15] comments on use of the Jewish scriptures in *Revelation* as a sign of intellectualism). See further Clackson's (*Language and Society*, 158) remarks on Christians using language to engage with intellectual society beyond Christian circles, as well as Coogan's observations on Hebrew competency as a mark of intellectual expertise: Jeremiah Coogan, "The Ways that Parted in the Library: The Gospels

94 *Julia D. Lindenlaub*

text's epistolary opening as a figurehead for his recipients and thereby sets a high standard for the interests and abilities of a reading community.

Not only is James an accomplished author, but he writes to likewise accomplished readers. One may immediately observe that this "letter" responds to an associate's prior request: "Since you asked that I send you a secret book ... [I have written] it in the Hebrew alphabet and sent it to you, and you alone" (1.8–18). The text's implied recipient seems to have shown special interest in obtaining a copy of a secret book: "[i]n a society where literacy and the ownership of books afforded social prestige, possessing books of secret revelation may have staked out a position of prestige within particular social circles, for oneself or one's group."[35] Though no specifics are given regarding this supposed prior request, we may recall the copies sought in P.Oxy. 2192 and readily imagine former epistolary correspondence requesting the specialist literature of the "revelatory book." Moreover, it seems the sender and recipient are socially acquainted through this practice, as James has already sent another text of his own composition, even specifying a time frame of ten months for this ongoing exchange. The practicality of circulation in this passage invites the further analogy of "pseudo-documentarism," which describes the discovery and circulation of purportedly authentic texts.[36] The *Apocryphon of James* here exhibits characteristics of "embedded" pseudo-documentarism, wherein books cited within a text artificially foster an air of authenticity. Taking this one step further, the circulation of literature embedded in the *Apocryphon of James'* epistolary opening artificially fosters a scholarly atmosphere. Insofar as the author and recipients share literary interests, a social identity for the reading community is shaped by their intellectual values. As the author and audience engage in the textual practices of composing, copying, and circulating literature of mutual interest, a kind of read-

---

according to Matthew and according to the Hebrews in Late Ancient Heresiology," *Journal of Ecclesiastical History* 74 (2023): 488.

[35] King, "'What Is an Author?'" 25. King makes this observation about the *Apocryphon of John* and posits that such posturing for status may be directed beyond Christian circles (i.e., toward "non-Christian philosophical or theurgic groups") or within Christian contests over accepted tradition.

[36] Lundhaug ("Fictional Books in Coptic Apocrypha," 331) relates the function of unnamed books in Coptic literature, including the *Apocryphon of James*, to the pseudo-documentary strategies of contemporaneous literary culture, citing: William Hansen, "Strategies of Authentication in Ancient Popular Literature," in *The Ancient Novel and Beyond*, ed. Stelios Panayotakis, Maaike Zimmerman, and Wytse Keulen, Mnemosyne Supplements 241 (Leiden: Brill, 2003), 302; Karen ní Mheallaigh, "Pseudo-Documentarism and the Limits of Ancient Fiction," *American Journal of Philology* 129 (2008): 424. On epistolary features as a tool for pseudo-documentarism, see further: Karen ní Mheallaigh, *Reading Fiction with Lucian: Fakes, Freaks, and Hyperreality* (Cambridge: Cambridge University Press, 2014), 152. See also Geue on the documentary preoccupations of this milieu: Tom Geue, "Keeping/Losing Records, Keeping/Losing Faith: Suetonius and Justin Do the Document," in *Literature and Culture in the Roman Empire, 96–235: Cross-Cultural Interactions*, ed. Alice König, Rebecca Langlands, and James Uden (Cambridge: Cambridge University Press, 2020), 203–22.

The Fictive Author and the Reading Community in the Apocryphon of James 95

ing community coalesces around James – "James' circle" – a circle perhaps not unlike that of Diodorus or Harpocration.

The analogous reading communities suggested by the epistolary features of P.Oxy. 2192 and the *Apocryphon of James* can be further explored with respect to *how* the imagined reading circle reads in addition to *what* they read. As Johnson remarks regarding elite reading communities in the imperial context: "The system is symbiotic, in that the focal text provides fodder for the community's activity ... while the interrogation of the text validates the community's sense of self-identity as the educated, able to derive special meaning from this exclusive text."[37] With reference to both P.Oxy. 2192 and the *Apocryphon of James* among other instances, Jeremiah Coogan has presented Christian literature as a type of disciplinary knowledge in antiquity, governed by the same norms of bibliographic gatekeeping as in other fields like medicine and law: "In these ancient discourses, it was not sufficient to have access to a wide range of books; one also needed to exercise the judgment cultivated by advanced education."[38] These observations shed light on how the depiction of literary circulation in *Ap. Jas.* reflects intellectual concerns of disciplinary expertise. In the *Apocryphon of James'* epistolary frame, we can see a construct of authorship by which textual circulation is restricted and comprehension is made paramount. James' epistolary introduction to his secret book carefully admonishes his recipient regarding the text's intended readership: "since you are a minister of the salvation of the saints, endeavour earnestly and take care not to rehearse this text to many – this that the Savior did not wish to tell to all of us, his twelve disciples" (1.18–25). The audience for this text is a reading community of those interested in revelatory texts, but more importantly those capable of understanding and appreciating them.[39] As the learned reader rightly discerns the value of Greek literature sought after by the correspondents in P.Oxy. 2192, so also the discerning recipient of revealed knowledge will seek out – and gatekeep – James' writings.

This motif is developed from the epistolary opening into the next passage following interruption by a lacuna. The text continues: "the twelve disciples were all sitting together and recalling what the Savior had said to each one of them, whether in secret or openly, and putting it in books" (2.8–15). In this scene, the

---

[37] Johnson, *Readers and Reading Culture*, 22.

[38] Coogan ("Disciplinary Knowledge and Gospel Bibliography") cites the examples of Seneca, *Tranq.* 9.4–8 and Lucian, *Ind.* regarding the undiscerning book collector. Howley's (*Aulus Gellius and Roman Reading Culture*, 66–111) discussion of Aulus Gellius' *Noctes Atticae* provides further examples of the importance of intellectual ability in sophisticated reading practices of the milieu. See also Secord's (*Christian Intellectuals and the Roman Empire*, 2) comments on the ancient intellectual expressing their knowledge in a range of subject areas on the mutual ground of classical education and knowledge.

[39] One may compare the epistolary frame in *Revelation*, which specifies a privileged readership receiving the revelation (*Rev* 1.4) but also admonishes great care in the textual practices applied even by such a privileged group (*Rev.* 22.18–19) (King, "'What Is an Author?'" 28–29; cf. Nicklas, "Crazy Guy or Intellectual Leader?" 12–13).

96   *Julia D. Lindenlaub*

disciples as a group – presumably including James and Peter before they are drawn aside whilst their fellows continue – form a scholarly "circle" of their own. James' participation in the remarkable production of this collection of specialised literature broadens his composition's "narrative boundaries and widen[s] its intertextual context, giving the impression of there being much more out there to be known and read, and that would bolster the argument of the referring text."[40] Here the fictive author appears within a scribally educated social circle of disciple peers, but he alone becomes arbiter of this bibliographic context for the *Apocryphon of James'* readers.[41] While the other disciples are excluded from the privileged revelation shared with James in the ensuing narrative, the audience of *Ap. Jas.* is admonished to study James' insights in the secret book(s) he writes and sends. The expert knowledge James provides to his readers supersedes even the corpus of apostolic literature to which he was ostensibly a contributor.[42] The *Apocryphon of James'* authorial fiction deploys a literate intellectual skilled in elite textual practices, with the self-authorisation of superior expertise.[43] As recipients of this figure's writings, the audience of *Ap. Jas.* is thus able to continue in this tradition of the imagined apostolic author's own scholarly community – to even better result. Not unlike the related-but-distinct reading circles of P.Oxy. 2192, James is part of the circle of disciples as well as his own circle of recipients.

The *Apocryphon of James'* purported authorship orients the text within an acknowledged disciplinary corpus of gospel writings, but it also links James' textual

---

[40] Lundhaug, "Fictional Books in Coptic Apocrypha," 333.

[41] Compare the roughly contemporaneous example of Origen as arbiter of the bibliography of gospel writings (Coogan, "Disciplinary Knowledge and Gospel Bibliography"). The language of the "text-broker" is similarly illuminating: H. Gregory Snyder, *Teachers and Texts in the Ancient World: Philosophers, Jews, and Christians*, Religion in the First Christian Centuries (London: Routledge, 2000).

[42] On the degree of "collaborative" gospel writing implied in this passage, see Jeremiah Coogan's contribution to this volume.

[43] I have argued elsewhere that the roots of the *Apocryphon of James'* posturing relationship to other Jesus books can be traced to the model of disciple authorship provided by the *Gospel of John*: Julia D. Lindenlaub, "The Gospel of John as Model for Literate Authors and their Texts in Epistula Apostolorum and Apocryphon of James (NHC I,2)," *Journal for the Study of the New Testament* 43 (2020): 3–27. Relatedly, see Keith's argument for the *Apocryphon of James'* role in the "competitive textualization" of gospel literature: Chris Keith, *The Gospel as Manuscript: An Early History of the Jesus Tradition as Material Artifact* (Oxford: Oxford University Press, 2020), 156. I recognise a competitive relationship between the *Apocryphon of James* and prior gospels while maintaining that it is intended to coexist with its rivals rather than eliminate them (cf. Brakke, "Parables and Plain Speech," 216; Elaine Pagels, "Gnosticism and the New Testament: The Apocryphon of James [NHC I,2] from Nag Hammadi," in *Method and Meaning: Essays on New Testament Interpretation in Honor of Harold W. Attridge*, ed. Andrew McGowan and Kent Harold Richards, Resources for Biblical Study 67 [Atlanta: Society of Biblical Literature, 2012]: 297–309; *contra* Francis Watson, "Against the Twelve: The Apocryphon of James and the Status of the Apostles," in *Texts in Context: Essays on Dating and Contextualising Christian Writings from the Second and Early Third Centuries*, ed. Joseph Verheyden, Jens Schröter, and Tobias Nicklas [Leuven: Peeters, 2021], 209–30).

The Fictive Author and the Reading Community in the Apocryphon of James 97

community within the narrative to that outside of the narrative. As Brakke notes in his connection of the *Apocryphon of James* with a sophisticated intellectual milieu in Egyptian Christianity: "the author of this work has given his study circle a past in Christian history."[44] Here is author-function deployed in a way that blurs the boundaries between the reading community of the revered past and the reading community of the historical present. Imitating the imperial milieu's standards for intellectualism, the author of *Ap. Jas.* fictively self-presents as "an impeccably well-connected, authoritatively knowledgeable member of that community, and as such supremely well qualified to act as arbiter and voice of its self-evident insider consensus."[45] James' concluding address to the reader at the text's close speaks directly to the privileged few to whom the text was circulated on behalf of a learned apostolic community. Moreover, the audience is invited to see their own privileged status as exceeding that of their legendary forebears through the intellectual pursuits and practices James models: "And I pray that the beginning may come from you, for thus I shall be capable of salvation, since they will be enlightened through me" (16.12–16). To this end, the *Apocryphon of James*' authorial fiction makes clever use of "strategies that emphasize elite status associated with literacy, education, and scribal activity."[46] The epistolary framing device in this text bridges the fictional author's heritage as a member of a revered scholarly community with the writer's vision for his own intellectual community.

---

[44] Brakke, "Parables and Plain Speech," 217; cf. Kloppenborg's ("Literate Media in Early Christ Groups") extension of Brakke's argument.

[45] Eshleman, *Social World of Intellectuals*, 176. Eshleman's comments here regarding Christian heresiologists are apt for application to the *Apocryphon of James*. If an aspiring Christian intellectual was not able to gain patronage or successfully attain recognition in the fashion of a figure like Origen, pseudepigraphy may have presented an appealing prospect for representing oneself fictionally with the elite values one espouses (cf. King, "'What Is an Author?'" 39). Individuals not conforming to the ideal of the *pepaidoumenoi* – such as a woman or enslaved person – would be prime candidates for such a tactic. On classed and gendered discourses around authorship in early Christian texts and the wider Roman Mediterranean literary context, see: Jeremiah Coogan and Candida R. Moss. "The Textual Demiurge: Social Status and the Academic Discourse of Early Christian Forgery," *New Testament Studies* 70 (2024): forthcoming. See further the ongoing research into the significance of the enslaved in the production of early Christian literature: Candida R. Moss, "Between the Lines: Looking for the Contributions of Enslaved Literate Laborers in a Second Century Text (P. Berol. 11632)," *Studies in Late Antiquity* 5 (2021): 432–52; eadem, "Fashioning Mark: Early Christian Discussions about the Scribe and Status of the Second Gospel," *New Testament Studies* 67 (2021): 181–204; eadem, God's Ghostwriters: Enslaved Christians and the Making of the Bible (New York: Little, Brown and Company, 2024); Jeremiah Coogan, Candida R. Moss, and Joseph A. Howley, "The Socioeconomics of Fabrication: Textuality, Authenticity, and Class in the Roman Mediterranean," *Arethusa* (2024): forthcoming. The contributions of Chance Bonar and Emily Mitchell to this volume provide additional insights into the voices of the enslaved in authorial constructs.

[46] Fewster, "Ancient Book Culture," 416.

4. Conclusion

Having compared the epistolary features of the *Apocryphon of James* with those of P.Oxy. 2192, I conclude that the author of the Nag Hammadi tractate was likely steeped in a cultural milieu like that glimpsed in the Oxyrhynchus papyrus. Within such a setting, this author would be well equipped to evoke correspondence readily recognisable from that of contemporary intellectual reading communities. An author aspiring to the status of such social groups could find compelling verisimilitude for their authorial fiction by employing the generic strategies found in *Ap. Jas.*: "the real world of the reader imprints itself upon the world of the fiction – and the fictional world of the book absorbs and dramatizes the world of the reader."[47] While the authorship of the disciple James remains a fictive literary conceit, the text's epistolary character portrays the apostolic age in terms familiar – and attractive – to scholarly minded elites in the author's own milieu. The recipients of this text are thus inheritors of an apostolic tradition they would esteem in their own terms. By examining a learned reading community through the lens of P.Oxy. 2192, we can better understand the *Apocryphon of James*' epistolary details. The writer's sophisticated grasp of the appropriate conventions for correspondence concerning textual practices positions the audience of *Ap. Jas.* among an even more privileged group than the apostles themselves. Like the study circles of Diodorus and Harpocration, or of Clement and Origen, the "study circles" of James and the disciples or of James and his readers share fundamental assumptions about identity formation as an elite reading culture in Roman Egypt. Most importantly for the purposes of this volume, the analogy provided by the Oxyrhynchus evidence contextualises the literary use of epistolary framing in terms of author-function in order to reveal a clear rhetorical purpose.[48] Attribution to James installs the text's author as a champion of scholarly pursuits orbited by a community of like-minded, expert readers.

I close with a final reflection on the fourth-century monastic preservation of the *Apocryphon of James* in the Nag Hammadi codices.[49] In this later period, the legacy of scholarly circles like those of Clement and Origen – or indeed of Diodorus or Harpocration – remained influential.[50] The *Apocryphon of James*

---

[47] ní Mheallaigh, *Reading Fiction with Lucian*, 144.

[48] My reading of the *Apocryphon of James*' authorial fiction is intended to dovetail with Brakke's case that the text's logic of "parables and plain speech" emulates scholarly Christian communities that elevated the status of an educated elite over those unable to penetrate a text's intellectual significance. I see the complementary contexts provided by Alexandria and Oxyrhynchus as working together to support an Egyptian provenance for this text and moreover to explain the text's unusual epistolary construct and authorial fiction.

[49] For the foundational study on the monastic context for the Nag Hammadi Codices, see: Hugo Lundhaug and Lance Jenott, *The Monastic Origins of the Nag Hammadi Codices*, Studien und Texte zu Antike und Christentum 97 (Tübingen: Mohr Siebeck, 2015).

[50] One may also compare an imagined past study circle in: Elizabeth C. Penland, "The His-

The Fictive Author and the Reading Community in the Apocryphon of James 99

appears to have been received in this setting as an ideal opening to follow the brief introductory tractate of Codex I, *Prayer of the Apostle Paul* (NHC I,1). Through the epistolary framing and authorial fiction of *Ap. Jas.*, the readers of this codex are invited to draw the same conclusions as indicated by the text's second-century provenance. The *Apocryphon of James*' readership – though expanded by its preservation in the codex – remains limited to a select number: those who take seriously the discerning study of chosen literature, in this case the whole of Codex I itself.[51] Befitting this position, *Ap. Jas.* "hits the rhetorical-esoteric sweet spot: openly sharing the content of an explicitly secret teaching from Jesus, but shrouding it in the intimate form of a letter, supposedly for the eyes of the addressee only."[52] Moreover, *Ap. Jas.* is immediately followed in the codex by the *Gospel of Truth* (NHC I,3), emerging from a context of scholarly minded Valentinians also in the second century. The *Apocryphon of James*' elevation of textual study is thus capitalised on by the placement of another revealed book preoccupied with shaping the textual practices of its intended reading community. In the *Gospel of Truth*, "[b]elievers are invited to receive this revealed book, distribute it, and publish their own texts."[53] As such, the *Gospel of Truth* is "advanced-level curriculum"[54] for the intellectual reader envisioned in *Ap. Jas.* and carries forward its fixation on literary pursuits. The *Apocryphon of James*' compositional strategies thus map conveniently onto the later concerns of those who selected this text for inclusion in the codex from which we know it. Such continuity between the intellectually oriented influences upon the text's origin and its preservation highlights simultaneous evolution and stability in Egyptian Christian reading culture – seen through the lens of the fictive author and the reading community in the *Apocryphon of James*.

---

tory of the Caesarean Present: Eusebius and Narratives of Origen," in *Eusebius of Caesarea: Tradition and Innovations*, ed. Jeremy M. Schott, and Aaron P. Johnson (Cambridge, MA: Harvard University Press, 2013), 83–95.

[51] These observations on the *Apocryphon of James*' context in Nag Hammadi Codex I are put forward in: Lance Jenott and Elaine Pagels, "Antony's Letters and Nag Hammadi Codex I: Sources of Religious Conflict in Fourth-Century Egypt," *Journal of Early Christian Studies* 18 (2010): 557–89. Their discussion is framed by Athanasius' opposition to academically oriented Christian communities following a teacher like Origen or Antony. See also Given's affirmation of this proposal: J. Gregory Given, "Four Texts from Nag Hammadi amid the Textual and Generic Fluidity of the 'Letter' in Late Antique Egypt," in *Snapshots of Evolving Traditions: Jewish and Christian Manuscript Culture, Textual Fluidity, and New Philology*, ed. Liv Ingeborg Lied and Hugo Lundhaug, Texte und Untersuchungen zur Geschichte der altchristlichen Literatur 175 (Berlin: De Gruyter, 2017): 201–20.

[52] Given, "Four Texts from Nag Hammadi," 217.

[53] Anne Kreps, "The Passion of the Book: The Gospel of Truth as Valentinian Scriptural Practice," *Journal of Early Christian Studies* 24 (2016): 314 (note Kreps' use of "scriptural practices," following Brakke, "Scriptural Practices in Early Christianity"); cf. Anne Kreps, *The Crucified Book: Sacred Writing in the Age of Valentinus*, Divinations: Rereading Late Antique Religion (Philadelphia: University of Pennsylvania Press, 2022).

[54] Jenott and Pagels, "Antony's Letters and Nag Hammadi Codex I," 584–85.

Bibliography

Ayres, Lewis and H. Clifton Ward III. "Introduction and Acknowledgments." Pages 1–6 in *The Rise of the Christian Intellectual*. Edited by Lewis Ayres and H. Clifton Ward III. Arbeiten zur Kirchengeschichte 139. Berlin: De Gruyter, 2020.

Blumell, Lincoln H. *Lettered Christians: Christians, Letters, and Late Antique Oxyrhynchus*. New Testament Tools, Studies and Documents 39. Leiden: Brill, 2012.

Brakke, David. "Parables and Plain Speech in the Fourth Gospel and the Apocryphon of James." *Journal of Early Christian Studies* 7 (1999): 187–218.

Brakke, David. "Scriptural Practices in Early Christianity: Towards a New History of the New Testament Canon." Pages 263–280 in *Invention, Rewriting, Usurpation: Discursive Fights over Religious Traditions in Antiquity*. Edited by David Brakke, Anders-Christian Jacobsen, and Jörg Ulrich. Early Christianity in the Context of Antiquity 11. Frankfurt: Peter Lang, 2012.

Braund, David, John Wilkins, and Glen Bowersock, eds. *Athenaeus and His World: Reading Greek Culture in the Roman Empire*. Oxford: Oxford University Press, 2000.

Clackson, James. *Language and Society in the Greek and Roman Worlds*. Key Themes in Ancient History. Cambridge: Cambridge University Press, 2015.

Coogan, Jeremiah. "Failed Gospels and Disciplinary Knowledge in Origen's *Hom. Luc.* 1." Forthcoming in *Unruly Books: Rethinking Ancient and Academic Imaginations of Religious Texts*. Edited by Esther Brownsmith, Marianne B. Kartzow, and Liv Ingeborg Lied. London: Bloomsbury T&T Clark, 2024.

Coogan, Jeremiah. "Meddling with the Gospel: Celsus, Early Christian Textuality, and the Politics of Reading." *Novum Testamentum* 65 (2023): 400–422.

Coogan, Jeremiah. "The Ways that Parted in the Library: The Gospels according to Matthew and according to the Hebrews in Late Ancient Heresiology." *Journal of Ecclesiastical History* 74 (2023): 473–490.

Coogan, Jeremiah and Candida R. Moss. "The Textual Demiurge: Social Status and the Academic Discourse of Early Christian Forgery." *New Testament Studies* 70 (2024): forthcoming.

Coogan, Jeremiah, Candida R. Moss, and Joseph A. Howley. "The Socioeconomics of Fabrication: Textuality, Authenticity, and Class in the Roman Mediterranean." *Arethusa* (2024): forthcoming.

Crawford, Matthew R. "Tatian, Celsus, and Christianity as 'Barbarian Philosophy' in the Late Second Century." Pages 45–80 in *The Rise of the Christian Intellectual*. Edited by Lewis Ayres and H. Clifton Ward III. Arbeiten zur Kirchengeschichte 139. Berlin: De Gruyter, 2020.

Eshleman, Kendra. *The Social World of Intellectuals in the Roman Empire: Sophists, Philosophers, and Christians*. Cambridge: Cambridge University Press, 2012.

Fewster, Gregory P. "Ancient Book Culture and the Literacy of James: On the Production and Consumption of a Pseudepigraphal Letter." *Zeitschrift für Antikes Christentum* 20 (2016): 387–417.

Foucault, Michel. "What Is an Author?" Pages 205–222 in *Aesthetics, Method, and Epistemology*. Edited by James D. Faubion and translated by Robert Hurley et al. New York: The New Press, 1998.

Gamble, Harry Y. *Books and Readers in the Early Church: A History of Early Christian Texts*. New Haven, CT: Yale University Press, 1995.

The Fictive Author and the Reading Community in the Apocryphon of James 101

Gamble, Harry Y. "The Book Trade in the Roman Empire." Pages 23–36 in *The Early Text of the New Testament*. Edited by Charles E. Hill and Michael J. Kruger. New York: Oxford University Press, 2012.

Geue, Tom. "Keeping/Losing Records, Keeping/Losing Faith: Suetonius and Justin Do the Document." Pages 203–222 in *Literature and Culture in the Roman Empire, 96–235: Cross-Cultural Interactions*. Edited by Alice König, Rebecca Langlands, and James Uden. Cambridge: Cambridge University Press, 2020.

Given, J. Gregory. "Four Texts from Nag Hammadi amid the Textual and Generic Fluidity of the 'Letter' in Late Antique Egypt." Pages 201–220 in *Snapshots of Evolving Traditions: Jewish and Christian Manuscript Culture, Textual Fluidity, and New Philology*. Edited by Liv Ingeborg Lied and Hugo Lundhaug. Texte und Untersuchungen zur Geschichte der altchristlichen Literatur 175. Berlin: De Gruyter, 2017.

Hansen, William. "Strategies of Authentication in Ancient Popular Literature." Pages 301–314 in *The Ancient Novel and Beyond*. Edited by Stelios Panayotakis, Maaike Zimmerman, and Wytse Keulen. Mnemosyne Supplements 241. Leiden: Brill, 2003.

Hartenstein, Judith and Uwe-Karsten Plisch. "'Der Brief des Jakobus' (NHC I,2)." Pages 10–17 in *Nag Hammadi Deutsch 1: NHC I,1–V,1*. Edited by Hans-Martin Schenke et al. Berlin: De Gruyter, 2001.

Heath, Jane M. F. *Clement of Alexandria and the Shaping of Christian Literary Practice: Miscellany and the Transformation of Greco-Roman Writing*. Cambridge: Cambridge University Press, 2020.

Heath, Jane M. F. "'Textual Communities': Brian Stock's Concept and Recent Scholarship on Antiquity." Pages 5–35 in *Scriptural Interpretation at the Interface between Education and Religion: In Memory of Hans Conzelmann*. Edited by Florian Wilk. Themes in Biblical Narrative 22. Leiden: Brill, 2018.

Heilmann, Jan. *Lesen in Antike und frühem Christentum: Kulturgeschichtliche, philologische sowie kognitionswissenschaftliche Perspektiven und deren Bedeutung für die neutestamentliche Exegese*. Texte und Arbeiten zum Neutestamentlichen Zeitalter. Tübingen: Narr Francke Attempto, 2021.

Howley, Joseph A. *Aulus Gellius and Roman Reading Culture: Text, Presence, and Imperial Knowledge in the* Noctes Atticae. Cambridge: Cambridge University Press, 2018.

Jenott, Lance and Elaine Pagels. "Antony's Letters and Nag Hammadi Codex I: Sources of Religious Conflict in Fourth-Century Egypt." *Journal of Early Christian Studies* 18 (2010): 557–589.

Johnson, William A. *Readers and Reading Culture in the High Roman Empire: A Study of Elite Communities*. Oxford: Oxford University Press, 2010.

Kreps, Anne. *The Crucified Book: Sacred Writing in the Age of Valentinus*, Divinations: Rereading Late Antique Religion. Philadelphia: University of Pennsylvania Press, 2022.

Kreps, Anne. "The Passion of the Book: The Gospel of Truth as Valentinian Scriptural Practice." *Journal of Early Christian Studies* 24 (2016): 311–335.

Lindenlaub, Julia D. "The Gospel of John as Model for Literate Authors and their Texts in Epistula Apostolorum and Apocryphon of James (NHC I,2)." *Journal for the Study of the New Testament* 43 (2020): 3–27.

Löhr, Winrich A. *Basilides und seine Schule: Eine Studie zur Theologie- und Kirchengeschichte des zweiten Jahrhunderts*. Tübingen: Mohr Siebeck, 1996.

Luijendijk, AnneMarie. "Books and Private Readers in Early Christian Oxyrhynchus: 'A Spiritual Meadow and a Garden of Delight.'" Pages 101–136 in *Books and Readers in the Premodern World: Essays in Honour of Harry Gamble*. Edited by Karl Shuve. Writings from the Greco-Roman World Supplements 12. Atlanta: Society of Biblical Literature, 2018.

Luijendijk, AnneMarie. *Greetings in the Lord: Early Christians and the Oxyrhynchus Papyri*. Harvard Theological Studies 60. Cambridge, MA: Harvard University Press, 2008.

Lundhaug, Hugo. "Fictional Books in Coptic Apocrypha." *Journal for the Study of the Pseudepigrapha* 32 (2023): 323–342.

Lundhaug, Hugo and Lance Jenott. *The Monastic Origins of the Nag Hammadi Codices*. Studien und Texte zu Antike und Christentum 97. Tübingen: Mohr Siebeck, 2015.

Keith, Chris. *The Gospel as Manuscript: An Early History of the Jesus Tradition as Material Artifact*. Oxford: Oxford University Press, 2020.

King, Karen L. "'What Is an Author?': Ancient Author-Function in the *Apocryphon of John* and the Apocalypse of John." Pages 15–42 in *Scribal Practices and Social Structures among Jesus Adherents: Essays in Honour of John S. Kloppenborg*. Edited by William E. Arnal et al. Leuven: Peeters, 2016.

Kloppenborg, John S. "Literate Media in Early Christ Groups: The Creation of a Christian Book Culture." *Journal of Early Christian Studies* 22 (2014): 21–59.

Last, Richard. "Communities That Write: Christ-Groups, Associations, and Gospel Communities." *New Testament Studies* 58 (2012): 173–198.

Last, Richard. "The Social Relationship of Gospel Writers: New Insights from Inscriptions Commending Greek Historiographers." *Journal for the Study of the New Testament* 37 (2015): 223–252.

Markschies, Christoph. "Intellectuals and Church Fathers in the Third and Fourth Centuries." Pages 239–256 in *Christians and Christianity in the Holy Land: From the Origins to the Latin Kingdoms*. Edited by Ora Limor and Guy G. Stroumsa. Turnhout: Brepols, 2006.

Markschies, Christoph. "Preface." Pages vii–xii in *Rise of the Christian Intellectual*. Edited by Lewis Ayres and H. Clifton Ward III. Arbeiten zur Kirchengeschichte 139. Berlin: De Gruyter, 2020.

Mheallaigh, Karen ní. "Pseudo-Documentarism and the Limits of Ancient Fiction." *American Journal of Philology* 129 (2008): 403–431.

Mheallaigh, Karen ní. *Reading Fiction with Lucian: Fakes, Freaks, and Hyperreality*. Cambridge: Cambridge University Press, 2014.

Moss, Candida R. "Between the Lines: Looking for the Contributions of Enslaved Literate Laborers in a Second Century Text (P. Berol. 11632)." *Studies in Late Antiquity* 5 (2021): 432–52.

Moss, Candida R. "Fashioning Mark: Early Christian Discussions about the Scribe and Status of the Second Gospel." *New Testament Studies* 67 (2021): 181–204.

Moss, Candida R. *God's Ghostwriters: Enslaved Christians and the Making of the Bible*. New York: Little, Brown and Company, 2024.

Moss, Candida R. "The Secretary: Enslaved Workers, Stenography, and the Production of Early Christian Literature." *Journal of Theological Studies* 74 (2023): 20–56.

Myllykoski, Matti. "James the Just in History and Tradition: Perspectives of Past and Present Scholarship (Part II)." *Currents in Biblical Research* 5 (2007): 73–122.

Nasrallah, Laura Salah. "Mapping the World: Justin, Tatian, Lucian, and the Second Sophistic." *Harvard Theological Review* 98 (2005): 283–314.

Nicklas, Tobias. "Crazy Guy or Intellectual Leader? The Seer of Revelation and his Role for the Communities of Asia Minor." Pages 7–24 in *Rise of the Christian Intellectual*.

Edited by Lewis Ayres and H. Clifton Ward III. Arbeiten zur Kirchengeschichte 139. Berlin: De Gruyter, 2020.

Pagels, Elaine. "Gnosticism and the New Testament: The Apocryphon of James [NHC I,2] from Nag Hammadi." Pages 297–309 in Method and Meaning: Essays on New Testament Interpretation in Honor of Harold W. Attridge. Edited by Andrew McGowan and Kent Harold Richards. Resources for Biblical Study 67. Atlanta: Society of Biblical Literature, 2012.

Parkhouse, Sarah. Eschatology and the Saviour: The 'Gospel of Mary' among Early Christian Dialogue Gospels. Society for New Testament Studies Monograph Series 176. Cambridge: Cambridge University Press, 2019.

Peirano Garrison, Irene. The Rhetoric of the Roman Fake: Latin Pseudepigrapha in Context. Cambridge: Cambridge University Press, 2012.

Penland, Elizabeth C. "The History of the Caesarean Present: Eusebius and Narratives of Origen." Pages 83–95 in Eusebius of Caesarea: Tradition and Innovations. Edited by Jeremy M. Schott, and Aaron P. Johnson. Cambridge, MA: Harvard University Press, 2013.

Secord, Jared. Christian Intellectuals and the Roman Empire: From Justin Martyr to Origen, Inventing Christianity. University Park, PA: Pennsylvania State University Press, 2020.

Snyder, H. Gregory. Teachers and Texts in the Ancient World: Philosophers, Jews, and Christians, Religion in the First Christian Centuries. London: Routledge, 2000.

Stock, Brian. The Implications of Literacy: Written Language and Models of Interpretation in the Eleventh and Twelfth Centuries. Princeton: Princeton University Press, 1983.

Stock, Brian. Listening for the Text: On the Uses of the Past. Philadelphia: University of Pennsylvania Press, 1990.

Walsh, Robyn Faith. The Origins of Early Christian Literature: Contextualizing the New Testament within Greco-Roman Literary Culture. Cambridge: Cambridge University Press, 2021.

Watson, Francis. "Against the Twelve: The Apocryphon of James and the Status of the Apostles." Pages 209–230 in Texts in Context: Essays on Dating and Contextualising Christian Writings from the Second and Early Third Centuries. Edited by Joseph Verheyden, Jens Schröter, and Tobias Nicklas. Leuven: Peeters, 2021.

Wendt, Heidi. At the Temple Gates: The Religion of Freelance Experts in the Roman Empire. Oxford: Oxford University Press, 2016.

Wendt, Heidi. "Christians as and among Writer-Intellectuals in Second-Century Rome." Pages 84–108 in Christian Teachers in Second-Century Rome: Schools and Students in the Ancient City. Supplements to Vigiliae Christianae 159. Leiden: Brill, 2020.

White, Peter. "Bookshops in the Literary Culture of Rome." Pages 268–278 in Ancient Literacies: The Culture of Reading in Greece and Rome. Edited by William A. Johnson and Holt N. Parker. Oxford: Oxford University Press, 2009.

Williams, Francis E. "The Apocryphon of James." Pages 13–53 in Nag Hammadi Codex I (The Jung Codex): Introductions, Texts, Translations, Indices. Edited by Harold W. Attridge. Leiden: Brill, 1985.

Yadin-Israel, Azzan. "Christian, Jewish, and Pagan Authority and the Rise of the Christian Intellectual." Pages 165–192 in The Rise of the Christian Intellectual. Edited by Lewis Ayres and H. Clifton Ward III. Arbeiten zur Kirchengeschichte 139. Berlin: De Gruyter, 2020.

Writing Truth and Secrets

Authorship and the Legitimising Role of Apocalyptic in Manichaeism

Nicholas Baker-Brian

1. Introduction: Apocalyptic in the Sasanian Court and the *Shābuhragān*

In light of recent research on the apocalyptic traditions of late antiquity, the topic of Mani and his followers' interest in apocalyptic literature is ripe for re-appraisal. This contribution develops the argument that Mani's authority as an "Apostle of God" (cf. Bīrūnī, *Vestiges* [*Āthār*] 207)[1] derived from his persona as an author whose ideas aligned with the prevailing "apocalypticism" (a prophetically orientated current of eschatological thought and/or practice manifest as a "sociological ideology," à la John J. Collins)[2] of the third century CE. Not perhaps a spectacular claim but one which is rarely raised in Manichaean studies, most likely because Mani's writings survive largely in fragmentary form or as verbatim citations and jaundiced summaries in the works of his opponents. As such, commentators have been hesitant to discuss the literary forms and ideas utilised by Mani to promote his teachings, the one exception being a developing body of research highlighting Mani's prolific use of the letter form.[3]

A number of recent contributions examining the significance of apocalypses in gnostic traditions and Manichaeism have highlighted the important intellectual and cultural role of apocalypses in relation to the philosophical and theological concerns of the second and third centuries. John Reeves' important work from 1996, *Heralds of that Good Realm: Syro-Mesopotamian Gnosis and Jewish Traditions*, examined the excerpted pseudepigraphic apocalypses attributed to the antediluvian figures Adam, Sethel, Enosh, Shem, and Enoch, which appear in the Greek *Life* of Mani (otherwise known as the *Cologne Mani Codex* [*CMC*]),

---

[1] John C. Reeves, *Prolegomena to a History of Islamicate Manichaeism* (Sheffield: Equinox, 2011), 102–3.

[2] Defined as a "sociological ideology" by John J. Collins, "Introduction: Towards the Morphology of a Genre," *Semeia* 14 (1979): 3–4.

[3] Most recently, see Iain Gardner, *Mani's Epistles: The Surviving Parts of the Coptic Codex Berlin P.15998*, Manichäische Handschriften der Staatlichen Museen zu Berlin (Stuttgart: Kohlhammer, 2022).

106   Nicholas Baker-Brian

an early Byzantine-era work (fourth/fifth century)[4] in which Mani's early life
and earliest missions are portrayed in a hagiographic style. Reeves demonstrates
convincingly that all five excerpted apocalypses (*CMC* 48.16–62.9), cited in
the course of testimony supplied by Baraiēs, a key figure in the early history of
Manichaeism who carried the senior honorific "The Teacher" (ὁ διδάσκαλος),[5]
represent creative adaptations of existing works and traditions about these
"primal ancestors" held in high esteem by "'native' forms of gnosticism"[6] from
the regions comprising ancient Syria and Mesopotamia. In the context of the
Life, the excerpts served to demonstrate that Mani's teachings had derived from
his own revelatory experiences, guided by his divine twin (Gk. *Syzygos*), and
that he shared the same experiences with his revered ancestors from the deepest
reaches of antiquity.

Moving on to other dualist cosmologies from regions east of the Roman empire,
Plotinus' censure of various apocalypses with roots in the gnostic traditions of
late antiquity as narrated by Porphyry in his biography of the philosopher-sage,[7]
are the subject of a perceptive study by Dylan Burns from 2014, *Apocalypse of the
Alien God: Platonism and the Exile of Sethian Gnosticism.* Burns identifies these
writings as apocalyptic pseudepigrapha of a "Sethian" gnostic persuasion and
argues that the Manichaean interest in apocalypses (the excerpted apocalyptic
works in the Greek *Life* of Mani are his main source of evidence in this regard)[8]
derives from the same Jewish-Platonising theological traditions as Sethianism
and the same geographical area, namely Mesopotamia.[9] Most recently, Paul
Dilley has examined the broader appeal of "apocalypticism" to Manichaeism by

---

[4] See the recent reappraisal in favour of an earlier date by Cornelia Römer, "Die Datierung
des Kölner Mani-Kodex," *Zeitschrift für Papyrologie und Epigraphik* 220 (2021): 94–96.

[5] See esp. Julien Ries, "Baraiès le Didascale dans le Codex Mani: Nature, Structure et Valeur
de son Témoignage sur Mani et sa Doctrine," in *Atti del Terzo Congresso Internazionale di Studi:
Manicheismo e Oriente Cristiano Antico,* ed. Luigi Cirillo and Alois van Tongerloo (Leuven:
Brepols, 1997), 305–11. On the title, "Teacher," see the comments by Iain Gardner, *The Founder
of Manichaeism: Rethinking the Life of Mani* (Cambridge: Cambridge University Press, 2020),
50.

[6] John C. Reeves, *Heralds of That Good Realm: Syro-Mesopotamian Gnosis and Jewish
Traditions* (Leiden: Brill 1996), 209.

[7] § 16 *Life of Plotinus*; Lloyd P. Gerson, ed., *Plotinus. The Enneads* (Cambridge: Cambridge
University Press, 2018); cf. Dylan Burns, *Apocalypse of the Alien God: Platonism and the Exile of
Sethian Gnosticism* (Philadelphia: University of Pennsylvania Press, 2014), 161–63.

[8] Burns is incorrect in the claim that the apocalypses cited by Baraiēs were "circulating in
the community of Mani's childhood" (*Apocalypse,* 58–59): the *CMC* makes no such claim, and
the work's citation of the excerpts belongs to the portions of text associated with the testimony
of Baraiēs, most likely an independent unit of text or texts deriving from Baraiēs himself rather
than Mani. On the homiletic structure of Baraiēs' testimony, see Eibert Tigchelaar, "Baraies on
Mani's Rapture, Paul, and the Antediluvian Apostles," in *The Wisdom of Egypt. Jewish, Early
Christian, and Gnostic Essays in Honour of Gerard P. Luttikhuizen,* ed. Anthony Hilhorst and
George H. van Kooten (Leiden: Brill, 2001), 429–41.

[9] Burns, *Apocalypse,* 140–59.

Writing Truth and Secrets

exploring the links between visionary, revelatory experiences and the profile of the religious clientele of the Sasanian court of the third century, by way of investigating the presentation of Mani's apostolic predecessors in the recently published edition (pp. 343–442) of the Chester Beatty *Kephalaia* ("The Chapters of the Wisdom of My Lord Mani"; cited as 2 Ke),[10] specifically Mani's admission in chapter 342[11] (424:7–11) to have seen both the Land of Light and Hell during the course of his own rapture.

This contribution builds on these studies and other influential scholarly treatments of recent years dealing with questions of authorship in Manichaeism in order to develop a better understanding of Mani's claim to a highly elevated form of authorial authority. The essay considers how Mani deployed apocalyptic language and imagery in his own writings for the purpose of developing and enhancing his apostolic status among his followers. It begins by contextualising Mani's engagement with the phenomenon of apocalypticism within elite Sasanian circles, arguing that in this way Mani was able to legitimise the religious pre-eminence which he claimed for himself. The essay then moves on to consider the reception of Mani's authorial persona as a writer of apocalyptic by key figures in the nascent Manichaean community of the late third century (notably, in the work of Baraiēs) and evaluate reactions *against* Mani's persona as an author of apocalyptic-leaning literature by his opponents, notably the followers or students of Bardaisan, the influential thinker of the late second/early third century.

In Dilley's analysis of Mani's *Shābuhragān*, an association is thus proposed between the chapter of that work entitled "The Coming of the Apostle" (Bīrūnī, *Āthār* 208),[12] and chapter 342 of the Coptic *Kephalaia*, together with the testimony attributed to Baraiēs in the Greek *Life*, where Mani's apostolic predecessors are identified and the details of their raptures are conveyed via the excerpted apocalypses. Dilley's proposal that chapter 342 is linked to the *Shābuhragān* is especially significant for a number of reasons. The *Shābuhragān* is one of Mani's earliest works, composed between 240–42 CE, at the point when he had begun to teach publicly, and it was written to attract the support of Shapur I, the ruling *šāh* of the Sasanian dynasty (translation, "Dedicated to Shapur").[13] However, the

---

[10] Paul Dilley, "'Hell Exists, and We Have Seen the Place Where It Is': Rapture and Religious Competition in Sasanian Iran," in *Mani at the Court of the Persian Kings: Studies on the Chester Beatty* Kephalaia Codex, ed. Iain Gardner, Jason BeDuhn, and Paul Dilley, Nag Hammadi and Manichaean Studies 87 (Leiden: Brill, 2015), 211–46.

[11] Iain Gardner, Jason BeDuhn, and Paul C. Dilley, eds., *The Chapters of the Wisdom of My Lord Mani, Part III: Pages 343–442 (Chapters 321–347)*, Nag Hammadi and Manichaean Studies 92 (Leiden: Brill, 2018). All translations from the *Kephalaia* are taken from this volume.

[12] Reeves, *Prolegomena*, 103.

[13] Christiane Reck, "*Shābuhragān*," *Encyclopaedia Iranica* 2010, https://iranicaonline.org/articles/sabuhragan (accessed November 2022).

108   Nicholas Baker-Brian

Shābuhragān survives only in fragments and via testimonia from Islamic authors, such as al-Nadīm (d. 995), Bīrūnī (d. 1050) and Shahrastānī (d. 1153). According to the testimony of Bīrūnī, one of the work's aims was to locate Mani's place in the catena of apostles sent from God to bring "wisdom and knowledge" to humanity, among whom were included Budda, Zoroaster, and Jesus – all "regional" apostles – and finally Mani, as "the apostle of the God of truth to Babylonia."[14] Chapter 342 of the *Kephalaia* refers to these figures and others as being "seized" (Coptic: *autarpou*)[15] and "taken up; they went, they saw, they came (back), they bore witness; they have told [that the] land of light exists and that we have come from it. Also, hell exists, and we have seen the place where it is."[16] The ascent experiences of the antediluvian patriarchs – those whose pseudepigrapha are cited by Baraiēs in the *CMC* – are also described by the author of the chapter (2 Ke 423.23 to 424.4–5: similar to the regional apostles mentioned earlier, the patriarchs' "testimony" [*marturia*] was also recorded in writing [424.4–5]). Next in line in the Chapter is Mani's confession: "I, myself, whom you are looking at: I went to the land of light Indeed, I have seen the land of light with my eyes, the way that it exists. Again, I have [seen] hell with my eyes, the way it exists ... I have revealed this place (i.e., the land of light) in this world. I preached the word of God" (2 Ke 424.7–10; 11–12).

Dilley argues that the material from the *Kephalaia* and the *Life* are "reworkings" of the "Coming of the Apostle" chapter from the *Shābuhragān* with the implication that the work for Shapur I also promoted Mani as one who had experienced divine rapture.[17] This is an important argument in light of the fact that the *Shābuhragān* almost certainly conveyed autobiographical details about Mani's rapture and subsequent apostleship, an argument developed by Werner Sundermann whose study of Middle Iranian Manichaean texts from 1981 proposed the idea that a number of fragments (M49, M464a, M3414, M805a) should on palaeographic and thematic grounds be assigned to the *Shābuhragān*.[18] These fragments describe Mani's experience with his divine twin (Pahlavi: *nrjmyg* = *Syzygos*)[19] and his early mission under the guidance of his twin to the Sasanian

---

[14] Reeves, *Prolegomena*, 102–3.

[15] Cf. Dilley, "Hell Exists," 218 (together with the philological comment at n. 29), and the association with 2 Cor 12:1–5, raised previously by Tigchelaar, "Baraies on Mani's Rapture."

[16] 2 Ke 423, 15–18; Gardner, BeDuhn, and Dilley, *The Chapters of the Wisdom of My Lord Mani*, 167.

[17] Dilley, "Hell Exists," 214.

[18] Werner Sundermann, *Mitteliranische manichäische Texte kirchengeschichtlichen Inhalts*, with an Appendix by Nicholas Sims-Williams, Berliner Turfantexte XI (Berlin: Akademie, 1981), 91–98; Mary Boyce, *A Reader in Manichaean Middle Persian and Parthian*, Acta Iranica 9 (Leiden: Brill, 1975), 31–32.

[19] "Male-Twin": Sundermann, *Mitteliranische*, 91; Desmond Durkin-Meisterernst, *Dictionary of Manichaean Texts, Volume III: Texts from Central Asia and China* (Turnhout: Brepols, 2004), 244.

Writing Truth and Secrets 109

province of Bēt ʿArbāyē (Arbāyistān). Indeed, it was the disclosure of Mani's own ascent experience and his teachings about the fate of souls following the physical death of the body (cf. al-Nadīm, *Fihrist* 69.16–72.8,[20] likely drawn from three chapters of the *Shābuhragān* dealing in turn with the release of the souls of the Elect, the Hearers, and "Wrongdoers"),[21] both at court and in his writings, which appear to have elicited a response from Kartīr, the Mazdayasnian high priest at the Sasanian court with whom Mani had an antagonistic relationship.[22] Kartīr memorialised his career and religious deeds in a series of inscriptions within the vicinity of Naqsh-i Rustam, the imperial necropolis close to Persepolis.[23] The inscriptions convey a vision granted to Kartīr following an invocation to the gods of the Mazdayasnian faith: "And I prayed towards the gods, then I set this sign that, '[If you] gods are able, then show me the nature of heaven and hell'" (§ 22).[24] Kartīr's vision (characterised across § 22–§ 36 by the Middle Persian phrase, *ʾdwyn mhly*, translated as, "a kind of death")[25] is presented as a journey where his double (twin!) and a woman from the east traverse hell and heaven and return to a palace where a meal is shared with its princely inhabitant to whom Kartīr's double pays reverence (§ 34). Kartīr discloses the importance of his vision since it strengthened his piety: "then I became more obedient and well-wishing towards the gods and more liberal and true to my own soul and I became more confident about this worship and the rites which are performed in the empire" (§ 36).[26] As Prods Oktor Skjærvø has argued, the inscriptions (which date from the reign of Bahram II [276–293])[27] were set up in part to refute Mani's teachings and to challenge his authority in the period immediately following his death,[28] a goal which Kartīr undertook by utilising themes and motifs – a revelatory experience involving visions of heaven and hell under the guidance of a divine twin – em-

---

[20] Reeves, *Prolegomena*, 316–19.

[21] Reeves, *Prolegomena*, 101. A further link may also be drawn here with the references to the fate of the souls of the "Evildoers" in M805a (Sunderman, *Mitteliranische manichäische Texte*, 96–97).

[22] See esp. Iain Gardner, "Mani's Last Days," in *Mani at the Court of the Persian Kings: Studies on the Chester Beatty Kephalaia Codex*, ed. Iain Gardner, Jason BeDuhn, and Paul Dilley, Nag Hammadi and Manichaean Studies 87 (Leiden: Brill, 2015), 159–201.

[23] For a discussion of the inscriptions together with a synoptic edition and English translation, see D. N. MacKenzie, "Kerdir's Inscription," in *The Sasanian Rock Reliefs at Naqsh-i Rustam*, ed. Georgina Herrmann (Berlin: D. Reimer, 1989), 35–72.

[24] MacKenzie, "Kerdir's Inscription," 59.

[25] See the discussion by MacKenzie, "Kerdir's Inscription," 67–68.

[26] MacKenzie, "Kerdir's Inscription," 61.

[27] Notably, MacKenzie, "Kerdir's Inscription," 71–72.

[28] The areas of difference between Mani's theology and Kartīr's exposition of Mazdayasnian thought in light of the inscriptions are discussed at length by Prods Oktor Skjærvø, "Counter-Manichaean Elements in Kerdir's Inscriptions: Irano-Manichaica II," in *Atti del Terzo Congresso Internazionale di Studi: Manicheismo e Oriente Cristiano Antico*, ed. Luigi Cirillo and Alois van Tongerloo (Leuven: Brepols, 1997), 313–42.

110   Nicholas Baker-Brian

ployed by Mani previously.[29] The promotion of rapture-like experiences clearly
served a legitimising purpose aimed at obtaining patronage from royal audiences
for whom their disclosure was primarily intended.

Although different layers of patronage were sought and subsequently achieved
by Mani and Kartīr, both individuals demonstrated the benefits accruing to the
soul of the *šāh* as a reward for his patronage: In the case of Mani and Kartīr,
the highlighting of their understanding of the fate of souls as a result of the
knowledge gained from their raptures was, in Dilley's words, "an essential aspect
of obtaining and sustaining patronage."[30] Indeed, Kartīr emphatically draws
attention to this feature following his prayer: "[A]s I [prayed] from the beginning
and have endured trouble and pains (for) the gods, so too henceforth with regard
to the hereafter may I be better and more confident in the matter than [anybody]
else" (§ 22). While Kartīr's inscriptions disclose a key element of apocalyptic
in the guise of his otherworldly vision, his testimony would likely not qualify
as a work of ancient apocalyptic – the texts are primarily concerned with pro-
moting Kartīr's achievements, foremost of which include the oft-repeated claim
of having founded "many Wahram fires" (i. e. the highest grade of fire temple),[31]
which is achieved in lock-step with Sasanian martial success including into
Anērān, the Roman empire (§ 15) – although the inclusion of a vision narrative
in which otherworldly beings reveal to Kartīr "the nature of heaven and hell, and
righteousness and unrighteousness" (§ 36) demonstrates the important role that
apocalyptic thought and imagery played in legitimising religious authority within elite circles of Sasanian society during the third century.

As Dilley demonstrates, Mani understood the importance of this prevailing
trend in the context of elite Sasanian culture and responded with acumen in
the guise of his *Shābuhragān*. To what extent should this work be considered
an apocalypse? The prevailing trend among scholars has been to view the
Shābuhragān as a work akin to a systematic theology in which Mani outlined
his teachings for Shapur I in the Persian language of the royal court.[32] This is
certainly correct, although the driving mechanism underlying the themes in the
Shābuhragān is evidently apocalyptic. The fragments of the work[33] classified as
eschatological by scholars including David MacKenzie,[34] Manfred Hutter,[35] and

---

[29] A point emphasised by Dilley, "Hell Exists," 222–23.

[30] Dilley, "Hell Exists," 235.

[31] Notably, see Mary Boyce, *Textual Sources for the Study of Zoroastrianism* (Manchester:
Manchester University Press, 1984), 61–62.

[32] Notably in the valuable summary of the work by Reck, "*Shābuhragān.*"

[33] Outlined by D. N. MacKenzie, "Mani's *Shābuhragān*," *Bulletin of the School of Oriental and
African Studies* 42 (1979): 500–3, with an updated discussion by Reck, "*Shābuhragān.*"

[34] MacKenzie, "Mani's *Shābuhragān*," 502–503.

[35] Manfred Hutter, *Manis kosmogonische Šābuhragān-Texte: Edition, Kommentar und literaturgeschichtliche Einordnung der manichäischmittelpersischen Handschriften M98/99I und
M7980-7984* (Wiesbaden: Otto Harrassowitz, 1992), 130–34.

Writing Truth and Secrets

Hans-Joachim Klimkeit[36] outline the appearance of Xradeshahr ("The God of the World of Wisdom," otherwise Jesus the Splendour serving as Judge)[37] and the subsequent judgement conducted by Xradeshahr, during which a separation of the righteous from the evildoers takes place (the righteous and their helpers are the Elect and Hearers), the earths are destroyed and the evil archons including Āz,[38] and Ahriman and all demons and archdemons are immolated in "the great fire." An additional series of fragments (M98I, M99I, M7980, and M7984) have also been identified as belonging to the *Shābuhragān* and are classified as cosmological in orientation.[39] These fragments narrate the creation of the cosmos and the lower earths by key figures in the Manichaean pantheon, including the Living Spirit and the Mother of Life and their role in the creation of the purificatory structures of the cosmos, the evocation of Rōshnshahr ("the God of the World of Light") and Xradeshahr, and their role in "the seduction of the Archons,"[40] which leads in turn to the creation of plants and animals, the construction of the great prison by the Great Builder to house Āz and Ahriman and the New Paradise, a description of the cycles of the sun and moon, and finally an account of the creation by Āz of Gēhmurd (=Gayomard) and Murdiyānag (Adam and Eve).[41] If we compare the contents of these fragments with the elements comprising the "Master-Paradigm" for the identification of the genre of apocalyptic literature devised by John J. Collins, the contents map comfortably onto key areas for the determination of apocalyptic including: Theogony, Cosmogony, Eschatological Crisis, and Judgement.[42] However, absent from these fragments are details regarding the manner of revelation (i.e. the way in which Mani gained his knowledge of these events). There is no account of a vision or an "otherworldly journey," such as we read about in Kartīr's inscriptions, and there is no dialogue between the mediator and the recipient of the revelation (the eschatological portions of the *Shābuhragān* contain some dialogue although it is restricted to the characters in the narrative). As Collins highlights, "[n]ot every writing which expresses apocalyptic eschatology can be classified as an apocalypse,"[43] although the contents and orientation of the fragments identified

---

[36] Hans-Joachim Klimkeit, *Gnosis on the Silk Road. Gnostic Parables, Hymns and Prayers from Central Asia* (New York: Harper Collins, 1993), 242–47.

[37] Thus Reck, "*Shābuhragān*": "His function in *Shābuhragān* as Jesus the Splendour, the origin on Nous, is discussed several times. The function as deliverer of the redeeming wisdom and knowledge belongs to the tasks of the Nous, but the Judge is Jesus himself."

[38] See the discussion by Susanna Towers, *Constructions of Gender in Late Antique Manichaean Cosmological Narrative*, Studia Traditionis Theologiae 34 (Turnhout: Brepols, 2019), 192–210.

[39] Notably, see Hutter, *Manis kosmogonische Šābuhragān-Texte*, 225–35.

[40] See Towers, *Constructions of Gender*, 245–49.

[41] Concerning Gayomard, see the comments by Shaul Shaked, *Dualism in Transformation: Varieties of Religion in Sasanian Iran* (London: School of Oriental and African Studies, 1994), 68–69.

[42] Collins, "Introduction."

[43] Collins, "Introduction," 3.

112   *Nicholas Baker-Brian*

by Sundermann as deriving from the *Shābuhragān* (M 49, etc.; see previously) hint at some level of dialogic exchange on the matter of revelation between Mani and his twin (*nrjmyg*).

2. Mani's Revelatory Self-Authorization in other Manichaean literature

However, there are other works by Mani which emphasize both the manner of the revelation that forms the basis for his theology and his status as a privileged recipient of revelation. The remains of Mani's letter to (it is presumed) his followers in Edessa (likely the same letter identified by al-Nadīm in his list of Mani's letters as the one "to al-Rūhā," the Arabic name for Edessa),[44] the principal city of Osrhoene, present an encounter between Mani and his twin in the following terms:[45]

> The truth and the secrets of which I speak (τὴν ἀλήθειαν καὶ τὰ ἀπόρρητα ἅπερ διαλέγομαι), as well as the laying on of hands which is mine, I did not receive from men or beings of flesh, nor from the intercourse with writings; but when my most blessed father who called me to his grace and did not wish me and the others in the world to perish, saw and pitied me, with the purpose of offering well-being to those who were ready to be chosen by him from the religions, then by his grace he took me away from the council of the multitude which did not know the truth. And he disclosed to me his secrets and those of his undefiled father and of the whole world (καὶ ἀπεκάλυψέ μοι τά τε αὐτοῦ ἀπόρρητα καὶ πατρὸς αὐτοῦ τοῦ ἀχράντου καὶ παντὸς τοῦ κόσμου). He revealed to me how they existed before the creation of the world, and how the foundation for all works, good and evil, was laid, and how they manufactured from the mixture in those times.

In this portion of the letter, which is preserved in Greek translation in a section of the *Life* of Mani (*CMC*) immediately following the excerpts from the apocryphal pseudepigrapha discussed above, Mani recounts in a compressed fashion the encounter with his divine twin (*Syzygos*: here referred to as the "most blessed father" and distinguished from God *qua* God, the "undefiled father") during the period of his youth, and the role played by the twin in his final separation from the southern Mesopotamian Baptist community (Elchasaites?)[46] of this

---

[44] Bayard Dodge, *The Fihrist of al-Nadīm: A Tenth-Century Survey of Muslim Culture*, Volume II (New York and London: Columbia University Press, 1970), 799; cf. Reeves, *Prolegomena*, 117.

[45] *CMC* 64.8–65.22 (Ludwig Koenen and Cornelia Römer, eds., *Der Kölner Mani-Kodex: Über das Werden seines Leibes. Kritische Edition* (Opladen: Westdeutscher, 1988); Iain Gardner and Samuel N. C. Lieu, trans., *Manichaean Texts from the Roman Empire* (Cambridge: Cambridge University Press 2004), 166.

[46] Cf. the critical analysis developed by Gerard P. Luttikhuizen, *The Revelation of Elchasai: Investigations into the Evidence for a Mesopotamian Jewish Apocalypse of the Second Century and Its Reception by Judeo-Christian Propagandists* (Tübingen: Mohr Siebeck, 1985), 153–64.

Writing Truth and Secrets 113

time.[47] There are clear shades of Paul's statement in Gal 1:1 ("an apostle commissioned not by any human authority or human act") in Mani's claim to have received "truth and secrets" not from "men or beings of flesh." There is an additional Pauline parallel in the letter in the description of Mani's dramatic separation from the Baptist council and the abruptness of Paul's rapture in 2 Cor 12:2–4; the aorist ἀπέσπασε (ἀποσπάω: "dragged/torn away from") in the Edessene letter corresponds to ἁρπάζω ("seized/snatched away") in Corinthians and implies an abrupt action befitting, for instance, the impact of divine revelation on a recipient.

Similarly, an excerpt from Mani's *Gospel* also included in the Greek *Life* contains a series of claims about Mani having "seen" (εἶδον) eternal truth. The opening of the *Gospel* begins with a statement of Mani's apostolic credentials: "I, Mannichaeus, apostle of Jesus Christ, through the will of God, the Father of Truth, from whom I came into being." It continues:[48]

From him [sc. God] I have my being, and I exist according to this will. And from him all that is true was revealed to me and from (his) truth I exist. I have seen (the truth of eternity which he revealed). And I declared the truth to my companions; I preached peace to the children of peace; I proclaimed hope to the undying generation; I chose the elect and showed the path leading to the height to those who will go up according to this truth. I have proclaimed hope and revealed this revelation; and have written this immortal gospel, in which I have put down these pre-eminent secret rites and declared great deeds (καὶ τόδε τὸ ἀθάνατον εὐαγγέλιον γέγραφα ἐνθέμενος αὐτῶι ταῦτα τὰ τῆς ὑπεροχῆς ὄργια καὶ μέγιστα ἔργα ἐκφήνας ἐν αὐτῶι), indeed the greatest and holiest of supreme deeds of power. (And) these things which (he revealed) I have made known (to those who live in accordance with) the vision of supreme truth which I have seen, and the most glorious revelation which was revealed to me.

Neither the *Gospel* nor the Edessene letter constitute (by definition of genre) apocalypses, but they are evidently informed by the prevailing spirit of apocalypticism as evidenced by the fact that both excerpts present a causal relationship between the act of revelation, the contents of revelation (comprising "truth and secrets," "the truth of eternity," and "pre-eminent secret rites"), and the consolidation of Mani's authority as the recipient of revelation on his roles as apostle and author. As Mani states clearly in the *Gospel*, his authority derived from his role in the apocalyptic cycle: as the recipient of revelation, he was qualified to teach about "hope and peace," and in turn, he established a community by choosing his Elect and Hearers. As Dilley notes, the association between apocalyptic truth and individual authority seems to have been especially prized in the context of Sasanian society of the third century. To return to the epigraphic texts memorialising the achievements of Kartīr dating from the reign of Bahram II,

---

[47] On the role of the twin in the *Life*, see esp. Charles Stang, *Our Divine Double* (Cambridge, MA: Harvard University Press, 2016), 145–84.

[48] *CMC* 66.18–68.5; Gardner and Lieu, trans., *Manichaean Texts*, 157.

114   *Nicholas Baker-Brian*

it is worthwhile repeating the following statement (§ 36) in order to highlight the association between revelation and the consolidation of religious authority: "But afterwards, when once the gods had shown me these matters concerning the hereafter in this way, then I became more obedient and well-wishing towards the gods and more liberal and true to my own soul and I became more confident about this worship and the rites which are performed in the empire."[49]

Authority determined by apocalyptic was not, however, always accepted. It is no coincidence that the clearest examples of Mani's revelatory experiences are preserved in the Greek *Life* of the apostle. Both excerpts are cited at the end of a section (pp. 45–72 of the Codex) attributed to Baraiēs in which citations from the antediluvian pseudepigrapha of Adam, Sethel, Enosh, Shem, and Enoch, in addition to Paul's revelation of Christ from 2 Cor 12:2–5 and Gal 1:11–12, are also included. (The *Life* is arranged according to tradents and key individuals from the early Manichaean community, including Baraiēs, Timotheos, Abiesus, Innaios, Zacheas, Koustaios, and Ana, who provide [idealised] details of key events from Mani's life.)[50] In a lacunose portion of the Codex, Baraiēs introduces his concerns: to interpret Mani's apostleship for the sake of "this generation," to explain the significance of the Paraclete to Mani's apostleship, and – the first sign of dissent – to challenge the idea that Mani's followers had written about his rapture for boastful reasons alone (with an intertextual echo here of 2 Cor 12:1). In this regard, Baraiēs sets out carefully the precedents for the apostleship of "our generation" together with precedents for writing down the details of prior revelations for the sake of posterity, a concern which he summarises in the following way:[51]

In short all the most blessed apostles, saviours, evangelists and prophets of truth – each of them observed, as the living hope was revealed to him for proclamation, and wrote and has handed it down and deposited it for the reminding of the future sons of (the holy) spirit who would know the perception of his voice.

Baraiēs was evidently a highly privileged witness to the story of Mani's life. In the *Life*, his testimony includes a first-person account (i. e., presented as Mani's own words) of Mani's encounter with his twin and the nature of Mani's earthly existence (pp. 18–26), Mani's apostolic credentials (pp. 45–72), the early stages of his separation from the Baptists (pp. 72–74), and a further first-person narrative in which Mani debates with the Baptist elders and repudiates their rites and way of life (pp. 80–93). As Sam Lieu notes, these sections give the impression of being

---

[49] MacKenzie, "Kerdir's Inscription," 60–61.

[50] Many are known from other Manichaean (and non-Manichaean) sources; notably, see Jürgen Tubach, "Die Namen von Manis Jüngern und Ihre Herkunft," in *Atti del Terzo Congresso Internazionale di Studi: Manicheismo e Oriente Cristiano Antico*, ed. Luigi Cirillo and Alois van Tongerloo (Leuven: Brepols, 1997), 375–93.

[51] *CMC* 62.9–63.1; Gardner and Lieu, trans., *Manichaean Texts*, 57.

Writing Truth and Secrets   115

early and independent.[52] It is likely the case that Baraiēs was one of Mani's very first disciples, possibly a Syriac-speaking follower of the apostle whose name derives from the honorific, Bar Ḥayyē, "Son of Life."[53] He is a tradent in the *Life* alongside other known early disciples of Mani (including Innaios, the successor of Sisinnios who had been the first head of the Manichaean church after Mani), and he is recalled as an early follower by posterity, as seen by his inclusion among Mani's disciples in the Byzantine-era abjuration formulas.[54] As noted, he is also referred to in the *Life* as "the Teacher," a term denoting a senior leadership role in the early Manichaean church. In this regard, Baraiēs was charged with the serious responsibility of defending Mani against those who had doubted his apocalyptic credentials (emphasis added):[55]

In all the books of our father there are very many other extraordinary events similar to these, which make known his revelation and the rapture of his mission. For great is this magnificent coming which comes to (us) through the Paraclete, the spirit of truth. For what purpose and what reason have we dealt with such things, when we have been convinced once for all that this mission excels in its revelations? *It is because of the reasonings of those who have clothed themselves in unbelief and think nothing of this revelation and vision of our father, that we have repeated from our forefathers their rapture and each one's revelation, so that we may realise that the commission of the (earlier) apostles was likewise of (this nature).* For when each of them was seized, (everything he saw) and heard he wrote down and made known, and himself became a witness of his own revelation; while his disciples became the seal of his sending.

Eibert Tigchelaar argues that the strand in the *Life* which emphasises the apocalyptic credentials of Mani's apostleship (pp. 45–72 of the codex) was developed by the editor(s) of the work from a homily originally delivered by Baraiēs in which he addressed the community directly and imparted a lesson about discipleship.[56] The homily culminated with a clear allusion to 1 Cor 9:2 on the issue of remaining loyal even when confronted by doubters: "you are the very seal of my apostleship." In light of the contemporary complaints outlined by Baraiēs, primarily the impugning of the authenticity of Mani's apostleship, one imagines that the need to strengthen the resolve of Mani's followers was a pressing matter indeed. Therefore, the charge against Mani was old and dated from the first generation of his disciples, even perhaps from the time of Mani himself. Understandably, Tigchelaar does not attempt to excavate the context for the complaint about Mani's authenticity. However, the question of who and what constitutes an authentic teacher of divine revelation is one that engaged Mani deeply, which is apparent also in the remains of the *Shābuhragān*.

---

[52] Samuel N.C. Lieu, *Manichaeism in Mesopotamia and the Roman East* (Leiden: Brill, 1994), 81.

[53] Tubach, "Die Namen von Manis Jüngern," 382–83.

[54] Lieu, *Manichaeism in Mesopotamia and the Roman East*, 236–37.

[55] *CMC* 70.10–72.4; Gardner and Lieu, trans., *Manichaean Texts*, 58. My emphasis.

[56] Tigchelaar, "Baraies on Mani's Rapture," 435.

116 Nicholas Baker-Brian

According to *Shābuhragān* (M473, etc.), in the period prior to the appearance of Xradeshahr in the "last age," false prophets will appear and proclaim:

"[w]e are the ones who obey the instructions of the gods, [and you should go] along this path of ours." Most men [are] deceived and walk according to their (the false prophets') will (to do) evil deeds. And the righteous one who does not believe in his own religion will also follow suit.[57]

According to Mani in the work dedicated for Shapur I, believers at this time will be led astray by the teachings of false prophets, and those who consider themselves or are considered by others to be righteous (*dynwr*: "a relapsing Manichaean")[58] will also fall foul of spurious religions because they have ceased to believe in the true religion. In Manichaean terms, false prophets can be identified as those whose teachings lack the divine commission of Jesus the Splendour, "hypostasized" as the Light-Nous or Light Mind,[59] the figure responsible for inspiring all apostles: Xradeshahr also serves as Jesus the Splendour in this portion of the work since he is the one who, "first [gave] that male creation, the original first human being (Adam), wisdom and knowledge, and (who) afterwards from time to time and from age to age sent wisdom and knowledge to man[kind]."[60] Mani's claim regarding the existence of false prophets is clearly an aspect of his theology of apostleship whereby a catena of apostles, stretching all the way back to Adam but also accommodating "regional" apostles, including Buddha and Zoroaster (see previously), culminates in the time of his own apostleship: On the one hand, authentic teachers of "wisdom and knowledge" are present in the world at specific points in time, while *correlatively* a chain of false prophets are also engaged in misleading humankind with an antithetical message. The italic emphasis here highlights the absence of clear evidence regarding the precise identities of these false prophets, although Patristic-era testimony from figures such as Faustus, the bishop of the Manichaean community in Numidian Milevis, indicate Manichaean contempt of Moses (Faustus *apud* Augustine, *Contra Faustum* 14.1), a detail which correlates with later testimony from Islamic sources for Mani (see the following). Guy Stroumsa has argued that Mani's conception of false prophecy is best understood as residing in the nexus of traditions positing the doctrine of the "true prophet," which crystallises in the Pseudo-Clementine literature (viz. *Homilies*) of the third (?) century.[61] Stroumsa pro-

---

[57] Klimkeit, trans., *Gnosis on the Silk Road*, 242; Boyce, *A Reader in Manichaean Middle Persian and Parthian*, 77, n. 1: "the speakers are the false prophets who will appear at this time."

[58] MacKenzie, "Mani's *Shābuhragān*," 522 n. 9.

[59] Cf. Charles Stang, *Our Divine Double*, 168.

[60] Klimkeit, trans., *Gnosis on the Silk Road*, 242.

[61] Guy G. Stroumsa, *The Making of the Abrahamic Religions in Late Antiquity* (Oxford: Oxford University Press, 2015), 66–69. Regarding the dating of the Pseudo-Clementine literature, see F. Stanley Jones, "The Pseudo Clementines: A History of Research," *The Second Century: A Journal of Early Christian Studies* 2 (1982): 1–33, 63–96.

Writing Truth and Secrets 117

poses the transmission of this doctrine to Mani via the Elchasaites (the Baptisers of the *Life*) and the recapitulation of the idea in the lost *Book of Elchasai* (see the testimony of Hippolytus, *Refutations* 9.15.3).[62] Keeping in mind the numerous uncertainties raised by the influence and adaptation of this doctrine in Clementine literature, and among the Elchasaites and the Manichaeans, Mani's conception of false prophets could well have approximated to the description offered by Stroumsa: "In each generation ... the true prophet is preceded by a false prophet, an impostor sent by Satan who masquerades as the true prophet. Truth and falsehood are thus for ever coupled, throughout the ages, in 'syzygies' of opposites. The false prophets are 'the prophets of this world,' who remain forever ignorant of eternal truth."[63] This is certainly the underlying meaning of Mani's interest in false prophets in the *Shābuhragān*.

3. Bardaisan and Mani on Revelatory Authorization

Turning to another book by Mani, the *Book of Mysteries*, we encounter testimony in the ninth-century *Chronicle of Ibn Wadih* by Ya'qūbi claiming that Mani in the *Book of Mysteries* sought to "discredit the signs of the prophets."[64] The historic defence of prophecy (*Kitāb a'lām al-nubuwwa*) by Abū Ḥātim al-Rāzī from the following century preserves Abū Bakr al-Rāzī's (against whom Abū Ḥātim was writing) high praise of Mani's *Book of Mysteries* on the basis of its characterisation of Moses as a false prophet:[65] "[al- Rāzī] cited the claim of the Manichaeans that Moses was among the apostles of the satans, and he [al- Rāzī] said: 'Let anyone who is concerned about this read the *Book of Books* of the Manichaeans. Then he will become acquainted with the admirable things in their statements about Judaism from the time of Abraham until the time of Jesus'."[66] Furthermore, a tenth century manuscript attributed to a Mu'tazilite author states that Mani's *Book of Mysteries*, "impugned the miracles performed by Moses."[67] Evidently, therefore, Mani was concerned with disputing the teachings of prophets whom he regarded as spurious in more than one of his works. The *Book of Mysteries* is lost to posterity,[68] although a detailed description of its contents by way of

---

[62] Collected by Luttikhuizen, *The Revelation of Elchasai*, 49.

[63] Stroumsa, *The Making of the Abrahamic Religions*, 66.

[64] Reeves, trans., *Prolegomena*, 105; see also the comments by Konrad Kessler, *Mani: Forschungen über die manichäische Religion* (Berlin: Georg Reimer, 1889), 191–93.

[65] The broader anti-Jewish and anti-Torah ideas of al-Rāzī are discussed by Steven M. Wasserstrom, *Between Muslim and Jew: The Problem of Symbiosis under Early Islam* (Princeton: Princeton University Press, 1995), 148–55.

[66] Reeves, trans., *Prolegomena*, 105–6.

[67] Reeves, trans., *Prolegomena*, 108; Richard C. Martin, "The Identification of Two Mu'tazilite MSS," *Journal of the American Oriental Society* 98 (1978): 389–93.

[68] Michel Tardieu (*Manichaeism*, trans. M. B. DeBevoise [Urbana and Chicago: University

118   Nicholas Baker-Brian

summation of its chapters was included by al-Nadīm in his *Fihrist*. According
to the testimony of this witness, the work comprised eighteen chapters and was
oriented – not entirely, but largely – along apocalyptic lines. The second chapter
was dedicated "to the testimony of Yistāsar about the Beloved,"[69] a section based
on a Christianised portion of the apocalyptic work, the Parthian-era *Oracles
of Hystaspes*, the legendary king converted by Zoroaster.[70] Mani's exegesis of
apocalypses continued across the third chapter and the tenth chapter and appear
to have been concerned with an Apocalypse of James (*Yaʿqūb*), the brother of
Jesus, and an Apocalypse (Testament?) of Adam respectively, and the way in
which both works related to the apostleship of Jesus and of Mani.[71] Chapter sev-
enteen comprised an assessment of the prophets, presumably the polemic against
false prophets indicated by Yaʿqūbi.[72] The terminal chapter concerned "The Final
Judgement" and was framed according to the relationship between the *eschaton*
and resurrection (Arabic: *al-qiyama*).[73]

Among the other chapter summations for the *Book of Mysteries* supplied by
al-Nadīm, we also encounter "a chapter [ch. 1] discussing the Dayṣāniyya ... a
chapter [ch. 12] (on) the teachings of the Dayṣāniyya about the soul and the
body [and] a chapter [ch. 13] (containing) a refutation of the Dayṣāniyya on the
Living Soul."[74] The Dayṣāniyya are the Bardaiṣanites, the putative followers of
Bardaiṣan, the philosopher-theologian of Edessa who died in 222 CE, shortly
after the birth of Mani (ca. 216 CE). Bardaiṣan developed his reputation as a
deeply learned figure during his time embedded in the court of Abgar VIII, the
ruler of Edessa, prior to the awarding of Roman *colonia* status in 214 during
the reign of Caracalla. After his death, his followers remained concentrated in
Osrhoene but also in Mesopotamia.[75] Intellectual histories of early Syrian Christianity traditionally propose an association between the teachings of Bardaiṣan
and Mani that is not wholly unwarranted,[76] although significant differences are
evident between their respective theologies, a feature which is apparent in Mani's

---

of Illinois Press, 2008], 41) situates the *Book of Mysteries* between 260–270 CE and states that it
"was composed while Mani was in contact with the Christian communities of Syria and Mesopotamia."

[69] Reeves, trans., *Prolegomena*, 106.

[70] Brilliantly demonstrated by John C. Reeves, "An Enochic Citation in *Barnabas* 4:3 and
the *Oracles of Hystaspes*," in *Pursuing the Text: Studies in Honor of Ben Zion Wacholder on the
Occasion of his Seventieth Birthday*, ed. John C. Reeves and John Kampen (Sheffield: Sheffield
Academic Press, 1994), 269–72; cf. the analysis by Tardieu, *Manichaeism*, 38.

[71] See the commentary by Reeves, *Prolegomena*, 106–7; cf. Tardieu, *Manichaeism*, 38–39.

[72] Tardieu, *Manichaeism*, 41.

[73] Tardieu, *Manichaeism*, 41; cf. Reeves, *Prolegomena*, 107.

[74] Reeves, trans. *Prolegomena*, 107.

[75] Prods Oktor Skjærvø, "Bardesanes," *Encyclopaedia Iranica*, https://www.iranicaonline.
org/articles/bardesanes-syr (accessed November 2022).

[76] For a summary of scholarly arguments, see H. J. W. Drijvers, *Bardaisan of Edessa* (Piscataway, NJ: Gorgias Press, 2014), 47–67.

Writing Truth and Secrets 119

dedication of chapters in his *Book of Mysteries*, designed to refute the teachings of Bardaiṣan's school. The dispute between Mani and the Dayṣāniyya over the Living Soul is a case in point. The orientation of chapter thirteen is preserved by Bīrūnī in his survey of India (*Taḥqīq mā lil-Hind*) in which it is reported that Mani challenged the Bardaiṣanites' conception of the soul's purification. Bīrūnī claims to cite directly from the *Book of Mysteries* and the citation indicates that it is the Bardaiṣanites rather than Bardaiṣan himself which are Mani's direct target: "For [Mani] says also: 'The Dayṣāniyya are of the opinion that the ascension and purification of the Living Soul [i.e., divine light imprisoned into matter] takes place in the body. They do not know that the body is the enemy of the soul and that [the body] forbids [the soul] to make ascent, for it [the body] is a prison and an instrument of torture for it [the soul]. If this human form was associated with Truth, its creator would not let it wear out or experience harm, and he would not need it to propagate sexually by means of semen in wombs.'"[77] Bardaiṣan's theology – here encompassing his anthropology also – is generally regarded as more "optimistic"[78] than Mani's, for whom the body and the *genus* Matter were regarded as irredeemably evil, in contrast to Bardaiṣan's positive evaluation of the created order: "... the discussion of Mani with Bardaiṣan indirectly confirms our view of Bardaiṣan, as the 'Book of Mysteries' is of the third century and belongs to the Manichaean canon, Bardaiṣan has a positive attitude towards matter, and consequently towards sexuality, which is a form of purification."[79]

Drawing on the *Book of the Law of Countries*, a late third century work by a disciple of Bardaiṣan[80] ("the only contiguous text from Bardaiṣan's community that has come down to us"),[81] Ute Possekel has highlighted Bardaiṣan's rejection of any form of apocalypse or apocalyptic imagery in communicating his understanding of the final outcome of the world at the point of its judgement.[82] Similar to Mani, Bardaiṣan had developed a theology of creation based around the idea of the mixing of the cardinal elements, but in contrast to Mani it was God rather than an evil power who had fashioned the world out of this mixture. A primary factor in Bardaiṣanite cosmology, therefore, was the promotion of the inherent goodness of creation, a position deriving in part from Bardaiṣan's rejection of the Marcionite theology of two gods, one of whom (the less good one) was the creator. In light of this cosmology, human beings had enormous potential

---

[77] Reeves, trans., *Prolegomena*, 108; cf. Tardieu, *Manichaeism*, 40.

[78] Cf. Gardner, *The Founder of Manichaeism*, 90–91.

[79] Drijvers, *Bardaisan of Edessa*, 228.

[80] H. J. W. Drijvers, *The Book of the Laws of Countries: A Dialogue on Fate of Bardaisan of Edessa* (Piscataway, NJ: Gorgias Press, 2007).

[81] Ute Possekel, "Expectations of the End in Early Syriac Christianity," *Hugoye: Journal of Syriac Studies* 11 (2011): 65.

[82] Possekel, "Expectations of the End," 63–94; also, Ilaria L. E. Ramelli, *Bardaisan of Edessa: A Reassessment of the Evidence and a New Interpretation* (Piscataway, NJ: Gorgias Press, 2009), 90.

120 Nicholas Baker-Brian

to be forever good and, as such, a key feature of Bardaiṣan's theology was the promotion of human free-will which stood in contradistinction to prevailing theologies of astral determinism.[83] For Bardaiṣan, the final judgement will comprise the perfecting of creation where opportunities for strife and harm will be eradicated. Thus, in Bardaiṣanite theology irenic imagery of the final times replaced apocalyptic scenes of disorder, conflict, and chaos, where the possibility of harm arising from mixing of the natural elements will be replaced, according to the author of the *Book of the Law of Countries,* by: "a different intermixture. In this new world all evil damaging influences will have ceased and all revolts will have ended, the foolish will be convinced and every lack supplied, and peace and perfect quiet will reign through the gift of the Lord of all natures."[84]

As Possekel highlights, Bardaiṣan's eschatology stands in contrast to the prevailing culture of apocalypticism which, as an intellectual operating in Edessa during the late second/early third century, he would have been more than familiar with.[85] Possekel adduces two reasons behind Bardaiṣan's rejection of apocalypticism. The first, as noted above, derived from "one of his major goals [which] was to refute the Marcionite claim of the two gods ... [which would have provided] reason enough to avoid images of a final cosmic battle."[86] (Apocalypticism for Possekel is almost entirely oriented towards eschatology rather than experiences of rapture and the disclosure of heavenly secrets.) The second reason derives from the thesis developed by scholars from the 1970s onwards which viewed apocalypticism as a genre utilised largely by individuals and groups residing on the margins of society.[87] As an intellectual with connections at court, Bardaiṣan – so the argument goes – had no reason to utilise apocalyptic imagery or the genre of the apocalypse as a medium for his theology. This point is somewhat unconvincing in light of the important role we know apocalyptic themes, imagery, and literature played in the elite circles of Sasanian society during the third century. Kartīr's use of apocalyptic imagery in his inscriptions demonstrates elite engagement with apocalypticism, as does Mani's promotion of his theology via the apocalyptic and eschatologically themed *Shābuhragān,* a work directed at the heart of the Sasanian court. It is unlikely then that a genre with marginal appeal would have been chosen to engage the most powerful individuals and parties in west Asia.

Nevertheless, Possekel's argument regarding Bardaiṣan and his followers' repudiation of apocalypticism is valid and should certainly be regarded as one of the defining features of Bardaiṣan's contribution to the theological culture of

---

[83] See Ramelli, *Bardaisan of Edessa*, 115–45.
[84] *The Book of the Laws of Countries* 46 (Drijvers, *Book of the Laws of Countries*, 62, 15–18).
[85] Possekel, "Expectations of the End," 75–77.
[86] Possekel, "Expectations of the End," 77.
[87] Possekel, "Expectations of the End," 77–80 (including a useful summary of the scholarship, n. 43).

Writing Truth and Secrets 121

the late second and early third century.[88] Indeed, of all the suspects we could consider to be behind Baraiēs' complaint from p. 71 of the codex about the critics of Mani who reject his theology on the basis of its apocalyptic frame ("those who have clothed themselves in unbelief and think nothing of this revelation and vision of our father [Mani]"), it is Bardaiṣan and the Bardaiṣanites who would most fit the bill. If we regard Baraiēs as a first-generation or even – at the latest – a second-generation disciple of Mani, the rejection of Mani's theology as a result of the prominence of his apocalypticism emerges very early in the development of Mani's religion and, in light of Baraiēs' apology comprising the parabiblical and biblical material assembled to defend the revelatory core of Mani's theology (preserved across pp. 45–72 of the Greek *Life*), the Bardaiṣanites' challenge must have been deemed a very serious threat to the credibility of Mani's message. Indeed, on the basis of the evidence for the *Book of Mysteries*, there are grounds to believe that the Bardaiṣanites had challenged Mani directly on this very matter and that the *Book of Mysteries* was Mani's response to them. The testimony of Islamic-era authors highlights the apocalyptic orientation of Mani's work, which interestingly appropriates the identical title of a "Book of Mysteries" credited by Ephrem of Nisibis to Bardaiṣan himself.[89] As noted, al-Nadīm's reliable summary of the *Book of Mysteries* indicates that the work was directed against the Bardaiṣanites, and that it utilised pseudepigraphic apocalypses (James; Adam) and oracular material with a visionary bent (Hystaspes: cf. Lactantius, *Divine Institutes* 7.18.2),[90] and included a chapter on "the prophets," which as we know from other witnesses engaged with the notion of false prophets, and which in all likelihood also included a discussion of the parallel conception of true prophets. Furthermore, a number of the remaining chapters focused on apocalyptic and eschatological themes including, as noted, a chapter on the fate of souls (collectivised as the Living Soul) at the point of judgement (which Mani set against Bardaiṣanite soteriology), a chapter [16] on the Three days, a "shorthand" formula for a description of Mani's own eschatological position (which is described in detail in a chapter [no. 39] entitled, "Concerning the Three Days and the Two Deaths," from the *Kephalaia of the Teacher*), and a chapter [18] on the final judgement and the resurrection.

Should the association between the testimony of Baraiēs and the rejection of apocalypticism by Bardaisan and his followers be valid, we are witness to an early challenge to Mani's authority, one indeed dating from his own lifetime. We know

---

[88] As argued by Ramelli, *Bardaisan of Edessa*, 13.

[89] Cf. Drijvers, *Bardaisan of Edessa*, 181; Tardieu, *Manichaeism*, 38. On the significance of this title and the secret, cosmological teachings revealed in books bearing it, see Guy G. Stroumsa, *The Scriptural Universe of Ancient Christianity* (Cambridge, MA: Harvard University Press, 2016), 21.

[90] Notably, Reeves, "An Enochic Citation," 265–68.

122   *Nicholas Baker-Brian*

very little about the historical circumstances behind the *Shābuhragān*,[91] but it is clear from the fragments and testimony of the work that Mani privileged the revelatory orientation of his teachings for the benefit of Shapur I in the awareness that his ideas would be readily received by an audience that was both familiar with and valued "discourse on otherworldly realms."[92] Indeed, as Dilley has argued, the visions of these otherworldly realms – Heaven and Hell – in this work and cognate texts (including 2 Ke 342 and the Baraiēs material from the *CMC*) ultimately had an ethical orientation: "The common message of these texts was two-fold: First, that good deeds will aid the soul in its ascent to heaven; second, that bad deeds will be punished in hell, often in a spectacular manner related to the crime, known in Latin as the *lex talionis*."[93] Such a point of emphasis in the *Shābuhragān* (cf. al-Nadīm's summary of the "three paths apportioned for the souls of humans")[94] would make the work effectively a *mirror* for Shapur I. However, the apocalyptic orientation for Mani's eschatology faced a serious challenge, a fact made clear by the testimony of Baraiēs, who records that the "revelation and vision of our father" had been rejected by an unnamed party: "those who have put on unbelief." Among the most likely suspects for those repudiating Mani's revelation are the followers of Bardaisan who, in line with the theology of their teacher, also chose to frame the arrival of the eschatological aeon in a form very different from established apocalyptic narratives of cosmic conflict and redemption.

Decades of research into Manichaeism have demonstrated that the religion did not arrive pristine and fully-formed in the years of Mani's active life as teacher and prophet. In the case highlighted by Iain Gardner, Mani's authority as the pre-eminent teacher of theological dualism among his followers emerged only in the period after his death, when Mani's own emphasis on Jesus as the pre-eminent teacher of the two natures (e.g. Mt 7:17–19) was displaced by Mani's followers, who asserted Mani as the progenitor of the religion's fundamental dualistic datum.[95] A similar development is also discernible in the matter of Mani's authorial status. In a move intended to defend Mani's work against its detractors, it was Baraiēs, an early disciple, who aligned Mani's *Living Gospel* and

---

[91] Notably, the caveat by Paul Dilley, "Mani's Wisdom at the Court of the Persian Kings: The Genre and Context of the Chester Beatty *Kephalaia*," in *Mani at the Court of the Persian Kings: Studies on the Chester Beatty* Kephalaia *Codex*, ed. Iain Gardner, Jason BeDuhn, and Paul Dilley, Nag Hammadi and Manichaean Studies 87 (Leiden: Brill, 2015), 39–40.

[92] Dilley, "Hell Exists," 245.

[93] Dilley, "Hell Exists," 225.

[94] Reeves, trans., *Prolegomena*, 218.

[95] Iain Gardner, "Dualism in Mani and Manichaeism," *Chora* 13 (2015): 417–36; on the "Two Trees" in Mani's thought, see John Kevin Coyle, "Good Tree, Bad Tree: The Matthean/Lukan Paradigm in Manichaeism and Its Opponents," in *The Reception and Interpretation of the Bible in Late Antiquity: Proceedings of the Montreal Colloquium in Honour of Charles Kannengiesser, 11–13 October 2006*, ed. Lorenzo Di Tomasso and Lucian Turcescu (Leiden: Brill, 2006), 121–44.

Writing Truth and Secrets 123

Letter to Edessa with the purportedly ancient *Apocalypse of Adam, Apocalypse of Sethel, Apocalypse of Enosh, Apocalypse of Shem,* and *Apocalypse of Enoch* in addition to Paul's Second Letter to the Corinthians and his Letter to the Galatians. Baraiēs' endeavour proposed that Mani's writings were on a par with these mysterious and revered testaments authored by prophetically inspired figures from the past, a position of rank and authority that was demonstrably absent from Mani's writings during his lifetime – a conclusion which derives from the fact of their repudiation by the Bardaiṣanites. In the case of Mani, therefore, the relationship between authorship and authority – specifically the question of religious authority framed according to apocalyptic theology – was in the late third century at least, a matter of considerable negotiation.

Bibliography

Boyce, Mary. *A Reader in Manichaean Middle Persian and Parthian.* Acta Iranica 9. Leiden: Brill, 1975.

Boyce, Mary. *Textual Sources for the Study of Zoroastrianism.* Manchester: Manchester University Press, 1984.

Burns, Dylan. *Apocalypse of the Alien God: Platonism and the Exile of Sethian Gnosticism.* Philadelphia: University of Pennsylvania Press, 2014.

Collins, John J. "Introduction: Towards the Morphology of a Genre." *Semeia* 14 (1979): 1–20.

Coyle, John Kevin. "Good Tree, Bad Tree: The Matthean/Lukan Paradigm in Manichaeism and Its Opponents." Pages 121–144 in *The Reception and Interpretation of the Bible in Late Antiquity: Proceedings of the Montreal Colloquium in Honour of Charles Kannengiesser, 11–13 October 2006.* Edited by Lorenzo Di Tomasso and Lucian Turcescu. Leiden: Brill, 2006.

Dilley, Paul. "'Hell Exists, and We Have Seen the Place Where It Is': Rapture and Religious Competition in Sasanian Iran." Pages 211–246 in *Mani at the Court of the Persian Kings: Studies on the Chester Beatty Kephalaia Codex.* Edited by Iain Gardner, Jason BeDuhn, and Paul Dilley. Nag Hammadi and Manichaean Studies 87. Leiden: Brill, 2015.

Dilley, Paul. "Mani's Wisdom at the Court of the Persian Kings: The Genre and Context of the Chester Beatty *Kephalaia.*" Pages 15–51 in *Mani at the Court of the Persian Kings: Studies on the Chester Beatty Kephalaia Codex.* Edited by Iain Gardner, Jason BeDuhn, and Paul Dilley. Nag Hammadi and Manichaean Studies 87. Leiden: Brill, 2015.

Dodge, Bayard. *The Fihrist of al-Nadīm: A Tenth-Century Survey of Muslim Culture.* Vol. 2. New York and London: Columbia University Press, 1970.

Drijvers, H. J. W. *Bardaisan of Edessa.* Piscataway, NJ: Gorgias Press, 2014.

Drijvers, H. J. W. *The Book of the Laws of Countries: A Dialogue on Fate of Bardaisan of Edessa.* Piscataway, NJ: Gorgias Press, 2007.

Durkin-Meisterernst, Desmond. *Dictionary of Manichaean Texts, Volume III: Texts from Central Asia and China.* Turnhout: Brepols, 2004.

Gardner, Iain. "Dualism in Mani and Manichaeism." *Chora* 13 (2015): 417–436.

Gardner, Iain. *The Founder of Manichaeism: Rethinking the Life of Mani.* Cambridge: Cambridge University Press, 2020.

124   *Nicholas Baker-Brian*

Gardner, Iain. *Mani's Epistles: The Surviving Parts of the Coptic Codex Berlin P.15998*. Manichäische Handschriften der Staatlichen Museen zu Berlin. Stuttgart: Kohlhammer, 2022.

Gardner, Iain. "Mani's Last Days." Pages 159–201 in *Mani at the Court of the Persian Kings: Studies on the Chester Beatty* Kephalaia *Codex*. Edited by Iain Gardner, Jason BeDuhn, and Paul Dilley. Nag Hammadi and Manichaean Studies 87. Leiden: Brill, 2015.

Gardner, Iain, Jason BeDuhn, and Paul C. Dilley, eds. *The Chapters of the Wisdom of My Lord Mani, Part III: Pages 343–442 (Chapters 321–347)*. Nag Hammadi and Manichaean Studies 92. Leiden: Brill, 2018.

Gardner, Iain and Samuel N. C. Lieu, trans. *Manichaean Texts from the Roman Empire*. Cambridge: Cambridge University Press 2004.

Gerson, Lloyd P., ed. *Plotinus. The Enneads*. Cambridge: Cambridge University Press, 2018.

Hutter, Manfred. *Manis kosmogonische Šābuhragān-Texte: Edition, Kommentar und literaturgeschichtliche Einordnung der manichäischmittelpersischen Handschriften M98/ 99I und M7980–7984*. Wiesbaden: Otto Harrassowitz, 1992.

Kessler, Konrad. *Mani: Forschungen über die manichäische Religion*. Berlin: Georg Reimer, 1889.

Klimkeit, Hans-Joachim. *Gnosis on the Silk Road. Gnostic Parables, Hymns and Prayers from Central Asia*. New York: Harper Collins, 1993.

Koenen, Ludwig and Cornelia Römer, eds. *Der Kölner Mani-Kodex: Über das Werden seines Leibes. Kritische Edition*. Opladen: Westdeutscher, 1988.

Luttikhuizen, Gerard P. *The Revelation of Elchasai: Investigations into the Evidence for a Mesopotamian Jewish Apocalypse of the Second Century and Its Reception by Judeo-Christian Propagandists*. Tübingen: Mohr Siebeck, 1985.

MacKenzie, D. N. "Kerdir's Inscription." Pages 35–72 in *The Sasanian Rock Reliefs at Naqsh-i Rustam*. Edited by Georgina Herrmann. Berlin: D. Reimer, 1989.

MacKenzie, D. N. "Mani's *Shābuhragān*." *Bulletin of the School of Oriental and African Studies* 42 (1979): 500–503.

Martin, Richard C. "The Identification of Two Muʿtazilite MSS." *Journal of the American Oriental Society* 98 (1978): 389–393.

Possekel, Ute. "Expectations of the End in Early Syriac Christianity." *Hugoye: Journal of Syriac Studies* 11 (2011): 63–94.

Ramelli, Ilaria L. E. *Bardaisan of Edessa: A Reassessment of the Evidence and a New Interpretation*. Piscataway, NJ: Gorgias Press, 2009.

Reck, Christiane. "*Shābuhragān*." *Encyclopaedia Iranica* 2010, https://iranicaonline.org/ articles/sabuhragan.

Reeves, John C. "An Enochic Citation in *Barnabas* 4:3 and the *Oracles of Hystaspes*." Pages 269–272 in *Pursuing the Text: Studies in Honor of Ben Zion Wacholder on the Occasion of his Seventieth Birthday*. Edited by John C. Reeves and John Kampen. Sheffield: Sheffield Academic Press, 1994.

Reeves, John C. *Heralds of That Good Realm: Syro-Mesopotamian Gnosis and Jewish Traditions*. Leiden: Brill 1996.

Reeves, John C. *Prolegomena to a History of Islamicate Manichaeism*. Sheffield: Equinox, 2011.

Ries, Julien. "Baraiès le Didascale dans le Codex Mani: Nature, Structure et Valeur de son Témoignage sur Mani et sa Doctrine." Pages 305–311 in *Atti del Terzo Congresso Inter-*

nazionale di Studi: Manicheismo e Oriente Cristiano Antico. Edited by Luigi Cirillo and Alois van Tongerloo. Leuven: Brepols, 1997.

Römer, Cornelia. "Die Datierung des Kölner Mani-Kodex." *Zeitschrift für Papyrologie und Epigraphik* 220 (2021): 94–96.

Shaked, Shaul. *Dualism in Transformation: Varieties of Religion in Sasanian Iran.* London: School of Oriental and African Studies, 1994.

Skjærvø, Prods Oktor. "Bardesanes." *Encyclopaedia Iranica.* https://www.iranicaonline.org/articles/bardesanes-syr.

Skjærvø, Prods Oktor. "Counter-Manichaean Elements in Kerdīr's Inscriptions: Irano-Manichaica II." Pages 313–342 in *Atti del Terzo Congresso Internazionale di Studi: Manicheismo e Oriente Cristiano Antico.* Edited by Luigi Cirillo and Alois van Tongerloo. Leuven: Brepols, 1997.

Stang, Charles. *Our Divine Double.* Cambridge, MA: Harvard University Press, 2016.

Stroumsa, Guy G. *The Making of the Abrahamic Religions in Late Antiquity.* Oxford: Oxford University Press, 2015.

Stroumsa, Guy G. *The Scriptural Universe of Ancient Christianity.* Cambridge, MA: Harvard University Press, 2016.

Sundermann, Werner. *Mitteliranische manichäische Texte kirchengeschichtlichen Inhalts.* Berliner Turfantexte XI. Berlin: Akademie, 1981.

Tardieu, Michel. *Manichaeism.* Transltaed by M. B. DeBevoise. Urbana and Chicago: University of Illinois Press, 2008.

Tigchelaar, Eibert. "Baraies on Mani's Rapture, Paul, and the Antediluvian Apostles." Pages 429–441 in *The Wisdom of Egypt. Jewish, Early Christian, and Gnostic Essays in Honour of Gerard P. Luttikhuizen.* Edited by Anthony Hilhorst and George H. van Kooten. Leiden: Brill, 2001.

Towers, Susanna. *Constructions of Gender in Late Antique Manichaean Cosmological Narrative.* Studia Traditionis Theologiae 34. Turnhout: Brepols, 2019.

Tubach, Jürgen. "Die Namen von Manis Jüngern und Ihre Herkunft." Pages 375–393 in *Atti del Terzo Congresso Internazionale di Studi: Manicheismo e Oriente Cristiano Antico.* Edited by Luigi Cirillo and Alois van Tongerlo. Leuven: Brepols, 1997.

Wasserstrom, Steven M. *Between Muslim and Jew: The Problem of Symbiosis under Early Islam.* Princeton: Princeton University Press, 1995.

Coauthorial Attribution and the *Teachings of Silvanus* (NHC VII,4)

CHANCE E. BONAR

1. Introduction

One of the codices rediscovered near Nag Hammadi in the 1940s contains a text that is still underexplored, in part for not matching a recognizable New Testament genre (e. g., gospels, acts, letters) and in part for being attributed to an otherwise obscure figure: Silvanus. The *Teachings of Silvanus* (ⲛ̄ⲥⲃⲟⲩ ⲛ̄ⲥⲓⲗⲟⲩⲁⲛⲟⲥ; NHC VII,4), a third-century production of an Alexandrian Christian, survives only in one fourth-century Coptic copy alongside the *Paraphrase of Shem, Second Treatise of Great Seth, Apocalypse of Peter,* and *Three Steles of Seth.* The codex containing the *Teachings of Silvanus* was likely produced in a Pachomian monastic context, given the types of literary and documentary texts used as cartonnage to produce the codex's cover.[1] While most scholarship on the *Teachings of Silvanus* from the 1970s onward has focused on its relationship to Alexandrian philosophical-theological thought or to Jewish wisdom traditions,[2] the problem of the text's authorship is often discussed as a later addition or *non sequitur* to the text itself. The attachment of a certain "Silvanus" to a text of gnomic wisdom is treated either as a somewhat nonsensical attempt to connect the literature to a broader Christian storyworld, or perhaps to a late ancient theologian named Silvanus whose thoughts are developed in this text.

Here, I want to suggest that the *Teachings of Silvanus* is entitled as such not totally by accident, but that some portions of *Silvanus* may interpret or expand upon literature associated with the Silvanus mentioned in the New Testament.

---

[1] J. W. B. Barns, G. M. Browne, and J. C. Shelton, *Nag Hammadi Codices: Greek and Coptic Papyri from the Cartonnage of the Covers,* Nag Hammadi Studies 16 (Leiden: Brill, 1981), 4–11, 52–86; Hugo Lundhaug and Lance Jenott, *The Monastic Origins of the Nag Hammadi Codices,* Studien und Texte zu Antike und Christentum 97 (Tübingen: Mohr Siebeck, 2015).

[2] Some examples of the most prominent trends in *Silvanus* scholarship include W. R. Schoedel, "Jewish Wisdom and the Formation of the Christian Ascetic," in *Aspects of Wisdom in Judaism and Early Christianity,* ed. R. L. Wilken (Notre Dame, IL: University of Notre Dame, 1975), 169–99; Roelof Van den Broek, *Studies in Gnosticism and Alexandrian Christianity,* Nag Hammadi and Manichaean Studies 39 (Leiden: Brill, 1996); Jan Zandee, *"The Teachings of Silvanus" and Clement of Alexandria: A New Document of Alexandrian Theology* (Leiden: Ex Oriente Lux, 1977).

128   *Chance E. Bonar*

I will divide this contribution into three sections. In the first, I will provide an overview of Silvanus' role in both Pauline and Petrine literature, highlighting his treatment as a coauthorial figure and messenger. Second, I will lay out how recent scholarly literature explains the attribution of *Silvanus* to someone named Silvanus. Third, I will offer a comparison between *Silvanus* and some New Testament passages to suggest that the writer of *Silvanus* is building upon the scaffolding of a New Testament figure who coauthored with Paul, although deeply infusing their own Alexandrian Christian context into their authorial standpoint as Silvanus.

My approach to authorship in this contribution is heavily informed by the scholarship of Hindy Najman, Irene Peirano Garrison, and Karen King. In their work across the fields of ancient Judaism and Classics, Najman and Peirano Garrison examine pseudepigraphy not as explicitly and inevitably forgery, but as "creative acts of interpretation" and imposed frameworks through which to approach a text.[3] Texts that we typically deem pseudepigraphic, including *Silvanus*, can be read as attempts to continue an authorial thread, imitate, and explore how to refresh the meaning of a text for a new generation of readers. In the case of *Silvanus* and the circles it most likely circulated in – Alexandrian Christian philosophers and Egyptian ascetic monastics – this might mean attributing a text to Silvanus because he is treated as a figure whose teachings could be teased out, if only through reading the lines of Silvanean texts (1–2 Thess, 1 Pet) and creatively supplementing his words.

Similarly, Karen King's work on the *Apocryphon of James* and Revelation updates a Foucauldian approach to author-function that compels us to ask *why* and *in what ways* it matters to know the author of a text.[4] King points especially to a goal of attributing authors to texts in order to demonstrate that the text comes from a trustworthy source and has a stable line of transmission, among other possible concerns like literary prestige or filling an expected position within a social field. Attribution of *Silvanus* to the figure of Silvanus known through Pauline and Petrine correspondence might allow the text to have recognizable apostolic authority and be trustworthy by association. Likewise, as I'll note below regarding 2 Thess 2, *Silvanus* can be read as filling a gap in the storyworld of Silvanus as a Pauline coauthor and Petrine letter-carrier, in which a later Chris-

---

[3] Hindy Najman and Irene Peirano Garrison, "Pseudepigraphy as an Interpretative Construct," in *The Old Testament Pseudepigrapha: Fifty Years of the Pseudepigrapha Section at the SBL*, ed. Matthias Henze and Liv Ingeborg Lied (Atlanta: Society of Biblical Literature, 2019), 331–55, 343, and more broadly 343–51; Irene Peirano Garrison, *The Rhetoric of the Roman Fake: Latin Pseudepigrapha in Context* (Cambridge: Cambridge University Press, 2012).

[4] Karen L. King, "'What Is an Author?': Ancient Author-Function in *the Apocryphon of John* and the Apocalypse of John," in *Scribal Practices and Social Structures among Jesus Adherents: Essays in Honour of John S. Kloppenborg*, ed. William E. Arnal, et al. (Leuven: Peeters, 2016), 15–42. See also Robyn Faith Walsh's contribution to this volume.

tian writer imaginatively builds upon the scaffolding of what they know about Silvanus to produce or associate a text with him. *Silvanus* is a helpful example of one of King's questions about authorship and social prestige – "Who *can be* an author?" – since Silvanus' status as a named figure within three New Testament epistles made him recognizable enough to have at least one text produced in his name.[5] While contemporaneous Alexandrian Christians decided to write orthonymously (e. g., Clement, Origen, perhaps Cyril, Athanasius), the decision of an Egyptian contemporary to write pseudonymously may tell us something about the writer themselves, and about the decision for the writer or later scribe to view this text as Silvanus's.[6]

2. Coauthorship and Silvanus in the New Testament

The figure of Silvanus appears in three different places in the New Testament. Most prominently, he appears as Paul's coauthor in both 1 Thessalonians and 2 Thessalonians, listed alongside Paul and Timothy in this correspondence. While it is commonplace to read the Pauline corpus as belonging exclusively to Paul, there are plenty of contributors involved in the production of these epistles – most prominently, enslaved and formerly enslaved scribal workers and coauthors. In his account of Paul's use of secretaries, E. Randolph Richards concludes by noting that "it is not acceptable to sideline the issue [of Paul's secretarial use] and proceed as if the letters were solely the words and thoughts of Paul."[7] Here, I am suggesting we share the same concern for Pauline coauthors like Silvanus, whose role in the production of Pauline correspondence is often downplayed or ignored, and yet whose authorial persona is picked up by the *Teachings of Silvanus*. As Bruno Latour famously put it in his discussion of the proliferation of human and non-human actors that worked alongside Louis Pasteur to make vaccination possible: "There are more of us than we thought."[8] There are more writers and thinkers in the "Pauline epistles" than we thought, and their ascription does something *to* and *for* texts that goes beyond Paul.

---

[5] King, "What Is an Author?" 39.

[6] For example, Van den Broek (*Studies in Gnosticism,* 256) scathingly claims that *Silvanus* is a good example of "a mediocre orthodox contemporary of Eusebius and Athanasius" and that it provides us "insight into the state of mind and interests of the second-rate theologians." If this harsh critique of *Silvanus*'s theology holds any weight, it may hint at an Alexandrian writer who (for a multitude of possible reasons) felt that Silvanus's name would do a particular type of work to frame the text to make it readable and distributable.

[7] E. Randolph Richards, *The Secretary in the Letters of Paul,* Wissenschaftliche Untersuchungen zum Neuen Testament 2.42 (Tübingen: Mohr Siebeck, 1991), 201. Cf. Michael Prior, *Paul the Letter-Writer and the Second Letter to Timothy,* Journal for the Study of the New Testament Supplement Series 23 (Sheffield: Sheffield Academic Press, 1989), 37–39.

[8] Bruno Latour, *The Pasteurization of France,* trans. Alan Sheridan and John Law (Cambridge, MA: Harvard University Press, 1988), 35.

130   *Chance E. Bonar*

Both 1 Thess and 2 Thess predominantly use first-person plural language (e. g., "we," "our") throughout with only rare first-person singular interjections by Paul and/or others. Silvanus is not named again in 1 Thess, but only appears in the use of "we" throughout. By contrast, Paul makes a few individual appearances in the letter, particularly in 2:18 when he interjects and notes his intense desire to visit the Thessalonians: "Therefore we wanted to come to you – certainly I, Paul, [did] over and over" (διότι ἠθελήσαμεν ἐλθεῖν πρὸς ὑμᾶς – ἐγὼ μὲν Παῦλος, καὶ ἅπαξ καὶ δίς). Here we find Paul not only interrupting his coauthors, but also adding his own name to clarify who the "I" is that so strongly wants to be in Thessalonica. The use of "I, Paul" with the attached orthonym suggests that, at least on some occasions like this one, Paul felt the need to clarify that *he* is the "I" who is speaking. By doing so, this means that readers of Paul's letters may not always assume that *Paul* is the "I" who interjects. Perhaps Silvanus or Timothy could be presumed to be speaking more directly to their Thessalonian audience in other instances.[9]

The case of 2 Thess is slightly trickier, given that scholarly consensus tends to view it as a pseudepigraphic letter built upon the foundation of 1 Thess. The letter claims the same three coauthors as 1 Thess and mimics its plural writing style, only interjecting with a singular figure twice: an "I" claiming to have previously taught the Thessalonians about the coming man of lawlessness (2:5) and an "I" claiming to be Paul that nearly exaggerates their authorial presence: "The greeting with my own hand – Paul, which is my sign in every letter. I write this way" (ὁ ἀσπασμὸς τῇ ἐμῇ χειρὶ – Παύλου, ὅ ἐστιν σημεῖον ἐν πάσῃ ἐπιστολῇ. Οὕτως γράφω; 3:17).[10] Nevertheless, Silvanus is depicted as one of Paul's coauthors and a voice present in most of the letter.

Most of Paul's epistles are coauthored with either Silvanus, Timothy, or Sosthenes, and they likely include voices beyond Paul's own. This reality of Pauline coauthorship disrupts the idea that Paul is the sole authorial figure and "Great Man" sitting behind each of his letters.[11] Coauthorship was not a

---

[9] Prior (*Paul the Letter-Writer*, 39–40) shares this point in the interpretation of ἐγώ in 1 Thess.

[10] On Pseudo-Paul's association between Paul's signature and authenticity in 2 Thess, see Bart D. Ehrman, *Forgery and Counterforgery: The Use of Literary Deceit in Early Christian Polemics* (Oxford: Oxford University Press, 2013), 170–71. On the lack of uniqueness of Paul's epistolary sign-off, see Steve Reece, *Paul's Large Letters: Paul's Autographic Subscriptions in the Light of Ancient Epistolary Conventions* (London: Bloomsbury, 2017).

[11] On the role of enslaved scribal labor in the production of Pauline letters, see Candida R. Moss, "The Secretary: Enslaved Workers, Stenography, and the Production of Early Christian Literature," *Journal of Theological Studies* 74 (2023): 1–37 and more broadly, eadem, *God's Ghostwriters: Enslaved Christians and the Making of the Bible* (New York: Little, Brown and Company, 2024). On taking Pauline coauthorship seriously as a mode of writing that might impact when and where Paul's coauthors have a more prominent place in the correspondence, see Gordon J. Bahr, "Paul and Letter Writing in the First Century," *Catholic Biblical Quarterly* 28 (1966): 476, Jerome Murphy-O'Connor, "Co-Authorship in the Corinthian Correspondence," *Revue biblique* 100 (1993): 562–79; E. Randolph Richards, *Paul and First-Century Letter Writing:*

Coauthorial Attribution and the Teachings of Silvanus 131

common phenomenon in Mediterranean antiquity, but it certainly was not unknown either. While E. Randolph Richards has argued that coauthorship was functionally a "Christian phenomenon," since (according to him) elite Roman authors like Pliny, Cicero, and Seneca did not coauthor texts,[12] he misrepresents our evidence and excludes many papyrological examples. Jerome Murphy-O'Connor in particular has pointed to various letters that were coauthored in antiquity, including various letters sent by Cicero and his family members (Marcus, Terentia, Tullia) to Tiro or his brother Quintus,[13] Cicero's note on Atticus's coauthoring of letters,[14] and various letters preserved in Egypt regarding debts or weddings.[15] We might also add the substantial number of coauthored tax-related letters that have been overlooked in the discussion of the (relative) rarity of coauthorship in antiquity.[16] If we treat coauthorship as a recognizable authorial practice in the ancient Mediterranean, then we might better understand how figures like Silvanus could be conceptualized as an authorial figure to whom texts and ideas could be attributed.

Coauthorship in 1–2 Thess, however, has often been contested or downplayed. For example, Adolf Harnack disapproved of the idea of coauthorship based on how 1 Thess 3:2 describes "we" sending Timothy, and found it preposterous that Timothy could speak in the third person about his own sending.[17] In doing so, Harnack effectively ignored Silvanus's presence in the letter and failed to allow for the possibility of Paul, Silvanus, and Timothy to switch between using "we" to refer to all three of them, just two of them, or themselves and the people to whom they wrote. Some like C. E. B. Canfield argue that the "we" of 1–2 Thess was comparable to a "royal we" or a first-person singular disguised as a plural,

---

Secretaries, Composition and Collection (Downers Grove, IL: InterVarsity Press, 2004). Bruce J. Malina (*Timothy: Paul's Closest Associate* [Collegeville, MN: Liturgical Press, 2008], 70–94) also begins the work of viewing Timothy as cowriter. Silvanus is also depicted with Paul and Timothy once more as a preacher among the Corinthians in 2 Cor 1:19.

[12] Richards, *Paul and First-Century Letter Writing*, 33–36; cf. Richards, *The Secretary*, 47–48.

[13] Murphy-O'Connor, "Co-Authorship"; cf. Cicero, *Fam.* 14.14.1 (145.1); 14.18.2 (144.2); 16.1 (120); 16.3 (122); 16.4 (123); 16.5 (124); 16.6 (125); 16.11 (143).

[14] Cicero, *Atticus* 11.5.1.

[15] Richards, *Paul and First-Century Letter Writing*, 33–36; Murphy-O'Connor, "Co-Authorship," 564. Richards lists primarily second- and third-century letters: P.Oxy. 2.118, 8.1158, 9.1167, 42.3064, 43.3094, 46.3313, and maybe P.Zen. 35.

[16] For a small sampling, see: P.Oxy. 1.185; P.Tebt. 1.37; O.Amst. 46; O.Ashm. 43–44; O.Ash. Shelf 17; O.Berenike 2.140; O.Berl. 27, 47; O.Bodl. 1.251, 2.569; O.Cair. 89; O.Wilcken 2.801; SB 1.4333, 5.7570, 16.13003, 18.32279, 18.14031, 22.15387; UPZ 2.172; ZPE 209.217; cf. Tab.Vindol. I 21 (no. 248).

[17] Adolf von Harnack, *Die Briefsammlung des Apostels Paulus, und die anderen vorkonstantinischen christlichen Briefsammlungen: Sechs Vorlesungen aus der altkirchlichen Literaturgeschichte* (Leipzig: J. C. Hinrichs, 1926), 12. F. F. Bruce (*1 & 2 Thessalonians*, World Books Commentaries 45 [Waco, TX: World Books, 1982], 61) suggests that Paul originated the plan to send Timothy to Thessalonica, so the "I" of 1 Thess 3:5 is Paul and the "we" of 3:2 is their collective agreement with Paul's plan.

132   Chance E. Bonar

despite how a previous generation of scholars had convincingly demonstrated that Paul remains comfortable in joint authorship in his earlier letters.[18] Others like Leon Morris claimed that 1–2 Thess could not be truly coauthored because they are too stylistically similar to other (mostly coauthored) Pauline epistles, such that coauthorship with Paul must have been "largely a matter of courtesy."[19] Such an argument does not hold up well, since it fails to explain why Paul would include *some* names as coauthors but not the names of others who are explicitly noted to be present with him at the time of composition (e. g., those listed in 1 Cor 16). In any case, Paul's addition of Silvanus as a coauthor for 1–2 Thess opens up the interpretative possibility of viewing Silvanus as a writer whose voice might be found in the text – or that readers of Paul's letters may consider Silvanus as someone whose teachings are contained within.

Along with appearing as coauthor of two Pauline epistles, the writer of 1 Peter likewise claims to have written to the diasporic communities in Asia Minor "through Silvanus, a loyal brother to you as I consider him" (διὰ Σιλουανοῦ, ὑμῖν τοῦ πιστοῦ ἀδελφοῦ ὡς λογίζομαι; 5:12). This phrasing has led to a substantial debate as to whether Silvanus was a scribe, letter-carrier, or previously-uncredited coauthor of 1 Peter.[20] Most likely, the Silvanus of 1 Peter functioned as a letter-carrier, although some have sought out deeper connections between the

---

[18] C. E. B. Canfield, "Changes of Person and Number in Paul's Epistles," in *Paul and Paulinism: Essays in Honour of C. K. Barrett*, ed. Morna D. Hooker and Stephen G. Wilson (London: SPCK, 1982), 280–89. Examples of scholars who find Pauline coauthorship in 1–2 Thess convincing include E. H. Askwith, "'I' and 'We' in the Thessalonian Epistles," *Expositor* 8 (1911): 149–59; W. F. Lofthouse, "Singular and Plural in St. Paul's Letters," *Expository Times* 58 (1947): 179–82; idem, "'I' and 'We' in the Pauline Letters," *Expository Times* 64 (1953): 241–45; Prior, *Paul the Letter-Writer*, 40.

[19] Leon Morris, *The First and Second Epistles to the Thessalonians*, New International Commentary on the New Testament (Grand Rapids: Eerdmans, 1959), 46–47. Against the argument from courtesy, see Otto Roller, *Das Formular der paulinischen Briefe: Ein Beitrag zur Lehre vom antiken Briefe* (Stuttgart: Kohlhammer, 1933), 153.

[20] E. Randolph Richards ("Silvanus Was Not Peter's Secretary: Theological Bias in Interpreting Σιλουανοῦ … ἔγραψα in 1 Peter 5:12," *Journal of the Evangelical Theological Society* 43 [2000]: 417–32) argues that Silvanus must have been a letter-carrier. Reece (*Paul's Large Letters*, 41–42) notes that Richards's argument is not conclusive and that Silvanus may have also been the scribe of 1 Pet. For Silvanus as a scribe, see Curtis Vaught and Thomas Lea, *1, 2 Peter, Jude* (Grand Rapids: Zondervan, 1988), 132; Thomas Lea, *The New Testament: Its Background and Message* (Nashville, TN: Broadman, 1996), 535. Often, claiming Silvanus as a scribe is tied to academic concerns over the authorship of 1–2 Peter and the attempt to house both letters under the same authorial figure despite their differences. For an overview of letter carriers in early Christian literature, see Peter Head, "Named Letter-Carriers Among the Oxyrhynchus Papyri," *Journal for the Study of the New Testament* 31 (2009): 279–99; idem, "'Witnesses Between You and Us': The Role of the Letter-Carriers in 1 Clement," in *Studies on the Text of the New Testament and Early Christianity: Essays in Honor of Michael W. Holmes on the Occasion of His 65th Birthday*, ed. Daniel M. Gurtner, Jean Hernández Jr., and Paul Foster, New Testament Tools, Studies and Documents 50 (Leiden: Brill, 2015), 477–93; idem, "Onesimus the Letter Carrier and the Initial Reception of Paul's Letter to Philemon," *Journal of Theological Studies* 71 (2020): 628–56.

Coauthorial Attribution and the Teachings of Silvanus 133

three Silvanus texts. While it is not immediately obvious that 1 Peter's Silvanus is the same as that of 1–2 Thess, Benjamin Sargent has suggested there is shared terminology between the letters that might link them to a shared Silvanean character.[21] Like with 1–2 Thess, the presence of Silvanus in 1 Peter opens the door to reading the Petrine epistles with Silvanus in mind.

Silvanus is often also identified with Silas, a figure that first appears at the Jerusalem council in Acts 15 as a prophet and messenger of the letter to eastern Mediterranean gentiles regarding their food requirements. When Paul and Barnabas part ways, Paul chooses Silas as a travel companion (Acts 15:40), and thereafter Timothy joins Paul and Silas at Lystra (16:1). Afterwards, Paul and Silas are incarcerated (16:19–40), and Silas and Timothy remain at Berea before eventually rejoining Paul (17:14 and 18:5). Acts never explicitly identifies Silas as the Silvanus that coauthored letters with Paul or as the letter-carrier for Peter, but scholars have often debated whether these two figures are intended to be the same person.[22] Even though Silvanus never takes center stage in any of the New Testament references to him, an early Christian reader of such literature might begin to construct a biography of Silvanus: a prominent early Jesus adherent who functioned within the epistolary and travel networks of both Peter and Paul, and who was trusted multiple times with handling ecclesiastical issues at places like Corinth, Lystra, and Berea. Silvanus can be construed as a literary figure whose biographical gaps may be filled in by curious early Christians, as I will argue below.

2 Thess in particular provides a space for readers to interpret the coauthored letter as mentioning avenues through which Silvanus's words or teachings were disseminated. One of the coauthors claims to have warned the Thessalonians about the lawless one and son of perdition: "Do you not remember that I told you these things when I was still with you?" (2 Thess 2:5). While often read as Paul, the referent of the "I" is unclear between the three coauthors; we need not presume that only Paul has the capacity to interrupt the plural flow of the letters to the Thessalonians. Given this ambiguity, a late ancient Christian could interpret this time of one-on-one instruction as time spent between Silvanus and the Thessalonians. Later in that chapter, the three writers mention that the Thessalonians ought to do as they were instructed "either by word or by our letter" (εἴτε διὰ λόγου εἴτε δι' ἐπιστολῆς ἡμῶν; 2 Thess 2:15). It is unclear whether "our letter" refers to 1 Thess, 2 Thess, or another writing that they are imagined to have provided for the Thessalonians. Certainly, the pseudepigraphic coauthors express a fear that some other letter may have arrived with teachings contrary to theirs

---

[21] Benjamin Sargent, "Chosen Through Sanctification (1 Pet 1,2 and 2 Thess 2,13): The Theology or Diction of Silvanus?" *Biblica* 94 (2013): 117–20.

[22] Paul J. Achtemeier, *1 Peter: A Commentary on First Peter*, Hermeneia (Minneapolis, MN: Fortress, 2016 [1996]), 349–52.

134   *Chance E. Bonar*

(2 Thess 2:2). Nevertheless, 2 Thess suggests that Paul, Timothy, and Silvanus have provided teachings to the Thessalonians beyond those contained merely in these two letters, which would allow a later Christian writer to attribute a text to Silvanus and imagine what teachings might be passed down.

3. Scholarship on the Authorship of *Silvanus*

Scholarship on the *Teachings of Silvanus* has typically labeled the text something along the lines of a non-"gnostic" Christian wisdom tradition emerging from Egypt. The text of *Silvanus* itself is not a series of disconnected gnomic statements like the *Sentences of Sextus*, but contains shorter coherent lines of argumentation. Birger Pearson divides *Silvanus* into two sections. In the first, the writer expounds a mixture of Jewish, Stoic, and Middle Platonic thought that encourages self-control via mind (νοῦς) and reason (λόγος). The writer especially points to Jesus and understanding one's own tripartite self (body, mind, soul), as well as discourages any reliance on knowledge or friendship of others beyond Jesus.[23] The second section reflects Alexandrian Christian theological and Christological speculation, with a heavy focus on Jesus as light and incomprehensible as well as on his incarnational descent. *Silvanus* ends with a discussion of how Jesus crowns those who fight well against the adversary and maintain their self-control in the face of danger. As Blossom Stefaniw has convincingly argued, *Silvanus* is deeply concerned with producing a late Roman masculinist "plan of escape from vulnerability" – a guide to self-control in a world in which Roman Egyptian monastic ideals of masculinity are constantly under threat by worldly and demonic forces.[24]

Given its Alexandrian philosophical and theological milieu, *Silvanus*'s titular attribution to a figure named Silvanus has puzzled scholars. The large majority of scholars who have dealt with *Silvanus* have viewed its attribution to Silvanus as part and parcel of the common early Christian trend to attach later texts to first-century figures in the Jesus movement. Malcolm Peel and Jan Zandee have suggested such in their edition of the text:

[W]e look in vain for something that might link the tractate with the Silvanus of the New Testament. Missing from the document, also, are those devices commonly used in New

---

[23] Birger A. Pearson, "The Teachings of Silvanus," in *The Nag Hammadi Scriptures: The International Edition*, ed. Marvin Meyer (New York: HarperOne, 2007), 499–501. A portion of this section of *Silvanus* (97.3–98.22) is shared with a text attributed to St. Antony, suggesting that both pulled from a shared *Urtext*. On this Antony text, see Wolf Peter Funk, "Ein doppelt überliefertes Stück spätägyptischer Weisheit," *Zeitschrift für Ägyptische Sprache und Altertumskunde* 103 (1976): 8–21.

[24] Blossom Stefaniw, "Masculinity as Flight: Vulnerability, Devotion, Submission and Sovereignty in the *Teachings of Silvanus*," *Journal of Early Christian History* 11 (2021): 66–87.

Coauthorial Attribution and the Teachings of Silvanus 135

Testament apocryphal writings to support the claims of a pseudonymous text to apostolic authorship. Such considerations suggest that the title was probably added by a later copyist.[25]

Others like Birger Pearson agree that there are no indications within the *Teachings of Silvanus* to suggest that the original writer of the text imagined it to be explicitly connected to Silvanus, and that a later scribe decided to boost *Silvanus'* authorial status through attaching it to a coworker of Paul.[26] Yvonne Janssens, on the other hand, suggests that the writer of *Silvanus* "no doubt wanted to link his treatise in this way to a supposedly apostolic tradition, as was often done with the apocrypha of the first centuries."[27] Janssens, in contrast to Peel, Zandee, and Pearson, considers it more possible that the writer of *Silvanus* incorporated aspects of texts that relate to Silvanus (1 Thess, 2 Thess, 1 Pet) such that this authorial attribution is not a *non sequitur* with the context of the text itself. Ironically, although she is comfortable with the hints of Pauline and Petrine epistles influencing the authorial attribution of *Silvanus*, Janssens denies the possibility that Silvanus's coauthorial status in 1 Thess 1:1 and 2 Thess 1:1 or status as a messenger for Peter in 1 Pet 5:12 could be at play. Commenting on how Peter "wrote through Silvanus" [διὰ Σιλουανοῦ [...] ἔγραφα], she argues:

This simple little phrase, which fits so well with *Silv*, might it not be at the origin of the claims of our pseudepigrapher? *Silv* would thus have attributed to the scribe the teaching of Peter himself. Moreover, it has sometimes been hypothesized that Silvanus's collaboration was not limited to the work of a secretary [...] See also X. Léon-Dufour, who in his "Dictionnaire du Nouveau Testament" (p. 497), sees Silas as a "coauthor of the Epistles to the Thessalonians and First Peter" – which is perhaps debatable![28]

While Janssens is correct in doubting whether we can go so far as to attribute authorial status to Silvanus in 1 Peter, she overlooks the likelihood that Silvanus

---

[25] Malcolm Peel and Jan Zandee, "NHC VII,4: *The Teachings of Silvanus*," in *Nag Hammadi Codex VII*, ed. Birger A. Pearson, Nag Hammadi and Manichaean Studies 30 (Leiden: Brill, 1996), 249–50. See also Malcolm Peel and Jan Zandee, "The Teachings of Silvanus (VII,4)," in *The Nag Hammadi Library in English*, ed. James Robinson, 4th rev. ed (Leiden: Brill, 1996), 380.

[26] Pearson, "The Teachings of Silvanus," 502.

[27] Yvonne Janssens, *Les Leçons de Silvanos (NH VII, 4)*, Bibliothèque Copte de Nag Hammadi 13 (Québec: L'Université Laval, 1983), 3: "a sans doute voulu rattacher ainsi son traité à une tradition prétendûment apostolique, comme on le faisait souvent pour les Apocryphes des premiers siècles."

[28] Janssens, *Les Leçons*, 3–4: "Cette simple petite phrase, qui s'accorde si bien avec Silv, ne pourrait-elle pas être à l'origine des prétentions de notre pseudépigraphe? Silv aurait ainsi attribué au scribe l'enseignement de Pierre lui-même. On a d'ailleurs émis parfois l'hypothèse que la collaboration de Silvain ne se serait pas limitée au travail d'un secrétaire [...] Voir aussi X. Léon-Dufour qui dans son 'Dictionnaire du Nouveau Testament' (p. 497), voit en Silas un 'coauteur des Épîtres aux Thessaloniciens et de la Ire de Pierre' – ce qui est peut-être contestable!" See also Jannsens, "Les *Leçons de Silvanos* et le monachisme," in *Colloque international sur les textes de Nag Hammadi*, ed. Bernard Barc, Bibliothèque Copte de Nag Hammadi, Textes 1 (Québec: L'Université Laval, 1981), 352–56.

136   *Chance E. Bonar*

was a Pauline coauthor. She also too quickly presumes that all early Christian authors were concerned about uncovering the teachings of the twelve apostles (and Paul), and so suggested that if the author of *Silvanus* was writing as if the Silvanus of 1 Pet 5:12, they should have more naturally claimed to be Peter's scribe who merely passes along Peter's teachings. Despite this, Janssens opens the door for further exploration into the relationship between the title of *Silvanus* and content that may be connected to the New Testament figure of Silvanus.

On the other end of authorial claims about *Silvanus*, Roelef Van den Broek has extensively argued that attribution to the New Testament figure of Silvanus is unlikely, and that we ought to seek a late ancient philosopher named Silvanus instead:

> For obscure reasons, he is generally identified with the Silas or Silvanus who is mentioned in the New Testament as a companion of the apostles Paul and Peter. The author would have attached the name of an apostolic figure to his writing in order to enhance its authority. But the work contains nothing which points in that direction. Nowhere is the suggestion made that the author was a contemporary of the apostles; the name of Silvanus is only mentioned in the title.[29]

Unlike Janssens, Van den Broek sees no points of comparison between *Silvanus*, 1–2 Thess, and 1 Peter to justify its attribution, and so offers other possibilities from various philosophical Silvanuses that lived in the third and fourth centuries. While Van den Broek is convinced that the author must be a Silvanus who was "a mediocre orthodox contemporary of Eusebius and Athanasius,"[30] I am not as convinced that its Alexandrian philosophical milieu would disqualify it from being attributed to a first-century figure. After all, Pseudo-Dionysius and his clearly Neoplatonic philosophical writings were attributed to a first-century figure, with near-contemporaries like Severus of Antioch, Leontius of Jerusalem, and John Philoponus accepting such texts as written by Dionysius the Areopagite.[31] Belief that a text attributed to a certain Silvanus is meant to stem from Paul's coworker would not be unimaginable. By offering this argument, Van den Broek questions whether *Silvanus* fits the common mold of attributing early Christian literature to prominent first-century figures because so many of those types of texts contain explicit context relating to the named figure.

In my contribution to these debates over the authorship of *Silvanus*, I fall closest to Janssens and want to expand on her work. Resonances with texts related to the New Testament figure of Silvanus – which I will occasionally call

---

[29] Van den Broek, *Studies in Gnosticism*, 257.

[30] Van den Broek, *Studies in Gnosticism*, 256.

[31] See Ronald F. Hathaway, *Hierarchy and the Definition of Order in the Letters of Pseudo-Dionysius: A Study in the Form and Meaning of the Pseudo-Dionysian Writings* (The Hague: Martinus Nijhoff, 1969), esp. 9–21. Hathaway notes that Hypatius of Ephesus is one of the earliest voices to deny Pseudo-Dionysius's authorial authenticity based on its monophysite features and lack of citation by prominent Alexandrian figures like Cyril and Athanasius.

Coauthorial Attribution and the Teachings of Silvanus 137

"Silvanean literature" here – in the *Teachings of Silvanus* suggest that the writer had reason to connect the text to an admittedly-small Silvanean corpus.

4. Resonances of Silvanus

In this section, I want to explore some of the aforementioned resonances between *Silvanus* and texts associated with Silvanus in the New Testament: 1 Thess, 2 Thess, and 1 Peter. By doing so, I hope to demonstrate that, contrary to most scholarship on the authorship of *Silvanus*, its authorial attribution is not completely nonsensical or random, but rather recognizes subtle hints of an authorial Silvanus peeking through Alexandrian theological exposition. There are a few themes that appear in both *Silvanus* and Silvanus-related epistles: living a quiet and pleasing life to God, controlling and combating the passions, and overcoming the deceitful Adversary and his powers. In highlighting the commonalities between these two textual corpora, my analysis will be guided by Stefaniw's treatment of *Silvanus* as a roadmap of sorts for late Roman constructions of masculinity in a Christian ascetic milieu:

> But what happens if we think more carefully about wisdom literature as a place where men talk to each other about how to be men? This particular text is a site of masculine subjectification like getting a talking-to in a locker room or barracks or boarding school or being kept back after practice to be told off for slacking.[32]

Silvanus's vision of piety, bodily and spiritual vulnerability, and spiritual combat are tied up with the writer's vision of an ideally self-sufficient, isolated, Christ-submissive masculine figure. Here, I want to add one more layer: *Silvanus*'s vision is not merely built out of Jewish wisdom literature and Alexandrian theology, but also finds scaffolding and justification for its vision in the words of Silvanean literature like 1 Thess, 2 Thess, and 1 Peter.

4.1 Education and Imitation

Befitting *Silvanus*'s wisdom and *paideia*-based genre, the text reads as a one-sided conversation between a teacher and student.[33] The writer multiple times makes clear that they are addressing "my son" (ⲡⲁϣⲏⲣⲉ) and encouraging them to accept the teaching provided to them.[34] Along with being a common dialogical framework for wisdom and educational literature, such an appellation resonates with how the coauthors of 1 Thess talk about their pedagogical relationship to the Thessalonians:

---

[32] Stefaniw, "Masculinity in Flight," 70.
[33] Schoedel, "Jewish Wisdom," 172–73, 175–77.
[34] Some examples include *Silv* 85.30, 86.24, 87.4–12, 19–20, 88.22–23, 91.20–21. All Coptic citations of *Silvanus* in this contribution come from Malcolm Peel and Jan Zandee, "NHC VII,4."

138   *Chance E. Bonar*

As you know, we dealt with each one of you like a father with his children, urging and encouraging you and pleading that you lead a life worthy of God.[35]

Paul and Silvanus's paternalistic approach at Thessalonica helps set the stage for a text like *Silvanus* to be read as an expansion of what such a conversation may have looked like – albeit filled with Alexandrian philosophical thought that the first-century Silvanus would not have been privy to. The reference to previous moments of education opens up a space to expand Silvanus's biography and posit what type of Pauline-inflected teaching would be passed on.

Part of how *Silvanus* fulfills this goal of teaching its readers what a life worthy to God looks like is to encourage imitation of God. Fearing God and following the rational guiding principle provided by God through Christ, according to *Silvanus*, allows one to:

make himself like God. But he who makes himself like God (ⲡⲉⲧⲧⲟⲛⲧ̅ⲛ̅ ⲁⲉ ⲙⲙⲟϥ ⲉⲡⲛⲟⲩⲧⲉ) is one who does nothing unworthy of God, according to the statement of Paul who has become like Christ (ⲡⲁⲓ̈ ⲛ̅ⲧⲁϥϣⲱⲡⲉ ⲉϥⲧ̅ⲛⲧⲱⲛ ⲉⲡⲉⲭⲥ̅).[36]

To reach the life that the Thessalonian coauthors want their readers to achieve, *Silvanus* finds imitation to be a helpful avenue. Imitation is a common Pauline trope, as the writer of *Silvanus* knows and acknowledges through their sole explicit reference to Paul. However, the writer seems to be blending a few different verses in their recollection of Paul's words through their own Silvanean text. Paul claims to be an imitator of Christ in 1 Cor and encourages his and Sosthenes' readers to do the same: "Be imitators of me, as I am of Christ" (μιμηταί μου γίνεσθε, καθὼς κἀγὼ Χριστοῦ; 1 Cor 11:1).[37] But imitating God appears more explicitly in 1 Thess, in which the three coauthors urge the Thessalonians that they "became imitators of us, and of the Lord" (μιμηταί ἡμῶν ἐγενήθητε καὶ τοῦ κυρίου; 1 Thess 1:6) so as to become exemplary among their ecclesial peers across Greece and Macedonia.[38]

This language of imitation shifts between 1 Thess and *Silvanus*. In the former, Silvanus and his coauthors use it to praise the Thessalonians for persisting through discrimination and persecution, purportedly by local Jewish figures both in Thessalonica and Judea who disapprove of how Paul and his colleagues conceptualize gentile inclusion.[39] The function of imitation shifts substantially in

---

[35] 1 Thess 2:11–12.
[36] *Silv* 108.26–32. The language of being worthy of God is also closely shared with 1 Thess 2:12 in its Sahidic form (ⲡⲉⲙⲡϣⲁ ⲙ̅ⲡⲛⲟⲩⲧⲉ). Coptic text from George W. Horner, *The Coptic Version of the New Testament in the Southern Dialect*, vol. 5: The Epistles of S. Paul (Oxford: Clarendon Press, 1920), 380.
[37] Cf. 1 Cor 4:16.
[38] Cf. 1 Thess 2:14, where they claim the Thessalonians are properly imitating the Judean *ekklesia*; Eph 5:1.
[39] M. Eugene Boring, *I & II Thessalonians: A Commentary*, New Testament Library (Louis-

Coauthorial Attribution and the Teachings of Silvanus

this Alexandrian theological milieu in which the incarnation is an act of descent by God that allows (especially ascetic) humans to ascend to a divine status, as near contemporaries like Cyril and Athanasius attest to.[40] Christ's incarnation in *Silvanus* is not only described as a descent into the underworld through which he ransomed his own life to free humanity (*Silv* 103.34–104.14), but the incarnation is described as the method through which Christ exalts humans through his own divine status: "He who has exalted the human became like God (ⲁϥϫ̄ⲱⲡⲉ ⲉϥⲧ̄ⲛ̄ⲧⲱⲛ ⲉⲡⲛⲟⲩⲧⲉ), not in order to bring God down to the human, but that the human might become like God (ⲁⲗⲗⲁ ⲉⲧⲣⲉⲡⲣⲱⲙⲉ ϣⲱⲡⲉ ⲉϥⲧ̄ⲛ̄ⲧⲱⲛ ⲉⲡⲛⲟⲩⲧⲉ)."[41] *Silvanus* thus reads Pauline and Silvanean calls toward mimicry through this Alexandrian lens of theosis. Paul – and any manly ascetic reader – might achieve deification through Jesus's incarnation and through living a pious life defined by combating the passions and demonic powers, avoiding potentially-dangerous relationships beyond God, and protecting one's vulnerable body from the perceived dangers of this world.

4.2 A Pleasing and Quiet Ascetic Life

Silvanus is often concerned with what a life pleasing to God ought to look like, particularly as part of its construction of a self-sufficient and self-controlled masculine ideal. Part of this vision of self-sufficiency includes not befriending others in the world, but rather treating God and Christ as one's only friend since they are the only ones deemed trustworthy.[42] *Silvanus* connects such self-sufficiency to what God expects of the ideal man: "Be pleasing to God, and you will not need anyone" (ϣⲱⲡⲉ ⲉⲕⲣ̄ ⲁⲛⲁϥ ⲙ̄ⲡⲛⲟⲩⲧⲉ ⲁⲩⲱ ⲛ̄ⲅⲛⲁⲣ̄ ⲭⲣⲉⲓⲁ ⲁⲛ

---

ville: Westminster John Knox, 2015), 65–67, 98–101; Ben Witherington III, *1 and 2 Thessalonians: A Socio-Rhetorical Commentary* (Grand Rapids: Eerdmans, 2006), 65–83.

[40] Athanasius, *On the Incarnation* 54.3. On deification in Alexandrian theological circles, see Ben C. Blackwell, *Christosis: Pauline Soteriology in Light of Deification in Irenaeus and Cyril of Alexandria*, Wissenschaftliche Untersuchungen zum Neuen Testament 2.314 (Tübingen: Mohr Siebeck, 2011), esp. 71–98; Norman Russell, *The Doctrine of Deification in the Greek Patristic Tradition* (Oxford: Oxford University Press, 2004), 115–205; Jonathan Morgan, "The Role of Asceticism in Deification in Cyril of Alexandria's Festal Letters," *Downside Review* 135 (2017): 144–53.

[41] *Silv* 111.8–13.

[42] While Stefaniw does not focus on it in "Masculinity as Flight," friendship in *Silvanus* emerges from a paranoid masculinist stance based on a fear of vulnerability to flattery, temptation, and codependence. It is in many ways a heightened version of Paul's balance between friendship and self-sufficiency grounded in God as discussed in John T. Fitzgerald, "Christian Friendship: John, Paul, and the Philippians," *Interpretation* 61 (2007): 295–96; Abraham J. Malherbe, "Paul's Self-Sufficiency (Philippians 4:11)," in *Friendship, Flattery, and Frankness of Speech: Studies on Friendship in the New Testament World*, ed. John T. Fitzgerald, Novum Testamentum Supplements 82 (Leiden: Brill, 1996), 125–40. More broadly on the construction of masculinity in early Christian literature, see Eric C. Stewart, "Masculinity in the New Testament and Early Christianity," *Journal of Bible and Culture* 46 (2016): 91–102.

140   Chance E. Bonar

ⲛ̅ⲗⲁⲁⲩ; *Silv* 98.18–20). Likewise, those who guard themselves through God-granted wisdom and rationality against the passions are treated as both imitative of God and pleasing to God: "For who reveres God while not wanting to do things that please him?" (ⲛⲓⲙ ⲅⲁⲣ ⲡⲉ ⲡⲉⲧⲣ̅ⲥⲉⲃⲉⲥⲑⲁⲓ ⲉⲡⲛⲟⲩⲧⲉ · ⲉϥⲟⲩⲱϣ ⲉⲓⲣⲉ ⲁⲛ ⲛ̅ⲛⲉⲧⲣ̅ ⲁⲛⲁϥ ⲙ̅ⲡⲛⲟⲩⲧⲉ; *Silv* 108.32–35). *Silvanus* goes on to define piety as actions stemming from the heart that is near to God, particularly in those whose souls are clothed with Christ. Silvanus and his coauthors in 1 Thess use similar language regarding their promulgation of the gospel, claiming against Thessalonian opposition that their teaching is not deceitful (a key term for *Silvanus*) and "not to please mortals, but to please God who tests our hearts" (οὐχ ὡς ἀνθρώποις ἀρέσκοντες, ἀλλὰ θεῷ τῷ δοκιμάζοντι τὰς καρδίας ἡμῶν; 1 Thess 2:4). The coauthors go on to remind the Thessalonians that they have already taught them "how you ought to live and to please God" (πῶς δεῖ ὑμᾶς περιπατεῖν καὶ ἀρέσκειν θεῷ; 1 Thess 4:1), focusing particularly on avoiding fornication and maintaining the holiness of one's body.

Both texts propose pleasing God as key to living the right type of life, with special attention paid to what one does with their body. *Silvanus* develops these ideas further by conceptualizing Jesus as an indwelling being and Wisdom incarnate who makes it possible for the believer to live by God's standards.[43] Piety from the heart makes Jesus's descent and ransom for humanity efficacious in *Silvanus*'s reading, leaving the believer to choose to assent (ⲧⲡⲣⲟⲋⲉⲣⲉⲥⲓⲥ in 104.16–18) and offer "a contrite heart, [which] is the acceptable sacrifice" (ⲑⲩⲥⲓⲁ ⲉⲧϣⲏⲡ ⲡⲉ ⲟⲩϩⲏⲧ ⲉϥⲧⲛ̅ⲛⲟⲉⲓⲧ; *Silv* 104.20). Such language has parallels in 1 Pet 2:5, in which the writer urges diasporic readers to come to God and be built as a spiritual house and priesthood – an image I will return to later – "to offer spiritual sacrifices acceptable to God through Jesus Christ" (ἀνενέγκαι πνευματικὰς θυσίας εὐπροσδέκτους θεῷ διὰ Ἰησοῦ Χριστοῦ; 1 Pet 2:5).[44] While 1 Peter does not provide much detail on what these spiritual sacrifices might look like,[45] *Silvanus* understands such a sacrifice as submitting one's heart as a proper response to Jesus's offer of salvation. This sacrifice involves an ascetic and philosophical masculinism – a removal from the world and a combative stance against the passions.[46]

We find another echo between *Silvanus* and 1 Peter in its treatment of humility and exaltation as part of its discussion of what makes an acceptable sacrifice. *Silvanus*'s vision of theosis mentioned above depends in part on what the writer

---

[43] On Jesus as Wisdom incarnate, see *Silvanus* 107.3; Schoedel, "Jewish Wisdom," 191–93, particularly on *Silvanus*'s relationship to Wis 7 and John 1.

[44] Also see the Sahidic version of 1 Pet 2:5 for lexical similarities: ⲉⲧⲁⲗⲟ ⲉϩⲣⲁⲓ ⲛ̅ϩⲉⲛⲑⲩⲥⲓⲁ ⲙ̅ⲡⲛⲉⲩⲙⲁⲧⲓⲕⲟⲛ ⲉⲩϣⲏⲡ ⲙ̅ⲡⲛⲟⲩⲧⲉ ϩⲓⲧⲛ̅ ⲓⲥ̅ ⲡⲉⲭⲥ̅. Coptic text from George W. Horner, *The Coptic Version of the New Testament in the Southern Dialect*, vol. 7: *The Catholic Epistles and the Apocalypse* (Oxford: Clarendon Press, 1924), 18.

[45] Achtemeier, *1 Peter*, 155–58.

[46] Stefaniw, "Masculinity as Flight," esp. 76–78.

Coauthorial Attribution and the Teachings of Silvanus   141

deems "humility of the heart" – that is, assenting to Christ's gift of wisdom and "treating Christ as an appropriate object of submission."[47] While *Silvanus* goes on to describe the incarnation as a moment of humility on Christ's part and exaltation of humanity toward deification (*Silv* 110.35–111.13), the writer sets the stage for discussing deification through proper submission to Christ:

> If you humble yourself, you will be greatly exalted; and if you exalt yourself, you will be exceedingly humbled.[48]

Such language, as Peel and Zandee note, has parallels in Matt 23:12. However, the order of humility and exaltation presented in *Silvanus* more closely matches 1 Pet 5:6 and Jas 4:10.[49] The 1 Peter parallel comes from a passage that shares multiple themes with *Silvanus*: humility, casting anxiety on God, the concept of a demonic adversary, contending for crowns, and staying sober and awake. Given the importance of 1 Pet 5 to the thematic scaffolding of *Silvanus*, it is possible that the writer of 1 Peter's call for younger folk in the diaspora to be humble before their elders is reformulated as Silvanus's teaching about humility and submission before Christ.

Part of the ability to successfully live a passionless and holy life in both Silvanus's Pauline letters and *Silvanus* is to live a peaceful or quiet life, expressed in 1 Thess as "striving to live quietly and keep to your own affairs and work with your own hands, just as we commanded you" (φιλοτιμεῖσθαι ἡσυχάζειν καὶ πράσσειν τὰ ἴδια, καὶ ἐργάζεσθαι ταῖς ἰδίαις χερσὶν ὑμῶν, καθὼς ὑμῖν παρηγγείλαμεν; 1 Thess 4:11) and in *Silvanus* as a "quiet life" (ⲛ̄ⲛⲟⲩⲃⲓⲟⲥ ⲉϥⲥⲟⲣⲁϩⲧ̄; *Silv* 85.7) and "passing your life in quiet" (ⲉⲣ̄ ⲡⲉⲕⲁϩⲉ ⲉⲕⲥⲟⲣⲁϩⲧ̄; *Silv* 98.14–15). *Silvanus*'s concept of a quiet life, once more, extends 1 Thessalonians's call to "have need of no one" (μηδενὸς χρείαν ἔχητε; 1 Thess 4:12) by claiming that living a quiet life involves not keeping any company, almost anxiously avoiding potentially harmful friendships, and being pleasing to God by which "you will not need anyone" (ⲛ̄ⲅ̄ⲛⲁⲣ̄ ⲭⲣⲉⲓⲁ ⲁⲛ ⲛ̄ⲗⲁⲁⲩ; *Silv* 98.19–20). Befitting its ascetic milieu, *Silvanus* urges severing contact with those who might distract from or contradict what the writer deems proper Christological, theological, and social standards, and finds evidence in some Silvanus-related correspondence that bolsters their argument for a solitary lifestyle.

4.3 Christ the Gift-Giver and Indweller

Unsurprisingly, the ascetic masculinist roadmap contained in *Silvanus* views the human body as a powerful and dangerously porous battlefield upon which the (ideal male) reader of the text keeps the passions at bay and exhibits self-control.

---

[47] Stefaniw, "Masculinity as Flight," esp. 78; *Silv* 104.18–19.
[48] *Silv* 104.21–24.
[49] Peel and Zandee, "NHC VII,4," 330.

142   Chance E. Bonar

As part of *Silvanus*'s urge for the reader to accept the wisdom given by and through Christ, the writer calls to "end the sleep which weighs heavily upon you. Depart from the forgetfulness which fills you with darkness" (ⲚⲄⲗⲁϭⲉ ⲉϥⲓⲛⲏⲃ ⲉⲧ︦ϩⲟⲣ︦ϣ︦ ⲉ︦ϫⲱⲕ · ⲁⲙⲟⲩ ⲉⲃⲟⲗ ϩⲛ̄ ⲧⲃ︦ϣ︦ⲉ ⲧⲁ︦ⲓ ⲉⲧⲙⲟϩ ⲙ̄ⲙⲟⲕ ⲛ̄ⲕⲁⲕⲉ; *Silv* 88.24–27). This intertwining of sleep, forgetfulness, and darkness is not only a common trope among Alexandrian thinkers – for example, the writer of the *Gospel of Truth*[50] – but bears some similarities to the warning about the coming day of the Lord in 1 Thess. In the Pauline (and Silvanean) eschatological scheme, those who are children of the light and of the day – including the Thessalonians – ought not fall asleep or become drunk, but avoid the associations of sleep and drunkenness with the dark nighttime (1 Thess 5:4–8).[51] Likewise, near the writer of 1 Peter's acknowledgement of Silvanus's role in the letter, they urge their diasporic audience to "be sober; be alert" (νήψατε γρηγορήσατε; 1 Pet 5:8) in a pericope that links to other aspects of *Silvanus*, as we will see soon. While the immediacy of the Pauline message about the end of the world is lacking in *Silvanus*, darkness, drunkenness, and sleep persist as activities to be avoided since they lend themselves to missing or misunderstanding Christ's gift of wisdom and enlightenment.[52] In the midst of *Silvanus*'s encouragement to accept Christ's wisdom and abandon sleepy darkness, the text once more evokes the end of 1 Peter through urging the ascetic reader to "cast your anxiety upon God alone" (ⲛⲟⲩϫⲉ ⲙ̄ⲡⲉⲕⲣⲟⲟⲩϣ ⲉⲡⲛⲟⲩⲧⲉ ⲟⲩⲁⲁϥ; *Silv* 89.16–17). Such language closely mirrors how 1 Peter calls upon the reader to humble themselves before God and "cast all your anxiety upon him, because he cares for you" (πᾶσαν τὴν μέριμναν ὑμῶν ἐπιρίψαντες ἐπ᾽ αὐτόν, ὅτι αὐτῷ μέλει περὶ ὑμῶν; 1 Pet 5:7), before turning to the call to keep sober and alert.[53] The Sahidic version of 1 Pet 5:7 even more closely matches the phrasing of *Silvanus* (ⲉⲧⲉⲧⲛ̄ⲛⲟⲩϫⲉ ⲙ̄ⲡⲉⲧⲛ̄ⲣⲟⲟⲩϣ ⲧⲏⲣϥ̄ ⲉⲣⲟϥ), suggesting that the writer had this epistle in mind when producing this exhortation.[54] The writer of *Silvanus* closely entangles their treatment of proper wakeful discipline and transferring anxieties to God with the language used in 1 Thess and 1 Peter, but modifies them toward a solitary relationship with God through the gift of wisdom.

Jesus is also conceptualized by *Silvanus* through spatial language. In its description of how a pure soul and pious heart would act, the writer urges ascetic

---

[50] *Gospel of Truth* 28.23–30.23. Darkness and forgetfulness are also linked in *Silv* 89.14–16.

[51] See Peel and Zandee. "NHC VII,4," 290–91. Exhortations to avoid sleep and stay alert are not, however, innocent. Rather, they are often shaped by logics of torture and bodily control of the enslaved. See Mitzi J. Smith, "Slavery, Torture, Systemic Oppression, and Kingdom Rhetoric: An African American Reading of Matthew 25:1–13," in *Insights from African American Interpretation*, ed. Mitzi J. Smith and Mark Allen Powell (Minneapolis, MN: Fortress Press, 2017), 87–91.

[52] Christ's figuration as a reason-filled light is expounded most fully at *Silv* 99.2–20. See Van den Broek, *Studies in Gnosticism*, 240–47.

[53] Peel and Zandee. "NHC VII,4," 292–93.

[54] Horner, *The Coptic Version*, 7:60.

Coauthorial Attribution and the Teachings of Silvanus 143

readers to allow Christ to dwell in their world and subdue the passion-causing powers within. In particular, *Silvanus* pulls on temple language:

Let him enter the temple which is within you so that he may cast out the merchants. Let him dwell in the temple which is within you, and may you become for him a priest and a Levite, entering in purity. Blessed are you, o soul, if you find this one in your temple. Blessed are you still more if you perform his service.[55]

While this passage certainly pulls from 1 Cor 3 and its portrayal of the body as God's temple and the holy spirit as an indwelling figure, there are also resonances with 1 Pet 2. There, the writer urges readers to be built into a spiritual house and to "be a holy priesthood" (ἱεράτευμα ἅγιον; 1 Pet 2:5) and offer acceptable sacrifices. Unlike 1 Corinthians, which only portrays the believer's body as a building, 1 Peter and *Silvanus* understand the believer's body to be a building and that believers function as priests for God.

4.4 Adversaries, Powers, and Crowns

As a final point: *Silvanus* is replete with similar themes to Silvanean epistles regarding the inevitable struggle against powers and the Adversary, as well as the goal of attaining a crown through such suffering. As David Brakke has convincingly demonstrated, Egyptian monastic writers developed elaborate demonologies (standing on the shoulders of Origen) and understood spiritual combat as part of the production of a masculine, solitary, pious self.[56] *Silvanus* joins these ranks as a text likely read by monastics that conceptualized the ideal Christian life as one of isolation and struggle against worldly and spiritual powers, with support stemming from Christ and God alone.

Silvanus pulls its language around demonic opponents most clearly from 2 Thess 2, a section that I noted above breaks from the plurality of the "we" language used throughout 2 Thess to remind the reader that an ambiguous "I" (perhaps Paul, perhaps Silvanus) warned them about this in person. Near the end of *Silvanus*, the writer describes God's act of descent into the underworld and suggests that every person who fails to please God "is the son of perdition" (ⲡϣⲏⲣⲉ ⲙ̄ⲡⲧⲁⲕⲟ ⲡⲉ; *Silv* 114.24–25). Surprisingly, only Janssens's commentary recognizes the lexical relationship between this statement and 2 Thess 2:3, one of the famous passages utilized in the late ancient construction of the Antichrist.[57] *Silvanus*'s borrowing of the phrase "son of perdition" is not only clear

---

[55] *Silv* 109.15–25. Cf. Origen, *Comm. Io.* 2.10 on how wise ones are priests and know how to serve God.

[56] David Brakke, *Demons and the Making of the Monk: Spiritual Combat in Early Christianity* (Cambridge, MA: Harvard University Press, 2006), esp. 182–212 on (en)gendering spiritual combat.

[57] Janssens notes that *Silv* 114.23 has some reminiscences of New Testament epistles without further comment (*Les Leçons*, 3), and does not note this feature again in the commentary's ap-

144 Chance E. Bonar

in the Greek (ὁ υἱός τῆς ἀπωλείας), but even more so matches the Sahidic New Testament's translation of 2 Thess 2:3 (πϣηρε ⲙ̄ⲡⲧⲁⲕⲟ).[58] Likewise, *Silvanus* refers multiple times to "the Adversary" (ⲡⲁⲛⲧⲓⲕⲉⲓⲙⲉⲛⲟⲥ) who delegates powers to harass believers, provides false knowledge, and attempts to befriend and flatter.[59] Like the son of perdition, this figure appears to be an expansion upon the description of the lawless one who comes with lying wonders and tricks believers while declaring himself to be God (2 Thess 2:3–12). The substantive adjectival form of "the adversary" or "opposer" is rarely used in the New Testament, and most clearly in this passage: "the one who opposes (ὁ ἀντικείμενος; ⲡⲁⲛⲧⲓⲕⲉⲓⲙⲉⲛⲟⲥ) and exalts himself above every so-called god or object of worship" (2 Thess 2:4).[60] A similar conceptualization of the devil as a singular adversary appears in 1 Pet 5:8, right after the aforementioned passage on casting one's anxieties on God and staying sober and awake: "Your adversary, the devil, (ὁ ἀντίδικος ὑμῶν διάβολος; ⲡⲉⲧⲛ̄ⲁⲛⲧⲓⲇⲓⲕⲟⲥ ⲡⲇⲓⲁⲃⲟⲗⲟⲥ) prowls around like a roaring lion."[61] 2 Thess, and 1 Peter to a lesser degree, provide lexical scaffolding for *Silvanus* to conceptualize the demonic force against which ascetic men needed to defend themselves.

The crown stands out as one more point of contact. While the earlier portion of *Silvanus* mentions crowns multiple times as something that the ideal man produces himself when he accepts the *paideia* given through rationality and wisdom (*Silv* 87.11, 89.21–31), in the latter part of the monologue the crown appears as a prize for those who have successfully participated in spiritual combat and have properly imitated God. The writer posits a renewal of life through which believers are clothed in shimmering garments and during which time some are crowned:

Christ, being the contest's judge, is the one who crowned everyone, who taught everyone how to contend.[62]

Silvanus goes on to claim that winning the crown from Christ allows one to gain strength and give light to others, mirroring how Christ is described as an enlightening agent earlier in the text. To win the crown is to become more like Christ and to be rewarded for such mimicry. We find two parallels in Silvanean related literature, although crowns and competition are not rare themes through-

---

paratus (138). Likewise, Peel and Zandee, "NHC VII,4," 358–59 note a similarity to Rom 8:7–8, but not 2 Thess 2:3.

[58] Horner, *The Coptic Version*, 5:416.

[59] *Silv* 91.20, 95.1, 106.1, 114.6.

[60] Horner, *The Coptic Version*, 5:416. Cf. 1 Tim 5:14 for a singular satanic adversary, as opposed to the plural "opponents" of 1 Cor 16:9 and Phil 1:28.

[61] Horner, *The Coptic Version*, 7:60. The devil only appears by name once in *Silv* 88.12, seemingly synonymous to the Adversary. The term *antidikos* only elsewhere appears in Jesus's discussions of legal contexts in the New Testament (Matt 5:25, Luke 12:58, 18:3).

[62] *Silv* 112.19–22.

Coauthorial Attribution and the Teachings of Silvanus   145

out New Testament epistles, particularly in 1 Cor 9:24–25 and its description of athletes who compete for a perishable wreath.[63] The relationship between the crown given by Christ and exemplarity appears in 1 Pet 5:3, in which the head shepherd appears to those who are proper examples of conduct to their congregants. On the other hand, 1 Thess 2:19 treats the Thessalonians as the crown of boasting for Silvanus and his coauthors at Jesus's second coming because of their perseverance through suffering and their imitation of Judean *ekklesiai*, which made them examples to Greek and Macdeonian *ekklesiai*. Despite parallels of competition for crowns elsewhere in the Pauline and Catholic epistles, only two of the Silvanean epistles connect the granting of crowns at the eschaton to exemplarity in the way *Silvanus* does. Christ in *Silvanus* is the teacher and giver of wisdom behind the narrator, who gives believers the raw material from which to contend and through whom dominion is granted, as Stefaniw has demonstrated. Christ the light paves the way for other enlightened and exemplary ascetic men.

5. Conclusion

I have argued that, contrary to the consensus on *Silvanus's* authorship as merely a feature of early Christian literature with no clear connection to the context of the text, *Silvanus* may be more deeply tied to Silvanean literature (1 Thess, 2 Thess, 1 Pet) than previously assumed. While it is unclear whether the attribution to Silvanus stems from the original Greek writer or a later Greek or Coptic scribe, there are enough resonances with New Testament epistles related to Silvanus to suggest that either a writer or scribe associated the text with the first-century author and letter-carrier.

Some sections of Silvanean literature – especially 1 Thess 4, 2 Thess 2, and 1 Pet 5 – particularly influence *Silvanus'* sapiental and Christological pedagogical model. With the exception of the discussion of crowns in 1 Pet 5:4 examined above, *Silvanus* primarily pulls in 1 Pet 5 from the pericope filled with advice intended not for elders (1 Pet 5:1–4), but for a younger audience (1 Pet 5:5–11). The Sahidic version of *1 Pet* calls this audience "young children" (ⲛ̄ϣⲏⲣⲉ ϣⲏⲙ), which more closely matches *Silvanus'* language for its interlocutor "son" than the Greek term "younger ones" (νεώτεροι).[64] Perhaps the writer or a later scribe of *Silvanus* understood this part of 1 Pet 5 (or more of the text) to be attributable to Silvanus, given that the writer goes on immediately after to mention Silvanus' role in the letter's distribution (1 Pet 5:12).

---

[63] See Janssens (*Les Leçons*, 137) on crowns and competition in 1 Tim 6:12 and 2 Tim 4:7–8, and a smaller parallel in *Silv* 114.1–2.

[64] Horner, *The Coptic Version*, 7:58.

146   *Chance E. Bonar*

For a text so deeply concerned with proper *paideia*, we might also read *Silvanus* itself through the process of Hellenistic and Roman education. As Najman and Peirano Garrison note in their work on pseudepigraphy, "the line is often blurred between impersonation, fiction, forgery, and writing in the style of another."[65] Advanced Latin and Greek students were often trained through *imitatio* and *prosopopoeia*, producing literature attributed to writers beyond themselves, both as part of school exercises and beyond. Raised in a similar pedagogical environment as the writer of *Silvanus*, Hellenistic Jewish writers (likely from Alexandria) wrote defenses of Jewish practices and beliefs under the names of Hellenic authors like Homer and Hesiod,[66] and nearby texts from the Bodmer Papyri attest to fifth-century CE Christian *ethopoeia*, imagined speeches produced in the *persona* of Cain after murdering Abel.[67] We might imagine that an Alexandrian Christian could produce *Silvanus* by utilizing their training in *imitatio* to generate a text that creatively expands the literary corpus of an otherwise supporting actor in the apostolic storyworld and that allows for philosophical and sapiential speculation.

If the attribution does not stem from the writer but is added on by a scribe later in the third or fourth centuries, we might read it as an attempt by a scribe or book-handler to organize *Silvanus* alongside others by assigning an author based on Silvanean resonances in the text. Perhaps something along the lines of a "special library" – a collection of books by a particular *collegium* or special-interest group, such as Alexandrian theologians or Upper Egyptian monastics – could have acquired *Silvanus* and found it useful for its synthesis of Greek philosophy, Jewish wisdom, and Christology, and masculinist ascetic framing.[68] If it did not already have a title attached to it, it may have been organized in a larger collection and given a plausible author.[69] While this is possible, Jocelyn

---

[65] Najman and Peirano Garrison, "Pseudepigraphy," 347. They cite as helpful resources the work of Stanley Frederick Bonner, *Roman Declamation in the Late Republic and Early Empire* (Berkeley, CA: University of California Press, 1949); Raffaella Cribiore, *Gymnastics of the Mind: Greek Education in Hellenistic and Roman Egypt* (Princeton, NJ: Princeton University Press, 2001).

[66] Justin P. Jeffcoat Schedtler, "Perplexing Pseudepigraphy: The Pseudonymous Greek Poets," *Journal of Ancient Judaism* 8 (2018): 69–89. See Maren R. Niehoff, *Jewish Exegesis and Homeric Scholarship in Alexandria* (Cambridge: Cambridge University Press, 2011) on the centrality of both Moses and Homer as central authorial figures whose texts are expanded upon by Alexandrian Jewish writers.

[67] André Hurst and Jean Rudhardt, *Papyri Bodmer XXX–XXXVIII, "Codex des Visions,"* *Poèmes divers* (Munich: K.G. Saur, 1999), 119–26, 150–80.

[68] On special libraries in antiquity, see Victor M. Martínez and Megan Finn Senseney, "The Professional and His Books: Special Libraries in the Ancient World," in *Ancient Libraries*, ed. Jason König, Katerina Oukonomopoulou, and Greg Woolf (Cambridge: Cambridge University Press, 2013), 401–17; cf. Jörg Rüpke, "Ennius's *Fasti* in Flavius's Temple: Greek Rationality and Roman Tradition," *Arethusa* 39 (2006): 489–512.

[69] While *Silvanus* was likely originally produced in codex format, authorial attribution may have functioned similar to the *sillybos* attached to rolls in the late Republican and early Imperial periods to assist in organizing and identifying texts without having to open them. A *sillybos*

Penny Small has rightly noted that "by the time of Cicero, titles were generally assigned by the authors themselves and not by scholars or librarians, as during the Hellenistic period."[70] I consider it more likely that the writer of *Silvanus* attributed the text to Silvanus as part of a creative pseudepigraphic theological project.

There is still plenty more to be said about the *Teachings of Silvanus*. As Blossom Stefaniw has correctly pointed out:

> The *Teachings of Silvanus* is not usually treated as an important text for early Christianity, nor even for ascetic Christianity in Egypt, because it was unavailable to European scholars at the time of our map of late antiquity and early Christianity was being drawn and is not attested in those writers who are not marked as the most important and most-Christian Christians of late antiquity.[71]

Beyond Coptic philology and the oddity of a non-"gnostic" text stitched together with "gnostic" ones, the text has been marginal in early Christian scholarship. Its pseudepigraphic attribution to Silvanus has likely not helped with that situation, since it does not capture the attention of scholars in the same way that a primordial hero (e. g., Adam, Moses, Enoch) or an apostolic hotshot (e. g., Paul, Peter) would. While perhaps not as appealing as such big names in early Christian conceptualizations of the past, my suggestion is that we not too quickly overlook how some early Christians could have found Silvanus tantalizing. He is depicted as being entrusted with cowriting letters with Paul, sending letters and potentially influencing the writing of Peter, and teaching across Greece. Much like how the brief conversion episode of Dionysius the Areopagite allowed for the development of a late ancient Neoplatonic authorial figure, Silvanus's presence in New Testament literature and coauthorial status may have made him an appealing first-century figure to think through. Who better to memorialize with such an attribution?

Bibliography

Achtemeier, Paul J. *1 Peter: A Commentary on First Peter*. Hermeneia. Minneapolis, MN: Fortress, 2016 [1996].
Askwith, E. H. "'I' and 'We' in the Thessalonian Epistles." *Expositor* 8 (1911): 149–159.
Bahr, Gordon J. "Paul and Letter Writing in the First Century." *Catholic Biblical Quarterly* 28 (1966): 465–477.

---

title similar to that of the *Teachings of Silvanus* can be found in P.Oxy. 3.201, of Sophron's *Mimes of Women*. See Sarah Bond, "It's on the Sillybos: The Birth of the Book Title," 16 May 2016, https://sarahemilybond.com/2016/05/16/its-on-the-sillybos-the-birth-of-the-book-title/. While codex titles are internalized within the codex page rather than stuck out the side like a *sillybos*, they serve a similar function of organizing material by book title and/or authorial attribution.

[70] Jocelyn Penny Small, *Wax Tablets of the Mind: Cognitive Studies of Memory and Literacy in Classical Antiquity* (London: Routledge, 1997), 33–35, 48–49, quote on 34.

[71] Stefaniw, "Masculinity as Flight," 70.

148 Chance E. Bonar

Barns, J.W.B., G.M. Browne, and J.C. Shelton. *Nag Hammadi Codices: Greek and Coptic Papyri from the Cartonnage of the Covers.* Nag Hammadi Studies 16. Leiden: Brill, 1981.

Blackwell, Ben C. *Christosis: Pauline Soteriology in Light of Deification in Irenaeus and Cyril of Alexandria.* Wissenschaftliche Untersuchungen zum Neuen Testament 2.314. Tübingen: Mohr Siebeck, 2011.

Bond, Sarah. "It's on the Sillybos: The Birth of the Book Title." 16 May 2016. https://sarahemilybond.com/2016/05/16/its-on-the-sillybos-the-birth-of-the-book-title/.

Bonner, Stanley Frederick. *Roman Declamation in the Late Republic and Early Empire.* Berkeley, CA: University of California Press, 1949.

Boring, M. Eugene. *I & II Thessalonians: A Commentary.* New Testament Library. Louisville: Westminster John Knox, 2015.

Brakke, David. *Demons and the Making of the Monk: Spiritual Combat in Early Christianity.* Cambridge, MA: Harvard University Press, 2006.

Broek, Roelof van den. *Studies in Gnosticism and Alexandrian Christianity.* Nag Hammadi and Manichaean Studies 39. Leiden: Brill, 1996.

Bruce, F. F. *1 & 2 Thessalonians.* World Books Commentaries 45. Waco, TX: World Books, 1982.

Canfield, C. E. B. "Changes of Person and Number in Paul's Epistles." Pages 280–289 in *Paul and Paulinism: Essays in Honour of C.K. Barrett.* Edited by Morna D. Hooker and Stephen G. Wilson. London: SPCK, 1982.

Cribiore, Raffaella. *Gymnastics of the Mind: Greek Education in Hellenistic and Roman Egypt.* Princeton, NJ: Princeton University Press, 2001.

Ehrman, Bart D. *Forgery and Counterforgery: The Use of Literary Deceit in Early Christian Polemics.* Oxford: Oxford University Press, 2013.

Fitzgerald, John T. "Christian Friendship: John, Paul, and the Philippians." *Interpretation* 61 (2007): 284–296.

Funk, Wolf Peter. "Ein doppelt überliefertes Stück spätägyptischer Weisheit." *Zeitschrift für Ägyptische Sprache und Altertumskunde* 103 (1976): 8–21.

Harnack, Adolf von. *Die Briefsammlung des Apostels Paulus, und die anderen vorkonstantinischen christlichen Briefsammlungen: Sechs Vorlesungen aus der altkirchlichen Literaturgeschichte.* Leipzig: J.C. Hinrichs, 1926.

Hathaway, Ronald F. *Hierarchy and the Definition of Order in the Letters of Pseudo-Dionysius: A Study in the Form and Meaning of the Pseudo-Dionysian Writings.* The Hague: Martinus Nijhoff, 1969.

Head, Peter. "Named Letter-Carriers Among the Oxyrhynchus Papyri." *Journal for the Study of the New Testament* 31 (2009): 279–299.

Head, Peter. "Onesimus the Letter Carrier and the Initial Reception of Paul's Letter to Philemon." *Journal of Theological Studies* 71 (2020): 628–656.

Head, Peter. "'Witnesses Between You and Us': The Role of the Letter-Carriers in 1 Clement." Pages 477–493 in *Studies on the Text of the New Testament and Early Christianity: Essays in Honor of Michael W. Holmes on the Occasion of His 65th Birthday.* Edited by Daniel M. Gurtner, Jean Hernández Jr., and Paul Foster. New Testament Tools, Studies and Documents 50. Leiden: Brill, 2015.

Horner, William G. *The Coptic Version of the New Testament in the Southern Dialect.* Vol. 5: The Epistles of S. Paul. Oxford: Clarendon Press, 1920.

Horner, George W. *The Coptic Version of the New Testament in the Southern Dialect.* Vol. 7: The Catholic Epistles and the Apocalypse. Oxford: Clarendon Press, 1924.

Coauthorial Attribution and the Teachings of Silvanus 149

Hurst, André and Jean Rudhardt. *Papyri Bodmer XXX–XXXVIII, "Codex des Visions,"* *Poèmes divers.* Munich: K. G. Saur, 1999.

Janssens, Yvonne. *Les Leçons de Silvanos (NH VII, 4).* Bibliothèque Copte de Nag Hammadi 13. Québec: L'Université Laval, 1983.

Jannsens, Yvonne. "Les Leçons de Silvanos et le monachisme." Pages 352–361 in *Colloque international sur les textes de Nag Hammadi.* Edited by Bernard Barc. Bibliothèque Copte de Nag Hammadi, Textes 1. Québec: L'Université Laval, 1981.

King, Karen L. "'What Is an Author?': Ancient Author-Function in the Apocryphon of John and the Apocalypse of John." Pages 15–42 in *Scribal Practices and Social Structures among Jesus Adherents: Essays in Honour of John S. Kloppenborg.* Edited by William E. Arnal et al. Leuven: Peeters, 2016.

Latour, Bruno. *The Pasteurization of France,* trans. Alan Sheridan and John Law. Cambridge, MA: Harvard University Press, 1988.

Lofthouse, W. G. "'I' and 'We' in the Pauline Letters." *Expository Times* 64 (1953): 241–245.

Lofthouse, W. F. "Singular and Plural in St. Paul's Letters." *Expository Times* 58 (1947): 179–182.

Lundhaug, Hugo and Lance Jenott. *The Monastic Origins of the Nag Hammadi Codices.* Studien und Texte zu Antike und Christentum 97. Tübingen: Mohr Siebeck, 2015.

Malherbe, Abraham J. "Paul's Self-Sufficiency (Philippians 4:11)." Pages 125–140 in *Friendship, Flattery, and Frankness of Speech: Studies on Friendship in the New Testament World.* Edited by John T. Fitzgerald. Novum Testamentum Supplements 82. Leiden: Brill, 1996.

Malina, Bruce J. *Timothy: Paul's Closest Associate.* Collegeville, MN: Liturgical Press, 2008.

Martínez, Victor M. and Megan Finn Senseney. "The Professional and His Books: Special Libraries in the Ancient World." Pages 401–417 in *Ancient Libraries.* Edited by Jason König, Katerina Oukonomopoulou, and Greg Woolf. Cambridge: Cambridge University Press, 2013.

Morgan, Jonathan. "The Role of Asceticism in Deification in Cyril of Alexandria's Festal Letters." *Downside Review* 135 (2017): 144–153.

Morris, Leon. *The First and Second Epistles to the Thessalonians.* New International Commentary on the New Testament. Grand Rapids: Eerdmans, 1959.

Moss, Candida R. *God's Ghostwriters: Enslaved Christians and the Making of the Bible.* New York: Little, Brown and Company, 2024.

Moss, Candida R. "The Secretary: Enslaved Workers, Stenography, and the Production of Early Christian Literature." *Journal of Theological Studies* 74 (2023): 1–37.

Murphy-O'Connor, Jerome. "Co-Authorship in the Corinthian Correspondence." *Revue biblique* 100 (1993): 562–579.

Najman, Hindy and Irene Peirano Garrison. "Pseudepigraphy as an Interpretative Construct." Pages 331–355 in *The Old Testament Pseudepigrapha: Fifty Years of the Pseudepigrapha Section at the SBL.* Edited by Matthias Henze and Liv Ingeborg Lied. Atlanta: Society of Biblical Literature, 2019.

Niehoff, Maren R. *Jewish Exegesis and Homeric Scholarship in Alexandria.* Cambridge: Cambridge University Press, 2011.

Pearson, Birger A. "The Teachings of Silvanus." Pages 499–522 in *The Nag Hammadi Scriptures: The International Edition.* Edited by Marvin Meyer. New York: HarperOne, 2007.

150 Chance E. Bonar

Peel, Malcolm and Jan Zandee. "NHC VII,4: *The Teachings of Silvanus.*" Pages 249–369 in *Nag Hammadi Codex VII*. Edited by Birger A. Pearson. Nag Hammadi and Manichaean Studies 30. Leiden: Brill, 1996.

Peirano Garrison, Irene. *The Rhetoric of the Roman Fake: Latin Pseudepigrapha in Context*. Cambridge: Cambridge University Press, 2012.

Prior, Michael. *Paul the Letter-Writer and the Second Letter to Timothy*. Journal for the Study of the New Testament Supplement Series 23. Sheffield: Sheffield Academic Press, 1989.

Reece, Steve. *Paul's Large Letters: Paul's Autographic Subscriptions in the Light of Ancient Epistolary Conventions*. London: Bloomsbury, 2017.

Richards, E. Randolph. *Paul and First-Century Letter Writing: Secretaries, Composition and Collection*. Downers Grove, IL: InterVarsity Press, 2004.

Richards, E. Randolph. *The Secretary in the Letters of Paul*, Wissenschaftliche Untersuchungen zum Neuen Testament 2.42. Tübingen: Mohr Siebeck, 1991.

Richards, E. Randolph. "Silvanus Was Not Peter's Secretary: Theological Bias in Interpreting Σιλουανοῦ ... ἔγραψα in 1 Peter 5:12." *Journal of the Evangelical Theological Society* 43 (2000): 417–432.

Roller, Otto. *Das Formular der paulinischen Briefe: Ein Beitrag zur Lehre vom antiken Briefe*. Stuttgart: Kohlhammer, 1933.

Rüpke, Jörg. "Ennius's *Fasti* in Flavius's Temple: Greek Rationality and Roman Tradition." *Arethusa* 39 (2006): 489–512.

Russell, Norman. *The Doctrine of Deification in the Greek Patristic Tradition*. Oxford: Oxford University Press, 2004.

Sargent, Benjamin. "Chosen Through Sanctification (1 Pet 1,2 and 2 Thess 2,13): The Theology or Diction of Silvanus?" *Biblica* 94 (2013): 117–120.

Schedtler, Justin P. Jeffcoat. "Perplexing Pseudepigraphy: The Pseudonymous Greek Poets." *Journal of Ancient Judaism* 8 (2018): 69–89.

Schoedel, W. R. "Jewish Wisdom and the Formation of the Christian Ascetic." Pages 169–199 in *Aspects of Wisdom in Judaism and Early Christianity*. Edited by R. L. Wilken. Notre Dame, IL: University of Notre Dame, 1975.

Small, Jocelyn Penny. *Wax Tablets of the Mind: Cognitive Studies of Memory and Literacy in Classical Antiquity*. London: Routledge, 1997.

Smith, Mitzi J. "Slavery, Torture, Systemic Oppression, and Kingdom Rhetoric: An African American Reading of Matthew 25:1–13." Pages 77–97 in *Insights from African American Interpretation*. Edited by Mitzi J. Smith and Mark Allen Powell. Minneapolis, MN: Fortress Press, 2017.

Stefaniw, Blossom. "Masculinity as Flight: Vulnerability, Devotion, Submission and Sovereignty in the *Teachings of Silvanus.*" *Journal of Early Christian History* 11 (2021): 66–87.

Stewart, Eric C. "Masculinity in the New Testament and Early Christianity." *Journal of Bible and Culture* 46 (2016): 91–102.

Vaught, Curtis and Thomas Lea. *1, 2 Peter, Jude*. Grand Rapids: Zondervan, 1988.

Melito's Enoch

Anti-Judaism and the Transmission of the Pseudepigrapha*

ELENA DUGAN

It is not unusual for Christian manuscripts to contain a text attributed to a figure of pre-Jesus antiquity. In fact, as scholars of the pseudepigrapha know well, our modern access to these curious texts very often relies on Christian scribes preserving the works in manuscript traditions. In light of this reality, scholarship on the pseudepigrapha has been more and more cognizant of "Jewish texts and their Christian contexts," as Robert Kraft dubbed the conundrum.[1] When Christian manuscripts contain a text attributed to a figure of pre-Jesus antiquity – Abraham, Baruch, Enoch, Solomon, and so on – we should not simply think of this manuscript as a box in which an earlier tradition is stored, but as a repackaging for a purpose.

In this contribution, I will think about the problem of the "box": how to describe and evaluate the material context in which a pseudepigraphal text is found. Specifically, I will focus on the function of a pseudepigraphal attribution in its codicological context – when a book of Enoch appears in a Christian codex, how and why does it make a difference that it is a book of *Enoch*, and not Solomon, or Peter, or Mary? Why was Enoch, of all the figures in the early Christian imaginary, invited to be a member of this codex? And how does Enoch's presence shape how we evaluate the import and intended function of the codex, generally?

I will focus on the Epistle of Enoch in the fourth-century papyrus codex now split between the Chester-Beatty and University of Michigan's papyrological collections. I will argue that the Epistle must be understood alongside its companions in the codex – Melito's vitriolic supersessionist homily *Peri Pascha*, and the so-called Apocryphon of Ezekiel, both of which detail the historical failings of Israel to live up to its covenantal duties. I argue that the Epistle of Enoch was understood to be a valuable member of this codex pre-

---

* I presented versions of this work at the British New Testament Society's 2018 Annual Meeting, and the Society for Biblical Literature's 2021 Annual Meeting (Pseudepigrapha Section) and am grateful for the feedback of the participants. I am also grateful to Brent Nongbri, Garrick Allen, AnneMarie Luijendijk, Martha Himmelfarb, Stanley Porter, and Tommy Wassermann for answering questions as this contribution developed.

[1] Robert A. Kraft, *Exploring the Scripturesque: Jewish Texts and Their Christian Contexts* (Leiden: Brill, 2009).

152 *Elena Dugan*

cisely because it is chronologically pre-Christian, describing a moment of Israelite history in a manner consonant with a Christian's understanding of the same. The Epistle of Enoch is valued less as a timeless witness to certain ethical truths, and more as a time-and-spaced marker of a period when a certain patriarch saw deficiencies in his own tradition. In this case, the Epistle of Enoch became materially meaningful not only as it was tied to a particular historical person, but also to a definite historical time. This work therefore fulfills a literary function that moves beyond pseudepigraphy, to something like pseudo-chronography, and grafts Enoch into a historiography of Israel serving an anti-Jewish literary agenda.

1. Contents

In 1930, Alfred Chester-Beatty, an American mining magnate, purchased leaves of a papyrus codex from the Cairo dealer Maurice Nahman (P. Chester Beatty XII). The leaves were, and still are, of uncertain archaeological provenance, though were almost certainly unearthed in Egypt.[2] Also in 1930, the coincidentally named Enoch Peterson, director of the University of Michigan's excavation at Karanis, purchased what turned out to be two leaves of the Epistle of Enoch (p. Mich. inv. 5552), and four leaves of Melito's homily (p. Mich. inv. 5553).[3] Additional fragments belonging to this manuscript are currently held by the Chester-Beatty – previously labeled as BP 185, they are now considered to be part of P. Chester Beatty XII – and have been identified as part of an "Apocryphon of Ezekiel." The codex, as all its leaves are reassembled from across the two libraries in the imagination of scholars, is known as the Chester Beatty-Michigan Codex (TM 61462/LDAB 2608), a practice I will adopt below.

There was once more in the codex than we possess today. As it currently stands, the manuscript is made up of fourteen leaves of papyrus. The page dimensions seem to have been 14 cm x 27 cm, but the best preserved is 14 cm x 25 cm.[4] The three identified works belonging to the codex seem to have been written by the

---

[2] See Brent Nongbri, *God's Library: The Archaeology of the Earliest Christian Manuscripts* (New Haven: Yale University Press, 2018), 119–30. The leaves themselves can be accessed at https://viewer.cbl.ie/viewer/image/BP_XII_f_8/1/.

[3] See Brent Nongbri, "The Acquisition of the University of Michigan's Portion of the Chester Beatty Biblical Papyri and a New Suggested Provenance," *Archiv für Papyrusforschung und verwandte Gebiete* 60 (2014): 93–116. The leaves themselves can be accessed at: https://quod.lib.umich.edu/a/apis/x-3967/5552_19v.tif.

[4] Frederic G. Kenyon, *Fasciculus 8: Enoch and Melito*, The Chester Beatty Biblical Papyri: Descriptions and Texts of Twelve Manuscripts on Papyrus of the Greek Bible (London: Walker, 1941), 5. The reconstructed page dimensions are from Eric Gardner Turner, *The Typology of the Early Codex*, Haney Foundation Series 18 (Philadelphia: University of Pennsylvania Press, 1977), 132.

Figure 1. End of Enoch, beginning of Melito. BP XII f.13. © The Trustees of the Chester Beatty Library, Dublin.

154   *Elena Dugan*

same scribal hand, though the original publishers, Frederic Kenyon and Campbell Bonner, believe the page-numbers were added by a different hand.[5] Numbers ranging from 17–36 are preserved on the extant leaves, and we can use what we know of the order of Enoch from Ethiopic versions to line up what must be pages 15 and 16 at the beginning of the progression. We are therefore missing pages 1–14, or seven leaves of papyrus, if the numbering can be trusted as a guide to the codex's one-time shape. It is possible we are missing even more, depending on how scholars reconstruct the codex.[6] It seems to have been produced in the fourth or fifth century.[7]

We do know the Epistle of Enoch preceded Melito's homily – we know this because the Epistle ends on page 26 (as numbered in the codex), followed by a herring-bone decoration serving as a dividing line, then the beginning of Melito on the very same page (Figure 1). There are fragments of a third work, which has been identified as the Apocryphon of Ezekiel. But there are also fragments belonging to the manuscript that have not been satisfactorily identified as belonging to any of the three works, and it is possible there were one or more additional short works belonging to this codex.[8]

The easiest of the three works to describe may be Melito's homily – a stridently anti-Jewish sermon. The homily is infamous for its explicit supersessionism, deriding the events of the Passover as devoid of spiritual significance now that they have reached culmination in the crucifixion of Jesus as Christ. The most "horrendous novelty" introduced by Melito herein was the charge of deicide: he insisted upon Jewish culpability for the death of Jesus, and therefore the death of God.[9] But the Passover, and explicit typological connections to the crucifixion of Jesus, are not Melito's only concerns. In verses 49–56, Melito outlines the twisted inheritance of humans, as the generations after Adam were "seized by tyrannical sin (v. 49)," and "swamped by unsatiable pleasures (v. 49)."[10] This is the origin

---

[5] Campbell Bonner, *The Last Chapters of Enoch in Greek* (London: Christophers, 1937), 6; Kenyon, *Fasciculus 8: Enoch and Melito*, 6.

[6] In the initial publication, Kenyon observed that the first 7 leaves are verso-recto, while the next 7 are recto-verso. He proposed a codex constructed of one quire of 14 leaves, plus a smaller quire of 8 leaves, which would account for the 7 missing leaves needed to fill out the page numbering. He also suggested these 14 leaves might be the central portions of a quire of 28 leaves, which would suggest we are missing 7 leaves before and 7 leaves following the preserved leaves. This discussion can be found in Kenyon, *Fasciculus 8: Enoch and Melito*, 6. Brent Nongbri's recent re-evaluation of the Chester-Beatty Biblical papyri judiciously notes the number of quires was "probably 1," and the folia were "at least 15" in number, in Nongbri, *God's Library*, 132–33.

[7] Bonner, *The Last Chapters of Enoch in Greek*, 13; Kenyon, *Fasciculus 8: Enoch and Melito*, 12; Turner, *The Typology of the Early Codex*, 132; Nongbri, *God's Library*, 132–33.

[8] Some of these fragments can be seen at https://viewer.cbl.ie/viewer/image/BP_XII_i_1/2/.

[9] Stephen G. Wilson, "Melito and Israel," in *Anti-Judaism in Early Christianity*, ed. Stephen G. Wilson, Vol. 2: Separation and Polemic (Waterloo: Wilfred Laurier University Press, 1986), 81–102, n. 101.

[10] This is the translation of Stuart George Hall, *On Pascha and Fragments*, Oxford Early Christian Texts (Oxford: Clarendon Press, 1979). The original edition and translation, tied

Figure 2. Herring-bone decoration on fragment assigned to Apocryphon of Ezekiel. BP 185. © The Trustees of the Chester Beatty Library, Dublin.

of the wretched state of the world into which Jesus would one day be born. He stretches the story forward from Adam and suggests that Christ's suffering was prefigured in that of Abel, Isaac, Joseph, Moses, and David (v. 59), emphasizing that what has come to pass was "foreseen well in advance (57)." In that way, not just the Passover, but the whole of the tradition of Israel, with a focus on the antediluvian world (49–56), serves as a type for a sinful and oppressed world awaiting the salvation arriving with Jesus as Christ.

The Apocryphon of Ezekiel is fragmentary – it appears short, but because of its fragmentary preservation, we don't know just how short it once was! There are three fragments which Bonner's initial publication identified with this composition.[11] Of these three, it is the verso of the first and largest fragment that has guided identification, as the text overlaps with sayings attributed to Ezekiel by Clement of Alexandria in *Paedagogus* I. (9.)84.2–4.[12] The recto of the first fragment does not evidence any such overlap, nor do the other two fragments. Part of the reason Bonner included the third fragment in this grouping was because

---

to the Chester-Beatty-Michigan manuscript, is Campbell Bonner, *The Homily on the Passion: With Some Fragm. of the Apocryphal Ezekiel* (London: Christophers, 1940). I will generally rely on Bonner, as he was only attempting to translate the Chester-Beatty-Michigan Codex, which is helpful for our purposes. I do, however, appreciate many of Hall's turns of phrase, as here.

[11] The Chester Beatty has made these images available (as of November 2022), at https://viewer.cbl.ie/viewer/image/BP_185/1/LOG_0000/.

[12] For the initial publication, see Bonner, *The Homily on the Passion*, 183–90. More recent treatments include James R. Mueller and Stephen E. Robinson, "Apocryphon of Ezekiel," in *The Old Testament Pseudepigrapha*, ed. James H. Charlesworth, Vol. 1 (London: Darton, Longman & Todd, 1983), 91–203; James R. Mueller, *The Five Fragments of the Apocryphon of Ezekiel: A Critical Study*, Journal for the Study of the Pseudepigrapha Supplement 5 (Sheffield: Sheffield Academic Press, 1994), 149–56; Benjamin G. Wright, "The Apocryphal Ezekiel Fragments," in *The Apocryphal Ezekiel*, ed. Michael E. Stone, David Satran, and Benjamin G. Wright, Early Judaism and Its Literature 18 (Atlanta: Society of Biblical Literature, 2000), 28–34; Benjamin G. Wright, "The Apocryphon of Ezekiel," in *Old Testament Pseudepigrapha: More Noncanonical Scriptures*, ed. Richard Bauckham, James R. Davila, and Alexander Panayotov, vol. 1 (Grand Rapids: Eerdmans, 2013), 380–92.

156   *Elena Dugan*

of an aesthetic clue – it has a herring-bone decoration which seems to mark the end of a selection.[13]

But scholars are rightly cautious about assigning fragments 2 and 3 to a purported Apocryphon of Ezekiel, for all they have been grouped with it in the history of editing.[14]

What remains is a little hard to parse, but a core theme seems to be God's covenant with Israel. The verso of the first fragment, which runs parallel to the portion from Clement, is a passage inspired by Ezekiel 34, in which God reiterates his power to save and punish. The recto of the first fragment, though too damaged to be fully cohesive, features specific references to figures and places in Israelite history – beginning with something about "the Egyptians," followed by an injunction for Jerusalem to beg for mercy, and recounting a memory of mercy granted to Abraham, Isaac, and Jacob. Fragments 2 and 3, if they belong to this work, seem to mention a kind of visionary journey, but we know little else at this stage. The impression, though fragmented by poor preservation, is of a contested relationship between God and Israel, with specific memories of exemplary figures and places playing a key role.

The Epistle of Enoch is a title used to refer to 1 Enoch 91–108. This designation of chapters, and the whole of 108 chapters implied, is drawn from a longer version of a work known as *Henok* attested in Ethiopic manuscripts.[15] Within chapters 91–108, there are multiple identifiable works, though scholars differ on where, exactly, to draw the lines between them.[16] Most scholars agree on a few key component pieces making up the Epistle of Enoch – the Apocalypse of Weeks (1 Enoch 91, 93), the Body of the Epistle (roughly 1 Enoch 94–105), the Book of Noah (1 Enoch 106–107), and a standalone compilation that George Nickelsburg and James VanderKam's recent popular translation calls "A Final Book of Enoch."[17] The reason this matters is that not all of these component pieces are attested in the Chester-Beatty-Michigan manuscript. In fact, it seems we only have the Body of the Epistle and the Book of Noah, as the Chester Beatty codex contains text corresponding to 1 Enoch 97.6–107.3.[18] It would be inaccurate, then,

---

[13] Bonner, *The Homily on the Passion*, 183.

[14] As noted in in Mueller, *The Five Fragments of the Apocryphon of Ezekiel*, 156; Wright, "The Apocryphon of Ezekiel," 383.

[15] On Henok as the title of this work, see Ted M. Erho and Loren T. Stuckenbruck, "The Ge'ez Manuscript Tradition and the Study of 1 Enoch: Problems and Prospects" (10th Enoch Seminar: Enoch and Enochic Traditions in the Early Modern Period: A Reception History from the 15th to the End of the 19th Centuries, Florence, Italy, 2019).

[16] For one influential recent treatment, see Loren T. Stuckenbruck, *1 Enoch 91–108* (Berlin: De Gruyter, 2007), 5–13.

[17] George W. E. Nickelsburg and James C. VanderKam, *1 Enoch: A New Translation, Based on the Hermeneia Commentary* (Minneapolis: Fortress, 2004), 168.

[18] Note also these further fragment identifications, which might identify text outside the Body (1 Enoch 94–105) and Book of Noah (1 Enoch 106–107), but which I find unconvincing: 1) Milik proposed that a fragment assigned by Bonner to Pseudo-Ezekiel actually comprises 1 Enoch

Melito's Enoch 157

to say that the Chester-Beatty-Michigan manuscript contains the entirety of the Epistle of Enoch, in the way that scholars use that term to refer to a progression of text covering 1 Enoch 91–108. Funnily enough, though, the title "Epistle of Enoch" comes from this very manuscript and nowhere else – it is found in no other manuscript, in Ethiopia or otherwise. So, this manuscript does contain the Epistle of Enoch – or at least, that is its exact claim! But it does not contain what scholars mean by the Epistle – if we ask the manuscript to return 1 Enoch 91–108, we will be disappointed.

The text of Enoch included herein features Enoch at his most ethically interested – holding forth to a community on economic injustice and the divergent fates of the wicked and righteous, and issuing prophecies of a time in which all will receive their just deserts. Enoch pronounces woe unto the rich (97.8–10), who are suffused in decadence that will come to an inevitable end (98.1–3). He opines that lawlessness was not sent to the earth, but rather, humans brought it upon themselves (98.4) – the focus on human agency, and recompense based on what people have done, is pronounced throughout. He warns of the coming judgment, but encourages the righteous that, "you will shine; the gates

---

91.3–4. In J. T. Milik, *The Books of Enoch: Aramaic Fragments of Qumran Cave 4* (Oxford: Clarendon Press, 1976), 259. Cf. also Bonner, *The Homily on the Passion*, 187; Albert Pietersma, "New Greek Fragments of Biblical Manuscripts in the Chester Beatty Library," *Bulletin of the American Society of Papyrologists* 24 (1987): 44; Eibert Tigchelaar, "Evaluating the Discussions Concerning the Original Order of Chapters 91–93 and Codicological Data Pertaining to 4Q212 and Chester Beatty XII Enoch," in *Enoch and Qumran Origins: New Light on a Forgotten Connection*, ed. Gabriele Boccaccini (Grand Rapids: Eerdmans, 2005), 221. 2) Milik proposed that a fragment attests 1 Enoch 92.1. This is accepted by Pietersma and Stuckenbruck. Milik additionally suggests the recto contains 92.5, though this is rejected as improbable by Pietersma, and not adopted in Stuckenbruck. See Bonner, *The Last Chapters of Enoch in Greek*, 11; Milik, *Books of Enoch*, 261–62; Pietersma, "New Greek Fragments of Biblical Manuscripts in the Chester Beatty Library," 44; Stuckenbruck, *1 Enoch 91–108*, 218. 3) Pietersma places a fragment which he suggests attests 1 Enoch 93.12–13 and 1 Enoch 94.7, verses which may belong to the Body of the Epistle, or to transitionary material around the Apocalypse of Weeks. See Pietersma, "New Greek Fragments of Biblical Manuscripts in the Chester Beatty Library," 42–43. It is startling that none of these identifications establish text corresponding to the Apocalypse of Weeks proper (1 Enoch 93.1–10; 91.11–17). The second and third identifications, however, would seem to establish text (92.1 and 93.12–13) that finds parallel in 4Q212, a document which is largely taken up by the Apocalypse of Weeks. The problem is that these chapters are immensely difficult to subdivide into pieces, as most translations of the Epistle actually rearrange the Ethiopic to present a more original ordering of the various pieces of text housed in chapters 91–94, an order found in no manuscript anywhere. So, the presence of these particular verses in the Chester-Beatty codex does not necessarily clue us into the presence of the Apocalypse of Weeks, though it does point to a very complicated textual history surrounding these identifiable subsidiary works. Regardless of these problems, codicological discussions of the extent of 1 Enoch in the Chester-Beatty codex often proceed as if we are looking for the entirety of the Epistle, assuming the presence of the Apocalypse of Weeks (see, e. g., the calculations of the length of the missing pages of the Chester-Beatty Enoch by Pietersma and Tigchelaar, both of which look to 1 Enoch 91.1 as the presumed starting point). In light of the fragmentary nature of the evidence, I find this to be an unduly confident assumption.

158 Elena Dugan

of heaven will be opened to you (104.2)."[19] The reader might wonder about the particular community to which this epistle might have been composed and addressed, because of its continued emphasis on a righteous in-group, alongside its consistent complaints about a wealthy, decadent, idolatrous, and (percievedly) corrupt network of oppressors, though the concerns are enduring enough that they might apply to a number of settings.

In chapter 106, the tone shifts, as we leave the Body of the Epistle, and enter the Book of Noah. We read a story about the coming of Enoch's great-grandson Noah, who will "tame the earth from the corruption which is in it (106.17)." The very last line of the Epistle of Enoch is: "and his name was called Noah, consoling the earth from the destruction (107.3)." The Epistle of Enoch, as extant in the Chester-Beatty-Michigan codex, contains a strident condemnation of the oppressors of today, but with reference to a coming era in which justice will be done, and the consolation and hope that might be offered by a saving figure on the horizon: Noah.

This, then, is what we have in the Chester-Beatty-Michigan codex, in order: 1) an excoriation of the wicked rich, and exhortation to the righteous to hold fast until an era in which justice will be done, attributed to an antediluvian prophet (the Body of the Epistle); 2) A prophecy of the coming of a saving figure, to punish the wicked, cleanse the earth, and usher in a new age (the Book of Noah); 3) A supersessionist homily on the failings of Israel, with an interest in traditions of Israel as types for the advent of Christ (Melito). And somewhere in the codex, an Apocryphon of Ezekiel (or extracts) reflect on God's conflicted covenantal relationship with Israel.

2. George Nickelsburg and the Possibility of a Miscellany

In 1990, George Nickelsburg wrote an article on the only two long-form Greek manuscripts containing excerpts of Enoch extant to scholars today – the Chester-Beatty-Michigan manuscript, and the Codex Panopolitanus – suggesting their codicology might be interesting to scholars. Each of these two manuscripts contains multiple identifiable works, and Nickelsburg set himself the task of trying to discern "a rationale for the collection."[20] He undertook this goal in the hopes that each manuscript might not just be mined for text-critical details pertaining

---

[19] All translations of the Epistle of Enoch, unless otherwise noted, are from the translation of the Chester-Beatty-Michigan manuscript in Stuckenbruck, *1 Enoch 91–108*.

[20] George W. E. Nickelsburg, "Two Enochic Manuscripts: Unstudied Evidence for Egyptian Christianity," in *Of Scribes and Scrolls: Studies on the Hebrew Bible, Intertestamental Judaism, and Christian Origins Presented to John Strugnell on the Occasion of His Sixtieth Birthday*, ed. Harold W. Attridge, John J. Collins, and Thomas H. Tobin (Lanham, MD: University Press of America, 1990), 251.

Melito's Enoch　　　159

to Enoch, but might also be reclaimed as evidence for Egyptian Christianity. Nickelsburg was thereby an early adopter of an approach that would gain increasing popularity in pseudepigrapha studies, as scholars grew more thoughtful about the Christian manuscripts in which purportedly Jewish texts were embedded.[21]

Nickelsburg notes many of the larger themes I highlighted in my summary above, and that they work together in the codex to tell a particular kind of story.[22] In his words:

> The order of the three texts in the codex would have suggested the following interpretation. God promised that Israel would return from exile and live on the holy mountain in a new covenantal relationship with God (Ezekiel). Israel, however, has continued to sin. Therefore, God has rejected the nation and accepted the church as the holy people. The promises made through Ezekiel have failed because of Israel's renewed disobedience – their perversion of the ancient covenant (Enoch), and their rejection of the Christ (Melito).[23]

I think this intuition of a cohesive codex is broadly correct, and some of the below will serve to draw a version of this hypothesis out, highlighting particular connections between the texts, and updating Nickelsburg's suggestion with reference to contemporary scholarship on papyrology and codicology.

But Nickelsburg also suggests that the Epistle of Enoch was read without historical coding. He suggests "the Epistle would probably not have been understood as a Jewish product, but as writing by the ancient seer, addressed especially to 'the latter generations who will observe truth and peace (92:1).'"[24] The idea of the compiler would be that Enoch's prophecies were effectively dehistoricized, waiting for the arrival of Christian readers – Christians, thousands of years into the future, were Enoch's intended audience all along.

Against this, I think it crucial that the Epistle was coded as a "Jewish product," or at least, one that is chronologically pre-Christian. Melito's venomous anti-Judaism has a specific and manifest poison – *Peri Pascha* does not just recast people and events in Israelite history as "types" awaiting their fulfillment, but

---

[21] For some touchpoints in the literature, see Robert A. Kraft, "The Pseudepigrapha and Christianity, Revisited: Setting the Stage and Framing Some Central Questions," in *Exploring the Scripturesque: Jewish Texts and Their Christian Contexts* (Leiden: Brill, 2009), 35–61; Marinus de Jonge, *Pseudepigrapha of the Old Testament as Part of Christian Literature: The Case of the Testaments of the Twelve Patriarchs and the Greek Life of Adam and Eve* (Leiden: Brill, 2003); Liv Ingeborg Lied and Loren T. Stuckenbruck, "Pseudepigrapha and Their Manuscripts," in *The Old Testament Pseudepigrapha*, ed. Liv Ingeborg Lied and Matthias Henze, Fifty Years of the Pseudepigrapha Section at the SBL (Atlanta: Society of Biblical Literature, 2019), 203–30.

[22] Note that Nickelsburg places the Apocryphon of Ezekiel first in the progression, though he acknowledges there is little physical data to guide us in placing the fragments.

[23] Nickelsburg, "Two Enochic Manuscripts: Unstudied Evidence for Egyptian Christianity," 258.

[24] Nickelsburg, "Two Enochic Manuscripts: Unstudied Evidence for Egyptian Christianity," 256.

160 *Elena Dugan*

also goes out of its way to highlight Israel's wretched and sinful ways during the antediluvian period. The presence of Enoch in the codex is not just as a keeper of benignly inspirational exhortations for Christians, but becomes a chronicle of moments during the lifetime of Enoch that Israel failed.

3. Enoch in the Chester-Beatty-Michigan Codex

We can begin with two paratextual features of the Chester-Beatty-Michigan codex that highlight the person of Enoch.

The first, as previously mentioned, is the presence of the title "Epistle of Enoch" at the end of the work. There are some grounds for the title in the Greek text itself – 1 Enoch 100.6, as extant in the Chester-Beatty-Michigan manuscript, features a reference to "the words of this epistle (τοὺς λόγους τούτους τῆς ἐπιστολῆς ταύτης)," though exactly what is meant by "this epistle" is unclear (Just this section of the text? The entire work as extant in Greek? All of Enoch's writings?).[25] A hypothesis that titular practices belie the Chester-Beatty-Michigan codex's focus on historical personages might also be clarified by the very next title – just after Enoch, Melito begins, introduced simply as "μελιτων" (Figure 3). By comparision, in the Bodmer Miscellaneous Codex, the work is introduced as "μελιτωνος περι πασχα."[26] Perhaps, then, we have a codex unusually interested in its authors.

It is, however, ultimately uncertain just how remarkable or notable a title this might have been in the context of other biblical and parabiblical literature, as we lack a plethora of titles preserved on biblical papyri to provide contemporary comparanda.[27] P72, a title marker designating 1 and 2 Peter and Jude as extant in the Bodmer Miscellaneous Codex, includes both inscriptions and subscriptions for each work marking them off as epistles belonging to their respective men (e. g., πετρου επιστολη α, in Figure 4).[28]

It is generally the case that the literary genre of "epistle" implies a sender, and directly connects the attending text with a certain historical person.[29] In that

---

[25] For Aramaic and Ethiopic evidence concerning a possible title, see the discussion in Stuckenbruck, *1 Enoch 91–108*, 188. Note that neither Aramaic nor Ethiopic manuscripts provide clear additional evidence for the existence of the title "Epistle of Enoch."

[26] The page in question can be seen at: https://bodmerlab.unige.ch/fr/constellations/papyri/mirador/1072205366?page=056

[27] In what follows, I rely on the information assembled in Garrick V. Allen, "Titles in the New Testament Papyri," *New Testament Studies* 68 (2022): 156–71.

[28] Image from https://upload.wikimedia.org/wikipedia/commons/3/38/Papyrus_Bodmer_VIII.jpg

[29] On definitions of "epistle," and "letter," see Lutz Doering, *Ancient Jewish Letters and the Beginnings of Christian Epistolography*, Wissenschaftliche Untersuchungen zum Neuen Testament 298 (Tübingen: Mohr Siebeck, 2012), 17–28.

Figure 3. Titles for Enoch and Melito. BP XII f.13. © The Trustees of the Chester Beatty Library, Dublin.

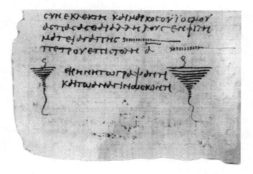

Figure 4. Ending of 1 Peter, with some similar decorations to the Epistle of Enoch. P72 X v. (p. 36).

case, the subscriptive labeling of this work "Epistle of Enoch," emphasizes (to the point of obviousness) what was already pretty clear throughout – that this is a missive sent by Enoch. But the titular practices of P46, a codex also belonging to the Chester-Beatty Biblical papyri and comprising the works which scholars now call the "Pauline Epistles" and Hebrews (P46), provides a helpful reminder that there was another option: the work could have been named after its recipient. After all, P46 never uses the term "epistle" in inscription or subscription, always identifying the letters by their recipients (e. g., προς εβραιους). So, when it came time to title the Epistle of Enoch, why not call it προς Μαθουσάλας (cf. 91.1, 106.1, or the reference to "my children" at 94.1)? In sum, the title of the Chester-Beatty-Michigan codex – "Epistle of Enoch" – might feel on-the-nose, but it is not devoid of information.

A second feature is the off-setting of woes in the body of the text itself, which may function as a kind of emphatic quotation, and draws further attention to Enoch as speaker. The Epistle of Enoch spends a good amount of time pronouncing woes upon ("οὐαὶ ὑμῖν ...") any number of wrongdoers: the "stiff-necked and hard of heart (99.11)," those who "write lying words (99.15)," "fools

Figure 5. "Woes" set off in the Chester-Beatty-Michigan Epistle. BP XII f.9. © The Trustees of the Chester Beatty Library, Dublin.

[who] will be destroyed because of your folly (99.9)," and so on. Many of these woes are set off with pericope dividers of some kind. In Figure 5, we can see examples of woes set off by spaces within a line, as well as woes set off with the aid of *ekthesis* (the projection of the first letter of the line following a break). The scribal patterns here are reminiscent of those used for Jesus' woes. Though we do not have many papyrus witnesses to Matthew 23 and Luke 11 (in fact, we only have 2), the sites of the infamous Woes of the Pharisees, P75 provides one apt comparison to the interactions between text and layout that we see in Enoch (Figure 6).[30] Of course, these passages from Matthew, Luke, and Enoch are not the only collections of woe oracles belonging to ancient Jewish and Christian literature! But we are dealing with Greek papyri, and material collections in

---

[30] See also the similar patterns of spacing and ekthesis used for the relevant portions of Matthew and Luke among the parchment codices – Vaticanus, Alexandrinus, Sinaiticus, Washingtonianus, and Bezae – collated in Charles E. Hill, "The Capitulatio Vaticana and Its Predecessors in the New Testament," in *The First Chapters: Dividing the Text of Scripture in Codex Vaticanus and Its Predecessors* (Oxford: Oxford University Press, 2022), 313–400.

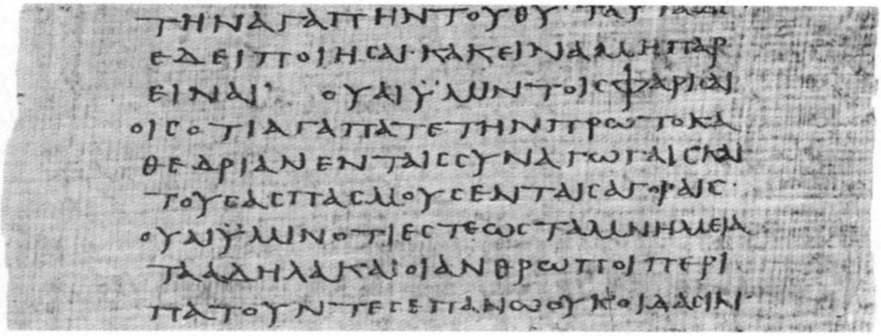

Melito's Enoch 163

Figure 6. Woes in Luke 11. P75.

orbit around works that would be deemed biblical. It is therefore striking to see Enoch's woe oracles materially arranged in a manner consonant with those ascribed to Jesus in Matthew and Luke. This may simply be a marker of the strength of Christian scribal reflexes, and the extent to which we must imagine our scribe of Enoch being cognizant of, and perhaps even trained on, works belonging to the New Testament. Or, it might be objected that markers like this are just an offhand device to keep things organized.

Stanley Porter, however, has suggested that pericope divisions in the papyri around Jesus' woes might represent "emphatic quotation."[31] I find this a helpful suggestion with reference to the Epistle of Enoch, as the effect in our codex is the identification of multiple utterances – woe after woe after woe. By setting off individual woe oracles, different moments of speech are created, and what was once a block utterance might break into multiple moments. What was one woe oracle becomes two, or three, or eight. The unifying element is the speaker to whom a manifold network of oracles is now attributed. I therefore take Porter's suggestion that we think about emphatic quotation to mean that we should think about the person being quoted – Enoch – and acknowledge the stress upon the figure to whom the woes are attributed accordingly. Moreover, the appearance of multiplication made possible by the continual offsetting of individual woes makes Israel's missteps seem voluminous indeed![32]

Though subtle, I suggest that both of these paratextual features serve to highlight the sender of the epistle: Enoch. They make it difficult to depersonalize the work, or to stretch it away from its imagined historical context. The naming of the work as an Epistle of Enoch – nothing more, nothing less – squarely em-

---

[31] See Porter's discussion of Matthew 23 in P77 and Luke 11 in P75 in Stanley E. Porter, "Pericope Markers in Some Early Greek New Testament Manuscripts," in *Layout Markers in Biblical Manuscripts and Ugaritic Tablets*, ed. Marjo C.A. Korpel and Josef M. Oesch. (Leiden: Brill, 2005), 161–76, esp. 165, 169.

[32] I am grateful to Chance Bonar for this suggestion.

164   *Elena Dugan*

phasizes the sender. And the delimitation of the woes mirrors the delimitation of woes we see in early manuscripts of Matthew and Luke – a curious material echo that may simply reveal trained Christian scribal reflexes, but which might also be a kind of emphatic quotation, revealing a heightened cognizance of a speaker. Paratextual features emphasize Enoch behind the Epistle. But what, exactly, is Enoch doing in this codex? I have suggested that part of the answer comes from Melito's account of the antediluvian period, worthy of being quoted in full:

> And when he (Adam) became prolific and lived long, through the tasting of the tree had returned to earth, there was bequeathed by him to his children an inheritance; for an inheritance he left them, not chastity, but fornication (πορνείαν), not incorruptibility but corruption (φθοράν), not honor but dishonor (ἀτιμίαν), not freedom but slavery (δουλείαν), not sovereignty but oppression (τυραννίδα), not life but death, not salvation but destruction (ἀπώλειαν). And strange and terrible was the destruction of men upon the earth. For these woes befell them; they were seized by tyrannous sin and led into the turmoils of desires (χώρους τῶν ἐπιθυμιῶν), in which they were buffeted about by insatiable pleasures (τῶν ἀκορέστων ἡδονῶν), by adultery (μοιχείας), by fornication (πορνείας), by lewdness (ἀσελγείας), by lust (ἐπιθυμίας), by avarice (φιλαργυρίας), by murders (φόνων), by bloodshed (αἱμάτων), by oppression wicked and lawless.

> Father drew sword against son, and son laid hands upon father, and impiously smote the breasts that nurtured him. Brother slew brother, and friend friend, and man slaughtered man with tyrannous hand. So all men became, some man-slayers, some father-slayers, some child-slayers upon the earth. But what ... and most terribly on the ... A father touched the flesh ... drinking ... no longer spared her children. Many deeds they also did which were accounted most ... among men; the father lusted for his child, the son for his mother, the brother for his sister, male for male, and each man for his neighbor's wife (48–52).[33]

In this passage, Melito recites a litany of crimes into which humanity fell, after Adam. Many of them have clear parallels in the Epistle of Enoch.

Motif	*Melito*	*Epistle of Enoch*
"Honor and dishonor"	... not honor, but dishonor (οὐ τιμὴν ἀλλὰ ἀτιμίαν) (49)	... honor into dishonor (καὶ τῆς τιμῆς εἰς ἀτιμίαν) (98.3)
Slavery	... not freedom, but slavery (ουκ ἐλευθερίαν ἄλλα δουλείαν). (49)	It was not ordained that a slave be a slave – it was not given from above – but came about because of oppression (ὅτι οὐχ ὡρίσθη δούλην εἶναι δούλην· ἄνωθεν οὐκ ἐδόθη ἀλλὰ ἐκ καταδυναστείας ἐγένετο). (98.5)
Murder	... they were swamped by insatiable pleasures ... by murder (φόνων) (50)	Woe to those who practice lawlessness and help unrighteousness, murdering (φονεύοντες) their neighbor (99.15)

---

[33] Translation from Bonner, *The Homily on the Passion.*

Melito's Enoch 165

Motif	Melito	Epistle of Enoch
Perversion of mothers[34]	... the strangest and most terrible thing happened on the earth: a mother touched the flesh which she has borne, and fastened onto those she had fed at the breast (52)	In that time, those who are giving birth will expel and put away and abandon the infant, and those with child will [abort], and those who suckle will cast their children, and they will not return to their infants (99.5)
Fathers killing sons, the killing of brothers, mass-murder	Father drew sword against son, and son laid hands upon father (χεῖρας προσήνεγκεν), and impiously smote the breasts that nurtured him. Brother slew (ἐφόνευσεν,) brother, and friend friend, man slaughtered man with tyrannous hand. So all men became, some man-slayers, some father-slayers, some child-slayers upon the earth (51)	And then in one place ... their blood ... and a man will not withhold his hand (οὐκ ἀφέξει τὴν χεῖρα αὐτοῦ) from his son nor from his beloved in order to kill him, and the sinner from an honest man, nor from his brother. From dawn until the sun sets, they will be murdered (φονευθήσονται) together (100.1)
Male sexual transgression/ gender confusion	Many deeds they also did which were accounted most ....among men; the father lusted for his child, the son for his mother, the brother for his sister, male for male, and each man for his neighbor's wife (53)	You will see many lawless things upon the earth. For men will be adorned with beautification like women, color more beautiful than virgins, in royalty, majesty, and power (98.2)

Although the phrasing is not always the same, the substance of the accounts is quite similar. The period after Adam, the era in which Enoch would purportedly issue his epistle, is characterized by intense moral degradation: by enslavement, dishonor, murder (and interfamilial murder!), by mothers forsaking and even perverting their duties to their children. The last two passages, which I have labeled "sexual transgression/gender confusion," overlap in that men are excoriated for transgressing heteronormative bounds. Melito objects to sexual pairings that cross boundaries – incest, men pursuing men, and adultery. And Enoch includes men "adorned with beautification like women" among a denunciation of the lawless, specifically those belonging to a decadent elite, prophesying that they will "perish together with all your possessions (98.3)." There is more in Enoch than might be picked up in Melito, of course, as the text has emphases of its own which have little or lesser echo in Melito – Enoch's focus

---

[34] This parallel has been previously noted by Loren T. Stuckenbruck: "The crimes described in this verse are included amongst the consequences of the fall of humanity in the Garden of Eden in Melito's sermon On the Passover 49–56 (esp. 51–52)" (1 Enoch 91–108, 392).

166 Elena Dugan

on the wickedness of the rich and economic injustice, for example, does not do too much for Melito. But there are remarkable similarities that suggest we might have passed the bounds of coincidence.

We also have a curious feature of the Chester-Beatty-Epistle that may be explained thanks to the presence of Melito in the codex – the inclusion of the Book of Noah, as an additional marker of Enoch's location in historical time. The Book of Noah (1 Enoch 106–107) marks a clear change of pace from the Body of the Epistle. It does not continue Enoch's remarks on the failings of the wicked and the promises due to the righteous, but switches to become a narrative about the birth of Noah, as Lamech fears that this shining child may not be a product of this earth. It is a curious inclusion especially because of the epistolary title given to the work in the codex – 1 Enoch 97–105 sounds like an epistle should, with lots of grandstanding and the delivery of unsolicited advice, but the Book of Noah is an abrupt change of pace.[35] There is even a marker in the text itself that something has shifted, as there is a striking space in the manuscript at the end of 1 Enoch 104.9, before the beginning of 1 Enoch 106.1 (Figure 7).

One thing accomplished with the inclusion of the Book of Noah, however, is that Enoch's historical location becomes crystal-clear. We are reminded of what the reader already knew, but perhaps did not have at the front of their mind – that Enoch was the father of Methuselah, who was the father of Lamech, and so on, and that he belongs to the antediluvian generation. At one point, when Methuselah asks Enoch's advice, Enoch replies with a historical prophecy (106.13–17) outlining what has already taken place (the transgressions of Enoch's age, and the age of his father), and what will come in the next crop of years (the Flood, and the coming of Noah to "tame the earth from the corruption which is in it" [106.17]). The arrival of Noah might of course have some typological significance for a Christian reader, though, interestingly, Noah does not play a role in Melito's homily here. (Note that other versions of Melito have verses 83–85 mention Noah in passing, but these lines are damaged in the Chester-Beatty-Michigan codex, and what remains does not mention Noah at all.)[36] Instead, it seems to me that the primary demonstrable function of the Book of Noah is to extend the Epistle into the historical narrative of the antediluvian period, and anchor its oracles in a particular chronographic landscape. Without the Book of Noah, much of the content of the Epistle of Enoch is flexible enough to be applied to a variety of temporal settings, which can frustrate both ancient and modern readers. Stuckenbruck notes, for example, that modern scholarly attempts to date the Epistle precisely are foiled by the reality that "the language of the Epistle in general is too imprecise to pin down on … particular

---

[35] Cf. Stuckenbruck's remark that "This subscription, ΕΠΙΣΤΟΛΗ ΕΝΟΧ, does not describe Birth of Noah or the Apoc. of Weeks very well," (1 Enoch 91–108, 606).

[36] See the translation and critical notes in Hall, On Pascha and Fragments, 46–47.

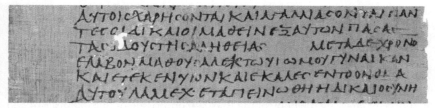

Figure 7. Transition from Body of the Epistle to Book of Noah. P Mich. inv. 5552, recto.

groups."[37] But, with the Book of Noah, a particular chronological framework is explicitly foregrounded (though this does not, of course, foreclose the possibility of more presentist reading strategies!).

My proposal is, then, that the Epistle of Enoch's primary function in the Chester-Beatty-Michigan codex is as a purported historical witness to a particular moment of catastrophe in the history of Israel. Paratextual features which emphasize Enoch, and the inclusion of the Book of Noah, make it hard to detach the message from the messenger. And the "message" itself bears striking resemblance to Melito's portrait of Israel as fallen into a post-Eden state of calamity.

An abiding concern of Melito's anti-Jewish homily is the failures of Israel to spot the workings of God in their lives (not least of which is displayed in the Jews' recent failure to recognize Jesus as their Messiah). Enoch, in this context, may be the shining exception, an Israelite (or, perhaps, a Jew – though it depends how we parse Enoch as a pre-Mosaic patriarch from the perspective of the Christian assembling the codex in the fourth century CE) who saw his people descending into sin and cried out against it. The Epistle of Enoch may thereby be a valuable member of this codex precisely because it is chronologically pre-Christian, describing a moment of Israelite history in a manner consonant with a Christian's understanding of the same. It might be subject to a kind of typological reading as a witness to the times of contemporary issues, but its tightest correspondences within its codicological context are with a passage that decries this very particular post-Adamic, pre-Noachic moment in Israelite history.

It is (of course!) not inherently anti-Jewish for prophets to be critical of the practices, excesses, or mistakes of their time. The Epistle of Enoch is not an inherently anti-Jewish text! This probably goes without saying. But in the earliest context in which it is documented, it seems to be presenting an anti-Jewish agenda. We have no earlier manuscripts of the so-called "body" of the Epistle of Enoch (1 Enoch 94–105), as it is not attested at Qumran, nor found in any other

---

[37] Stuckenbruck, *1 Enoch 91–108*, 212.

168   Elena Dugan

early Greek manuscripts.[38] The Chester-Beatty-Michigan manuscript therefore provides our earliest evidence for the text of this portion of the Epistle and represents our only evidence for the work in Greek. When we notice the ways in which this work functions in its place in a Christian codex, it may be tempting to phrase these features as "adaptations" from a previous or Jewish version. But, unfortunately, we have no evidence for any other version – in fact, every single manuscript attesting the body of the Epistle (comprising of this manuscript and the manifold Ge'ez witnesses) is Christian.[39]

Some of what we uncover in this exposition, then, may not just be happenstance similarities, but may indicate directions in which the text of the Epistle (and Melito, perhaps) grew over time. I do not mean to say that the demands of this particular codex drove the textual development of the Epistle. Instead, what I propose is that the particular functions of the Epistle of Enoch unearthed in an analysis of this codex might be indicators of wider patterns of use. It is possible, then, that lines or layers of the Epistle may have been generated by Christians, as a natural overflow of their interest in the text as a witness to antediluvian sin, and a particular moment in the history of Israel.

---

[38] On which, see my treatment in Elena Dugan, *The Apocalypse of the Birds: 1 Enoch and the Jewish Revolt against Rome* (Edinburgh: Edinburgh University Press, 2023), 23–26. But note that in Stuckenbruck's commentary, the work he calls "Epistle of Enoch B (94.6–104.8)" is affirmed to be "not attested among the Qumran Aramaic manuscripts" (Stuckenbruck, *1 Enoch 91–108*, 7). Note also that there *is* an attestation of the Book of Noah at Qumran (4Q204).

[39] This statement is contingent upon rejecting the identification of the 7Q fragments found at Qumran as the Epistle, as has been advanced by Nebe, Muro, and Puech. The 7Q fragments are sufficiently fragmentary that a wide variety of identifications might plausibly be made. 7Q5 was infamously identified by Jóse O'Callaghan as Mark 6.52–53. Maria Victoria Spottorno identified it (in an exploration of other possibilities) with 1 Enoch 15.9–10 (the Book of the Watchers), in addition to a variety of other identifications proposed with works ranging from Exodus, to the synoptic gospels, to Homer. In light of these ambiguities in interpretation, as well as the fragmentary nature of the material in question, scholars of 1 Enoch like Nickelsburg, Stuckenbruck, and Drawnel have proven unconvinced by the Body of the Epistle identifications of Puech, et al. In any event, even if the identification were adopted, the amount of text retrieved would be so slight as to be unhelpful in figuring out the shape and extent of the text at the time. See Gerhard-Wilhelm Nebe, "'7Q4' – Möglichkeit und Grenze einer Identifikation," *Revue de Qumrân* 13, no. 1/4 (49/52) (1988): 629–33; Ernest A. Muro, "The Greek Fragments of Enoch from Qumran Cave 7 ('7Q4, 7Q8, & 7Q12=7QEn Gr= Enoch' 103.3–4, 7–8)," *Revue de Qumrân* 18.2 (70) (1997): 307–12; Émile Puech, "Sept Fragments Grecs de la 'Lettre D'Hénoch' ('1 Hén' 100, 103 et 105) Dans La Grotte 7 de Qumrân (= '7QHéngr')," *Revue de Qumrân* 18.2 (70) (1997): 313–23; José O'Callaghan, "¿Papiros neotestamentarios en la cueva 7 de Qumrân?," *Biblica* 53 (1972): 91–100; Maria Victoria Spottorno, "Can Methodological Limits Be Set in the Debate on the Identification of 7Q5?," *Dead Sea Discoveries* 6 (1999): 66–77; George W. E. Nickelsburg, "The Greek Fragments of '1 Enoch' from Qumran Cave 7: An Unproven Identification," *Revue de Qumrân* 21.4 (84) (2004): 631–34; Stuckenbruck, *1 Enoch 91–108*, 7 n. 21; Henryk Drawnel, *Qumran Cave 4: The Aramaic Books of Enoch* (Oxford: Oxford University Press, 2019), 19–20.

Melito's Enoch 169

4. Miscellaneous Comparanda and Comparable Miscellanies

The retrieval of a denser network of connections between the texts attempted here is meant to tip the balance towards classifying this codex as a miscellany, of sorts. An argument of this sort should not proceed without caution. Scholars have no shortage of late-ancient and early-medieval manuscripts that attest multiple works, and it should not be taken for granted that every manuscript was compiled with exquisite care: scholars might easily project a nuanced and creative intentionality upon a codex thrown together with whatever was lying around.

We can think with a comparable manuscript – another fourth-century Greek multi-text compilation which attests *Peri Pascha* alongside other works, just like the Chester-Beatty-Michigan.[40] The Bodmer Miscellaneous Codex (LDAB 220465) is a Greek codex dated to the fourth century. When put together as it once was (it is currently split across a number of different modern libraries), the codex witnesses an assemblage of eleven different works, and is the product of multiple scribal hands. Scholars differ in their estimation of how, exactly, the codex was originally assembled.[41] They also differ, considerably, in their estimation of the logic of the codex's contents. In 1964, one of the codex's

---

[40] Another relevant example is the Crosby-Schøyen codex (LDAB 107771), a fourth-century Coptic codex which contains Melito's *Peri Pascha* alongside excerpts from 2 Maccabees, Jonah, 1 Peter, and Pachomius' *Homily on Easter*. Like the Chester-Beatty-Michigan codex, it seems to have been a single quire, and the product of a single hand. Shortly after the publication of the Crosby-Schøyen codex, Allen Cabaniss suggested the codex must have been a "Paschal lectionary" (Allen Cabaniss, "University of Mississippi Coptic Papyrus Manuscript: A Paschal Lectionary?" *New Testament Studies* 8 [1961]: 70–72). Recently, Albert Pietersma and Susan Comstock published fragments belonging to an additional leaf of this codex – identified from among the holdings of none other than the Chester-Beatty library – which they believe confirm the hypothesis that "the entire codex was intended to be the liturgy for the annual Easter celebration of the Pachomian koinonia of monasteries" (Albert Pietersma and Susan Comstock, "Two More Pages of Crosby-Schøyen Codex MS 193: A Pachomian Easter Lectionary?" *Bulletin of the American Society of Papyrologists* 48 [2011]: 40). The Crosby-Schøyen codex, like the Bodmer Miscellaneous Codex, is the subject of Brice C. Jones' critique, as Jones insists there are no thematic links binding the works together (Brice C. Jones, "The Bodmer 'Miscellaneous' Codex and The Crosby-Schøyen Codex MS 193: A New Proposal," *Journal of Greco-Roman Christianity and Judaism* 8 2011: 9–20). But in my estimation, the Crosby-Schøyen Codex does not benefit in the same way from my analysis here, as the "Old Testament" works in the codex – Jonah, and a martyrological excerpt from 2 Maccabees – seem to provide obvious "types" for the crucifixion and resurrection of Christ. In other words, over Jones' objection, I think the case for thematic coherence in this codex – that it is a collection of works oriented around the Easter event, as proposed by Cabaniss, Pietersma, and Comstock – is largely convincing already, and there is less of an intervention required. The Crosby-Schøyen Codex would thus represent a site at which Melito's *Peri Pascha* operated somewhat differently than it does in the Bodmer Miscellaneous Codex, and Chester-Beatty-Michigan Codex, as I have described them.

[41] On which, see Tommy Wasserman, "Papyrus 72 and the Bodmer Miscellaneous Codex," *New Testament Studies* 51 (2005): 137–54; Brent Nongbri, "The Construction of P.Bodmer Arm and the Bodmer 'Composite' or 'Miscellaneous' Codex," *Novum Testamentum* 58 (2016): 394–410.

170 *Elena Dugan*

original editors, Victor Martin, proposed that the texts were all theological literature and interested in somehow engaging orthodoxy or heresy.[42] Kim Haines-Eitzen found this all too vague, and instead suggested a theme of "the body."[43] Tommy Wasserman cautioned that a single theme might escape us and proposed a general tendency towards a Christological focus,[44] and in a later article with Tobias Nicklas, he classified this codex as "occup[ying] a middle position between codices which individual texts have been brought together rather consciously, united by one specific [*leitenden*] theme, and those [individual texts] which display no connection."[45]

Meanwhile, building on previous notes of scholarly dissent, Brice C. Jones denies the existence of a common theme for the contents of the Bodmer Miscellany, concluding it does not merit the marker of thematic coherence, as arguments have been advanced.[46] Part of Jones' objection stems from the possibility that codices were assembled just to be assembled – codices might be more like textual repositories, which are not necessarily assumed to have a conceptual unity in the same kind of way. But I think what warrants objection in part, though it is not explicitly named as such in Jones' article, are the nebulous standards of proof underlying all of these discussions. What quantity or quality of evidence would serve to convince us that a hypothesis of thematic coherence is something more than a clever scholar using their pattern-recognition skills to over-fit a theory to the evidence?

I think that the denser the network of conceptual connections upon which a hypothesis of thematic coherence might rest, the stronger the case – the kinds of parallels assembled above may tip the balance in our estimation of the Chester-Beatty-Michigan Codex. But there is an auxiliary benefit to our analysis that could help move the conversations on the Bodmer Miscellaneous Codex forward – the identification of Melito's *Peri Pascha* as a magnetic work, which might attract biblical works that would function in concert with its revisionist anti-Jewish historiography of Israel.

I have argued that the Epistle of Enoch is so-transformed in this context, becoming a witness to the antediluvian failures for which Melito excoriates Israel,

---

[42] Victor Martin, *Papyrus Bodmer XX: Apologie de Philéas, évêque de Thmouis*, Bibliotheca Bodmeriana (Cologny-Genève: Bibliotheca Bodmeriana, 1964), 9.

[43] Kim Haines-Eitzen, *Guardians of Letters: Literacy, Power, and the Transmitters of Early Christian Literature* (New York: Oxford University Press, 2000), 102–103.

[44] Wasserman, "Papyrus 72 and the Bodmer Miscellaneous Codex," 147–48.

[45] Translation from Tommy Wasserman, "Evangelical Textual Criticism: Bodmer 'Miscellaneous' or 'Composite' Codex?," *Evangelical Textual Criticism*, 8 September 2011, http://evangelicaltextualcriticism.blogspot.com/2011/09/bodmer-miscellaneous-or-composite-codex.html. Original citation from Tobias Nicklas and Tommy Wasserman, "Theologische Linien im Codex Bodmer Miscellani?" in *New Testament Manuscripts: Their Texts and Their World*, ed. Thomas J. Kraus and Tobias Nicklas, Texts and Editions for New Testament Study 2 (Leiden: Brill, 2006), 185.

[46] Jones, "The Bodmer 'Miscellaneous' Codex and The Crosby-Schøyen Codex MS 193."

Melito's Enoch 171

and I have even suggested that the text of the Epistle itself should be interrogated for signals that it transformed under these conceptual pressures.

In the Bodmer Miscellaneous Codex, Melito is preceded by Jude. The logic behind the inclusion of Jude is a bit opaque. David Horrell, for instance, suggests that "the inclusion of Jude might well be explained either on the grounds of the status of its author or because of the evident similarity of its material with 2 Peter."[47] Horrell's remarks, and appeal to the general "status of its author," should clarify that Jude is not exactly a load-bearing member of the codex and does not play a key role in discussions of the codex's purported thematic unity.[48] But one of the things that Jude does bring to the table is a litany of instances in which Israel has fallen short – the Israelites' unbelief after the Exodus (Jude 5), the errors of the fallen angels (6), the evils of Sodom and Gomorrah (7), and the failings of Cain, Balaam, and Korah (11). Jude famously appeals to none other than Enoch, to prophesy the coming of a day of judgment for these "grumblers and malcontents" (16). The exact phrasing in Jude is revealing: "It was also about these that Enoch, in the seventh [generation] from Adam, prophesied, saying ..."[49] Enoch's prophecy is introduced as if it were "about these" – about these mis-steppers drawn from the history of Israel. The prophecy itself points to a judgment that is not yet actualized (or that is currently breaking into the author's contemporary world), but the objects of its ire are drawn from a historical imaginary populated by long-gone Israelites.

The function of Jude as Melito's opening act in the Bodmer Miscellany proves to be surprisingly similar to that fulfilled by Enoch in the Chester-Beatty-Michigan codex. Both remind the reader of the historical failings of Israel, to be immediately followed by Melito's screed on the very same, and serve to set up his construction of a typological reading by which to make sense of the meaning of these failings. Even more curiously, both invoke Enoch as a historical figure who witnessed to these failings (recall the formulation of Jude that highlights Enoch's historical location: Enoch was the "seventh from Adam"), and as one who prophesied a day of judgment in which these individuals would receive their supposed just deserts. In both instances, the figure of Enoch is conjured to lay some of the groundwork for Melito's anti-Jewish historiographic project.

---

[47] David G. Horrell, "The Themes of 1 Peter: Insights from the Earliest Manuscripts (the Crosby-Schøyen Codex Ms 193 and the Bodmer Miscellaneous Codex Containing P72)," *New Testament Studies* 55 (2009): 512–13.

[48] Note some attempts to show how some small details in Jude might serve other proposed themes, like the body (Haines-Eitzen, *Guardians of Letters*, 103–4). or certain kinds of Christology (Nicklas and Wasserman, "Theologische Linien im Codex Bodmer Miscellani?" 177–79).

[49] Quotations from Jude are in keeping with the New Revised Standard Version, though note that I have checked the text against Wasserman's transcription of P72 in Tommy Wasserman, *The Epistle of Jude: Its Text and Transmission*, Coniectanea Biblica, New Testament Series 43 (Stockholm: Almqvist & Wiksell International, 2006).

172   *Elena Dugan*

5. Conclusion

This contribution has suggested that scholars of the pseudepigrapha in Christian transmission must attend to what, if anything, material attestations might be saying about Jews or Judaism, and the ways the manuscript might be imbricated in larger discourses of anti-Judaism. Here, I have proposed that Enoch is made to operate in service to Melito's anti-Jewish agenda in this codex, especially insofar as the Epistle of Enoch provides an account of the supposed horrors of the antediluvian period. There are undoubtedly more cases to be uncovered in which we might see pseudepigrapha fulfilling similar roles,[50] just as there are likely cases in which this is not a helpful or generative consideration. But especially for codices as early as the Chester-Beatty/Michigan, produced during centuries in which the proverbial ways between Judaism and Christianity had not yet parted – or, at least, not entirely and in every place – asking after manuscripts as artifacts of religious identity formation may yield dividends.[51]

Another conclusion is the need for caution in assuming that received attributions, as in the case of the Epistle, which is imagined to be composed earlier and elsewhere, are benign in their later material contexts. I have argued that the Chester-Beatty-Michigan codex shows a particular concern for the "Enoch" in the "Epistle of Enoch," as can be detected with careful attention to this manuscript's practices of titling, spacing, and textual selection. In this way, we can detect continued care for Enoch, and not just the copying of the words of his epistle, a conclusion that should prompt us to ask whether we might find similar practices in other manuscripts attributed to noteworthy figures.

Ultimately, this contribution has opened up a new avenue in the research of the pseudepigrapha, thinking about the extent to which not only their texts, but also the figures to whom the texts are attributed, might be generative figures in early Christian manuscript cultures – for better, and for worse.

---

[50] For one recent example, which I thought with often while preparing this essay, Liv Lied highlights some of the supersessionist and anti-Jewish functions that 2 Baruch serves in its current location in the Codex Ambrosianus, as the percievedly-violent end to the Old Covenant and harbinger of the New (Liv Ingeborg Lied, *Invisible Manuscripts: Textual Scholarship and the Survival of 2 Baruch*, Studien und Texte zu Antike und Christentum 128 [Tübingen: Mohr Siebeck, 2021]).

[51] I borrow the phrasing and insight that Judaism and Christianity represent the "ways that never parted" from Adam H. Becker and Annette Yoshiko Reed, ed., *The Ways That Never Parted: Jews and Christians in Late Antiquity and the Early Middle Ages*, Texte und Studien zum antiken Judentum 95 (Tübingen: Mohr Siebeck, 2003).

Bibliography

Allen, Garrick V. "Titles in the New Testament Papyri." *New Testament Studies* 68 (2022): 156–171.

Becker, Adam H. and Annette Yoshiko Reed, ed. *The Ways That Never Parted: Jews and Christians in Late Antiquity and the Early Middle Ages.* Texte und Studien zum antiken Judentum 95. Tübingen: Mohr Siebeck, 2003.

Bonner, Campbell. *The Homily on the Passion: With Some Fragm. of the Apocryphal Ezekiel.* London: Christophers, 1940.

Bonner, Campbell. *The Last Chapters of Enoch in Greek.* London: Christophers, 1937.

Cabaniss, Allen. "University of Mississippi Coptic Papyrus Manuscript: A Paschal Lectionary?" *New Testament Studies* 8 [1961]: 70–72.

Doering, Lutz. *Ancient Jewish Letters and the Beginnings of Christian Epistolography.* Wissenschaftliche Untersuchungen zum Neuen Testament 298. Tübingen: Mohr Siebeck, 2012.

Drawnel, Henryk. *Qumran Cave 4: The Aramaic Books of Enoch.* Oxford: Oxford University Press, 2019.

Dugan, Elena. *The Apocalypse of the Birds: 1 Enoch and the Jewish Revolt against Rome.* Edinburgh: Edinburgh University Press, 2023.

Erho, Ted M. and Loren T. Stuckenbruck. "The Ge'ez Manuscript Tradition and the Study of 1 Enoch: Problems and Prospects." 10th Enoch Seminar: Enoch and Enochic Traditions in the Early Modern Period: A Reception History from the 15th to the End of the 19th Centuries. Florence, Italy, 2019.

Haines-Eitzen, Kim. *Guardians of Letters: Literacy, Power, and the Transmitters of Early Christian Literature.* New York: Oxford University Press, 2000.

Hall, Stuart George. *On Pascha and Fragments.* Oxford Early Christian Texts. Oxford: Clarendon Press, 1979.

Hill, Charles E. "The Capitulatio Vaticana and Its Predecessors in the New Testament." Pages 311–400 in *The First Chapters: Dividing the Text of Scripture in Codex Vaticanus and Its Predecessors.* Oxford: Oxford University Press, 2022.

Horrell, David G. "The Themes of 1 Peter: Insights from the Earliest Manuscripts (the Crosby-Schøyen Codex Ms 193 and the Bodmer Miscellaneous Codex Containing P72)." *New Testament Studies* 55 (2009): 502–522.

Jones, Brice C. "The Bodmer 'Miscellaneous' Codex and The Crosby-Schøyen Codex MS 193: A New Proposal." *Journal of Greco-Roman Christianity and Judaism* 8 (2011): 9–20.

Jonge, Marinus de. *Pseudepigrapha of the Old Testament as Part of Christian Literature: The Case of the Testaments of the Twelve Patriarchs and the Greek Life of Adam and Eve.* Leiden: Brill, 2003.

Kenyon, Frederic G. *Fasciculus 8: Enoch and Melito.* The Chester Beatty Biblical Papyri Descriptions and Texts of Twelve Manuscripts on Papyrus of the Greek Bible. London: Walker, 1941.

Kraft, Robert A., ed. *Exploring the Scripturesque: Jewish Texts and Their Christian Contexts.* Leiden: Brill, 2009.

Kraft, Robert A. "The Pseudepigrapha and Christianity, Revisited: Setting the Stage and Framing Some Central Questions." Pages 35–61 in *Exploring the Scripturesque: Jewish Texts and Their Christian Contexts.* Leiden: Brill, 2009.

174   *Elena Dugan*

Lied, Liv Ingeborg. *Invisible Manuscripts: Textual Scholarship and the Survival of 2 Baruch.* Studien und Texte zu Antike und Christentum 128. Tübingen: Mohr Siebeck, 2021.

Lied, Liv Ingeborg and Loren T. Stuckenbruck. "Pseudepigrapha and Their Manuscripts." Pages 203–230 in *The Old Testament Pseudepigrapha.* Edited by Liv Ingeborg Lied and Matthias Henze. Fifty Years of the Pseudepigrapha Section at the SBL. Atlanta: Society of Biblical Literature, 2019.

Martin, Victor. *Papyrus Bodmer XX: Apologie de Philéas, évêque de Thmouis,* Bibliotheca Bodmeriana. Cologny-Genève: Bibliotheca Bodmeriana, 1964.

Milik, J. T. *The Books of Enoch: Aramaic Fragments of Qumran Cave 4.* Oxford: Clarendon Press, 1976.

Mueller, James R. and Stephen E. Robinson. "Apocryphon of Ezekiel." Pages 91–203 in *The Old Testament Pseudepigrapha.* Edited by James H. Charlesworth. Vol. 1. London: Darton, Longman & Todd, 1983.

Mueller, James R. *The Five Fragments of the Apocryphon of Ezekiel: A Critical Study.* Journal for the Study of the Pseudepigrapha Supplement 5. Sheffield: Sheffield Academic Press, 1994.

Muro, Ernest A. "The Greek Fragments of Enoch from Qumran Cave 7 ('7Q4, 7Q8, & 7Q12=7QEn Gr= Enoch' 103.3–4, 7–8)." *Revue de Qumrân* 18.2 (70) (1997): 307–312.

Nebe, Gerhard-Wilhelm. "'7Q4' – Möglichkeit und Grenze einer Identifikation." *Revue de Qumrân* 13, no. 1/4 (49/52) (1988): 629–633.

Nickelsburg, George W. E. "The Greek Fragments of '1 Enoch' from Qumran Cave 7: An Unproven Identification." *Revue de Qumrân* 21.4 (84) (2004): 631–634.

Nickelsburg, George W. E. "Two Enochic Manuscripts: Unstudied Evidence for Egyptian Christianity." Pages 251–260 in *Of Scribes and Scrolls: Studies on the Hebrew Bible, Intertestamental Judaism, and Christian Origins Presented to John Strugnell on the Occasion of His Sixtieth Birthday.* Edited by Harold W. Attridge, John J. Collins, and Thomas H. Tobin. Lanham, MD: University Press of America, 1990.

Nickelsburg, George W. E. and James C. VanderKam. *1 Enoch: A New Translation, Based on the Hermeneia Commentary.* Minneapolis: Fortress, 2004.

Nicklas, Tobias and Tommy Wasserman. "Theologische Linien im Codex Bodmer Miscellani?" Pages 161–188 in *New Testament Manuscripts: Their Texts and Their World.* Edited by Thomas J. Kraus and Tobias Nicklas. Texts and Editions for New Testament Study 2. Leiden: Brill, 2006.

Nongbri, Brent. "The Acquisition of the University of Michigan's Portion of the Chester Beatty Biblical Papyri and a New Suggested Provenance." *Archiv für Papyrusforschung und verwandte Gebiete* 60 (2014): 93–116.

Nongbri, Brent. "The Construction of P.Bodmer Arm and the Bodmer 'Composite' or 'Miscellaneous' Codex." *Novum Testamentum* 58 (2016): 394–410.

Nongbri, Brent. *God's Library: The Archaeology of the Earliest Christian Manuscripts.* New Haven: Yale University Press, 2018.

O'Callaghan, José. "¿Papiros neotestamentarios en la cueva 7 de Qumrán?" *Biblica* 53 (1972): 91–100.

Pietersma, Albert. "New Greek Fragments of Biblical Manuscripts in the Chester Beatty Library." *Bulletin of the American Society of Papyrologists* 24 (1987): 37–61.

Pietersma, Albert and Susan Comstock. "Two More Pages of Crosby-Schøyen Codex MS 193: A Pachomian Easter Lectionary?" *Bulletin of the American Society of Papyrologists* 48 (2011): 27–46.

Porter, Stanley E. "Pericope Markers in Some Early Greek New Testament Manuscripts." Pages 161–176 in *Layout Markers in Biblical Manuscripts and Ugaritic Tablets*. Edited by Marjo C. A. Korpel and Josef M. Oesch. Leiden: Brill, 2005.

Puech, Émile. "Sept Fragments Grecs de la 'Lettre D'Hénoch' ('1 Hén' 100, 103 et 105) Dans La Grotte 7 de Qumrân (= '7QHéngr')." *Revue de Qumrân* 18.2 (70) (1997): 313–323.

Spottorno, Maria Victoria. "Can Methodological Limits Be Set in the Debate on the Identification of 7Q5?" *Dead Sea Discoveries* 6 (1999): 66–77.

Tigchelaar, Eibert. "Evaluating the Discussions Concerning the Original Order of Chapters 91–93 and Codicological Data Pertaining to 4Q212 and Chester Beatty XII Enoch." Pages 220–223 in *Enoch and Qumran Origins: New Light on a Forgotten Connection*. Edited by Gabriele Boccaccini. Grand Rapids: Eerdmans, 2005.

Turner, Eric Gardner. *The Typology of the Early Codex*, Haney Foundation Series 18. Philadelphia: University of Pennsylvania Press, 1977.

Wasserman, Tommy. *The Epistle of Jude: Its Text and Transmission*. Coniectanea Biblica, New Testament Series 43. Stockholm: Almqvist & Wiksell International, 2006.

Wasserman, Tommy. "Evangelical Textual Criticism: Bodmer 'Miscellaneous' or 'Composite' Codex?" *Evangelical Textual Criticism*. 8 September 2011. http://evangelicaltextualcriticism.blogspot.com/2011/09/bodmer-miscellaneous-or-composite-codex.html.

Wasserman, Tommy. "Papyrus 72 and the Bodmer Miscellaneous Codex." *New Testament Studies* 51 (2005): 137–154.

Wilson, Stephen G. "Melito and Israel." Pages 81–102 in *Anti-Judaism in Early Christianity*. Edited by Stephen G. Wilson. Vol. 2: Separation and Polemic. Waterloo: Wilfred Laurier University Press, 1986.

Wright, Benjamin G. "The Apocryphon of Ezekiel." Pages 380–392 in *Old Testament Pseudepigrapha: More Noncanonical Scriptures*. Edited by Richard Bauckham, James R. Davila, and Alexander Panayotov. Vol. 1. Grand Rapids: Eerdmans, 2013.

Wright, Benjamin G. "The Apocryphal Ezekiel Fragments." Pages 28–34 in *The Apocryphal Ezekiel*. Edited by Michael E. Stone, David Satran, and Benjamin G. Wright. Early Judaism and Its Literature 18. Atlanta: Society of Biblical Literature, 2000.

From Beyond the Grave: 'Ventriloquizing' the Enslaved and the Emancipated in Latin Verse Epitaphs

EMILY MITCHELL

It is commonly acknowledged that authorship is notoriously difficult to determine in the case of Latin funerary inscriptions, not only for the incidental viewer but even for the scholar of Roman epigraphy. Many inscriptions include no explicit attribution of authorship; even in cases where such an attribution *is* included (e.g., with a standard formula such as "[Name] made this"), it is often unclear precisely what role the named individual played in the creation of the monument and inscription. While such statements may refer to the composition of the inscribed text, this is not necessarily the case, since the creation of a funerary monument comprised a number of different steps: e.g., the commissioning and financing of the monument; the choice of monument type and material; the physical creation and erection of the monument; the composition of the text to be inscribed thereon; the physical incision of this text into the monument.[1] Individuals named on the finished monument may have been responsible for just one of these components or for a combination of different components: for instance, while it is possible that the same person might have commissioned the monument and composed the text, it is equally plausible – and indeed attested in the epigraphic record – for these tasks to be allocated to different parties.[2] In addition, since it was common in the Roman world for individuals to design their own funerary monument and epitaph prior to their death, we may indeed, in many cases, be seeing an authentic self-representation on the part of the deceased.[3]

---

[1] On the process of designing and producing an inscription see Alison E. Cooley, "The Production and Design of Inscriptions," *The Cambridge Manual to Latin Epigraphy* (Cambridge: Cambridge University Press, 2012), 286–300, and Jonathan Edmondson, "Inscribing Roman Texts: *Officinae*, Layout, and Carving Techniques," *The Oxford Handbook of Roman Epigraphy*, ed. Christer Bruun and Jonathan Edmondson (Oxford; New York: Oxford University Press, 2015), 111–30.

[2] See, for instance, *Carmina Latina Epigraphica* (hereafter *CLE*) 578, in which the freedpeople Volussius (*sic*) and Sabatia attribute the text of the epitaph to their patrons while claiming responsibility for setting up the monument themselves, and *CLE* 1278, which states that the freedman Rufinus composed the text of his epitaph during his lifetime and his patron set up the monument after his death.

[3] See, for instance, *CLE* 67, a self-commemoration by the freedwoman Manlia Gnome, which states *ossa dedi terrae corpus Volchano dedi|di ego ut suprema mortis man|data edidi* ("My bones I gave to the earth and my body to Vulcan [i.e., the fire] when I made known my final directives

178 *Emily Mitchell*

Since antiquity, therefore, a viewer who encounters a Roman funerary monument for the first time typically has no means of determining who is responsible for which elements of the monument – and, crucially, who authored the text of the epitaph. In this paper, I argue that the ambiguity surrounding authorship of epigraphic texts was deliberately manipulated by individuals in the Roman world. It enables a phenomenon whereby the author of the epitaph uses the voice of the deceased commemorand to address, or to enter into a dialogue with, the living. The occurrence of this phenomenon in Latin epitaphs has been examined by Allison Boex in a 2018 article, where she terms it "fictive orality." Focusing primarily on epitaphs from the late republican period, Boex concludes that such "fictive orality" was most commonly used in cases of premature death and that one of its main functions was to provide consolation for those mourning the deceased.[4] While I concur with the former of these observations, I also posit, drawing on a selection of texts from the *Carmina Latina Epigraphica*, that this technique has a very specific purpose in verse epitaphs for enslaved and emancipated individuals.[5] In such epitaphs, "fictive orality" functions as more than a consolatory device: it constitutes a means through which the commemorator may advance their social and political agenda.

In what follows, I seek to demonstrate that, when an enslaved or emancipated person is commemorated by their enslaver, fictive orality is employed to create an idealized representation of slavery, with the voice of the deceased often used to praise their enslaver or patron, recount the benefactions that they provided, and express a wish or prayer that they may, in return for such benevolence, enjoy good fortune in the future. By contrast, when an enslaved or emancipated individual is commemorated by their loved ones, fictive orality is used to challenge this representation of slavery both implicitly and more overtly. I begin with some preliminary remarks on terminology and on critical frameworks for approaching the issue of authorship; I then examine a series of epitaphs authored by enslavers, before, finally, turning to the epitaphs authored by enslaved and emancipated people for their loved ones.

---

for my death"), and *CLE* 139, a self-commemoration by the freedman P. Atinius Nicepor, which states *monumentum | me uiuo aedific|aui* ("I built [this] monument during my lifetime").

[4] Allison Boex, "Cold Comfort: Speeches to and from the Prematurely Deceased in Early Roman Verse-Epitaphs," *Latomus* 77.1 (2018): 74–98, here 94.

[5] Throughout this paper, I use the terms "enslaved person" and "enslaver" rather than the terms "slave" and "master" in line with the guidance provided by P. Gabrielle Foreman et al., "Writing about Slavery/Teaching About Slavery: This Might Help," community-sourced document, accessed 12/15/2022 at 17:30 EST, https://docs.google.com/document/d/1A4TEdDgYslX-hlKezLodMIM71My3KTN0zxRv0IQTOQs/mobilebasic/. When translating the Latin words *seruus* and *dominus*, however, I use "slave" and "master" in order to represent as accurately as possible the tone conveyed by these words and the worldview that underpins them.

From Beyond the Grave   179

1. Terminology and authorship

In this paper, I follow Michel Foucault in treating the concept of "the author" as a function of discourse, and "author-function" as a literary and social construct that performs specific roles within discourse (and indeed society more broadly).[6] In Latin funerary inscriptions, author-function is typically constructed through a standard formula: the name of the commemorator is given in the nominative case, sometimes accompanied by the verb *fecit* ("he/she made [this]"); following this, the name of the deceased is given in the dative case. The complete phrase may be translated as "X made [this] for Y" or simply "X, for Y." More occasionally, verse inscriptions may deploy author-function by integrating an attribution into the body of the epigram: one such example would be the phrase *Cotta ... qui carmina tristis haec dedit* ("Cotta ... who has, in sadness, given these verses") in the epitaph of the freedman M. Aurelius Zosimus (*CLE* 990; *CIL* XIV 2298).[7] As mentioned above, the process of designing and constructing a funerary monument comprises multiple different steps and may thus have involved a number of individuals; author-function, however, tends to be attributed to one specific individual, thus eliding the different parties involved in the creation of the monument. Karen King notes in her discussion of author-function in ancient Mediterranean texts that it tends to be "deployed in specific contexts to do certain identifiable work" and that "works receive attribution only when it is useful to perform certain kinds of discursive work with regard to some present social enterprise."[8] In the case of epitaphs, as we will observe, author-function is deployed to showcase the generosity of the commemorator and/or to emphasize the closeness of their relationship with the deceased, thereby contributing to the rhetorical and ideological goals of the monument.

Foucault makes the following observations on the difference between author-function and the use of the first-person voice:

Everyone knows that, in a novel narrated in the first person, neither the first-person pronoun nor the present indicative refers exactly either to the writer or to the moment in which he writes, but rather to an alter ego whose distance from the author varies, often changing in the course of the work. It would be just as wrong to equate the author with the real writer as to equate him with the fictitious speaker; the author function is carried out and operates in the scission itself, in this division and this distance.[9]

---

[6] Michel Foucault, "What Is An Author?," *The Foucault Reader*, ed. Paul Rabinow (New York: Pantheon Books, 1984), 101–120.

[7] Discussed on p. 180–184.

[8] Karen King, "What Is an Author?: Ancient Author-Function in the Apocryphon of John and the Apocalypse of John," *Scribal Practices and Social Structures Among Jesus Adherents: Essays in Honour Of John S. Kloppenborg*, ed. William E. Arnal, Richard S. Ascough, Robert A. Derrenbacker, Jr., and Philip A. Harland (Leuven; Paris; Bristol, Leuven: Peeters, 2016), 15–42, here 18 and 41.

[9] Foucault, "What Is an Author?" 112.

180 *Emily Mitchell*

In a similar vein, Robert Matera observes in his analysis of *CLE* 1175 (*CIL* VI 29896), a Latin verse epitaph for a pet dog named Margarita ("Pearl"), that the text of the inscription, which is written in Pearl's voice, presents her as its author despite the obvious fictitiousness of such a conceit.[10] Matera concludes with the statement that "by presenting an impossible author as the only named candidate for author, Pearl's epitaph shows that the 'I' of a speaking epitaph cannot safely be taken as its author."[11] The distance, and dissonance, between the deployment of author-function and the use of the first-person voice within a given text is the primary focus of this paper. In what follows, I use the term "author-function" to denote the living individual to whom the inscription and monument are attributed, and the term "authorial fiction" to denote the phenomenon whereby this living individual uses the deceased's voice to narrate the epitaph, thus creating the impression that they are the originator of the sentiments expressed. I use "authorial fiction" interchangeably with Allison Boex's term "fictive orality." In addition, I use the metaphor of 'ventriloquism' to highlight the fact that it is the living author, not the deceased commemorand, who controls the content of the epitaph, and that the use of the first-person voice does not necessarily mean that the text reflects what the deceased themselves would have chosen to compose.

2. Commemorations by enslavers

I begin by examining three epitaphs which explicitly attribute author-function to the deceased's enslaver or patron. The first of these is the epitaph created by M. Aurelius Cotta Maximus Messalinus, *cos.* 20 CE, for his freedman Zosimus (*CLE* 990; *CIL* XIV 2298). This epitaph, composed in elegiac couplets and inscribed on a marble statue base, was recovered at Aricia in Latium (modern Ariccia) and can be dated to the period 21–50 CE. It reads as follows:[12]

M(arcus) Aurelius Cottae		Marcus Aurelius Zosimus,
Maximi l(ibertus) Zosimus		freedman of Cotta Maximus,
accensus patroni		his patron's attendant.
libertinus eram fateor	1	I was a freedman, I confess,
sed facta legetur		but my shade will be read to have been
patrono Cotta nobilis umbra mea		ennobled by my patron, Cotta –
qui mihi saepe libens census donauit		he who often willingly bestowed equestrian
equestris qui iussit natos	5	fortunes upon me, who ordered me to raise
tollere quos aleret		children so that he might provide for them,

[10] Robert Matera, "The Doctitude of Pearl the Dog in *CE* 1175 = *CIL* VI 29896," *Zeitschrift für Papyrologie und Epigraphik* 210 (2019): 91–103.

[11] Matera, "Doctitude of Pearl," 101.

[12] All transcriptions and translations of epigraphic texts are my own, except where otherwise indicated. I begin my line numbering from the first line composed in verse; where the epitaph includes a prose preface or postscript, this is not included in the numbering.

From Beyond the Grave   181

quique suas commisit opes		and who entrusted his wealth
mihi semper et idem dotauit		to me always, and likewise dowered
natas ut pater ipse meas		my daughters as if he were their own father,
Cottanumque meum produxit	10	and promoted my Cottanus to the rank
honore tribuni quem fortis		of tribune, which, with his bravery,
castris Caesaris emeruit		he earned in Caesar's camp.
quid non Cotta dedit qui nunc		What did Cotta not give? He has now,
et carmina tristis haec dedit		in sadness, given even these verses
in tumulo conspicienda meo	15	to be looked at on my tomb.

Aurelia Saturnina Zosimi (uxor)   Aurelia Saturnina, (wife) of Zosimus

Here, author-function is explicitly assigned to Zosimus' patron Cotta: we are told that it is Cotta who "has given these verses" (*carmina ... haec dedit*, 14). Whether this means that Cotta composed the epitaph himself or commissioned a poet to do so is not clear, but in either case we may safely assume that Cotta has exercised a significant degree of control over the content and phrasing of this text and that the sentiments expressed therein reflect his perspective as patron rather than that of Zosimus as freedman. Despite this attribution, however, the epitaph is written in the first-person voice and put into the mouth of the deceased Zosimus, which gives the impression that these statements come from him rather than from Cotta.[13] The purpose of this fictive orality becomes clear when we examine the content of the epitaph and the ideological standpoint that it takes.

The epitaph presents a rosy image of patron-freedperson relations. Cotta is portrayed as a crucial source of material and professional support for Zosimus, elevating his social status (*facta legetur | patrono Cotta nobilis umbra mea*, 2–3), and giving him the means to join the equestrian order (*qui mihi saepe libens census donauit | equestris*, 4–5) as well as other types of financial assistance (*quique suas commisit opes | mihi semper*, 7–8). In addition, he is said to exhibit grief at Zosimus' death (*tristis*, 14) and to honor him with commemoration (*qui nunc | et carmina ... haec dedit | in tumulo conspicienda meo*, 13–15). Cotta is thus depicted as an archetypal "good patron": benevolent, generous, and sincere in his affections. Zosimus too is suggested to be a "good freedman," since the use of his voice to enumerate Cotta's alleged benefactions and to pose a rhetorical question that highlights Cotta's generosity (*quid non Cotta dedit?* 13) gives the impression that he is appreciative.

As well as consciously advancing this ideological message, the epitaph also implicitly reinforces two phenomena that the sociologist Orlando Patterson has identified as essential characteristics of slavery across different historical and geographical contexts: namely, "social death" and "quasi-filial fictive kinship."

---

[13] Note also that this epitaph is inscribed on a statue base, which means that it may originally have been accompanied by a statue of Zosimus; one can imagine that such a statue, if present, would have strengthened the impression that the viewer of the monument is hearing from Zosimus himself.

182   *Emily Mitchell*

"Social death" refers to the rejection of enslaved people as full members of society and the denial to them of the right to form an independent social structure (including, e.g., the formation of legally recognized marriages and the production of legitimate offspring).[14] The related idea of "quasi-filial fictive kinship" denotes, in Patterson's words, "the practice of incorporating the slave as a fictive kinsman of his master in kin-based societies"; distinguishing this phenomenon from adoption, which involves "genuine assimilation by the adopted person of all the claims, privileges, powers, and obligations of the status he or she has been ascribed." Patterson writes that such relationships "use the language of kinship as a means of expressing an authority relation between master and slave, and a state of loyalty to the kinsmen of the master."[15] More recently, the anthropologist Todne Thomas has critiqued the use of the term "fictive" to describe non-biological kinship relationships, noting that such usage "presumes the singular authenticity of biological and genealogical kinship" and "assumes that family is fundamentally a construct of biogenetic descent"; in her work on Black evangelical sociality, Thomas uses instead the term "kincraft" to describe the creation and maintenance of non-biological kinship ties through "craftsmanship and collective labor."[16] Here and elsewhere in this paper, I retain Patterson's term "quasi-familial fictive kinship," as it denotes specifically the phenomenon whereby a slaveholder is conceptualized as a paternal figure towards their enslaved and emancipated dependents. Recognizing, however, that the term "fictive kinship" may not fully convey the nature of non-biological kinship ties and the processes through which they are created and maintained, I employ Thomas' term "kincraft" alongside the phrasing used by Patterson.

In Cotta's epitaph for Zosimus, the phenomena of "social death" and "quasi-filial fictive kinship" or "kincraft" are enacted through the language used to describe Cotta's relationship with Zosimus' family. Cotta is shown to supersede Zosimus as "father" both with respect to both the legal role of *pater familias*, understood to denote the male head of the Roman household,[17] and the role of the father *qua* social caregiver. The 'ventriloquized' Zosimus tells us that Cotta *iussit natos | tollere quos aleret*, "ordered [me] to raise children so that he might provide for them" (5–6): the phrase *natos tollere*, which literally means "raise children", may carry the same meaning as the corresponding modern English phrase,[18] or, alternatively, may be a reference to the alleged Roman custom whereby the father

---

[14] Orlando Patterson, *Slavery and Social Death: A Comparative Study* (Cambridge, MA: Harvard University Press, 1982), 38–45.

[15] *Ibid.*, 62–63.

[16] Todne Thomas, *Kincraft: The Making of Black Evangelical Sociality* (Durham: Duke University Press, 2021), 15.

[17] On the *pater familias* see further Richard P. Saller, "*Pater familias, mater familias*, and the gendered semantics of the Roman household," *Classical Philology* 94.2 (1999): 182–97.

[18] Lewis and Short s.v. *tollo* IA, 2a.

From Beyond the Grave   183

"raises" (*tollere*) a newborn child from the floor to signal his acknowledgement of them as legitimate offspring.[19] In either case, Cotta is portrayed as having the power of life and death over Zosimus' children: he is responsible for their presence within the family, and is the one who "nourishes" or "provides for" them (*aleret*) after their birth. Several years later, he likewise gives dowries to Zosimus' daughters "as if he were their own father" (*dotauit | natas ut pater ipse meas*, 8–9) and oversees the professional advancement of Zosimus' son Cottanus (10–12). Throughout this epitaph, therefore, it is Cotta who is established as the primary parental figure to Zosimus' children, while Zosimus' own relationship with them receives no comment at all. This is consistent with Patterson's concept of "social death," under which the social and familial relationships formed by enslaved people receive no formal acknowledgement or legitimation, and also with his idea of "quasi-filial fictive kinship," whereby the enslaver is conceptualized as a father-figure. Following Thomas, one might argue that Cotta's actions towards Zosimus' children over the course of their lives, as well as his narration of these actions in Zosimus' epitaph, constitute a form of "craftsmanship" through which a non-biological kinship tie is created and maintained.

Another way in which this epitaph enacts "social death" upon the emancipated people mentioned therein is in its sidelining of Aurelia Saturnina, Zosimus' wife. Saturnina's name is inscribed at the bottom of the monument, a detail for which there are two possible explanations. It may be the case that she is being posthumously commemorated along with Zosimus; since we have evidence that spouses from all strata of Roman society were frequently buried and commemorated together, this is a likely scenario. Alternatively, the presence of Saturnina's name may suggest that she played some role in the creation of the monument, perhaps by financing or overseeing its construction; since, as mentioned above,[20] there exist numerous commemorations in which different parties claim responsibility for the composition of the inscription and the establishment of the physical monument, this too is a plausible explanation. Crucially, however, the inscription neglects to tell us which of these two possibilities is the case. I would argue that, regardless of which interpretation we admit, the lack of information about Saturnina's role demonstrates the degree to which she is marginalized in this epitaph: if she is a commemorand, she receives no personalized memorialization, whereas, if she is a commemorator, she receives no explicit credit for her contribution, and is not assigned author-function as Cotta is. In addition, the epigram neglects to acknowledge her relationship with Zosimus

---

[19] *OLD* s.v. *tollo* 2a. However, Brent D. Shaw ("Raising and Killing Children: Two Roman Myths," *Mnemosyne* 54.1 [2001]: 31–77) has argued against the existence of such a custom, asserting that it is unsupported by Roman sources and is instead a narrative constructed by modern historians. He argues that *liberos tollere* simply means to "have" or "raise" children.

[20] See note 2.

184 *Emily Mitchell*

and her children, concentrating instead on these individuals' relationship with their patron, Cotta.

The 'ventriloquizing' of Zosimus, therefore, is more than simply a literary conceit: it functions as a rhetorical device intended to reinforce several crucial ideological tenets of Roman slavery. This phenomenon can be observed across a number of verse epitaphs for enslaved and emancipated people, as with, for instance, the epitaph of the freedwoman Tinuleia Musa, which seems to attribute author-function to her patron Sextus (*AE* 1946, 208).[21] This epitaph, composed in iambic senarii, is inscribed on a limestone tablet which was recovered at Regium Lepidum in Aemilia (modern Reggio Emilia) and is datable to the period between 30 BCE and 50 CE. It reads as follows:

Tinuleia [S]ex(ti) l(iberta) Musa	Tinuleia Musa, freedwoman of Sextus
si uoce superum ga[udent] qui a luce abierunt 1	If those who have departed from the
placuisse me patrono [mo]nimentum indicat	light of day rejoice at the voice of those
quo funere amplo per f[re]quentem gratiam	above, this monument indicates that
die supremo lacrumans [me] amissam intulit	I pleased my patron – the monument
in quo hoc effecit me feli[ce]m mortuam 5	into which, he, in tears, brought me
ut dicant omnes quod [pat]rono placuerim	on the day that I died, with generous
	funeral rites on account of my frequent
	service, and by means of which he has
	accomplished this: he has made every-
	one say that I am fortunate in death
	because I pleased my patron.

Like Zosimus, the deceased freedwoman Musa is 'ventriloquized' and made to recount the benefactions bestowed upon her by her patron, Sextus. We are told that Sextus granted her funeral rites (*funere amplo*, 3) as well as the monument itself, which entails public renown (*effecit me feli[ce]m mortuam | ut dicant omnes*, 5–6); in addition, he displayed grief at her death (*lacrumans*, 4). Musa is, in turn, praised for pleasing her patron and fulfilling her obligations to him (*placuisse me patrono [mo]nimentum indicat*, 2; *per frequentem gratiam*, 3; *ut dicant omnes quod [pat]rono placuerim*, 6); this is, in fact, the only detail we are told about her. Like Zosimus' epitaph, therefore, Musa's epitaph presents a rosy view of the patron-freedperson relationship in which the patron demonstrates

---

[21] Unlike Zosimus' epitaph, which unambiguously attributes the composition of the text to the patron (cf. *qui nunc | et carmina … haec dedit | in tumulo conspicienda meo*, CLE 990, 13–15), Musa's epitaph does not explicitly tell us that it was composed by her patron Sextus. However, I posit that the epitaph assigns author-function to Sextus on the following grounds: firstly, Musa's funerary monument, and her interment therein, are attributed to him (cf. *placuisse me patrono [mo]nimentum indicat | quo … [me] amissam intulit*, 2–4), indicating that he was closely involved in the burial and commemoration process; secondly, the epitaph makes repeated reference to events that occurred after Musa's death (cf. *quo funere amplo per f[re]quentem gratiam | die supremo lacrumans [me] amissam intulit | in quo hoc effecit me feli[ce]m mortuam | ut dicant omnes*, 3–6), highlighting the fact that she herself could not have been the author.

From Beyond the Grave

beneficence and the freedperson dutifulness; Musa herself is defined entirely in terms of her relationship with her patron, with no information offered about her origins, family members, or personality.

Some epitaphs 'ventriloquize' not only the deceased but also the slaveholder responsible for commemorating them, thus creating an imagined dialogue between the two parties that serves not only to portray their relationship in positive terms but also to attribute specific opinions and reactions to the deceased. This is the case in the epitaph of an enslaved sixteen-year-old boy named Hymnus, which attributes author-function to his patron Orestinus (*AE* 1997, 362 and 1998, 374). The epitaph consists of three elegiac couplets; it is inscribed on a limestone stele which can be dated to the late first or early second century CE, and was recovered at Larinum in Apulia (modern Larino). It reads as follows:[22]

Hymno	For Hymnus,
puero karissimo	dearest boy,
Orestinus dominus fecit	Orestinus, [his] master, made [this].
libertas promissa fuit <u>scio</u> morte perempta est 1	"Freedom was promised." <u>"I know."</u>
<u>*sentio* </u>*fallebam nil dominus <u>fateor</u>*	"It was taken away by death." <u>"I ob-</u>
quot potui lacrimas aeternaq(ue) munera misi	<u>serve [that]."</u> "I, as your master, was not
<u>*heu me libertas est dolor iste mihi*</u>	deceiving you at all." <u>"I confess [it]."</u>
debueras nostris potius tu flere sepulcris 5	"I sent as many tears and everlasting
<u>*uiue set atfectus sis memor oro mei*</u>	gifts as I could." <u>"Alas, that freedom</u>
uix(it) ann(os) XVI	<u>is a [source of] pain for me."</u> "You
	should have been the one weeping at
	my tomb." <u>"Live, but I ask that you</u>
	<u>remember my affection."</u>
	He [= Hymnus] lived sixteen years.

In this epitaph, the deceased Hymnus and his enslaver Orestinus discuss the fact that Hymnus died before securing his freedom, which his enslaver had apparently promised to grant him. The voice of Hymnus is used to exonerate and console Orestinus for failing to manumit the youth during his lifetime: Hymnus is made to assent explicitly to Orestinus' assertions that he did indeed promise to free him (*libertas promissa fuit*, 1), that it was death which interfered with the fulfilment of this promise (*morte perempta est*, 1) and that he was not actively deceiving Hymnus (*fallebam nil dominus*, 2). A few lines later, the dialogue between the two parties paints their relationship as tender and affectionate. Orestinus laments that Hymnus died before he did (*debueras nostris potius tu flere*

---

[22] Here, I follow Marco Buonocore ("Su due carmina epigraphica latina da Larinum," *Aufidus* 31 [1997]: 72–77) for both the transcription of the text and the division of the dialogue between Orestinus and Hymnus. I thus read the final line as *uiue set atfectus sis memor oro mei* ("Live, but I ask that you remember my affection") rather than the transcription provided at *AE* 1997, 362 and 1998, 374, which is *uiues et atlectus sis memor oro mei* ("You will live, and I ask that you remember my selection/appointment.") For the sake of clarity, I have underlined the words attributed to the deceased Hymnus in both the Latin transcription and the English translation.

186   *Emily Mitchell*

sepulcris, 5); the ventriloquized Hymnus responds by encouraging his enslaver to move on with his life (*uiue*, 6) while remaining mindful of the affection that Hymnus bore him (*set atfectus sis memor oro mei*, 6). The voice of the enslaved commemorand is thus used to suggest the presence of a strong emotional bond between enslaver and enslaved, to validate the enslaver's past, present, and future behavior, and to exonerate the enslaver of any blame for the fact that the deceased was never emancipated.

These are but three examples of an enslaved or emancipated commemorand being 'ventriloquized' to praise their enslaver or patron and to present an idealized image of enslavement and patronage; this phenomenon is widespread throughout the Roman world.[23] It is important to note that all of these examples contain clear attributions of author-function, assigning responsibility for the monument and epitaph to the deceased's enslaver or patron. A critical reader may thus look past the 'ventriloquizing' of the deceased to identify the epitaph's actual composer (and the rhetorical agenda that they seek to advance). Not all verse epitaphs, however, lay bare their authorial fiction in this way. In many cases, the fiction is taken further: the epitaph is written in the voice of the deceased without any attribution of author-function whatsoever, thus obscuring the ideological standpoint of the text and the agenda of its composer. Nevertheless, in several cases, we can ascertain from contextual details that the deceased could not possibly have composed the epitaph themselves; we may thus identify these texts not as authentic self-representations on the part of the enslaved and emancipated, but, once again, authorial fictions created by the slaveholder class to justify slavery as an institution.

The epitaph of the freedwoman Egnatuleia Urbana (*CLE* 963; *CIL* VI 17130), composed in elegiac couplets and inscribed on a marble tablet at Rome in the summer of 12 BCE, seems likely to be one such authorial fiction. It reads as follows:

Egnatuleia ((mulieris)) l(iberta) Urbana hic sita est	Here lies Egnatuleia Urbana, freedwoman of a woman.
O iucundum lumen superum O uitae iucunda uoluptas 1	Delightful were the light of the world above, and delightful the pleasure of
florenti si non succederet inuidia	life, had not envy come upon me in
inuidus aurato surrexit mihi Lucifer astro	my prime. For me the Morning Star,
cum miseram me urgeret inuidia	with his golden light, rose envious,
bis duodenos annos iam processerat aetas 5	when he was oppressing me –
cum me ex luce expulit officium	wretched one – with envy. My life had
sed te nunc Pietas uenerorque precorque	already advanced twice twelve years

---

[23] Further examples of fictive orality being employed for such ideological purposes include the epitaphs of M. Terentius Iucundus (*CLE* 1007; *CIL* XIII 7070), C. Seccius Lesbius (*CLE* 1116; *CIL* XIII 7105), Domesticus (*CLE* 1185; *CIL* VI 16913), Scope (*CLE* 1213; *CIL* IX 3122), M. Gellius Phoebus (*CLE* 1248; *CIL* XIV 2709), and Rodine (*CLE* 2092; *CIL* XIII 11889).

ut bene pro meriteis hilares Hilaram
quae me seruili nomine preiuat
et dulci suo participat cinerem   10
sed tu adulescens quem Phrycia edidit tellus
desiste lamenteis me exciere
namque tua officia grata mihi in luce fuerunt
et nunc demum ad cinerem IV kal(endas)
Sex(tiles) P(ublio) Q(uirinio) C(aio) V(algio)
c(onsulibus)

when duty drove me from the light of day. But you, Piety, I now venerate, and I pray that you may, in return for her benefactions, bestow lots of hilarity upon Hilara, who deprives me of [my] servile name and lets my ashes partake of her own sweet [name]. But you, young man, whom the land of Phrygia brought forth, stop rousing me with your lamentations; for your services were welcome to me in life and are now, at last, welcome at my grave. [Erected] 29th July in the consulship of P. Quirinius and C. Valgius.

Several details in this epitaph suggest that the deceased, Urbana, did not compose this epitaph herself; the most important of these is the statement made in lines 7–10, where Urbana is made to express gratitude to a woman named Hilara, whom she says "deprives me of [my] servile name and lets my ashes partake of her own sweet [name]." This is a clear reference to manumission, under which emancipated women would adopt the *nomen* (family name) of their patron or patroness. We may deduce, therefore, that the 'Hilara' mentioned is Urbana's enslaver; the use of the present tense to describe Urbana's manumission (*preiuat*, "deprives"; *participat*, "lets ... partake") and the fact that it is Urbana's "ashes" (*cinerem*) which are allowed to partake of her patroness's name indicates that the manumission occurred posthumously, thus making it impossible for Urbana to have composed this epitaph herself.

I would argue that, for three reasons, the composer is most likely Urbana's patroness Hilara. Firstly, the deceased is made to express appreciation for the slaveholder's benevolence: Urbana addresses *Pietas*, "Piety," and asks that Hilara might enjoy good fortune on account of her services to her freedwoman (*sed te nunc Pietas uenerorque precorque | ut bene pro meriteis hilares Hilaram*, 7–8). This is consistent with the rosy image of enslaver-enslaved and patron-freedperson relations presented in the epitaphs of Zosimus, Musa, and Hymnus, discussed above. Secondly, the mention of Hilara's manumission of Urbana strengthens the case for attributing the epitaph to the former, since the manumission of an enslaved person who died prematurely is something in which multiple slave-owning authors take pride;[24] by contrast, as we saw in Orestinus' epitaph for

---

[24] Compare, for instance, Martial *Epigrams* 1.101, in which the poet describes his deathbed manumission of his *amanuensis* Demetrius, or Pliny *Epistles* 8.16, in which Pliny relates the illness and death of some of his freedmen, consoling himself with the knowledge that he had manumitted them. In addition, Maureen Carroll ("The Mourning Was Very Good: Liberation and Liberality in Roman Funerary Commemoration," *Memory and Mourning: Studies on Roman Death*, ed. Valerie M. Hope and Janet Huskinson [Oxford; Oakville, CT: Oxbow Books,

188   Emily Mitchell

Hymnus, a slaveholder who failed to manumit an enslaved person prior to their death might feel a sense of guilt. Finally, Urbana's epitaph prioritizes her relationship with her patroness, to which her other personal and familial connections are subordinated. In lines 11–14, Urbana is made to address an unnamed *adulescens*, whom she encourages to cease from mourning (*sed tu adulescens quem Phrycia edidit tellus | desiste lamenteis me exciere | namque tua officia grata mihi in luce fuerunt | et nunc demum ad cinerem*). The identity of this *adulescens* is not specified. Based on the information provided in the epitaph, we can deduce that he is probably not Urbana's son, firstly because she is said to have been 24 years old at the time of her death (5–6), making her too young to have adolescent offspring, and secondly because this *adulescens* is said to originate from Phrygia, which, given Urbana's Latinate name, is unlikely to be her homeland. Since *adulescens* may denote an individual between the ages of approximately 15 and 30,[25] this person could be someone of Urbana's own age, possibly a partner or friend within the same household. In any case, the epitaph's failure to name this *adulescens* or to clarify his relationship with the deceased, as well as the fact that he is mentioned only after Urbana's patroness, fundamentally marginalizes him. This might remind us of the treatment of Aurelia Saturnina in Zosimus' epitaph, discussed above, and essentially constitutes an enactment of "social death" upon Urbana.[26]

What initially appears to be a testimony from the deceased herself is thus, in actual fact, most likely an authorial fiction created by her patroness to advance a specific agenda. One final example of such a fiction is the epitaph of an enslaved five-year-old boy named Vitalis (*CLE* 78; *CIL* XII 912). This epitaph, composed in iambic senarii, is inscribed on a limestone stele which was recovered at Arelate in Gallia Narbonensis (modern Arles, France) and can be dated to the first century CE. It reads as follows:

Vitalis M(arci)		Vitalis, [slave] of Marcus
Verati Clari		Veratius Clarus,
ann(orum) V hic s(itus) est		five years old, lies here.
inspexi lucem	1	I looked upon the light of day,
subito quae er-		which was suddenly
epta est mihi		snatched from me;

2011], 126–49) observes that Roman slaveholders often, in their own epitaphs, reference their manumissions of enslaved people as a point of pride; it is thus entirely plausible that Hilara might have wished to advertise publicly her manumission of Urbana.

[25] Cf. Lewis and Short s. v. *adulescens*, section I, B.

[26] Compare also the epitaph of the freedwoman Plotia Prune (*CLEHisp* 157; cf. *CIL* II 3495), which states *qualis fuerit contra patronum patron|am parentem coniugem monu|mentum indicat* ("How she conducted herself towards her patron, patroness, parent, and spouse, this monument indicates"). The choice to promote the words *patronum* and *patronam* ahead of *parentem* and *coniugem* suggests that Prune's relationship with her patron and patroness should be seen as more significant than her relationship with her parent and spouse.

From Beyond the Grave 189

ita neque dom-		thus it was not permitted
ino liquit[27] *e me*	5	for my master
gaudia percipe-		to derive joys from me,
re nec me sci-		nor for me to know
re quid natus		for what purpose
forem		I was born.

As with the epitaphs hitherto examined, this text serves to reinforce the ideology of slavery. Vitalis is defined entirely in terms of his relationship with his enslaver, Marcus Veratius Clarus: the enslaver is the only individual named on the epitaph, with no mention of Vitalis' parents or relatives, and the ventriloquized Vitalis explains that his premature death is lamentable because "it was not permitted for my master to derive joys from me" (*neque dom|ino liquit e me | gaudia percipe|re*, 4–7), thus implying that his primary function in life was to gratify his enslaver. Vitalis' closing statement, "it was not permitted ... for me to know for what purpose I was born" (*liquit ... nec me sci|re quid natus | forem*, 4–9) may also contribute to this idea, since it could be understood to imply that the purpose for which Vitalis was born was precisely to provide "joys" to his enslaver.

Although this epitaph is put into the mouth of the deceased Vitalis, his age at death (a mere five years old) makes it impossible for him to have composed such a poem himself. Like the epitaph of Egnatuleia Urbana, this inscription contains no explicit attribution of author-function. Based on its content, however, Vitalis' enslaver, Marcus Veratius Clarus, appears to be a plausible candidate. Although we will likely never have sufficient evidence definitively to attribute this epitaph to Clarus, the way in which the text is designed to reinforce several central ideological tenets of Roman slavery, and the parallels with other epitaphs where we do indeed have an explicit statement of authorship, strongly suggest that he was responsible for this text.

The last three epitaphs examined in this section – namely, those of Hymnus, Egnatuleia Urbana, and Vitalis – conform to the trend observed by Boex insofar as they utilize fictive orality to convey the tragedy of an individual's premature death. We should note, however, that these epitaphs emphasize not only the young age at which their subjects died, but also, in the cases of Hymnus and Urbana, the fact that they died prior to manumission, and, in all three cases, the impact of the deceased's premature death on their enslaver. In Hymnus and Urbana's epitaphs, the motif of death before manumission ultimately serves to underscore the benevolence and affection of the slaveholder. The imagined conversation between Orestinus and the deceased Hymnus, in which the latter reassures and comforts the former, suggests some lingering guilt on Orestinus' part for his failure to manumit Hymnus during his lifetime. Ultimately, however, it portrays Orestinus as feeling genuine affection for Hymnus and exhibiting the

---

[27] I interpret *liquit* here as an alternative spelling of *licuit*, "it was permitted."

190 Emily Mitchell

appropriate behaviors after losing him;[28] Hymnus' death prior to manumission is thus depicted as an unforeseeable tragedy rather than an injustice for which his enslaver bears responsibility. Urbana's manumission, which seems to have occurred on her deathbed, if not posthumously, is portrayed as a benefaction for which she is deeply grateful to her patroness.[29] The death of five-year-old Vitalis, meanwhile, is portrayed as tragic not in and of itself, but rather because of the loss that it entails, in practical terms, for his enslaver.[30] All three of these examples, therefore, employ fictive orality not just to create pathos for an individual who died young, but also to center the perspective of the enslaver and thereby reinforce the ideology of slavery.

We have thus observed that the phenomenon of fictive orality was, in verse epitaphs for enslaved and emancipated people, harnessed in service of an ideological agenda. Enslavers and patrons frequently utilized the voice of the deceased to paint a heavily sentimentalized picture of enslavement and patronage and to portray themselves in a positive light. This authorial fiction whereby the perspective of the slaveholder class is packaged as the testimony of the enslaved and emancipated, was not, however, universally effective or accepted. In the following section, I will examine how enslaved and emancipated people in the Roman world used fictive orality to challenge the portrayal of slavery constructed by their enslavers and patrons and to advance an alternative self-representation.

3. Commemorations by Enslaved and Emancipated People

As a counterpoint to the epitaphs hitherto examined, I will now consider two verse epitaphs authored by emancipated people. Each of these commemorates a deceased woman and attributes author-function to her surviving husband; both feature an imagined dialogue between husband and wife in which the wife is 'ventriloquized'. In this instance, however, fictive orality is used to challenge the ideological tenets of slavery and the image of enslavement and emancipation propagated by slaveholders.

Let us first examine the epitaph of the freedwoman Claudia Homonoea (*CLE* 995; *CIL* VI 12652), inscribed on a marble altar that was recovered at Rome and is datable to the reign of the emperor Tiberius (14–37 CE). The inscription spans

---

[28] Cf. *quot potui lacrimas aeternaq(ue) munera misi*, "I sent as many tears and everlasting gifts as I could" (*AE* 1997, 362 and 1998, 374, 3).

[29] Cf. *sed te nunc Pietas uenerorque precorque | ut bene pro meriteis hilares Hilaram | quae me seruili nomine preiuat | et dulci suo participat cinerem*, "But you, Piety, I now venerate, and I pray that you may, in return for her benefactions, bestow lots of hilarity upon Hilara, who deprives me of [my] servile name and lets my ashes partake of her own sweet [name]" (*CLE* 963, 7–10).

[30] Cf. *ita neque dom|ino liquit e me | gaudia percipe|re nec me sci|re quid natus | forem*, "thus it was not permitted for my master to derive joys from me, nor for me to know for what purpose I was born" (*CLE* 78, 4–8).

From Beyond the Grave 191

three faces of the altar (the front, left-hand, and right-hand faces). The front face holds a brief preface written in Latin prose, a short inscription written in Greek elegiac couplets, and a brief postscript, again written in Latin prose. The left-hand face contains a 26-line inscription in Latin elegiac couplets which dramatizes a dialogue between the deceased and her husband; similarly, the right-hand side contains a 25-line inscription in Latin elegiac couplets dramatizing a dialogue between the deceased and an imagined viewer of the monument. The full inscription may be transcribed and translated as follows:

Front face:

Atimetus Pamphili
Ti(beri) Caesaris Aug(usti) l(iberti) l(ibertus)
Anterotianus sibi et
Claudiae Homonoeae
conlibertae et
contubernali

Atimetus Anterotianus,
freedman of Pamphilus the freedman of Tiberius Caesar Augustus,
[made this] for himself
and for Claudia Homonoea,
his fellow-freedwoman and partner.

ἡ πολὺ Σειρήνων λιγυρωτέρη ἡ παρὰ Βάκχωι
καὶ θοίναις αὐτῆς χρυσοτέρη Κύπριδος
ἡ λαλίη φαιδρή τε χελειδονὶς ἔνθ' Ὁμόνοια
κεῖμαι Ἀτιμήτωι λειπομένη δάκρυα
τῶι πέλον ἀσπασίη βαιῆς ἄπο τὴν δὲ
τοσαύτην
δαίμων ἀπροϊδῆς ἐσκέδασεν φιλίην

I who was sweeter-voiced than the Sirens, I who, at drinking-parties and feasts, was more golden than Cypris herself, was I, the chattering and radiant swallow – here I, Homonoea, lie, leaving tears for Atimetus, to whom I was dear since I was a young girl; but a god unexpectedly disrupted such great love.

permissu patroni
in fronte longum p(edes) V latum p(edes) IV

By permission of the patron
Five feet wide at the front and four feet deep.

Left-hand face:

si pensare animas		[Anterotianus:] "If the cruel fates allowed us
sinerent crudelia fata		to exchange our souls
et posset redimi morte		and health could be bought
aliena salus		with another's death,
quantulacumque meae	5	whatever short time
debentur tempora uitae		be owed to my lifespan,
pensassem pro te cara		this I would have gladly exchanged
Homonoea libens		for you, dear Homonoea.
at nunc quod possum fugiam		But now (this I can do) I will flee the light of day
lucemque deosque ut te	10	and the gods in order to follow you through the
matura per Styga morte sequar		Styx by means of a timely death."
parce tuam coniu(n)x fletu		[Homonoea:] "Husband, cease disturbing
quassare iuuentam		your youth with weeping
fataque maerendo solli-		and, by grieving, bothering
citare mea	15	my shades.
ni(hi)l prosunt lacrimae nec		Tears are of no use, nor can

192 Emily Mitchell

possunt fata moveri uiximus	the fates be swayed. My life is done;
hic omnis exitus unus habet	this sole ending takes hold of everyone.
parce ita non unquam similem	Cease; so may you never experience
experiare dolorem et 20	a grief like this one,
faveant uotis numina	and may all the divinities give
cuncta tuis	assent to your prayers,
quodque mihi eripuit	and may my untimely death
mors immatura iuuen-	prolong for you, as you continue
tae id tibi uicturo 25	your life, that which it
proroget ulterius	snatched from my youth."

Right-hand face:

tu qui secura	[Homonoea:] "You who go forth
procedis mente	with a calm mind,
parumper siste gradum	halt your steps briefly,
quaeso uerbaque	I ask, and read
pauca lege 5	a few words.
illa ego quae claris	I am she who was pre-eminent
fueram praelata	among illustrious
puellis hoc Homonoea	girls; I, Homonoea, am
breui condita sum	buried in this little
tumulo 10	tomb,
cui formam Paphie	I to whom the Paphian gave
Charites tribuere deco-	beauty and the Graces charm,
rem quam Pallas	I whom Pallas
cunctis artibus erudiit	educated in all the arts.
nondum bis denos ae- 15	My age had not yet
tas mea uiderat annos	seen twice ten years [when]
iniecere manus inuida	the envious fates laid
fata mihi	their hands on me.
nec pro me queror hoc	Nor do I lament for myself;
morte est mihi tristior 20	sadder to me than my own death
ipsa maeror Atimeti	is the grief of Atimetus,
coniugis ille mei	my husband."
sit tibi terra leuis mulier dign-	[Viewer:] "May the earth be light upon you,
issima uita quaeque tuis	woman most worthy of life, you who would long
olim perfruerere bonis 25	since have been enjoying your blessings [if you
	were still alive]."

The 'ventriloquism' of Homonoea in this epitaph serves three important purposes. In the first place, it conveys her learnedness and artistic skill to the viewer. We are told in the Greek poem that Homonoea was a singer and possibly a poetess (ἡ πολὺ Σειρήνων λιγυρωτέρη, 1; ἡ λαλίη φαιδρή τε χελειδονίς, 3) and in the Latin poem that she was educated "in all the arts" (*quam Pallas | cunctis artibus erudiit,* 13–14);[31] moreover, we can deduce from her name, which

---

[31] The Greek word χελειδονίς (literally "female swallow") may indicate that Homonoea

From Beyond the Grave 193

is a Greek noun (ἡ ὁμόνοια, meaning "unanimity" or "concord") that she was of
Hellenic origin and thus presumably bilingual in Greek and Latin. The choice
to have the deceased Homonoea deliver her own verse epitaph in both these
languages, therefore, mimics the type of recitations or performances that she
likely gave in life, thus illustrating for the viewer the nature and extent of her
skill.

The second function of fictive orality here is to convey the depth and sincerity
of feeling between Homonoea and her husband Atimetus Anterotianus. On
all three faces of the monument, Homonoea is made to express awareness of
her husband's suffering and concern for his wellbeing (lines 4–6 in the Greek
epigram on the front face, lines 12–26 on the left-hand face, and lines 19–22 on
the right-hand face), a move which serves to characterize her as a devoted and
empathetic partner, and to indicate that Atimetus is exhibiting the appropriate
degree of grief at the loss of his wife. Moreover, in the inscription on the left-hand
face of the altar, which constitutes a dialogue between Homonoea and Atimetus,
both husband and wife are shown to be preoccupied with each other's welfare,
even at the cost of their own: Atimetus wishes that he could have given his own
life to save Homonoea (1–8) before announcing his intention to commit suicide
in order to join her (9–11); Homonoea replies with an exhortation to cease
mourning, since death is the common lot of all humans (12–18) and a wish that
Atimetus may enjoy better fortune in future (19–26). Throughout the inscription,
therefore, and particularly on the left-hand face, the ventriloquizing of Homonoea emphasizes the closeness of the bond between her and her husband.

The third and final intended function of this fictive orality is to induce in
the viewer empathy for the deceased Homonoea. The right-hand side of the inscription presents an imagined dialogue between Homonoea and the viewer.
Homonoea begins by addressing the viewer directly and asking them to read
her epitaph, a common trope in Latin funerary inscriptions (*tu qui secura* |
procedis mente | *parumper siste gradum* | *quaeso uerbaque* | *pauca lege*, 1–5). She
then introduces herself (6–14) before lamenting her premature death at the age
of nineteen (15–18) and her husband's suffering (19–22). This is followed by an
imagined response from the viewer, who expresses a formulaic wish for Homo-
noea to rest in peace (*sit tibi terra leuis*, 23), addressing her as *mulier dign|issima
uita quaeque tuis* | *olim perfruerere bonis* ("woman most worthy of life, you who
would long since have been enjoying your blessings [if you were still alive]," 23–

---

was a poetess. In his edition, Edward Courtney (*Musa Lapidaria: A Selection of Latin Verse
Inscriptions* [Atlanta, GA: Scholars Press, 1995]) translates this word literally; the *LSJ* entry
for χελειδονίς, however, citing this inscription, claims that it may be applied metaphorically
to a poetess. Further details provided in the Greek epigram (namely, that Homonoea was
Σειρήνων λιγυρωτέρη, "sweeter-voiced than the Sirens," and that she appeared παρὰ Βάκχωι
| καὶ θοίναις, "at the symposium and at feasts") also support the interpretation of her as a
bard or poet.

194 *Emily Mitchell*

25). This creation of a 'script' for the viewer is extremely unusual among Latin verse epitaphs and affords us some insight into the response that Homonoea's husband wished this monument to evoke. The description of Homonoea as "woman most worthy of life" and the comment that she "would long since have been enjoying [her] blessings" indicate that Anterotianus wished the epitaph to engender in the viewer a positive view of Homonoea and a sense of empathy with her misfortunes.

We may observe, therefore, that fictive orality is used to vastly different effect here than in the inscriptions authored by slaveholders. Rather than utilizing Homonoea's voice to affirm the benevolence of her patron and paint a rosy picture of enslavement and emancipation, the epitaph ventriloquizes her in order to impress upon the viewer the nature and extent of her accomplishments (we are shown, for instance, that she was bilingual and possessed considerable literary and artistic talent), to convey the depth and sincerity of her and her husband's affection for one another, and to prompt the viewer to empathize with her. This use of Homonoea's voice constitutes an implicit challenge to the ideology of slavery: Homonoea is defined not in terms of her relationship with her patron, which is not explicitly mentioned at any point in this inscription,[32] but rather in terms of her independent professional identity and marital relationship.[33]

A similar use of the deceased's voice to foreground interpersonal relationships and sideline the slaveholder can be observed in the funerary monument for the freedwoman Aurelia Philematium, which attributes author-function to her husband L. Aurelius Hermia (*CLE* 959; *CIL* I 1221, VI 9499). This monument, recovered at Rome and datable to the first half of the first century BCE, consists of a slab of limestone (specifically *lapis tiburtinus* or "Tiburtine stone") at the center of which a relief has been carved. The relief depicts a male and a female figure, presumably the deceased and her husband, holding hands. The verse epitaph,

---

[32] Atimetus' and Homonoea's patron, Pamphilus, is mentioned only in passing: once in the prose preface, as part of a standard Latin onomastic formula ("Atimetus Anterotianus, <u>freedman of Pamphilus the freedman of Tiberius Caesar Augustus,</u> [made this] for himself and for Claudia Homonoea ..."), and once in the prose postscript, which tells us that the monument was erected *permissu patroni*, "with the patron's permission." This contrasts sharply with the epitaphs examined in Part 1, where the benevolence of the slaveholder and their role in the deceased's life tend to be foregrounded.

[33] With its considerable emphasis on Homonoea's relationship with her husband Atimetus Anterotianus, this epitaph supports the observations of Henrik Mouritsen ("Freedmen and Decurions: Epitaphs and Social History in Imperial Italy," *Journal of Roman Studies* 95 [2005]: 38–63), who argues that the foregrounding of interpersonal relationships in funerary inscriptions created by freedpeople constitutes an emotional response to enslavement, under which they did not have the right to form legally recognized marriages and family units, and John Bodel ("Death and Social Death in Ancient Rome," *On Human Bondage: After Slavery and Social Death*, ed. John Bodel and Walter Scheidel [Malden, MA: Wiley, 2017], 81–108), who reads this foregrounding of relationships as a reaction against the "social death" imposed by enslavement.

From Beyond the Grave 195

which consists of mostly regular elegiac couplets, is inscribed to the left and right of the relief; on the left-hand side, the epitaph is written in the voice of the surviving husband, while on the right-hand side, it is written in the voice of the deceased wife. The text reads as follows:

Left-hand side:

[L(ucius) Au]relius L(uci) l(ibertus)		Lucius Aurelius Hermia,
[H]ermia		freedman of Lucius,
[la]nius de colle		a butcher of the
Viminale		Viminal Hill.
[h]aec quae me faato	1	This woman who preceded me
praecessit corpore		in death, chaste
casto		of body,
[c]oniunx{s} una meo		my wife, singularly endowed
praedita amans	5	with my spirit,
animo		loving,
[f]ido fida uiro ueix{s}it		lived faithful to her faithful husband,
studio parili qum		with affection equal [to her other virtues],
nulla in auaritie		since in no [moment of] selfishness
cessit ab officio	10	did she ever abandon her duties.
[A]urelia L(uci) l(iberta)		Aurelia, freedwoman of Lucius.

Right-hand side:

Aurelia L(uci) l(iberta)		Aurelia Philemation,
Philematio(n)		freedwoman of Lucius.
uiua Philematium sum	1	While I lived, I was known as
Aurelia nominitata		Philematium Aurelia:
casta pudens uolgei		chaste, modest, unknown to the
nescia feida uiro		common herd, faithful to my husband.
uir conleibertus fuit	5	My husband was a fellow-freedman –
eidem quo careo		he, the very one of whom I am now deprived,
eheu		alas!
ree fuit eeuero plus		In truth, he really was
superaque parens		over and above a parent [to me]:
septem me naatam	10	when I was seven years old,
annorum gremio		he himself took me
ipse recepit XXXX		onto his lap.
annos nata necis pot[ior]		Aged forty, I meet my death.
ille meo officio		Through my assiduous duties,
adsiduo florebat ad o[mnis]	15	he used to flourish in all circumstances.

Although this inscription predates Homonoea's epitaph, it exhibits several thematic similarities. Once again, the verse epitaph utilizes the voices of both the deceased wife and her widowed husband, with the ventriloquizing of the wife serving to emphasize their closeness. Here, L. Aurelius Hermia, the husband, speaks first. He attributes to Philematium not only conventional wifely virtues (e.g., chastity, lines 2–3; fidelity, line 7) but also a deep love for, and understanding of, her husband: he stresses the degree to which she understood him (*una meo | praedita ... animo*, "singularly endowed with my spirit," 4–6) and the fact that she was consistently affectionate and dutiful towards him (*studio parili qum | nulla in auaritie | cessit ab officio*, "with affection equal [to her other virtues], since in no [moment of] selfishness did she ever abandon her duties," 8–10). In the second column of the epitaph, the 'ventriloquized' Philematium echoes these sentiments. She is made to describe her own virtues using the same language employed by her husband: while Hermia described her as *corpore casto*, "with a chaste body" (2–3), she calls herself *casta*, "chaste" (3); similarly, Hermia called her *fido fida uiro*, "faithful to her faithful husband" (7), and she calls herself *feida uiro*, "faithful to my husband" (4); finally, as mentioned above, Hermia uses the word *officium*, "duty," in reference to Philematium (10), and Philematium later uses this same word herself when she states that *ille meo officio | adsiduo florebat ad omnis*, "through my assiduous duties, he [Hermia] used to flourish in all seasons" (14–15). These close linguistic correspondences between the two columns of the epitaph reinforce the idea that Philematium is "singularly endowed" with her husband's spirit, since the statements that she makes, and the words that she uses to do so, match the statements previously made by him.

One specific statement put into Philematium's mouth challenges the ideology of slavery more overtly. In lines 8–12, Philematium is made to state that *ree fuit eeuero plus | superaque parens | septem me naatam | annorum gremio | ipse recepit* ("In truth, [my husband] really was over and above a parent [to me]: when I was seven years old he himself took me onto his lap.") The use of fatherhood as a metaphor to describe other kinds of relationships recalls the first epitaph examined in this paper – namely, the senator Cotta's commeoration of his freedman Zosimus, where Zosimus is made to say that Cotta *dotauit | natas ut pater ipse meas*, "dowered my daughters as if he were their own father" (*CLE* 990, 8–9). In this case, however, the metaphor of fatherhood is applied not to the relationship between a slaveholder and his freedpeople, but rather to the relationship between two freedpeople who seem to have grown up in the same household. What is more, the epitaph makes no mention whatsoever of Hermia and Philematium's patron. When taken together, the 'snubbing' of these individuals' former slaveholder and the reassigning of the fatherhood metaphor to the relationship between husband and wife is a radical move: it suggests that the most important and beneficial relationship that Philematium had in her life was not with her enslaver, but rather with a fellow enslaved person in her household. This may be read as a challenge to the attempted imposition of "social death," under which an enslaved person's only significant relationship is with their slaveholder, and also to the phenomenon of "quasi-filial fictive kinship" (to use Patterson's terminology); following Thomas, we might also read this

From Beyond the Grave   197

reclamation of the language of paternalism as an instance of conscious "kincraft" on the part of Hermia.

From the examples of Homonoea and Philematium, therefore, we may observe that, in verse epitaphs authored by emancipated people for their loved ones, fictive orality was used primarily to emphasize the interpersonal relationships formed by the deceased beyond their patron and former enslaver. This use of fictive orality implicitly challenges a central ideological tenet of Roman slavery, namely, that the patron should play an integral role in the social and professional lives of their freedpeople even after manumission.

It could be argued that, since both the authors of these epitaphs (i.e., Atimetus and Hermia) and the women commemorated therein (i.e., Homonoea and Philematium) had been emancipated by the time of their death, they are likely to have enjoyed a greater degree of freedom of expression than they would have done had they still been enslaved. Perhaps surprisingly, however, the use of fictive orality to challenge the ideology of slavery may be observed even in commemorations created by and for enslaved people. One such commemoration is the epitaph of three-year-old Iucundus (*CLE* 987; *CIL* VI 19747). Composed in elegiac couplets, this epitaph is inscribed on a marble tablet which was recovered at Rome and may be dated to the first half of the first century CE. It reads as follows:

Iucundus Li[[uiae Drusi Caesar]]is[34] *f(ilius) Gryp{h}i et Vitalis* *in quartum surgens comprensus deprimor annum* 1 *cum possem matri dulcis et esse patri eripuit me saga manus crudelis ubique cum manet in terris et nocit arte sua uos uestros natos concustodite parentes* 5 *ni dolor in toto pectore fix{s}us est*	Iucundus, [slave] of Livia [wife] of Drusus Caesar,[35] son of Grypus and Vitalis. Attacked as I was growing into my fourth year, I am pressed down, when I had the potential to be sweet to my mother and father. I was seized by the hand of a witch, cruel everywhere when it remains on the earth and causes harm through its art. Parents, guard your children well, lest grief be driven into, and permeate, your whole heart.

---

[34] Part of Livia's name appears to have been deliberately effaced, which must have been done after her execution in 31 CE; Tacitus (*Annals* 6.2) reports that, the following year, the senate issued "terrible decrees against her very statues and memory" (*atroces sententiae ... in effigies quoque ac memoriam eius*).

[35] Although the epitaph does not explicitly attribute author-function to Iucundus' parents, we may infer that it was dedicated by them on the basis of circumstantial evidence. Livia's name, which is inscribed in cramped letters and actually spills over the border of the epitaph on the right-hand side, seems likely to have been added after the rest of the text. This makes it unlikely that she was the original dedicator, since, if she were, she would, presumably, have planned for the inclusion of her own name. The subsequent addition of her name may reflect a change of mind on the part of Iucundus' parents, or may even be the result of a directive from Livia herself.

198   Emily Mitchell

The prose preface explicitly tells us that Iucundus was enslaved by Livia, the
wife of Drusus Caesar. Since this Drusus was the adopted grandson and heir of
the emperor Tiberius, Livia, as his wife, was an extremely high-profile member
of the imperial family. Remarkably, however, the verse portion of the epitaph
neglects to mention Livia at all. Instead, the 'ventriloquized' Iucundus is made
to emphasize the pathos of his death at the age of just three (*in quartum surgens
comprensus deprimor annum*, "Attacked as I was growing into my fourth year, I
am pressed down," 1) and, most notably, the pain that this loss caused his parents (*cum possem matri dulcis et esse patri*, "when I had the potential to be sweet
to my mother and father," 2). The closing lines of the epitaph address all parents, warning them to safeguard their children in order to avoid such pain (*uos
uestros natos concustodite parentes | ni dolor in toto pectore fix{s}us est*, "Parents,
guard your children well, lest grief be driven into, and permeate, your whole
heart," 5–6). The appeal to "parents" in general, which is not qualified by any
reference to social status, establishes common ground between Iucundus' family
and any parents who might view the epitaph, regardless of whether or not they
themselves were enslaved. Like Homonoea's epitaph, therefore, this text seeks to
foreground the deceased's familial relationships and to engender empathy in the
viewer for their loss. This contrasts sharply with the epitaph of the enslaved five-
year-old boy Vitalis;[36] as mentioned, Vitalis' epitaph, authored by his enslaver,
makes no mention of his parents or family, or even the inherent pathos of his
premature death, focusing instead on the fact that Vitalis' death prevented his
enslaver from "deriving joys" from him.

A similar dynamic may be observed in the epitaph of an enslaved 30-year-old
woman named Urbana, which attributes author-function to her husband Atimetus (*CLE* 1310; *CIL* III 6475, 10762). Composed in elegiac couplets, this epitaph
is inscribed on a marble tablet, recovered at Emona in the province of Pannonia
Superior (modern Ljubljana, Slovenia) and datable to the first half of the first
century CE. It reads as follows:

Urbana Iuli		Urbana, [slave] of Iulius Salvius,
Salvi h(ic) s(ita)		lies here.
Atimetus conseru(us) fecit		Atimetus, her fellow-slave, made [this].
coniuge direpta meo direptaq(ue) natis	1	Snatched from my husband and
ei mihi fatales cur rapuere dei		snatched from my children – alas!
nam ter denos egi natales dum uita remansit		Why did the gods of death seize me?
nunc tumulus cineres ossaq(ue) lecta tegit		For, while life remained to me, I
uade age nunc hospes qua te uia ducit euntem	5	celebrated thrice ten birthdays; [but]
huc omnis fatis turba relicta ruit		now a tomb covers my ashes and my
		gathered bones. Come on now, guest,
		go where the road leads you on your
		journey; to this place rushes the whole
		crowd [of those] deserted by the fates.

___
[36] Discussed on p. 188–89.

From Beyond the Grave   199

Like the epitaphs examined in this section so far, Urbana's epitaph foregrounds her familial relationships: the first statement put into her mouth is the exclamation *coniuge direpta meo direptaq(ue) natis | ei mihi fatales cur rapuere dei* ("Snatched from my husband and snatched from my children – alas! Why did the gods of death seize me?" 1–2). Notably, although Urbana and her commemorator are explicitly stated in the prose preface to have been enslaved at the time this inscription was created, Atimetus is referred to as Urbana's *coniunx* ("husband"), a word that indicated the presence of a legally binding marriage, and was thus not applied to partnerships between enslaved individuals, which did not receive such legal recognition.[37] From the first word of the epitaph, therefore, the 'ventriloquizing' of Urbana serves not only to foreground her familial relationships but also to assert their legitimacy in the face of a social system which denied them formal recognition. The remainder of her epitaph utilizes similar techniques to the ones hitherto observed in other inscriptions: lines 3–4 highlight the tragedy of her untimely death, while lines 5–6 constitute a direct address to the viewer. This final address, in which Urbana instructs the living viewer to continue on their journey, in contrast to her own situation and that of other prematurely deceased persons, who are confined to their burial plots (*uade age nunc hospes qua te uia ducit euntem | huc omnis fatis turba relicta ruit*, "come on now, guest, go where the road leads you on your journey; to this place rushes the whole crowd [of those] deserted by the fates") once again works to create empathy on the viewer's part for the deceased, and perhaps to establish common ground with the viewer, who is indirectly reminded of their own mortality.

The use of fictive orality to challenge the prevailing ideology of slavery and to create a representation of the deceased that emphasized elements of their life that were not recognized or sanctioned by the slaveholder class is not, therefore, solely the preserve of emancipated people. As the epitaphs of Iucundus and Urbana indicate, enslaved people in the Roman world could, and did, make use of this rhetorical technique in their commemorations of loved ones. In both social groups, fictive orality was employed to the same effect: namely, to foreground the deceased's familial relationships, to generate empathy in the viewer both for the deceased's premature death and the grief of those who survived them, and to downplay the importance of the deceased's current or former enslaver in their life.

---

[37] The word used to denote an enslaved person's partner would typically be *contubernalis*, literally "tent-companion." For an in-depth discussion of partnerships between enslaved persons in the Roman world and the legal status thereof, see Marcel Simonis, *Cum seruis nullum est conubium: Untersuchungen zu den eheähnlichen Verbindungen von Sklaven im westlichen Mittelmeerraum des Römischen Reiches* (Hildesheim: Georg Olms Verlag, 2017).

200   *Emily Mitchell*

4. Conclusion

The common authorial fiction in Latin verse epitaphs whereby the deceased is made to address and/or to enter into dialogue with the viewer is much more than a literary conceit or consolatory device. In commemorations of enslaved and emancipated individuals, it constituted a powerful rhetorical technique which the author of the epitaph could utilize to advance their own social and political agenda. When members of the slaveholder class created epitaphs for enslaved and emancipated people, the voice of the deceased was frequently used to support several central ideological tenets of slavery and to portray the relationship between enslaver and enslaved (or patron and freedperson) in a favorable light. Conversely, on occasions where enslaved and emancipated people had the opportunity to commemorate their own loved ones, the deceased's voice was used primarily to emphasize the closeness of the familial bonds formed by the deceased during their lifetime, and thereby to contest one of the essential components of the ideology of slavery – namely, Patterson's concept of "social death", whereby the familial relationships formed by enslaved people were denied formal recognition. In such commemorations, the voice of the deceased could also be deployed with the aim of generating an empathetic response in the viewer, a usage not typically observed in epitaphs that attribute author-function to slaveholders.

Ultimately, these two contrasting uses of fictive orality bear testament to the poetic and rhetorical complexity of verse epitaphs. They serve as a reminder that, although these epigraphic texts may not constitute 'literature' in the conventional sense, and although, being inscribed in stone, they may present themselves as conveyors of objective, immutable fact, they are, in actuality, literary texts carefully constructed to advance their composers' social and political agendas. It is crucial, therefore, that we avoid taking such sources at face value. Only by recognizing, and critically analyzing, the authorial fictions at work in these epitaphs may we ascertain whose voice we are really hearing.

Bibliography

Bodel, John. "Death and Social Death in Ancient Rome." Pages 81–108 in *On Human Bondage: After Slavery and Social Death*. Edited by John Bodel and Walter Scheidel. Chichester; Malden, MA: John Wiley & Sons, Inc., 2017.

Boex, Allison. "Cold Comfort: Speeches to and from the Prematurely Deceased in Early Roman Verse-Epitaphs." *Latomus* 77.1 (2018): 74–98.

Buonocore, Marco. "Su due carmina epigraphica latina da Larinum." *Aufidus* 31 (1997): 72–77.

Carroll, Maureen. "The Mourning was Very Good: Liberation and Liberality in Roman Funerary Commemoration." Pages 126–149 in *Memory and Mourning: Studies on*

From Beyond the Grave 201

Roman Death. Edited by Valerie M. Hope and Janet Huskinson. Oxford; Oakville, CT: Oxbow Books, 2011.

Cooley, Alison E. "The Production and Design of Inscriptions." Pages 286–300 in *The Cambridge Manual of Latin Epigraphy*. Cambridge: Cambridge University Press, 2012.

Courtney, Edward. *Musa Lapidaria: A Selection of Latin Verse Inscriptions*. Atlanta, GA: Scholars Press, 1995.

Edmondson, Jonathan. "Inscribing Roman Texts: Officinae, Layout, and Carving Techniques." Pages 111–130 in *The Oxford Handbook of Roman Epigraphy*. Oxford: Oxford University Press, 2015.

Foreman, Gabrielle P., et al. "Writing About Slavery/Teaching About Slavery: This Might Help." Accessed 15 December 2022. URL: https://docs.google.com/document/d/1A4T EdDgYslX-hlKezLodMIM71My3KTN0zxRv0IQTOQs/mobilebasic

Foucault, Michel. "What Is an Author?" Pages 101–120 in *The Foucault Reader*. New York: Pantheon Books, 1984.

King, Karen L. "'What Is an Author?' Ancient Author-Function in the Apocryphon of John and the Apocalypse of John." Pages 15–42 in *Scribal Practices and Social Structures among Jesus Adherents: Essays in Honour of John S. Kloppenborg*. Edited by William E. Arnal et al. Leuven: Peeters, 2016.

Matera, Robert. "The Doctitude of Pearl the Dog in CE 1175 = *CIL* VI 29896." *Zeitschrift für Papyrologie und Epigraphik* 210 (2019): 91–103.

Mouritsen, Henrik. "Freedman and Decurions: Epitaphs and Social History in Imperial Italy." *Journal of Roman Studies* 95 (2005): 38–63.

Patterson, Orlando. *Slavery and Social Death: A Comparative Study*. Cambridge, MA: Harvard University Press, 1982.

Saller, Richard P. "*Pater familias, mater familias*, and the Gendered Semantics of the Roman Household." *Classical Philology* 94.2 (1999): 182–197.

Shaw, Brent D. "Raising and Killing Children: Two Roman Myths." *Mnemosyne* 54.1 (2001): 31–77.

Simonis, Marcel. *Cum seruis nullum est conubium: Untersuchungen zu den eheähnlichen Verbindungen von Sklaven im westlichen Mittelmeerraum des Römischen Reiches*. Hildesheim: Georg Olms Verlag, 2017.

Thomas, Todne. Kincraft: The Making of Black Evangelical Sociality. Durham, NC: Duke University Press, 2021.

Imagining Gospel Authorship

Anonymity, Collaboration, and Monography in a Pluriform Corpus*

JEREMIAH COOGAN

1. Introduction

In 1787 and 1788, as part of the raging debates over the ratification of the proposed United States Constitution, a series of essays were printed under the pseudonym "Publius." While the essays were published together as *The Federalist* in the spring of 1788, the names of the three collaborators – Alexander Hamilton, James Madison, and John Jay – did not appear on a title page until the French edition of 1792. Over the next several decades, the authorship of the essays continued to be reimagined; they were printed in the collected works of both Hamilton and Madison, and competing claims were advanced for the authorship of the individual essays. Through titles, prefaces, and other paratexts, the divergent moments of publication negotiated the tension between the essays as a collective project of "Publius" and as the work of monographic authors.

As legal historian Drew Starling describes, over time "certain modes of authorial attribution" prompt particular "ways of reading" this composite work.[1] How should one understand the collaborative nature of this text? Can individual essays – or the collection as a whole – be attributed to the authorial genius of any of the three collaborators? To what extent can one read the essays as part of the independent *oeuvres* of their authors? Reconfigured for varied editions, "Publius" appears in "many competing pseudonymous voices."[2] The publication history of these essays reflects readers' divergent constructions of their authorship, constructions which continue to shape their use today as a "canonical" text with a

---

* This project received funding from the European Commission's Horizon 2020 research and innovation program under Marie Skłodowska-Curie grant agreement no. 891569. I am also grateful for the support of the Oxford Centre for Hebrew and Jewish Studies and Keble College, Oxford. This research was first presented as part of the series "Authorial Fictions and Attributions in the Ancient Mediterranean" in autumn 2021. I am grateful to Tobias Nicklas for his insightful response, as well as to Gregory P. Fewster, Meghan Henning, David Lincicum, Julia Lindenlaub, and Candida R. Moss for their incisive feedback.

[1] Drew Starling, "Unmasking Publius: Authorial Attribution and the Making of *The Federalist*," *Book History* 25 (2022): 63–95. As Starling asks, "[W]hy were certain modes of authorial attribution chosen at particular moments in the essays' editorial history, and to what extent have these forms of authorial attribution invited new ways of reading *The Federalist*?" (63).

[2] Starling, "Unmasking Publius," 64.

204   Jeremiah Coogan

privileged role in US political and legal discourse.[3] The example of *The Federalist* offers critical leverage for interrogating constructions and reconfigurations of authorship for other textual corpora as well.

In this essay, I analyze similar dynamics in how late ancient readers conceptualized Gospel books. From the second century onward, readers reimagined authorial attributions in order to theorize multiple Gospels as a coherent corpus.[4] In a productive circularity, varied theorizations of Gospel literature exerted pressure on the divergent modes of authorship that Gospels were imagined to have. Readers developed varied models of authorship, balancing collaboration and monography.[5] Constructions of Gospel authorship shifted from initial anonymity, to models contrasting undifferentiated collaboration with distinct authorship, to schemata attempting (with varying degrees of success) to merge these alternatives. Imagined and reimagined, these ideas of authorship were entangled with novel ways of reading an emergent pluriform Gospel corpus.

When readers encounter a text, they frequently inquire, "Who wrote this?" This is not mere curiosity. Rather, the figure of the author serves a heuristic function. Whether for the essays of "Publius" or for early Christian Gospels, practices of reading – whether historical, literary, legal, or theological – invest authorship with hermeneutical weight. The reader who asks, "Who wrote this?" is often asking "How should I read this text?"[6]

---

[3] Starling, "Unmasking Publius," 63–65.

[4] I build on the work of other scholars who have analyzed early Christian conversations about Gospel authorship, especially Robert M. Grant's discussion of ancient debates over authenticity and attribution ("Literary Criticism and the New Testament Canon," *Journal for the Study of the New Testament* 5 [1982]: 24–44) and Annette Yoshiko Reed's study of efforts to conceptualize "Gospel" as a literary category, focused on Irenaeus ("Εὐαγγέλιον: Orality, Textuality, and the Christian Truth in Irenaeus' *Adversus haereses*," *Vigiliae christianae* 56 [2002]: 11–46). My essay challenges another strand of modern scholarship which asserts a "lack of interest in the question of authorship" among early Christian readers (e. g., Martin Hengel, "The Titles of the Gospels and the Gospel of Mark," in *Studies in the Gospel of Mark* [London: SCM, 1985], 68).

[5] For the language of "monographic" authors, I draw upon the work of Alice Savoie. Savoie contrasts historiographic discourses "that usually [call] for a monographic interpretation of events" with "the collaborative nature of most design processes" ("The Women Behind Times New Roman: The Contribution of Type Drawing Offices to Twentieth Century Type-Making," *Journal of Design History* 33 [2020]: 209–224, 210). We observe this monographic bias both in ancient discourses about textuality and in modern histories of textual practices; in this essay, I use the language of "monography" to describe this model of singular agency. Savoie's article attends in particular to the gendered dimensions of this historiographic distortion; especially in discussions of the Roman Mediterranean, we also note the ways that the labor and expertise of enslaved literary workers are occluded.

[6] On how readers use the "author" to guide their interpretation of a text, see Starling, "Unmasking Publius," 67–68. Starling assembles a number of eighteenth-century examples in which readers reflect on why a writer might prefer anonymity and on the ways that an author's (real or imagined) biography shapes the reception of a text. For parallel analysis of anonymity in Roman literature, see Tom Geue, *Author Unknown: The Power of Anonymity in Ancient Rome* (Cambridge, MA: Harvard University Press, 2019).

Imagining Gospel Authorship 205

In this essay, I build on Michel Foucault's influential account of the "author-function."[7] On this model, "authors" are the products of "texts"; they are the imagined figures who stand behind the literary work in order to give it a fictive unity. The "author" stands in for the complicated situations by which texts come to be, regardless of the conditions of textual production and apart from any attempt to reconstruct the interior states or intentions of the human agent or agents responsible for producing a text.[8] The "author" is a heuristic and hermeneutic reference point.[9]

Yet authorship is about more than attribution. Foucault's insight that authorship is manufactured and historically contingent enables us to recognize an inverse dynamic: Over time, readers and texts continue to transform the *function* of the author. As a result, even if the "author" of a text remains the same, their authorship might be reimagined to involve different kinds of labor, intention, or agency. Author-function changes. While the "author" shapes the text, texts also exert pressure on existing ideas of what it means to "author" a text and of who an "author" might be.[10] Authorial attribution becomes a "zone … of transaction" mediating between text and reader, a dynamic space in which new possibilities of interpretation and signification emerge.[11] Across genres and historical periods,

---

[7] Michel Foucault, "What is an Author?" in *Textual Strategies: Perspectives in Post-Structuralist Criticism*, ed. Josué V. Harari, (Ithaca: Cornell University Press, 1979 [1969]), 141–60; cf. Roger Chartier, *The Order of Books: Readers, Authors, and Libraries in Europe Between the Fourteenth and Eighteenth Centuries* (Stanford: Stanford University Press, 1994), 25–60; Robert J. Griffin, "Anonymity and Authorship," *New Literary History* 30 (1999): 877–95.

[8] Writing in Mediterranean antiquity and late antiquity frequently involved uncredited collaboration and complex processes of production. See *inter alia* William Fitzgerald, *Slavery and the Roman Literary Imagination* (Cambridge: Cambridge University Press, 2000); idem, "The Slave, Between Absence and Presence," in *Unspoken Rome: Absence in Latin Literature and Its Reception*, ed. Tom Geue and Elena Giusti (Cambridge: Cambridge University Press, 2021), 239–49; Candida R. Moss, "Between the Lines: Looking for the Contributions of Enslaved Literate Laborers in a Second-Century Text (P. Berol. 11632)," *Studies in Late Antiquity* 5 (2021): 432–52; Jeremiah Coogan, Candida R. Moss, and Joseph A. Howley, eds., *Writing, Enslavement, and Power in the Roman Mediterranean, 100 BCE–300 CE* (New York: Oxford University Press, 2024).

[9] As described by Gérard Genette, such "paratexts" are "thresholds of interpretation." They "ensure the text's presence in the world, its 'reception' and consumption in the form (nowadays at least) of a book" (*Paratexts: Thresholds of Interpretation* [Cambridge: Cambridge University Press, 1997], 1). Within this framework, Genette analyzes how "the name of the author" shapes readers' encounters with a work (*Paratexts*, 37–54). On paratexts in the Roman Mediterranean, see Laura Jansen, ed., *The Roman Paratext: Frame, Texts, Readers* (Cambridge: Cambridge University Press, 2014).

[10] On experiments with authorship in the Roman Mediterranean, see, e.g., Irene Peirano, *The Rhetoric of the Roman Fake: Latin Pseudepigrapha in Context* (Cambridge: Cambridge University Press, 2012); Geue, *Author Unknown*; Jeremiah Coogan, Candida R. Moss, and Joseph A. Howley, "The Socioeconomics of Fabrication: Textuality, Authenticity, and Class in the Roman Mediterranean," *Arethusa* (2024).

[11] Genette, *Paratexts*, 2.

206   Jeremiah Coogan

authorial attributions are never independent, but are networked into broader
bibliographic imaginaries that develop in this transactional space.[12]

In this essay, I analyze how figures from the second to fourth centuries CE
continued to reimagine Gospel authorship. Although scholars have often discussed how early readers made sense of the expanding landscape of books about
Jesus' words and deeds, scant attention has been devoted to how these divergent
theorizations of an emergent pluriform Gospel corpus centered on competing
models of authorship.

This omission results, at least in part, from the fact that modern discussions of authorship focus on the initial anonymity and subsequent attribution
of the Gospels according to Matthew, Mark, Luke, and John. The conventional
narrative understands these texts as initially untitled and perhaps anonymous
works.[13] On this model, the epigraphic κατά-title ("Gospel according to ...")
emerged in the second century as readers sought to organize the expanding literary field of Jesus books.[14] These epigraphic labels attribute individual agency

---

[12] See Eva Mroczek's groundbreaking work on the "literary imagination" of Second Temple
Judaism (*The Literary Imagination in Jewish Antiquity* [Oxford: Oxford University Press, 2016]),
as well as discussion of the early Christian "bibliographic imagination" in Jeremiah Coogan,
"Reading (in) a Quadriform Cosmos: Gospel Books and the Early Christian Bibliographic
Imagination," *Journal of Early Christian Studies* 31 (2023): 85–103; Jeremiah Coogan, "The Ways
that Parted in the Library: The Gospels *according to Matthew* and *according to the Hebrews* in
Late Ancient Heresiology," *Journal of Ecclesiastical History* 74 (2023): 473–90.

[13] For accounts of initial anonymity and secondary labeling see, e. g., Harry Y. Gamble, *Books
and Readers in the Early Church: A History of Early Christian Texts* (New Haven: Yale University
Press, 1995); Reed, "Εὐαγγέλιον," 16–21; Silke Petersen, "Die Evangelienüberschriften und die
Entstehung des neutestamentlichen Kanons," *Zeitschrift für die neutestamentliche Wissenschaft*
97 (2006): 250–74; Daniel Ullucci, "The Anonymity of the Gospels κατά Pac-Man," *Annali di
Storia dell'Esegesi* 36 (2019): 95–116. Others reject the idea of initial anonymity, although most
see the epigraphic titles as later than the composition of the texts to which they are attached
(e. g., Hengel, "Titles of the Gospels"; Adela Yarbro Collins, *Mark: A Commentary* [Minneapolis:
Fortress, 2007], 129; Simon J. Gathercole, "The Alleged Anonymity of the Canonical Gospels,"
Journal of Theological Studies 69 [2018]: 447–76). While broadly concurring with the conventional narrative, Larsen has challenged "authorship" as a relevant category for early Gospel
texts (Matthew D.C. Larsen, "Correcting the Gospel: Putting the Titles of the Gospels in Historical Context," in *Rethinking 'Authority' in Late Antiquity: Authorship, Law, and Transmission in Jewish and Christian Tradition*, ed. A.J. Berkovitz and Mark D. Letteney [New York:
Routledge, 2018], 78–103; idem, *Gospels Before the Book* [New York: Oxford University Press,
2018]; idem, "The Publication of the Synoptics and the Problem of Dating," in *The Oxford
Handbook of the Synoptic Gospels*, ed. Stephen P. Ahearne-Kroll [Oxford: Oxford University
Press, 2023], 175–76). Yet, by the later second century, readers attribute Gospel texts to particular
figures whose identities shape the reception of these texts. Instead of eschewing the category
of "author," then, I focus on how the "author" is imagined in these contexts. My argument thus
partly parallels Ullucci's emphasis on the importance of audience in the authorial (non-)at-
tribution of a text ("The Anonymity of the Gospels κατά Pac-Man"). Even so, Larsen is right to
mention varied "other possibilities of textual production," beyond a singular author at a single
point in time ("Publication of the Synoptics," 176).

[14] These arguments depend primarily on literary evidence. Physical traces of titles for the
New Testament Gospels appear in the late second century at the earliest. On the early manu-

Imagining Gospel Authorship 207

while also suggesting that the category "Gospel" unites and precedes these disparate texts. Scholars often treat the κατά-titles as endpoints, bibliographic labels that stabilize Gospel authorship into a durable configuration.

Yet this is not the conclusion of the story. Readers continued to reimagine Gospel authorship, for these four Gospel texts and for others. Titles and attributions invited creative reimaginations of the agency and circumstances of textual production. This set of shifting imaginations centers not on *who* the authors are, but on *what* an author is and does.

In this essay, I extend and nuance current discussions of Gospel authorship by analyzing three divergent theorizations of Gospel authorship from the second to fourth centuries. Drawing on Starling, we might describe these as "three key moments in the attribution history" of the Gospels.[15] How did these early Christian figures conceptualize Gospel authorship? The *Apocryphon of James* (NHC I,2), Origen of Alexandria (*Hom. Luc.* 1), and Epiphanius of Salamis (*Pan.* 51) each attest different theories of Gospel authorship. Each grapples with the tensions between individual and collective modes of authorship, between monography and multiplicity. The multiformity – the repetition and difference – within an emergent pluriform Gospel corpus modifies conceptions of "individual" authorship for particular Gospel books. This pluriform corpus exerts pressure on the extent to which the evangelists could be described as monographic authors, figures with distinct claims to authorial agency. The late ancient theorization of a pluriform Gospel corpus generates a quasi-pseudepigraphic construct of collective textual production even as it catalyzes new concepts of authorship.

2. The *Apocryphon of James* (NHC I,2)

The second-century *Apocryphon of James* (*Ap. Jas.*) demonstrates how readers grappled with a pluriform Gospel corpus.[16] The work exemplifies ongoing ef-

---

script evidence for Gospel titles, see Simon J. Gathercole, "The Titles of the Gospels in the Earliest New Testament Manuscripts," *Zeitschrift für die neutestamentliche Wissenschaft* 104 (2013): 33–76. For a survey of all titles in New Testament papyri, see Garrick V. Allen, "Titles in the New Testament Papyri," *New Testament Studies* 68 (2022): 156–71. The earliest extant Gospel title is probably found in 𝔓4 (Bibliothèque Nationale de France, suppl. gr. 1120 = LDAB 2936); cf. Jean Merell, "Nouveaux fragments du papyrus 4," *Revue biblique* 47 (1938): 6; Simon J. Gathercole, "The Earliest Manuscript Title of Matthew's Gospel (BnF Suppl. Gr. 1120 II 3 / 4)," *Novum Testamentum* 54 (2012): 209–35; Garrick V. Allen, "Titles in the New Testament Papyri," 160. Titles for both canonical and noncanonical Gospels in Coptic are attested by the third or fourth century (René Falkenberg, "Apocryphal Gospel Titles in Coptic," *Religions* 13 [2022], no. 796).

[15] Starling, "Unmasking Publius," 63.

[16] *Ap. Jas.* is extant in a single fourth-century Coptic manuscript (NHC I,2), although the work was likely composed in Greek in the late second or perhaps early third century CE. The work presents itself as written in Hebrew (*Ap. Jas.* 1.16), but this is a fiction. The *editio princeps*

208   Jeremiah Coogan

forts to craft monographic notions of Gospel authorship in a bibliographic landscape characterized by textual plurality. Unlike many other early Gospel texts,
the *Apocryphon* does not offer a narrative of Jesus' life; no biographical arc
leads from his baptism by John at the Jordan to a crucifixion and resurrection
at Jerusalem. Instead, the *Apocryphon* recounts an extended secret revelation of
Jesus to James and Peter that takes place after Jesus' resurrection (*Ap. Jas.* 1.1–35;
16.12–30). Despite differences in narrative content and literary form, the work
engages extensively with material from Gospel narratives that follow the biographical pattern.[17]

The relationship goes beyond shared material. Even while the *Apocryphon*
avoids the language of "Gospel" (τὸ εὐαγγέλιον/ⲡⲉⲩⲁⲅⲅⲉⲗⲓⲟⲛ), the work locates
itself in an expanding second-century landscape of books about Jesus. The
Apocryphon does not attest a fourfold Gospel, but it does imagine plurality and
textual diversity. In particular, the epistolary frame contrasts the *Apocryphon*'s
own textuality with other written Jesus traditions.[18] In this way, it enacts what
Chris Keith has termed "competitive textualization."[19]

---

is Michel Malinine, ed., *Epistula Iacobi apocrypha: Codex Jung F. Ir-F. VIIIv (p. 1–16)* (Zürich:
Rascher, 1968). In what follows, I have depended upon the more recent edition of Donald
Rouleau and Louise Roy, eds., *L'épître apocryphe de Jacques (NH 1,2)* (Québec: Presses de
l'Úniversité Laval, 1987). I follow the translation of Frank E. Williams in James M. Robinson,
ed., *The Nag Hammadi Library in English* (Leiden: Brill, 1996), 29–37. Bracketed words indicate
proposed restorations in the lacunose Coptic text. Reading *Ap. Jas.* in the context of NHC I as
a whole, see Lance Jenott and Elaine H. Pagels, "Antony's Letters and Nag Hammadi Codex I:
Sources of Religious Conflict in Fourth-Century Egypt," *Journal of Early Christian Studies* 18
(2010): 557–89. The conventional title "Apocryphon of James" is a modern editorial invention;
no title is preserved in the manuscript (cf. Falkenberg, "Apocryphal Gospel Titles," 11).

[17] On intersections with Synoptic and/or Johannine material, see Pheme Perkins, "Johannine Traditions in *Ap. Jas.* (NHC 1,2)," *Journal of Biblical Literature* 101 (1982): 403–14; David
Brakke, "Parables and Plain Speech in the Fourth Gospel and the *Apocryphon of James*," *Journal
of Early Christian Studies* 7 (1999): 187–218, esp. 189, 204, 206; Julia D. Lindenlaub, "The Gospel
of John as Model for Literate Authors and their Texts in Epistula Apostolorum and Apocryphon
of James (NHC I,2)," *Journal for the Study of the New Testament* 43 (2020): 3–27; Francis Watson, "Against the Twelve: The Apocryphon of James and the Status of the Apostles," in *Texts in
Context: Essays on Dating and Contextualising Christian Writings from the Second and Early
Third Centuries*, ed. Joseph Verheyden, Jens Schröter, and Tobias Nicklas (Leuven: Peeters,
2021), 225–26; Jeremiah Coogan and Jacob A. Rodriguez, "Ordering Gospel Textuality in the
Second Century," *Journal of Theological Studies* 74 (2023): 87 n. 104. Insofar as *Ap. Jas.* offers an
extended discourse by Jesus that reconfigures both Synoptic and Johannine material, the work
resembles *Ep. Apost.*; cf. Lindenlaub ("Gospel of John as Model"), who also draws attention to
parallels with John's authorial posture.

[18] On the epistolary framing of *Ap. Jas.*, see J. Gregory Given, "Four Texts From Nag Hammadi Amid the Textual and Generic Fluidity of the 'Letter' in the Literature of Late Antique
Egypt," in *Snapshots of Evolving Traditions: Jewish and Christian Manuscript Culture, Textual
Fluidity, and New Philology*, ed. Hugo Lundhaug and Liv Ingeborg Lied, (Berlin: De Gruyter,
2017), 201–20, as well as the contribution by Lindenlaub in this volume. Although Peter is also a
recipient of the revelation, the frame narrative attributes the work to James alone.

[19] On competitive textualization, see Chris Keith, *The Gospel as Manuscript: An Early History of the Jesus Tradition as Material Artifact* (Oxford: Oxford University Press, 2020), 103–5.

Imagining Gospel Authorship 209

The opening narrative describes "the twelve disciples all sitting together at the same time and recalling what the Savior had said to each one of them, whether in secret or openly, and [putting it] in books" (*Ap. Jas.* 2.8–15). The twelve are depicted as authors of multiple Jesus books. It is not clear how many separate books are imagined, although we might surmise that each disciple is producing his own. The imagined scene of synchronous and collaborative textual production results in a *corpus* of related books. This joint process limits individual claims of authorship. Even if Gospel texts might be named "according to" a particular figure, the collaborative process attenuates any singular attribution.[20]

This collaborative project of Gospel writing is mnemonic and revelatory. The disciples are "recalling" (ⲉⲩⲉⲓⲣⲉ ⲙ̄ⲡⲙⲉⲉⲩⲉ) what Jesus had said. The depiction of Jesus books as collections of remembered material resonates with other second-century imaginations of Gospel writing, from Papias of Hierapolis' collection of oral accounts (*apud* Eusebius, *Hist. eccl.* 3.39.3–4) to Justin of Rome's description of Gospels as apostolic "memoirs" (ἀπομνημονεύματα).[21] Moreover, the collab-

---

Keith defines "competitive textualization" as "the fact that in many cases an instance of tradition goes beyond reflecting on itself as written tradition and is also conscious of other written traditions that it holds in its direct or peripheral vision, *by which* or *with which* it is vying for (authoritative) status. […] this relationship is 'competitive' only in the sense that the tradition is aware of a prior tradition's social position and is vying for its own particular position by drawing parasitically upon that predecessor" (103). Keith notes *Ap. Jas.* as an example of competitive textualization (156). On how *Ap. Jas.* situates itself in relation to earlier Gospel writing, see *inter alia* Brakke, "Parables and Plain Speech," esp. 207; Keith, *Gospel as Manuscript*, 156; Lindenlaub, "Gospel of John as Model"; Watson, "Against the Twelve," 221–30. The Gospels that became canonical include two texts attributed to figures from among the twelve (Matthew and John). Yet we need not imagine that these are the only potential apostolic Gospel writers that the *Apocryphon* has in mind. As I discuss in the next section, Origen of Alexandria (*Hom. Luc.* 1.1–2) reports other Gospel books attributed to Jesus' various disciples. The "competitive textualization" visible in *Ap. Jas.* need not be limited to competition with the texts of the eventual fourfold collection. Indeed, the depiction of Gospel writing better fits an expansive landscape of Gospel writing like what Origen describes.

[20] *Ap. Jas.* is not the only second-century text that imagines collaborative Gospel authorship. *Ep. Apost.* offers another second-century example of apostles engaged in collective authorship. Yet in *Ap. Jas.* the collectivity authorizes a pluriform corpus of Gospel books, while in *Ep. Apost.* the result is a single text. On the interconnections between *Ep. Apost.* and *Ap. Jas.*, see Lindenlaub, "Gospel of John as Model"; Francis Watson, *An Apostolic Gospel: The 'Epistula Apostolorum' in Literary Context* (Cambridge: Cambridge University Press, 2020), 93; Watson, "Against the Twelve," 215.

[21] Numerous scholars have discussed Papias' preference for memory and the "living voice" (cf. Armin D. Baum, "Papias, der Vorzug der *Viva Vox* und die Evangelienschriften," *New Testament Studies* 44 [1998]: 144–51). Justin uses ἀπομνημονεύματα in parallel to εὐαγγέλια in *1 Apol.* 66.3. The term appears a total of fifteen times throughout his corpus. On Justin's ἀπομνημονεύματα, see *inter alia* Reed, "Εὐαγγέλιον," 16–17; Wally V. Cirafesi and Gregory P. Fewster, "Justin's ἀπομνημονεύματα and Ancient Greco-Roman Memoirs," *Early Christianity* 7 (2016): 186–212; Larsen, *Gospels Before the Book*, 90–91; Keith, *Gospel as Manuscript*, 52–53, 182–84; Jacob A. Rodriguez, "Justin and the Apostolic Memoirs," *Early Christianity* 11 (2020): 496–515. In emphasizing the role of memory in the composition of these other apostolic Gospels (*Ap. Jas.* 2.8–15), I differ from Keith, who describes them as "coming directly from Jesus" (*Gospel*

210   Jeremiah Coogan

orative apostolic texts in *Ap. Jas.* are revelatory. They textualize not only Jesus'
public teachings but also his secret instructions to the disciples.

The *Apocryphon* reframes multiplicity into collaborative unity by sub-
ordinating individual Gospel authorship to a collective process that produces
a cluster of interrelated (perhaps even interchangeable) texts.[22] Yet the *Apocryphon* claims to be a Jesus book unlike these others. While the other texts are
being written, Jesus takes Peter and James aside to give them the secret revelation
communicated by the *Apocryphon*. This diminishes the authority of other apostolic books (including the Gospels that would become canonical). True, when
Jesus arrives to deliver his new revelation to James, he allows the other disciples
to continue their work (*Ap. Jas.* 2.38–39). The *Apocryphon* thus acknowledges
the plurality of apostolic Jesus books and confers implicit divine approval on
the collaborative project.[23] Yet, even if other books are not rejected, they are
inferior to James' own text. Jesus' new revelation calls James away from the
collaborative process. Not only is the *Apocryphon* separate from the collective
project of authorship, but it contains material that "the Savior did not wish to
tell to all of us, his twelve disciples" (*Ap. Jas.* 1.23–25). As a result, the circulation
of the written work is to be limited.

As a project of competitive textualization, the *Apocryphon* reconfigures the
idea of Gospel authorship. It divides Jesus books into two categories, written
in distinct modes. Some Gospel texts are an interrelated corpus, the joint pro-

---

as Manuscript, 156). Watson ("Against the Twelve," 222) also notes the parallels between how
Ap. Jas. depicts collective Gospel authorship and the earlier approach of Justin and Papias; as
he writes, "Justin's terminology implies that these memoirs (ἀπομνημονεύματα) represent the
collective apostolic testimony" (216).

[22] Drawing on Brian Stock's idea of "textual communities" (Brian Stock, *The Implications of
Literacy: Written Language and Models of Interpretation in the Eleventh and Twelfth Centuries*
[Princeton: Princeton University Press, 1983]), Brakke locates this textual imagination of *Ap. Jas.*
in the social context of second-century Christian reading circles ("Parables and Plain Speech,"
203); cf. more recently John S. Kloppenborg, "Literate Media in Early Christian Groups: The
Creation of a Christian Book Culture," *Journal of Early Christian Studies* 22 (2014): 35, 43–44.
Johnson and Howley provide a robust contextual framework for understanding such reading
circles: William A. Johnson, *Readers and Reading Culture in the High Roman Empire: A Study
of Elite Communities* (Oxford: Oxford University Press, 2010); Joseph A. Howley, *Aulus Gellius
and Roman Reading Culture: Text, Presence, and Imperial Knowledge in the* Noctes Atticae
(Cambridge: Cambridge University Press, 2018). See also Lindenlaub's contribution in this
volume; through deft comparison with the reading circle attested by P. Oxy. 2192, Lindenlaub
argues that *Ap. Jas.* situates itself in a similar (imagined) reading community.

[23] In seeing this as Jesus' tacit endorsement of the project, I concur with Brakke, who observes that *Ap. Jas.* "celebrates the diversity of books left by the disciples, literature that contains
a mix of 'parables' and 'open' teachings" ("Parables and Plain Speech," 216, cf. 206). I disagree
with Francis Watson, who sees *Ap. Jas.* as rejecting all other apostolic Jesus books ("Against the
Twelve," 221–25). As Brakke notes ("Parables and Plain Speech," 216 n. 84), disparagement of
disciples is a common trope in early Christian literature and does not require rejecting apostolic figures altogether. Reading Jesus' actions as tacit approval of the ongoing project of apostolic Gospel writing, see also Lindenlaub, "Gospel of John as Model," 18.

Imagining Gospel Authorship 211

duction of an apostolic college remembering Jesus' teachings.[24] The *Apocryphon of James* is a different kind of book, reflecting a distinctive immediacy of individual revelatory experience.[25] These two bibliographic categories are marked by divergent dynamics of textual production and different modes of authorship. The individual and novel contrasts with the collaborative and remembered. Already in the second century, then, we see tension between ideas of apostolic collaboration and a monographic model of Gospel writing. These two contrasting modes continue to shape the subsequent Christian bibliographic imagination.

3. Origen of Alexandria (*Homily on Luke* 1)

Origen of Alexandria (*ca.* 185–*ca.* 255 CE) conceptualizes Gospel authorship in a different way than the *Apocryphon of James*.[26] The *Apocryphon* constructs a hierarchy of authorial modes, distinguishing its own novel, individual mode of composition from the collective, traditioned production of other Gospel texts. Origen redefines Gospel authorship in order to distinguish his ecclesial corpus from other texts that, in his view, fail to count as Gospels at all.

In a homily preached in Caesarea sometime in the years 239–242 CE, Origen explicates the beginning of Luke's prologue:[27] "Since many people have attempted to compose a narrative about the events that have been fulfilled among us ...." (1:1).[28] The prologue situates Luke's Gospel in a broader literary field, justifying its intervention in an increasingly crowded landscape of writings about Jesus.[29]

---

[24] One of the implications of this collaborative project is that redundancy, contradiction, and omission can all be understood as the effects of a singular and coherent project. *Ap. Jas.* thus offers a hermeneutical framework that can be used to fend off criticism and underwrite projects of reading multiple Gospels together.

[25] I am grateful to Tobias Nicklas for his insights on this contrast between the revelatory immediacy of *Ap. Jas.* and the role of memory in the other apostolic books.

[26] This passage has been central to scholarly discussions about non-canonical Gospels at least since Erwin Preuschen gave it pride of place in his *Antilegomena: Die Reste der ausserkanonischen Evangelien und urchristlichen Ueberlieferungen* (Berlin: De Gruyter, 1901), 1. It has been discussed in recent studies, although with limited attention to the question of authorship. Recent discussion includes Ronald Heine, *Origen: Scholarship in the Service of the Church* (Oxford: Oxford University Press, 2010), 79; Francis Watson, *Gospel Writing: A Canonical Perspective* (Grand Rapids: Eerdmans, 2013), 512–14; Keith, *Gospel as Manuscript*, 233; Samuel B. Johnson, "'A Sign for This Generation': The Life of Jesus in Origen's Gospel Commentaries" (PhD diss., University of Notre Dame, 2021), ch. 5; Jeremiah Coogan, "Failed Gospels and Disciplinary Knowledge in Origen's *Hom. Luc.* 1," in *Unruly Books: Rethinking Ancient and Academic Imaginations of Religious Texts*, ed. Esther Brownsmith, Marianne B. Kartzow, and Liv Ingeborg Lied (London: Bloomsbury T&T Clark, forthcoming).

[27] For the date, see Pierre Nautin, *Origène: Sa vie et son oeuvre* (Paris: Beauchesne, 1977), 389–412 (and especially the chronological table on pp. 410–12).

[28] Ἐπειδήπερ πολλοὶ ἐπεχείρησαν ἀνατάξασθαι διήγησιν περὶ τῶν πεπληροφορημένων ἐν ἡμῖν πραγμάτων.

[29] On the Lukan prologue in the context of Roman literary culture, see *inter alia* Loveday

212   Jeremiah Coogan

Subsequent readers, from antiquity to the present, have used the prologue in
their own reconstructions of the history of Gospel literature, and this is precisely
what we find Origen doing here. As he asserts,[30]

(1.1) ὥσπερ ἐν τῷ πάλαι λαῷ πολλοὶ προφητείαν ἐπηγγέλλοντο, ἀλλὰ τούτων τινὲς
μὲν ἦσαν ψευδοπροφῆται, τινὲς δὲ ἀληθῶς προφῆται, καὶ ἦν χάρισμα τῷ λαῷ διάκρισις
πνευμάτων, ἀφ' οὗ ἐκρίνετο ὅ τε ἀληθὴς προφήτης καὶ ὁ ψευδώνυμος· οὕτω καὶ νῦν ἐν
τῇ καινῇ διαθήκῃ τὰ εὐαγγέλια πολλοὶ ἠθέλησαν γράψαι, ἀλλ' οἱ δόκιμοι τραπεζῖται οὐ
πάντα ἐνέκριναν, ἀλλά τινα αὐτῶν ἐξελέξαντο. τάχα δὲ καὶ τὸ ἐπεχείρησαν λεληθυῖαν
ἔχει κατηγορίαν τῶν χωρὶς χαρίσματος ἐλθόντων ἐπὶ τὴν ἀναγραφὴν τῶν εὐαγγελίων.
Ματθαῖος γὰρ οὐκ ἐπεχείρησεν, ἀλλ' ἔγραψεν ἀπὸ ἁγίου πνεύματος, ὁμοίως καὶ
Μᾶρκος καὶ Ἰωάννης, παραπλησίως δὲ καὶ Λουκᾶς. (1.2) τὸ μέντοι ἐπιγεγραμμένον
κατὰ Αἰγυπτίους εὐαγγέλιον καὶ τὸ ἐπιγεγραμμένον τῶν Δώδεκα εὐαγγέλιον οἱ
συγγράψαντες ἐπεχείρησαν· ἤδη δὲ ἐτόλμησε καὶ Βασιλείδης γράψαι κατὰ Βασιλείδην
εὐαγγέλιον. πολλοὶ μὲν οὖν ἐπεχείρησαν· φέρεται γὰρ καὶ τὸ κατὰ Θωμᾶν εὐαγγέλιον
καὶ τὸ κατὰ Ματθίαν καὶ ἄλλα πλείονα. ταῦτά ἐστι τῶν ἐπιχειρησάντων· τὰ δὲ τέσσαρα
μόνα προκρίνει ἡ τοῦ θεοῦ ἐκκλησία.

(1.1) Just as many among the ancient people proclaimed prophecy, but some of these were
false prophets while others were truly prophets, the gift of the discernment of spirits was
given to the people, by which the true prophet and the falsely named one were discerned.
In the same way now, in the New Testament, many wished to write the Gospels, but the
"expert moneychangers" did not approve all [of the Gospels] but selected certain ones
of them. Perhaps "they attempted" has a subtle accusation of those who came to write
Gospels without the gift. For Matthew did not *attempt* but *wrote* by the Holy Spirit, just
as Mark and John, and similarly also Luke. (1.2) However, the ones composing the Gospel

---

Alexander, *The Preface to Luke's Gospel: Literary Convention and Social Context in Luke 1.1–4
and Acts 1.1* (Cambridge: Cambridge University Press, 1993); David P. Moessner, "The Appeal
and Power of Poetics (Luke 1:1–4): Luke's Superior Credentials (παρηκολουθηκότι), Narrative
Sequence (καθεξῆς), and Firmness of Understanding (ἀσφάλειαν) for the Reader," in *Jesus and
the Heritage of Israel*, ed. David P. Moessner (Harrisburg: Trinity Press International, 1999),
84–123; David P. Moessner, "Luke as Tradent and Hermeneut: 'As One Who Has a Thoroughly
Informed Familiarity With All the Events From the Top' (παρηκολουθηκότι ἄνωθεν πᾶσιν
ἀκριβῶς, Luke 1:3)," *Novum Testamentum* 58 (2016): 259–300; Janet E. Spittler, "The Acts of
Timothy, Luke's Prologue, and Gospel Prologues: Accounts of the Composition of Early Christian
Narratives," in *Narrative Hermeneutics, History, and Rhetoric*, ed. Margaret M. Mitchell,
Tobias Nicklas, and Janet Spittler (Leiden: Brill, 2023).

[30] Origen, *Hom. Luc.* 1.1–2. I translate from the GCS edition of Max Rauer, ed., *Origenes
Werke: Band 9. Die Homilien zu Lukas in der Übersetzung des Hieronymus und die griechischen
Reste der Homilien und des Lukas-Kommentars* (Berlin: De Gruyter, 1959 [repr. 2015]), 3–5. The
homily is also transmitted in Jerome's fourth-century Latin translation, produced in 393/94 CE.
This Latin text is edited in Henri Crouzel, François Fournier, and Pierre Périchon, eds., *Origène:
Homélies sur S. Luc* (Paris: Cerf, 1962), 98, 100, 102 and translated into English in Joseph T. Lienhard, *Origen: Homilies on Luke* (Washington: Catholic University of America Press, 1996),
5–6. Jerome's translation differs from the extant Greek texts. This results in part from the ex-
cerpting of Greek catenists, but Jerome has also rewritten and expanded Origen's material. The
passage from Origen is also rewritten in Ambrose, *Comm. Luc.* 1.2 (CSEL 32.11) and Jerome,
Comm. Matt. pr. 1. Ambrose's uncredited re-use of Origen's work prompts Jerome's translation
of Origen's homilies. Jerome's *Comm. Matt.* expands the list of Gospels and reworks Origen's
homily without attribution.

Imagining Gospel Authorship 213

titled *according to the Egyptians* and the Gospel titled *of the Twelve* attempted. Basilides, moreover, also dared to write a *Gospel according to Basilides*. Many indeed *attempted*, for also the *Gospel according to Thomas* and the one *according to Matthias* and many others are transmitted. These are [the Gospels] of those who attempted, but the church of God prefers the four [*sc.* Gospels] alone.

Like *Ap. Jas.*, Origen differentiates Gospel texts by their modes of authorship. He uses the Lukan phrase "many people have attempted" (πολλοὶ ἐπεχείρησαν) to distinguish his preferred Gospel corpus from other books that circulate with the title "Gospel" (εὐαγγέλιον).[31] These other texts are attributed to various figures, some apostolic, others not. Origen does not merely argue that these problematic texts are not accepted as ecclesial scriptures; rather, the crucial move is to assert that these other texts are not really Gospels at all. Their unqualified attempt at Gospel authorship has failed, as those with discernment readily recognize.[32] As Origen asserts, "perhaps [Luke's phrase] 'they attempted' has a subtle accusation of those who came to write Gospels without the gift. For Matthew did not *attempt* but *wrote* from the Holy Spirit, just as Mark and John, and similarly also Luke."[33] The divine "gift" (χάρισμα) is the *sine qua non* of effectual Gospel writing.

---

[31] This is one of numerous passages in which Origen engages the multiplicity of Gospel books; cf. Oscar Cullmann, "Die Pluralität der Evangelien als theologisches Problem im Altertum," *Theologische Zeitschrift* 1 (1945): 23–42, esp. 33–34.

[32] The saying about "expert moneychangers" is first attested in Clement, *Strom.* 1.28.177.2: εἰκότως ἄρα καὶ ἡ γραφὴ τοιούτους τινὰς ἡμᾶς διαλεκτικοὺς οὕτως ἐθέλουσα γενέσθαι παραινεῖ· γίνεσθε δὲ δόκιμοι τραπεζῖται, τὰ μὲν ἀποδοκιμάζοντες, τὸ δὲ καλὸν κατέχοντες (ed. Stählin GCS). Clement refers or alludes to this saying several times, including in his opening chapter, where it appears as a *leitmotiv* for the *Stromateis* as a whole. There is an irony in Origen's use of a non-canonical saying of Jesus to privilege the four Gospels that become canonical; Jerome unsurprisingly omits the reference to the moneychangers. On the reception of this saying, see Giovanni Bazzana, "'Be Good Moneychangers': The Role of an Agraphon in a Discursive Fight for the Canon of Scripture," in *Invention, Rewriting, Usurpation: Discursive Fights over Religious Traditions in Antiquity*, ed. Jörg Ulrich, Anders-Christian Jacobsen, and David Brakke (Frankfurt: Peter Lang, 2012), 297–311; Watson, *Gospel Writing*, 512–14. Bazzana examines several second- and third-century uses of the saying that differentiate "scriptural" or "canonical" texts, while Watson focuses on Origen. Although Origen maintains that these failed Gospels are rejected by the "experienced money-changers," this is not an assertion about episcopal or conciliar fiat. For Origen, this judgment derives from educated discernment rather than institutional authority. Contrasting these models of authority in debates about early Christian books, see, e. g., David Brakke, "Scriptural Practices in Early Christianity: Towards a New History of the New Testament Canon," in *Invention, Rewriting, Usurpation*, 263–80. On Origen's positioning of himself as a disciplinary expert, see Coogan, "Failed Gospels and Disciplinary Knowledge."

[33] Jerome rewrites this into punchier invective: "The words 'have tried' imply an accusation against those who rushed into writing Gospels without the grace of the Holy Spirit. Matthew, Mark, John, and Luke did not 'try' to write; they wrote their Gospels when they were filled with the Holy Spirit" (trans. Lienhard, *Origen*, 5). *Hoc quod ait: conati sunt, latentem habet accusationem eorum, qui absque gratia Spiritus sancti ad scribenda evangelia prosiluerunt. Mat-*

214   Jeremiah Coogan

According to Origen, the qualifications of the writers determine the success
or failure of their projects as "Gospel." The basis for this verdict is whether the
authors were qualified to write. The indispensable qualification is a kind of collaboration with the Holy Spirit.[34] According to Origen, the evangelists depend on
direct encounter with the divine Spirit and not merely on memory or historical
investigation. Yet he can also speak of the evangelists' individual intentions (*Hom.
Luc.* 1.3) and of the role of apostolic memory and tradition in Gospel writing
(*Hom. Luc.* 1.4, 6; cf. Luke 1:2–3). Origen's model thus synthesizes the individual-
revelatory and collaborative-traditioned models that we observed in the *Apocryphon of James*.

Origen's model of authorship performs different work than what we observed
in the *Apocryphon of James*. Yet the expanding landscape of Gospel books and the
increasingly authoritative status of these texts continues to exert pressure on what
it means to author a Gospel. For Origen, the title "Gospel" is no guarantee that a
Gospel has actually been written. The decisive factor is a qualified author, guided
by the Holy Spirit.[35] For this reason, the title "Gospel" must be policed and protected. "Real" Gospel authorship resembles the kind of revelatory encounter that
Apocryphon of James claims for itself. At least in this homily, Origen's definition
of Gospel literature – of what a Gospel really is – does not just exclude alternate
books as "bad" Gospels. Rather, these problematic texts are not Gospels at all.

4. Epiphanius of Salamis (*Panarion* 51)

In the late fourth century, the bishop and antiquarian Epiphanius of Salamis (*ca.*
320–403 CE) articulates a detailed theory of Gospel authorship.[36] Epiphanius' ex-

---

thaeus quippe et Marcus et Ioannes et Lucas non sunt conati scribere, sed Spiritu sancto pleni scri-
pserunt evangelia (ed. Crouzel et al., *Origène*, 100).

[34] While collaboration in *Ap. Jas.* is a way of grappling with Gospel multiplicity, Origen's model
centers on separating authentic and inauthentic Gospel writing. Although Origen privileges four
particular texts, this passage devotes less attention – less than either in the *Apocryphon*'s collaborative model or in Epiphanius' model that we will next discuss – to how different moments of
authentic Gospel writing work together within an emergent pluriform corpus.

[35] Discussing several first- and second-century Johannine texts, Karen King advances an
argument about failures of authorship that parallels the dynamics we see in Origen's homily:
"Such discourse helps clarify why charges of forgery ('false attribution') were so common in
these disputes, since author-function cannot be ascribed to heretics – that is, by definition they
cannot be reliable sources and traditors of truth. Only truth has 'authors'; falsehood can only
have forgers, fakes, counterfeits, frauds, false or flawed imitations. The same logic applied to
lines of transmission – the character of traditors will reflect that of the source" (Karen L. King,
"'What Is an Author?' Ancient Author-Function in *The Apocryphon of John* and *The Apocalypse
of John*," in *Scribal Practices and Social Structures among Jesus' Adherents: Essays in Honour of
John S. Kloppenborg*, ed. William E. Arnal et al. [Leuven: Peeters, 2016], 15–42, 36).

[36] As Andrew Jacobs has argued, Epiphanius uses heresiology to scaffold a capacious
antiquarian project of organizing knowledge: "Epiphanius of Salamis and the Antiquarian's

Imagining Gospel Authorship 215

pansive heresiological catalogue, the *Panarion*, enumerates eighty permutations of heresy. Among them is a heresy (αἵρεσις) that allegedly rejects the Gospel according to John and the λόγος which (or whom) it proclaims (*Pan.* 51).[37] On this basis, Epiphanius assigns them the name Ἄλογοι: those without reason, those without the (Johannine) λόγος.[38] The allusion to John's incipit is clear (ἐν ἀρχῇ ἦν ὁ λόγος [...], John 1:1), but Epiphanius uses λόγος in a multivalent way. The word refers to Jesus as λόγος, to John's Gospel as a written λόγος, and to λόγος as rational thought. By rejecting John, the Ἄλογοι also reject both human reason and the divine Word.

Within this lengthy chapter, however, Epiphanius devotes little energy to the Ἄλογοι or their ideas about John's Gospel.[39] He does not name even a single

---

Bible," *Journal of Early Christian Studies* 21 (2013): 437–64; idem, *Epiphanius of Cyprus: A Cultural Biography of Late Antiquity* (Berkeley: University of California Press, 2016); idem, "Epiphanius's Library," in *From Roman to Early Christian Cyprus: Studies in Religion and Archaeology*, ed. Laura Nasrallah, AnneMarie Luijendijk, and Charalambos Bakirtzis (Tübingen: Mohr Siebeck, 2020), 133–52. Both within and beyond the *Panarion*, Epiphanius engages in what I have termed "bibliographic thinking," categorizing books as a way of categorizing readers and ideas (Coogan, "The Ways that Parted," esp. 474–75; cf. Andrew Jacobs, "Matters (Un-)Becoming: Conversions in Epiphanius of Salamis," *Church History* 81 [2012]: 42–46).

[37] The chapter of the *Panarion* is titled "Against the heresy which does not accept the Gospel according to John and his Apocalypse" (κατὰ τῆς αἱρέσεως τῆς μὴ δεχομένης τὸ κατὰ Ἰωάννην εὐαγγέλιον καὶ τὴν αὐτοῦ Ἀποκάλυψιν). I translate from the GCS edition of Karl Holl, Christian-Friedrich Collatz, Arnd Rattmann, and Christoph Markschies, eds., *Epiphanius* (Leipzig; Berlin: J. C. Hinrichs; De Gruyter, 1915–2006), 2.249–311.

[38] The central characteristic of this group, for Epiphanius, is their rejection of the Gospel according to John and the Apocalypse of John. As Epiphanius writes, "the Ἄλογοι – for I apply this designation to them, for from now on thus they will be called and thus, beloved, let us apply to them the name, that is Ἄλογοι" (οἱ Ἄλογοι – ταύτην γὰρ αὐτοῖς ἐπιτίθημι τὴν ἐπωνυμίαν· ἀπὸ γὰρ τῆς δεῦρο οὕτως κληθήσονται καὶ οὕτως, ἀγαπητοί, ἐπιθῶμεν αὐτοῖς ὄνομα, τουτέστιν Ἀλόγων, *Pan.* 51.3.1 [ed. Holl et al., *Epiphanius*, 2.250]). The text of *Pan.* 51.3.2 is corrupt, but then continues "they reject the books of John. Therefore, since they do not accept the λόγος which is preached by John, they will be called Ἄλογοι" (ἀποβάλλουσαν Ἰωάννου τὰς βίβλους. ἐπεὶ οὖν τὸν λόγον οὐ δέχονται τὸν παρὰ Ἰωάννου κεκηρυγμένον, Ἄλογοι κληθήσονται, ed. Holl et al., *Epiphanius*, 2.250). On this passage, see Jacobs, *Epiphanius of Cyprus*, 152–54.

[39] Epiphanius' characterization of these Ἄλογοι may depend on earlier authors rather than reflecting fourth-century thinkers or groups. Irenaeus of Lyons briefly describes those who "do not receive that form [i. e., of the Gospel] which is the Gospel according to John" (*illam speciem non admittunt <eius> quod est secundum Iohannem Euangelium, Haer.* 3.11.9 [SC 211: 172]). Eusebius' juxtaposes Gaius' critique of Cerinthus' eschatology (*Hist. eccl.* 3.28.2) with Dionysius of Alexandria's third-century report of those who reject the Apocalypse of John (Eusebius, *Hist. eccl.* 3.28.4–5; cf. 7.25.1–3), but the excerpts from Dionysius do not name Gaius. Writings by Gaius are mentioned by Eusebius in *Hist. eccl.* 2.25.6–7; 3.28.2; 6.20.3. While Irenaeus describes only figures who reject John's Gospel, Dionysius describes only criticisms of the Apocalypse of John. According to the later Syriac authors Bar Salibi and ʿAbdishoʿ, Hippolytus of Rome offered more detail, attributing the rejection of both the Gospel and Apocalypse to a Roman presbyter named Gaius. Based on similarities between the Syriac sources and Epiphanius, Francis Watson argues that Epiphanius depends, at least in part, on Hippolytus (*Gospel Writing*, 477–93); at the very least, Epiphanius is not the only one to describe a group that rejects both the Gospel and Apocalypse of John. Scholars continue to disagree about various aspects of the second- and

216   Jeremiah Coogan

figure associated with the Ἄλογοι. Rather, the group's alleged rejection of John affords Epiphanius occasion for an extended account of Gospel writing and of the relationships between the four New Testament Gospels.[40] The Ἄλογοι are said to object to contradictions between John and the Synoptic Gospels (Pan. 51.4.5). Epiphanius instead harmonizes the conflicting details of his four Gospels, focusing on differences between John and the Synoptics. Even more vitally, Epiphanius provides a theory of Gospel authorship that explains the reason for these differences.

Epiphanius' account depends on two central ideas. First, the human evangelists are constrained by a divine plan. As Epiphanius writes, "For the will (θέλημα) was not theirs; both their sequence (ἀκολουθία) and their teaching (διδασκαλία) were from the Holy Spirit" (Pan. 51.4.11).[41] Both the form and the content are divine, not human. We might compare Epiphanius' emphasis on the Holy Spirit with Origen's, as well as with Ap. Jas.'s privileging of direct revelatory experience of Jesus. Yet while assertions of divine involvement in the writing of scriptural texts are widespread in early Christian literature, Epiphanius is remarkably hesitant to acknowledge human authorial agency. The evangelists do not enjoy authorial prerogatives. We see this in Epiphanius' discussion of the divergent infancy narratives in Matthew and Luke. Why does Matthew omit material that Luke provides, and vice versa (Pan. 51.5.9)? Because God gave the evangelists different assignments. The reason for difference is not the historian's prerogative to select material, nor is it the evangelists' own agency in addressing their varied audiences. Difference results from a divine masterplan for a multi-part Gospel anthology.

Second, the individual Gospels are insufficient on their own. The evangelists are not even authors of distinct works. The exceptional constraint that Epiphanius places upon human Gospel writers thus becomes explicable. Each evangelist

---

third-century debates over Johannine literature (e. g., Allen Brent, *Hippolytus and the Roman Church in the Third Century: Communities in Tension Before the Emergence of a Monarch-Bishop* [Leiden: Brill, 1995], 144–84; Charles E. Hill, *The Johannine Corpus in the Early Church* [Oxford: Oxford University Press, 2004], 172–204; Watson, *Gospel Writing*, 477–93), but these scholarly disagreements do not directly illuminate Epiphanius' theory of Gospel authorship. Epiphanius' discussion of the Apocalypse seems to respond more directly to the arguments and objections of those whom he calls Ἄλογοι than does his discussion of John's Gospel.

[40] This passage is not Epiphanius' only discussion of the relationships between Matthew, Mark, Luke, and John. Other examples include *Anc.* 13.1.5; 50.6; *Hom. in fest. palm.* (PG 43:432.8); *Mens.* 35 (64d–65a); and *Pan.* 64.8.5–9.1, as well as the dubiously Epiphanian *App. ad ind. apost. discip.* (Theodor Schermann, ed., *Prophetarum vitae fabulosae* [Leipzig: Teubner, 1907], 128–31). For Epiphanius' discussion of varied Gospel texts – including those used by Nazoreans, Ebionites, Marcionites, and Manichaeans – see *Anac.* 46; *Pan.* 28.5.1–3; 29.9.1; 30.3.7; 30.6.7–9; 30.11.5; 30.13.1–3; 30.13.6–8; 30.14.2–3, 5; 30.16.4–5; 30.22.4; 42 (*passim*); 46.1.1–5; 66.2.9; 66.35.6; 66.40.1; 66.78.1.

[41] οὐ γὰρ ἦν αὐτῶν τὸ θέλημα, ἀλλὰ ἐκ πνεύματος ἁγίου ἡ ἀκολουθία καὶ ἡ διδασκαλία (ed. Holl et al., *Epiphanius*, 2.252).

Imagining Gospel Authorship 217

writes to fill out a set. The τέλος of any individual canonical Gospel is to become part of this fourfold whole. Epiphanius works out the implications of this assumption in painstaking detail, arguing that the real meaning and context of the events becomes clear only through details provided in other Gospels (*Pan.* 51.17.3). The Gospels not only fit together but cannot stand apart. To read any individual Gospel requires reading the others. The four together constitute a single authorial project (*Pan.* 51.6.5). Moreover, Epiphanius claims, reading the four in any other way invites heresy. If one reads them as a single whole, however, "no sort of distortion or contradiction is found in the holy Gospels or among the evangelists, but everything is clear" (*Pan.* 51.15.14).[42]

Summarizing his theory of Gospel writing, Epiphanius writes, "other matters were not relevant to the other evangelists, because each [Gospel] is complemented (βοηθεῖσθαι) by each. For when the truth is assembled from all of [the Gospels], it is demonstrated to be something that is one and not in conflict with itself" (*Pan.* 51.17.3).[43] Under these conditions, the idea of Gospel authorship transforms almost beyond recognition. The fourfold Gospel emerges as a distinctive collective project.[44] This modifies the authorial agency imagined as generating any individual text. The decisions and speech-acts that attach to authorship dissolve into a new composite;[45] each subsequent evangelist writes

---

[42] ὥστε ἐξ ἅπαντος δείκνυσθαι ὅτι οὐδεμία σκολιότης οὐδ᾽ ἐναντιότης ἐν τοῖς ἁγίοις εὐαγγελίοις οὐδὲ παρὰ τοῖς εὐαγγελισταῖς εὑρίσκεται, ἀλλὰ πάντα σαφῆ (ed. Holl et al., *Epiphanius*, 2.270). In this context, one might read the prepositional phrase ἐξ ἅπαντος as indicating reading "from everything" in the Gospels. Epiphanius' reading of the four Gospels as narratively codependent is closely cognate to what we find, slightly later, in Augustine's *De consensu evangelistarum*. For a deft reading of Augustine's approach (focused on resurrection accounts), see Watson, *Gospel Writing*, ch. 1. Although Watson elsewhere discusses the circle around Gaius and their skepticism of John (*Gospel Writing*, 485–89), he does not devote attention to Epiphanius' project of reading the four Gospels together.

[43] καὶ πάλιν τοῖς ἄλλοις εὐαγγελισταῖς περὶ τῶν ἄλλων οὐ πεφρόντισται, διὰ τὸ ἕκαστον ἀφ᾽ ἑκάστου βοηθεῖσθαι. καὶ γὰρ παρὰ πάντων συλλεγομένη ἡ ἀλήθεια δείκνυται μία τις οὖσα καὶ πρὸς ἑαυτὴν μὴ στασιάζουσα (ed. Holl et al., *Epiphanius*, 2.273). In the immediate context, Epiphanius is explaining why John does not mention Jesus' forty days in the wilderness (ἤδη γὰρ ἦν τοῦτο διὰ τῶν τριῶν εὐαγγελιστῶν σημανθέν, *Pan.* 51.17.2), but he develops this argument in light of a broader hermeneutical strategy. As indicated by the construction in the neuter, the hermeneutical principle διὰ τὸ ἕκαστον ἀφ᾽ ἑκάστου βοηθεῖσθαι is about Gospels (εὐαγγέλια, neuter), not evangelists (εὐαγγελισταί, masculine).

[44] Epiphanius' approach resembles what Francis Watson describes as the "conventional" picture in modern Gospel scholarship, although Watson does not have Epiphanius in view: "While the four texts retain their individual integrity, each is what it is only in its relation to the other three. This fourfold gospel is also a singular entity in which each text is constrained by its relation to the other three" (Watson, "Against the Twelve," 209).

[45] For Epiphanius, evangelists do not have their own speech-acts. As divine secretaries or ghostwriters, they are extensions of the divine speaker without independent agency. Compare the ideologies of "masterly extensibility" (Brendon Reay, "Agriculture, Writing, and Cato's Aristocratic Self-Fashioning," *Classical Antiquity* 24 [2005]: 331–61) that shape notions of both enslavement and authorship in the Roman Mediterranean (Coogan et al., *Writing, Enslavement, and Power*).

218 *Jeremiah Coogan*

a subsection of the singular Gospel as a divinely commissioned ghostwriter.[46] As part of Epiphanius' construction of a fourfold Gospel corpus, monographic authorial agency is displaced from human evangelists to the divine author. What emerges in Epiphanius' model is a quasi-pseudepigraphic construct of collective textual production. There is only one Gospel – and the evangelists are not its authors.

5. Conclusion

Early Christian re-imaginations of Gospel authorship did not come to an end when κατά-titles were affixed in the second century. As I have argued in this essay, readers from the second to fourth centuries continued to reimagine Gospel authorship in light of an expanding constellation of Gospel books.

The *Apocryphon of James*, from the late second century, juxtaposes two different models of Gospel writing. Some texts are imagined as part of a collective and traditioned literature, the result of apostolic memory, textualized through human collaboration. But the *Apocryphon* offers a second model as well: an individual revelatory experience and a singular authorial voice. For the *Apocryphon*, these two modes of composition exist in parallel, and in some degree of competition.

Yet third- and fourth-century figures attempt to synthesize the competing dynamics exemplified in the *Apocryphon*'s two divergent models of Gospel authorship. They propose creative models of Gospel writing that seek to reconcile monographic authorship with textual plurality, human labor with divine agency.

Origen offers a model of Gospel writing in which human evangelists collaborate with the Holy Spirit; this divine "gift" is essential for effectual Gospel writing. Yet Origen's model of Gospel authorship involves a crucial human element as well. He emphasizes the evangelists' individual intentions, as well as the importance of apostolic memory and tradition. Origen thus combines the *Apocryphon*'s two models: Memory, collaboration, revelation, and individual authorship all work together.

In contrast to Origen, Epiphanius seeks to control the multiplicity and divergence of Gospel books by offering a model with a single divine author. It is not enough to exclude inauthentic Gospels, as Origen had attempted to do; one must also deploy a model of authorship that eliminates the possibility of contradiction.

---

[46] While Epiphanius' model of Gospel authorship is striking, various other early Christian figures experiment with ideas of humans as secretaries or ghostwriters for a divine author. On these dynamics, see Candida R. Moss, "The Secretary: Enslaved Workers, Stenography, and the Production of Early Christian Literature," *Journal of Theological Studies* 74 (2023): 20–56 (on secretaries, focusing on Pauline literature) and Candida R. Moss, *God's Ghostwriters: Enslaved Workers and the Making of Christianity* (New York: Little, Brown, and Company, 2024).

Imagining Gospel Authorship

For Epiphanius, a pluriform Gospel generates a quasi-pseudepigraphic conceit, constraining the "authorial" claims of any particular evangelist. Thus, for Epiphanius, the intention and cognition involved in gospel writing cannot be attributed to the human evangelists at all, but only to the divine spirit, the real monographic author of what turns out to be a singular fourfold Gospel.

In each of these examples, we observe how an ever-expanding constellation of Gospel literature prompted readers to reimagine what Gospels are and what it means to author one.[47] These three texts, spread over roughly two centuries, do not present a grand unified theory of Gospel authorship. Rather, each manifests broader dynamics and debates in a distinct way. Together, they offer a kaleidoscopic view of how a pluriform Gospel corpus exerted pressure on ideas of authorship. Early Christian thinkers resemble those who curated and transformed "Publius" into *The Federalist*, contesting the textual legacies of founding figures and reconfiguring earlier texts into new corpora. In each of our three examples, readers experiment with different models of collaboration, authorship, and authorization. In their differing approaches, we observe shifts in the imagination of Gospel authorship as the construction of a fourfold corpus displaces the possibility of monographic authorial agency and replaces it with a quasi-pseudepigraphic construct of collective textual production. Late ancient negotiations of Gospel authorship remind us that authorial attributions are exceptionally flexible, reflecting different models of agency, collaboration, and labor. These re-imaginations of Gospel authorship invite us to observe similar dynamics in how other textual collections – canonical or otherwise, ancient or modern – shape ideas of authorship as readers put their texts to work in changing contexts.

Bibliography

Alexander, Loveday. *The Preface to Luke's Gospel: Literary Convention and Social Context in Luke 1.1–4 and Acts 1.1*. Society for New Testament Studies Monograph Series 78. Cambridge: Cambridge University Press, 1993.

Allen, Garrick V. "Titles in the New Testament Papyri." *New Testament Studies* 68 (2022): 156–171.

Baum, Armin D. "Papias, der Vorzug der *Viva Vox* und die Evangelienschriften." *New Testament Studies* 44 (1998): 144–151.

Bazzana, Giovanni. "'Be Good Moneychangers': The Role of an Agraphon in a Discursive Fight for the Canon of Scripture." Pages 297–311 in *Invention, Rewriting, Usurpation:*

---

[47] Other texts discuss these questions as well. Eusebius of Caesarea seeks to define what makes an "evangelist" (εὐαγγελισταὶ τοῦ λόγου, *Hist. eccl.* 5.10.2–3). The fifth-century CE *Acts of Timothy* 8–10 reimagines the process by which Matthew, Mark, Luke, and John are crafted into a coherent corpus. Varied late ancient Gospel prefaces likewise offer accounts of Gospel writing and collecting.

220 Jeremiah Coogan

Discursive Fights over Religious Traditions in Antiquity. Edited by Jörg Ulrich, Anders-Christian Jacobsen, and David Brakke. Early Christianity in the Context of Antiquity 11. Frankfurt: Peter Lang, 2012.

Brakke, David. "Parables and Plain Speech in the Fourth Gospel and the *Apocryphon of James.*" *Journal of Early Christian Studies* 7 (1999): 187–218.

Brakke, David. "Scriptural Practices in Early Christianity: Towards a New History of the New Testament Canon." Pages 263–280 in *Invention, Rewriting, Usurpation: Discursive Fights over Religious Traditions in Antiquity.* Edited by Jörg Ulrich, Anders-Christian Jacobsen, and David Brakke. Early Christianity in the Context of Antiquity 11. Frankfurt: Peter Lang, 2012.

Brent, Allen. *Hippolytus and the Roman Church in the Third Century: Communities in Tension Before the Emergence of a Monarch-Bishop.* Supplements to Vigiliae Christianae 31. Leiden: Brill, 1995.

Chartier, Roger. *The Order of Books: Readers, Authors, and Libraries in Europe Between the Fourteenth and Eighteenth Centuries.* Stanford: Stanford University Press, 1994.

Cirafesi, Wally V., and Gregory P. Fewster. "Justin's ἀπομνημονεύματα and Ancient Greco-Roman Memoirs." *Early Christianity* 7 (2016): 186–212.

Collins, Adela Yarbro. *Mark: A Commentary.* Hermeneia. Minneapolis: Fortress, 2007.

Coogan, Jeremiah. "Reading (in) a Quadriform Cosmos: Gospel Books and the Early Christian Bibliographic Imagination." *Journal of Early Christian Studies* 31 (2023): 85–103.

Coogan, Jeremiah. "The Ways that Parted in the Library: The Gospels according to Matthew and according to the Hebrews in Late Ancient Heresiology." *Journal of Ecclesiastical History* 74 (2023): 473–490.

Coogan, Jeremiah. "Failed Gospels and Disciplinary Knowledge in Origen's *Hom. Luc.* 1." Forthcoming in *Unruly Books: Rethinking Ancient and Academic Imaginations of Religious Texts.* Edited by Esther Brownsmith, Marianne B. Kartzow, and Liv Ingeborg Lied. London: Bloomsbury T&T Clark, forthcoming.

Coogan, Jeremiah, Candida R. Moss, and Joseph A. Howley. "The Socioeconomics of Fabrication: Textuality, Authenticity, and Class in the Roman Mediterranean." *Arethusa* (2024).

Coogan, Jeremiah, Candida R. Moss, and Joseph A. Howley, eds. *Writing, Enslavement, and Power in the Roman Mediterranean, 100 BCE–300 CE.* Cultures of Reading in the Ancient Mediterranean. New York: Oxford University Press, 2024.

Coogan, Jeremiah and Jacob A. Rodriguez. "Ordering Gospel Textuality in the Second Century." *Journal of Theological Studies* 74 (2023): 57–102.

Crouzel, Henri, François Fournier, and Pierre Périchon, eds. *Origène: Homélies sur S. Luc.* SC 87. Paris: Cerf, 1962.

Cullmann, Oscar. "Die Pluralität der Evangelien als theologisches Problem im Altertum." *Theologische Zeitschrift* 1 (1945): 23–42.

Falkenberg, René. "Apocryphal Gospel Titles in Coptic." *Religions* 13 (2022), no. 796.

Fitzgerald, William. *Slavery and the Roman Literary Imagination.* Cambridge: Cambridge University Press, 2000.

Fitzgerald, William. "The Slave, Between Absence and Presence." Pages 239–249 in *Unspoken Rome: Absence in Latin Literature and Its Reception.* Edited by Tom Geue and Elena Giusti. Cambridge: Cambridge University Press, 2021.

Imagining Gospel Authorship 221

Foucault, Michel. "What is an Author?" Pages 141–160 in *Textual Strategies: Perspectives in Post-Structuralist Criticism*. Edited by Josué V. Harari. Ithaca: Cornell University Press, 1979 [1969].

Gamble, Harry Y. *Books and Readers in the Early Church: A History of Early Christian Texts*. New Haven: Yale University Press, 1995.

Gathercole, Simon J. "The Alleged Anonymity of the Canonical Gospels." *Journal of Theological Studies* 69 (2018): 447–476.

Gathercole, Simon J. "The Earliest Manuscript Title of Matthew's Gospel (BnF Suppl. Gr. 1120 II 3 / 4)." *Novum Testamentum* 54 (2012): 209–235.

Gathercole, Simon J. "The Titles of the Gospels in the Earliest New Testament Manuscripts." *Zeitschrift für die neutestamentliche Wissenschaft* 104 (2013): 33–76.

Gennette, Gerard. *Paratexts: Thresholds of Interpretation*. Cambridge: Cambridge University Press, 1997.

Geue, Tom. *Author Unknown: The Power of Anonymity in Ancient Rome*. Cambridge, MA: Harvard University Press, 2019.

Given, J. Gregory. "Four Texts From Nag Hammadi amid the Textual and Generic Fluidity of the 'Letter' in the Literature of Late Antique Egypt." Pages 201–220 in *Snapshots of Evolving Traditions: Jewish and Christian Manuscript Culture, Textual Fluidity, and New Philology*. Edited by Hugo Lundhaug and Liv Ingeborg Lied. Texte und Untersuchungen zur Geschichte der altchristlichen Literatur 175. Berlin: De Gruyter, 2017.

Grant, Robert M. "Literary Criticism and the New Testament Canon." *Journal for the Study of the New Testament* 5 (1982): 24–44.

Griffin, Robert J. "Anonymity and Authorship." *New Literary History* 30 (1999): 877–895.

Heine, Ronald. *Origen: Scholarship in the Service of the Church*. Oxford: Oxford University Press, 2010.

Hengel, Martin. "The Titles of the Gospels and the Gospel of Mark." Pages 64–84 in *Studies in the Gospel of Mark*. London: SCM, 1985.

Hill, Charles E. *The Johannine Corpus in the Early Church*. Oxford: Oxford University Press, 2004.

Holl, Karl, Christian-Friedrich Collatz, Arnd Rattmann, and Christoph Markschies, eds. *Epiphanius*. GCS. Leipzig; Berlin: J.C. Hinrichs; De Gruyter, 1915–2006.

Howley, Joseph A. *Aulus Gellius and Roman Reading Culture: Text, Presence, and Imperial Knowledge in the* Noctes Atticae. Cambridge: Cambridge University Press, 2018.

Jacobs, Andrew. *Epiphanius of Cyprus: A Cultural Biography of Late Antiquity*. Christianity in Late Antiquity 2. Berkeley: University of California Press, 2016.

Jacobs, Andrew. "Epiphanius's Library." Pages 133–152 in *From Roman to Early Christian Cyprus: Studies in Religion and Archaeology*. Edited by Laura Nasrallah, AnneMarie Luijendijk, and Charalambos Bakirtzis. Wissenschaftliche Untersuchungen zum Neuen Testament 437. Tübingen: Mohr Siebeck, 2020.

Jacobs, Andrew. "Epiphanius of Salamis and the Antiquarian's Bible." *Journal of Early Christian Studies* 21 (2013): 437–464.

Jacobs, Andrew. "Matters (Un-)Becoming: Conversions in Epiphanius of Salamis." *Church History* 81 (2012): 27–47.

Jansen, Laura, ed. *The Roman Paratext: Frame, Texts, Readers*. Cambridge: Cambridge University Press, 2014.

Jenott, Lance, and Elaine H. Pagels. "Antony's Letters and Nag Hammadi Codex I: Sources of Religious Conflict in Fourth-Century Egypt." *Journal of Early Christian Studies* 18 (2010): 557–589.

222 Jeremiah Coogan

Johnson, Samuel B. "'A Sign for This Generation': The Life of Jesus in Origen's Gospel Commentaries." PhD diss., University of Notre Dame, 2021.

Johnson, William A. *Readers and Reading Culture in the High Roman Empire: A Study of Elite Communities.* Oxford: Oxford University Press, 2010.

Lienhard, Joseph T. *Origen: Homilies on Luke.* FC 94. Washington: Catholic University of America Press, 1996.

Keith, Chris. *The Gospel as Manuscript: An Early History of the Jesus Tradition as Material Artifact.* Oxford: Oxford University Press, 2020.

King, Karen L. "'What Is an Author?': Ancient Author-Function in the Apocryphon of John and the Apocalypse of John." Pages 15–42 in *Scribal Practices and Social Structures among Jesus Adherents: Essays in Honour of John S. Kloppenborg.* Edited by William E. Arnal et al. Bibliotheca ephemeridum theologicarum lovaniensium 285. Leuven: Peeters, 2016.

Kloppenborg, John S. "Literate Media in Early Christian Groups: The Creation of a Christian Book Culture." *Journal of Early Christian Studies* 22 (2014): 21–59.

Larsen, Matthew D. C. "Correcting the Gospel: Putting the Titles of the Gospels in Historical Context. Pages 78–103" in *Rethinking 'Authority' in Late Antiquity: Authorship, Law, and Transmission in Jewish and Christian Tradition.* Edited by A. J. Berkovitz and Mark D. Letteney. New York: Routledge, 2018.

Larsen, Matthew D. C. *Gospels Before the Book.* New York: Oxford University Press, 2018.

Larsen, Matthew D. C. "The Publication of the Synoptics and the Problem of Dating." Pages 175–203 in *The Oxford Handbook of the Synoptic Gospels.* Edited by Stephen P. Ahearne-Kroll. Oxford: Oxford University Press, 2023.

Lindenlaub, Julia D. "The Gospel of John as Model for Literate Authors and their Texts in Epistula Apostolorum and Apocryphon of James (NHC I,2)." *Journal for the Study of the New Testament* 43 (2020): 3–27.

Malinine, Michel, ed. *Epistula Iacobi apocrypha: Codex Jung F. Ir-F. VIIIv (p. 1–16).* Zürich: Rascher, 1968.

Merell, Jean. "Nouveaux fragments du papyrus 4." *Revue biblique* 47 (1938): 5–22.

Moessner, David P. "The Appeal and Power of Poetics (Luke 1:1–4): Luke's Superior Credentials (παρηκολουθηκότι), Narrative Sequence (καθεξῆς), and Firmness of Understanding (ἀσφάλειαν) for the Reader." Pages 84–123 in *Jesus and the Heritage of Israel.* Edited by David P. Moessner. Harrisburg: Trinity Press International, 1999.

Moessner, David P. "Luke as Tradent and Hermeneut: 'As One Who Has a Thoroughly Informed Familiarity With All the Events From the Top' (παρηκολουθηκότι ἄνωθεν πᾶσιν ἀκριβῶς, Luke 1:3)." *Novum Testamentum* 58 (2016): 259–300.

Moss, Candida R. "Between the Lines: Looking for the Contributions of Enslaved Literate Laborers in a Second-Century Text (P. Berol. 11632)." *Studies in Late Antiquity* 5 (2021): 432–452.

Moss, Candida R. *God's Ghostwriters: Enslaved Workers and the Making of Christianity.* New York: Little, Brown, and Company, 2024.

Moss, Candida R. "The Secretary: Enslaved Workers, Stenography, and the Production of Early Christian Literature." *Journal of Theological Studies* 74 (2023): 20–56.

Mroczek, Eva. *The Literary Imagination in Jewish Antiquity.* Oxford: Oxford University Press, 2016.

Nautin, Pierre. *Origène: Sa vie et son oeuvre.* Paris: Beauchesne, 1977.

Peirano, Irene. *The Rhetoric of the Roman Fake: Latin Pseudepigrapha in Context.* Cambridge: Cambridge University Press, 2012.

Perkins, Pheme. "Johannine Traditions in *Ap. Jas.* (NHC 1,2)." *Journal of Biblical Literature* 101 (1982): 403–414.

Petersen, Silke. "Die Evangelienüberschriften und die Entstehung des neutestamentlichen Kanons." *Zeitschrift für die neutestamentliche Wissenschaft* 97 (2006): 250–274.

Preuschen, Erwin. *Antilegomena: Die Reste der ausserkanonischen Evangelien und urchristlichen Ueberlieferungen.* Berlin: De Gruyter, 1901.

Rauer, Max, ed. *Origenes Werke: Band 9, Die Homilien zu Lukas in der Übersetzung des Hieronymus und die griechischen Reste der Homilien und des Lukas-Kommentars.* GCS. Berlin: De Gruyter, 1959 [repr. 2015].

Reay, Brendon. "Agriculture, Writing, and Cato's Aristocratic Self-Fashioning." *Classical Antiquity* 24 (2005): 331–361.

Reed, Annette Yoshiko. "Εὐαγγέλιον: Orality, Textuality, and the Christian Truth in Irenaeus' *Adversus Haereses.*" *Vigiliae christianae* 56 (2002): 11–46.

Robinson, James M., ed. *The Nag Hammadi Library in English*, rev. ed. Leiden: Brill, 1996.

Rodriguez, Jacob A. "Justin and the Apostolic Memoirs." *Early Christianity* 11 (2020): 496–515.

Rouleau, Donald, and Louise Roy, eds. *L'épître apocryphe de Jacques (NH 1,2).* Bibliothèque copte de Nag Hammadi. Section "Textes" 18. Québec: Presses de l'Úniversité Laval, 1987.

Savoie, Alice. "The Women Behind Times New Roman: The Contribution of Type Drawing Offices to Twentieth Century Type-Making." *Journal of Design History* 33 (2020): 209–224.

Schermann, Theodor, ed. *Prophetarum vitae fabulosae.* Leipzig: Teubner, 1907.

Spittler, Janet E. "The Acts of Timothy, Luke's Prologue, and Gospel Prologues: Accounts of the Composition of Early Christian Narratives." Forthcoming in *Narrative Hermeneutics, History, and Rhetoric.* Edited by Margaret M. Mitchell, Tobias Nicklas, and Janet Spittler. Leiden: Brill, 2023.

Starling, Drew. "Unmasking Publius: Authorial Attribution and the Making of *The Federalist.*" *Book History* 25 (2022): 63–95.

Ullucci, Daniel. "The Anonymity of the Gospels κατά Pac-Man." *Annali di Storia dell'Esegesi* 36 (2019): 95–116.

Watson, Francis. "Against the Twelve: The Apocryphon of James and the Status of the Apostles." Pages 209–230 in *Texts in Context: Essays on Dating and Contextualising Christian Writings from the Second and Early Third Centuries.* Edited by Joseph Verheyden, Jens Schröter, and Tobias Nicklas. Bibliotheca ephemeridum theologicarum lovaniensium 319. Leuven: Peeters, 2021.

Watson, Francis. *An Apostolic Gospel: The 'Epistula Apostolorum' in Literary Context.* Society for New Testament Studies Monograph Series 179. Cambridge: Cambridge University Press, 2020.

Watson, Francis. *Gospel Writing: A Canonical Perspective.* Grand Rapids: Eerdmans, 2013.

Janus-Faced Authors

Production or Presentation?

Sophus Helle

Authorship, as it is currently studied in literary history, can refer to two things: the production of a text and the depiction of how that production took place. In the first sense, authorship refers to the collection of people and practices that create a given text. Studying authorship in this sense may involve tracing the author's biography, determining the exact identity of an anonymous writer, studying the circumstances of the text's composition or its sources of inspiration and input, the co-authorship or editorial intervention that shaped its final form, and so on. In the second sense, authorship refers to how readers have since imagined this act of textual creation. Authorship, in this sense, is an almost totemic symbol that comes to cleave to a given work over the course of its circulation. As Alexander Beecroft puts it, authorship can be seen as "a property ascribed to a text rather than a fact about its origins,"[1] or as Claire Rachel Jackson argues in this volume, authors "are as much a function of reception as composition." Studying authorship in this sense is an attempt to understand what, say, an authorial attribution, a deliberate anonymity, or an anecdote about the author is doing on its own terms – regardless of their historical accuracy.

The difference between the two approaches is the difference between studying how the *Odyssey* and the *Iliad* were composed, (e. g. by reconstructing the oral background from which they emerged) and studying how the figure of Homer came to be understood by ancient readers and how that understanding shaped the reception of the epics.[2] The two approaches are temporally distinct. The first understands authorship as something that *precedes* the text, as the convergence of context, creativity, and collaboration that results in the making of a work. The second understands authorship as something that *follows* the text: a set of images, narratives, and discursive functions that emerge from and in turn inflect the work's circulation. The author is thus a Janus-faced figure, looking back at the text's creation and forward to its reception.

---

[1] Alexander Beecroft, *Authorship and Cultural Identity in Early Greece and China: Patterns of Literary Circulation* (Cambridge: Cambridge University Press, 2010), 17.

[2] Barbara Graziosi, *Inventing Homer: The Early Reception of Epic*, Cambridge Classical Studies (Cambridge: Cambridge University Press, 2002).

226   *Sophus Helle*

However, the first approach has traditionally dominated the study of literary authorship. Asking about the authorship of the Babylonian epic *Gilgamesh*, for example, mostly means asking where, when, how, and by whom it was written. The narratives about the text's composition that circulated in the ancient world are thus treated as so many layers of potentially misleading evidence to be peeled away before one reaches a core of historical truth. As I return to below, pseudepigraphy and other forms of potentially misleading information about authors are treated almost with vehemence in this approach, as falsities to be discarded so that the truth of authorship may be firmly established.

This resistance to pseudepigraphy is an index of how invested philology has traditionally been in the study of what I will call *authorship-as-production*. This is not surprising, since the critical questioning of how texts were "really" produced has been central to philology at various key junctures of its history. For example, Lorenzo Valla's exposure of the *Donation of Constantine* as a forgery in the fifteenth century and Friedrich August Wolf's critique of Homer's authorship in the nineteenth have taken on an almost mythical status in the field's self-understanding. Both interventions consisted in using the tools of linguistic and historical analysis to establish the reality of the text's authorship in the face of a received narrative about it – that is, exposing an authorial fiction as a fiction. Whether Wolf was correct in his attack on Homer's authorial unity is not important here; what matters is rather that the explosion of philological activity in Germany that his work inaugurated began with a search for the historical truth behind authorial stories that had circulated for millennia.[3] No wonder, then, that the field preserves an investment in the historical truth of authorship and an accompanying unease around authorial fictions.

The present volume is a deliberate attempt to shift our focus towards what I will call *authorship-as-presentation*, in which authorial narratives are seen not as an imperfect set of sources for reconstructing how texts came into being, but as valuable objects of research in their own right. However spurious and inaccurate an authorial attribution might be, its significance to the text's reception is hard to overstate. The representation of a text's author – whether in the form of attributions, anecdotes, debates, visual images, or, as the title of this volume would have it, fictions of all sorts – is often a crucial source of insight about how those texts were understood by their earliest readers.

By turning our attention to this sense of the word "authorship" – the forward face of the Janus-like author – the volume builds on a fascinating history of research. An early example is the Russian Formalist Boris Tomashievsky,

---

[3] See the introduction to Wolf's thought, background, and legacy in Anthony Grafton, Glenn W. Most, and James E. G. Zetzel's "Introduction" to Friedrich August Wolf, *Prolegomena to Homer, 1795*, trans. and ed. Anthony Grafton, Glenn W. Most, and James E. G. Zetzel (Princeton: Princeton University Press, 1985), 3–36.

Janus-Faced Authors

who coined the term "biographical legends" to describe how Romantic poets would consciously shape the public's understanding of their lives and so enfold them in their literary oeuvre.[4] Undoubtedly the most famous study of authorship as an aspect of textual reception and not production is the essay "Qu'est-ce qu'un auteur?" by Michel Foucault, whose ideas recur in many of the contributions gathered in this volume.[5] With this essay, Foucault established the idea that authorship was, among other things, a way of structuring the literary field, linking some texts together (such as the *Odyssey* and the *Iliad*) while excluding others, establishing some texts as imbued with a special value (such as Nietzsche's authored books) while demoting others (such as Nietzsche's laundry bills), and so on. Other key figures in this approach to authorship include Rita Felski, who coined the term "allegories of authorship" in her study of female writers, and Andrew Bennett, who showed that the modern figure of the author is caught in an never-ending oscillation between biographical reality and cultural construction (that is, between what I would call authorship-as-production and authorship-as-presentation).[6] Within the field of ancient literature, I would highlight the approaches of Barbara Graziosi, who turned from the unanswerable question of who really wrote the *Iliad* and the *Odyssey* to the much more rewarding question of how ancient writers engaged with Homer as a cultural icon, and of Alexander Beecroft, who used ancient accounts of authorship to study the circulation of literary works in early Greece and China.[7]

In my own research, I set out to study the authorship of cuneiform literature and soon realized that, if I were to study the authorship-as-production of a text like the Babylonian epic *Gilgamesh* or the Sumerian *Exaltation of Inana*, my project was bound to fail.[8] The sources for how these texts were produced are either non-existent, unreliable, or so beset by methodological quandaries as to make any solid conclusions impossible. What I could study, however, was how the ancient scribes and scholars thought that such texts had been produced. As is generally the case in the ancient world, the sources for studying authorship-as-presentation in the cuneiform world are much more abundant than those

---

[4] Boris Tomashevsky, "Literature and Biography," in *Biography in Theory*, ed. Wilhelm Hemecker and Edward Saunders (Berlin: De Gruyter, 2017), 83–90.

[5] Michel Foucault, "What Is an Author?," in *Language, Counter-Memory, Practice: Selected Essays and Interviews*, trans. Donald Bouchard and Simon Sherry (Ithaca: Cornell University Press, 1977), 113–38.

[6] Rita Felski, *Literature after Feminism* (Chicago: University of Chicago Press, 2003), chap. 2; Andrew Bennett, *The Author*, New Critical Idiom (London: Routledge, 2005), 118–23.

[7] Graziosi, *Inventing Homer*; Beecroft, *Authorship and Cultural Identity*.

[8] Sophus Helle, "The First Authors: Narratives of Authorship in Akkadian Literature" (PhD diss., Aarhus University, 2020); the methodological considerations behind this project are summarized in: Sophus Helle, "Narratives of Authorship in Cuneiform Literature," in *Authorship and the Hebrew Bible*, ed. Katharina Pyschny, Sonja Ammann, and Julia Rhyder (Tübingen: Mohr Siebeck, 2022), 17–35.

228   *Sophus Helle*

that can be reliably used to study authorship-as-production. Further, with such an approach, one is freed from the suspicion that these sources deviate from historical reality – since the whole point is to study how they depict historical reality, rather than the reality itself.[9] I became particularly interested in how the presentation of authorship often takes on a distinctly narrative quality, and how, in the cuneiform world, narratives of authorship tended to be produced at times of cultural crisis, perhaps as a way to provide a concise overview of the scholars' literary heritage when their social position came under threat.[10] But that is a story for another time.

In the following, I discuss three features of the study of authorship-as-presentation that are brought out by the contributions to this volume. The first is that authorship-as-presentation invites a focus on the collaborative and contributory aspects of the literary field. The second is that authorial attributions are almost inevitably tied up with value judgments – a point that will bring me back to the resistance-to-presentation that characterizes many traditional approaches to authorship. My third claim is that, in the ancient world especially, narratives of authorship often serve to link text to context, providing readers with a frame of reference by which they could make sense of a given work.

1. Collaborative Fictions

Much of the animus that motivates contemporary work on authorship is a resistance to the Romantic idea of the solitary genius – the myth of the exceptional, often male individual who is credited with the creation of great art. This myth has been critiqued in various ways, from the historical work of Jack Stillinger, who sought to show that coauthorship and collaboration is the norm rather than the exception, to the theoretical postulates of T. S. Eliot and Roland Barthes, who stressed the impersonal and collective nature of literary creativity.[11] Often, the presentation of authorship in our sources, if examined uncritically, can skew our understanding of authorial production by *singularizing* it, focusing our attention on the figure of the author and so suppressing the contributions of others – as in the case of Homer, where a single man stands in for an entire tradition of oral composers and performers. This singularizing tendency is almost always a dis-

---

[9] In "Narratives of Authorship" (21–25), I further argue that the study of authorship-as-production in the ancient world is often plagued by a set of methodological pitfalls that are avoided in this alternative approach.

[10] These findings are presented in Part I and Part II of "The First Authors," respectively.

[11] Jack Stillinger, *Multiple Authorship and the Myth of Solitary Genius* (Oxford: Oxford University Press, 1991); Thomas Stearns Eliot, "Tradition and the Individual Talent, Part 2," *The Egoist* 6 (1919): 72–73; Roland Barthes, "The Death of the Author," trans. Richard Howard, *Aspen* 5–6 (1967).

Janus-Faced Authors

tortion of historical reality, because, as Stillinger would argue, almost all literary production entails a greater degree of collaboration than our sources tend to admit.

However, the study of authorship-as-presentation can just as easily be used to foreground the collaborative nature of literary production and circulation, as is the case in many contributions to this volume. As Robyn Faith Walsh concludes in her study of the *Epistle to the Laodiceans*, "the relationship between author and audience is, in some measure, reciprocal," since the audience actively (if often unintentionally) participates in the construction and modification of the authorial figure. The ongoing reception, reinvention, and adaptation of an authorial persona – which is what a focus on authorship-as-presentation highlights – is a perfect way to show that literature is not created and determined by a single person once and for all, but breathes, moves, and acquires meaning to the extent that it is appropriated and reshaped by others. Take the case of Lal Ded, a Kashmiri mystic poet from the fourteenth century. In his introduction to a translation of her poems, Ranjit Hoskote argues that her works allowed for the emergence of a "contributory lineage" that many generations of scribes and performers participated in by expanding and remaking both the poetic corpus and the authorial figure of Lal Ded, like coders working on open-source software.[12]

Chance Bonar draws on Bruno Latour's analysis of Louis Pasteur to make a similar point: behind, besides, and beyond the figure of the famous genius, one can discover a host of other agents that made his discoveries possible. Bonar deftly applies Latour's conclusion to authorship in general and premodern authorship in particular: "There are more of us than we thought."[13] The text discussed by Bonar is a particularly interesting example, as the attribution of the *Teachings of Silvanus* (NHC VII,4) to a minor figure from the New Testament gives voice and authorial "depth" to a character that would otherwise be relegated to the margins of literature, a little-known figure whose contribution to Paul's and Peter's letters rests somewhere on the sliding scale between scribe and co-author. By taking this figure out of Paul's literary penumbra and attributing to him a body of teachings, the text highlights the collaborative nature of texts in general – even texts that, as in the case of Paul's letters, we have become accustomed to treating as single-authored works.

Crucially, it is not only texts that are coauthored – so is the authorial figure itself.[14] No author can ever completely create or control the persona that readers associate with their writing. That persona is always co-created by a host of

---

[12] Ranjit Hoskote, "Introduction," in *I, Lalla: The Poems of Lal Děd*, Penguin Classics (London: Penguin Books, 2013), xxxiii–xxxiv.

[13] Bruno Latour, *The Pasteurization of France*, trans. Alan Sheridan and John Law (Cambridge, MA: Harvard University Press, 1988), 35.

[14] Sophus Helle, "The Birth of the Author: Co-Creating Authorship in Enheduana's *Exaltation*," *Orbis Litterarum* 75 (2020): 55–72.

230   *Sophus Helle*

people, which may, depending on the context, include editors, scribes, scholars, performers, readers, reviewers, disciples, detractors, publicists, translators, and so on.[15] For example, in the case of Mani, as discussed by Nicholas Baker-Brian, there was a real person who sought to shape his authorial persona (in this case, one inflected by the authority of apocalyptic insight), and then that persona was developed further by his disciples through a series of challenges and defenses.

Of course, the collaborative nature of the authorial figure is especially evident in the case of texts that received a pseudepigraphic attribution at a later point in their circulation. Here, the creator of the text and the creator of the authorial figure are two different persons altogether, and they may have entirely different relations to the text in question. As the example of *The Epistle of Enoch* discussed by Elena Dugan shows, a pseudepigraphic attribution can serve to reroute the "original" meaning of a text: the "real" author who created the text and the authorial persona created around it may thus invest the same words with divergent or even contradictory meanings, as in Dugan's case study of a Jewish text being reframed to promulgate anti-Jewish sentiment.

This potential tension between the different faces of authorship and the collaboration involved in each comes to the foreground in Emily Mitchell's study of the Latin verse epitaphs, where "tension" is perhaps too mild a world to describe the domination and resistance of enslaved voices within their posthumous addresses. By layering voice upon voice, the epitaphs create a palimpsest of erasures. In the epitaphs commissioned by enslavers, the enslaved are made to speak words of appreciation that erase the reality of their condition, their view of their own situation, their bonds to their family members, and their lives outside their relation to their enslavers, as well as the labor of the poets who composed the verses and the enslaver's control over the textual situation. All this is erased to present a simple picture of gratitude, though the erasures are not fully successful, since markers of each survive.

The two most influential essays on the theory of authorship, Barthes' "The Death of the Author" and Foucault's "What Is an Author?," are framed by the same question: "Does it actually matter who is speaking?" (it is the first question in Barthes's essay and the last in Foucault's).[16] The question takes on a particular moral weight in the context of this essay: it matters a good deal who is speaking in these texts, in part because the question of "Who is speaking?" can be rephrased

---

[15] On the institutional framework that shapes the figure of the author in the modern world, see Jason Puksar, "Institutions: Writing and Reading," in *The Cambridge Handbook of Literary Authorship*, ed. Ingo Berensmeyer, Gert Buelens, and Marysa Demoor (Cambridge: Cambridge University Press, 2019), 429–43.

[16] Barthes ("Death of the Author") asks "Who is speaking in this way?" in a literary text (the character, the author, ideology, the period), only to suggest that it is impossible to know and that it may therefore not matter. The last sentence of Foucault in "What Is an Author?" (138), is: "What matter who's speaking?"

as "Who is *not* speaking?" and "Who is speaking *on behalf of whom*?" In this case, then, the distance between the authorship-as-production and the authorship-as-presentation is crucial for understanding both, since the goal of the latter is to efface the former. Indeed, this authorial arrangement can be taken as a crisp representation of slavery in general, which as an organization of labor seeks to maximize the enslavers' control over not just the means but also the agents of production while obscuring the circumstances under which this production takes place, presenting the finished product as untarnished by the working condition of the enslaved. In the case of the epitaphs, the words of the enslaved are taken from them by the enslaver, given to a third person, the poet, whose labor also goes uncredited, and presented back to the audience as the poetic product of the happy enslaved. It is the economy of slavery in literary form.

The collaboration involved in the making of both texts and authorial personae can thus be a relation of partial reciprocity and mutual constitution, as we saw with Hoskote's "contributory lineage," but it can also be a relation of exploitation and erasure. Either way, prying apart the two faces of authorship allows us to see that both are shaped by a multitude of people whose voices and contributions are subsumed under the deceptively singular notion of "the author." In reality, texts are always shaped and reshaped within a complex field of power and collaboration, and the concept of authorship can be used to obscure that complexity as well as to expose it.

2. Authorship and Value

In November 2017, the painting *Salvator Mundi* was sold for a record 450 million dollars by the auction house Christie's to the Saudi prince Badr bin Abdullah al-Saud. The painting, whose aesthetic value can most optimistically be described as "elusive," fetched such an eye-watering sum for one reason only: Christie's had convinced the buyer and the mainstream media that the painting could with reasonable certainty be attributed to the Italian Renaissance painter Leonardo da Vinci. As it turned out, this attribution was considerably more disputed than Christie's had let on, but by the time this became apparent, the deal had been struck.[17]

What the story shows – should further proof be needed – is that authorial attributions almost always entail a value judgment, sometimes in the most literal sense (the "value judgment" here amounting to almost half a billion dollars). Whereas authorship-as-production remains a fixed feature of a work's history, since it is securely stowed away in the past, our understanding of that history is

---

[17] Charles Hope, "A Peece of Christ," *London Review of Books*, 2 January 2020, https://www.lrb.co.uk/the-paper/v42/n01/charles-hope/a-peece-of-christ.

232   *Sophus Helle*

anything but fixed: authorship-as-presentation can be consciously or unconsciously manipulated in an ongoing negotiation that can directly impact the status of a given work. Attributing a text to a famous author can elevate it to canonical fame; disproving that attribution can consign it to oblivion.[18]

The most interesting cases are those that fall somewhere between these two extremes, that is, cases in which an ambiguous attribution reflects an ambiguous value judgment, as in Rebecca Scharbach Wollenberg's study of authorial attributions as a strategy for containment in rabbinic literature. Opinions that were held to be both worthy of consideration and in need of rejection are attributed within the rabbinic corpus to Christian characters: the "negative" attribution of an opinion to a character that a Jewish reader would be inclined to dismiss balances the "positive" fact of its inclusion in the corpus. A structurally similar, but religiously inverse case is Dugan's aforementioned study of a Jewish text being included in a Christian codex but attributed to Enoch *in such a way* as to enlist the text in an anti-Jewish rhetoric: it is because these pro-Christian sentiments are allegedly being spoken by a Jewish patriarch in a pre-Christian antiquity that they gain the force of authority and prophecy.

The three examples show three different ways in which authorial attributions can serve as value judgments. The text can be (mis)attributed to a canonical author to enhance its value, to an unreliable author to decrease its value, or to an author whose historical situation establishes the text as a reliable witness, thus also increasing its value. But in the contributions collected in this volume, it also becomes clear that a text's value is affected not just by the object, but also by the nature of the authorial attribution. It matters not just who a text is attributed to, but also how secure that attribution is. A text that is suspected of an unreliable attribution loses value, as if the authorial question somehow contaminated the status of the work itself.

A crisp example of this dynamic is Walsh's study of the *Epistle of Laodiceans*. As Walsh notes, a perception of a text as pseudepigraphic changes its treatment in the scholarly literature. The exact same literary feature, the copying of passages from other texts, will be praised as a sophisticated practice of citationality in a work whose authorship is solidly established and as a transparent, clumsy attempt at plagiarism in a work whose authorship is contested. The difference reveals the underlying assumption that those works whose authorship is most reliable – that is, works for which the authorship-as-presentation corresponds most exactly to the authorship-as-production – are also "better" in some vague aesthetic sense.

---

[18] The example also shows how the question of value intersects with the question of collaboration: some critics of the painting allow for a *partial* attribution to Leonardo, but the establishment of value often requires an erasure of the collaborative nature of creativity, since the presence of other contributions is often perceived as damaging the value bestowed by the attribution to a famous artist.

Janus-Faced Authors 233

The same bias against unreliable authorship is reflected in the vitriol that is directed at the potentially pseudepigraphic letter: the epithets catalogued by Walsh include "uninteresting," "remarkably incompetent," "colorless and dull," "stupid," "feebly constructed," "lackluster," a "worthless hodgepodge," and a confluence of "falsity and stupidity." That this text has so attracted the ire of modern scholars cannot only be due to its literary qualities or lack of the same. As Walsh argues, this almost corporeal, disgusted rejection must at least partly be due to the perception of the work as fake or mendacious *because* its authorship is suspect.

As I noted above, the strength of this anti-pseudepigraphic sentiment partly stems from the history of philology, which has historically defined itself by its ability to detect and expunge texts of spurious authorship – ranging from whole works to single sentences. I mentioned Valla and Wolf above, but this tradition goes all the way back to the beginning of Alexandrian philology. As Franco Montanari has argued, the birth of philology in the West can arguably be dated to Zenodotus of Ephesus' edition of Homer in the early third century BCE, in which Zenodotus established a new set of methods for determining which lines in the received corpus could *not* be attributed to Homer with certainty.[19] Textual editors have been raging against scribal interpolations and misattributed texts ever since, so modern scholars' frustration at *Laodiceans* builds on two millennia of inherited hate.[20] Pseudepigraphy acts as a disciplinary irritant, revealing what the field strives to repress.

In short, the perceived value of an authorial attribution extends to the perceived value of the text, which in turn affects how the text is treated. That is why the choice between the two approaches to authorship – a focus on authorship-as-production and on authorship-as-presentation – leads to a cascade of methodological consequences. Texts are read differently if one is not invested in reconstructing the exact circumstances under which they were composed: that is perhaps the strongest point of agreement between the essays in this volume. Walsh argues that pseudepigraphy need not be regarded as a flaw but can be a deliberate tactic, and viewed thus, what had seemed like the main defects of the text become its strengths, as we saw with the case of plagiarism being reconfigured as strategic citation. Likewise, Wollenberg treats pseudepigraphy not as

---

[19] Franco Montanari, "From Book to Edition: Philology in Ancient Greece," in *World Philology*, ed. Sheldon Pollock, Benjamin A. Elman, and Ku-ming Kevin Chang (Cambridge, MA: Harvard University Press, 2015), 25–44.

[20] This is, of course, a crude generalization. I am speaking of a mainstream attitude, but textual editors of all stripes have pushed against this straight-jacketed investment in reconstructing the author's exact words and eliminating all other contributions. See most notably Jerome McGann, *A Critique of Modern Textual Criticism* (Charlottesville: University Press of Virginia, 1992); Bernard Cerquiglini, *Éloge de la variante: Histoire critique de la philologie* (Paris: Édition du Seuil, 1989).

a problem to be resolved but as a generative site of meaning, and Bonar claims that we should see "pseudepigraphy not as explicitly and inevitably forgery, but as 'creative acts of interpretation' and imposed frameworks through which to approach a text."

While a focus on authorship-as-production does not always entail a vehement rejection or value judgment of pseudepigraphic texts (in fact, an understanding of the real circumstances of a text's composition can be necessary for understanding the meaning and effects of its pseudepigraphic attribution), it surprisingly often leads to a frustration with authorial fictions. And as the example of *Salvator Mundi* shows, sometimes the frustration is legitimate. Works can be misattributed as part of a deliberate deception that has profit as its only aim, and such misattributions will almost inevitably reflect badly on the work itself. Would my impression of *Salvator Mundi* be nearly as lackluster had I not first been led to believe that it had been painted by Leonardo? However much we may critique it intellectually, the link between authorship and value can be hard to escape emotionally.

3. Between Text and Context

There is a foundational irony in Roland Barthes' attack on the importance that literary critics have traditionally ascribed to authors. In "The Death of the Author," Barthes suggests that the author is of scarce importance to the interpretation of literature because "the writer can only imitate a gesture forever anterior, never original; his only power is to combine the different kinds of writing, to oppose some by others, so as never to sustain himself by just one of them."[21] In other words, the role of the author is not to create something new, but to combine existing strands of discourse – the impersonal realm of the "intertext" from which all text gains meaning, according to Barthes – into new configurations. As Barthes goes on to say: "if he wants to express himself, at least he should know that the internal 'thing' he claims to 'translate' is itself only a readymade dictionary whose words can be explained (defined) only by other words, and so on ad infinitum."[22] Authors do not express an interior world with a particular creative force, because everything about their work – from their innermost feelings to their most audacious experiments – relies on already existent literary codes and structures of meaning.

Let us grant, for a moment, that Barthes is right in his account of literary production (that is, of authorship-as-production). Historically speaking, the emergence of literary works from a matrix of meaning is a major reason why the

---

[21] Barthes, "Death of the Author."
[22] Barthes, "Death of the Author."

Janus-Faced Authors 235

figure of the author (that is, authorship-as-presentation) first gained importance in the ancient world. If literature really does gain meaning only within a culturally determined structure of signification (Barthes's "intertext" and "readymade dictionary"), then literary works would become all but illegible when they leave their culture of origin. And to an extent, this is true: modern philologists, for example, must reconstruct the literary codes and templates on which an ancient work is drawing for that work to be fully understood. A text without context is a challenge to make sense of. If readers are to appreciate what a text means, at least some link to its source and original context is often necessary – and in the ancient world, that link was often provided by the figure of the author. Authors, including the (often spurious) anecdotes about them, served to situate the works that were (again, often spuriously) attributed to them in a specific place, time, and social setting, giving ancient readers at least a bare-bones context in which to make sense of them. *Pace* Barthes, the intertextual origins of literary meaning thus makes the figure of the author more important, not less.

I am here drawing on the theory of Beecroft, who proposed that authorship in the ancient world served a form of paratextual "wrapping" that helped readers make sense of works that had been separated from their original context. Comparing the literary history of authorship in ancient Greece and China, Beecroft sees a parallel development, since authorship in both cultures gained in importance when texts began to move out of what he terms an "epichoric" (that is, highly localized) sphere into a "panchoric" (that is, transregional) sphere. While the meaning of a work was originally communicated to an epichoric audience through performance and references to local places and practices, this meaning was far less apparent to a transregional audience that encountered the work in writing and had little or no knowledge of its original setting. The figure of the author filled this gap, providing a series of anecdotes and coordinates in time and space that gave the text the contextual scaffolding it needed to mean anything at all. Beecroft thus concludes that "the birth of the author, then, is at once the death of performance and the emergence of a cultural world empire, a marker of a given literature's capacity to generate meaning far beyond and long after the creation of its central texts."[23]

This is a crucial aspect of authorship-as-presentation, which helps explain why authorial fictions were so useful in the ancient world, when many other kinds of paratextual scaffolding were not yet in place. Among the many functions of these fictions was to link a text to its (possibly fictitious) context and thereby make it meaningful. The *Apocryphon of James* (NHC I,2), which figures in both

---

[23] Beecroft, *Authorship and Cultural Identity*, 286. I reach a similar conclusion in my study of authorship in the cuneiform world: authorship became important when the living, breathing cultural framework within which cuneiform literature had been composed and circulated came under significant stress, necessitating a new and more concise framework for making sense of this literary heritage. See Part II of Helle, "First Authors."

236 *Sophus Helle*

Jeremiah Coogan's and Julia Lindenlaub's contributions, demonstrates the use of ancient authorial fictions in tying a text to its context. As Coogan argues, the text juxtaposes the wider literary context of a collective, collaborative apostolic memory with the single revelatory voice of its own apostolic author. In a similar vein, Lindenlaub examines how the authorial fiction in the *Apocryphon of James* emplaces the text within the intellectual culture of the Roman Mediterranean. From both vantage points, considering authorship-as-presentation reveals how the text was carefully packaged to yield a context-sensitive delivery.

One might compare the ancient author to an egg. For the embryo to survive and grow into a chick, it must be surrounded by the nutrition of the yolk and the protection of the shell. Likewise, written texts were protected and nourished by the paratextual framing of their authors and the anecdotes circulating about them. Or one might think of the author as an anchor. As Wollenberg notes, the ancient sources reveal an anxiety, best known from the writings of Plato,[24] about "how vulnerable written text is because it is socially anchorless – unless carefully guarded, it quickly passes beyond the control of both its author and its original recipient." The figure of the author provides the written text with a degree of anchoring, as Wollenberg also shows: the potential subversive force of some texts are contained when they are attributed to authors of dubious standing. The author here "anchors" the text in the sense that the reader is told how to feel about it; it is solidly placed within a specific cultural framework of readymade opinion.

Yet another metaphor is the one used by Dugan, who speaks of a Jewish text in a Christian "box," arguing that this box is no passive container but "a repackaging for a purpose."[25] As Dugan notes, the pseudepigraphy involved in attributing the *Epistle of Enoch* to Enoch is also, and perhaps more importantly, a form of pseudochronography. The manuscript employs several paratextual strategies that "make it hard to detach the message from the messenger," but this repeated emphasis on the author is not, or at least not solely, due to the identity of that author. The author matters to this manuscript specifically as a set of spatiotemporal coordinates, as shown by the codex's various attempts to ensure that "Enoch's historical location becomes crystal-clear." In other words, the text is attributed to this author *so that it may be placed in a specific historical context*, from which it will derive the meaning that the compiler of the codex wished to impute to it: an anti-Jewish screed that gains authority from its supposed Jewish origins, a Christian supersessionist narrative that is given a veneer

---

[24] Plato's skepticism about written texts and their vulnerability to misinterpretation when they are removed from their original context, and especially the presence of their authors, is most famously expressed in *Phaedrus* 275d.

[25] An egg is also, after all, a kind of box. *Vide* Bilbo Baggins: "A box without hinges, key or lid! Yet golden treasure inside is hid ..." (J. R. R. Tolkien, *The Hobbit, or There and Back Again* [London: George Allen & Unwin, 1937], 70).

Janus-Faced Authors 237

of external validation from its supposed pre-Christian source. Dugan also uses the metaphor of the anchor, when she argues that the inclusion of the *Book of Noah* in the epistle serves to "anchor its oracles in a particular chronographic landscape."

The authorial figure is thus important here not only for its own sake, but for the way it links text to context, even if that context is incorrect from the perspective of authorship-as-production. I noted already that Bennett sees the author in the modern world as oscillating between fiction and reality. The figure of an author is shaped by the myths that surround them and the persona that emerges from their works, but at the same time, we are invested in author in part because we feel that the reality of their lives will connect the realm of fiction to the real world we inhabit.[26] One cannot visit Pemberley, but one *can* visit Jane Austen's house in Hampshire. Yet as Bennet notes, when one visits such houses, there is often "something hollow in the experience,"[27] because the author is not only the biographical person who inhabited this space – they are always also the authorship-as-presentation that exceeds such biographical reality, and which cannot be captured by the bricks and mortar of even the quaintest Hampshire cottage. This ambivalence at the heart of literary authorship – the two faces of the authorial Janus – is what allows authors to link texts to contexts, and writers since antiquity have created authorial fictions that manipulate this link in ways that served their ideological agendas.

4. Summary

The volume's focus on authorial fictions reveals a premise that is often present but rarely made explicit in the historiography of authorship: namely, that authorship refers to two things at once, the creation of a text and the depiction of that creation in the text's circulation. This volume resolutely emphasizes the latter approach, which I have termed authorship-as-presentation, in a direct challenge to philology's traditional suspicion towards pseudepigraphic writings and other forms of unreliable attribution.

In this response, I have highlighted three strands that run through the book, and which characterize the study of authorship-as-presentation more broadly. The first is that a focus on the construction of the authorial figure invites us to consider the social dimensions of literary production. Rather than treating authors as lone, creative individuals, we come to see the authorial figure as part of a wider negotiation about the text's meaning and form, in which the author is

---

[26] Bennett, *The Author*, 118–23.

[27] Bennett, 120. Bennett uses the example of Thomas Hardy, *Tess of the d'Urbervilles*, and Max Gate.

238   *Sophus Helle*

but one of several players. The authorial figure is created, sustained, and modified by a host of actors, including editors, coauthors, performers, disciples, scribes, and more.

The second strand is that authorial attributions almost always entail value judgments, in two main ways. First, it matters who a text is attributed to, as this attribution can raise a text to canonical standing, contain its subversive energy, and much more besides, depending on the author. Second, it matters how secure the attribution is, since an unreliable authorship can itself change how the text is perceived, especially in modern scholarship. This is one reason why a focus on authorship-as-presentation matters: it can counteract the undue disdain of pseudepigraphy that often characterizes the study of authorship-as-production.

Finally, the contributions to this volume suggest that an important role of the authorial figure in the ancient world is to place a potentially unmoored text in a context that lends it meaning and import. The Janus-faced nature of authors allows them to link the world of texts and literature to the world of biographical and historical reality, and as ancient writers realized, this means that one can change the significance and social status of a text by changing the authorial narratives that accompany it.

The author, in short, is a creature of contradictions, a figure of fiction and a real individual, a singular being and a collective construction, the creator and the creation of the text, and a discursive hinge that points forward and backward in time, into the text and out into its context. The author, as the contributions gathered here show, is a battleground on which cultural tensions can meet and play themselves out in a complex dynamic of subversion and containment, domination and resistance.

Bibliography

Beecroft, Alexander. *Authorship and Cultural Identity in Early Greece and China: Patterns of Literary Circulation*. Cambridge: Cambridge University Press, 2010.
Barthes, Roland. "The Death of the Author." Translated by Richard Howard. *Aspen* 5–6 (1967).
Bennett, Andrew. *The Author*. New Critical Idiom. London: Routledge, 2005.
Cerquiglini, Bernard. *Éloge de la variante: Histoire critique de la philologie*. Paris: Édition du Seuil, 1989.
Eliot, Thomas Stearns. "Tradition and the Individual Talent, Part 2." *The Egoist* 6 (1919): 72–73.
Felski, Rita. *Literature after Feminism*. Chicago: University of Chicago Press, 2003.
Foucault, Michel. "What Is an Author?" Pages 113–138 in *Language, Counter-Memory, Practice: Selected Essays and Interviews*. Translated by Donald Bouchard and Simon Sherry. Ithaca: Cornell University Press, 1977.
Graziosi, Barbara. *Inventing Homer: The Early Reception of Epic*. Cambridge Classical Studies. Cambridge: Cambridge University Press, 2002.

Helle, Sophus. "The Birth of the Author: Co-Creating Authorship in Enheduana's *Exaltation*." *Orbis Litterarum* 75 (2020): 55–72.

Helle, Sophus. "The First Authors: Narratives of Authorship in Akkadian Literature." PhD diss., Aarhus University, 2020.

Helle, Sophus. "Narratives of Authorship in Cuneiform Literature." Pages 17–35 in *Authorship and the Hebrew Bible*. Edited by Katharina Pyschny, Sonja Ammann, and Julia Rhyder. Tübingen: Mohr Siebeck, 2022.

Hope, Charles. "A Peece of Christ." *London Review of Books*. 2 January 2020. https://www.lrb.co.uk/the-paper/v42/n01/charles-hope/a-peece-of-christ.

Hoskote, Ranjit. "Introduction." Pages xxxiii–xxxiv in *I, Lalla: The Poems of Lal Děd*. Penguin Classics. London: Penguin Books, 2013.

Latour, Bruno. *The Pasteurization of France*. Translated by Alan Sheridan and John Law. Cambridge, MA: Harvard University Press, 1988.

McGann, Jerome. *A Critique of Modern Textual Criticism*. Charlottesville: University Press of Virginia, 1992.

Montanari, Franco. "From Book to Edition: Philology in Ancient Greece." Pages 25–44 in *World Philology*. Edited by Sheldon Pollock, Benjamin A. Elman, and Ku-ming Kevin Chang. Cambridge, MA: Harvard University Press, 2015.

Puksar, Jason. "Institutions: Writing and Reading." Pages 429–443 in *The Cambridge Handbook of Literary Authorship*. Edited by Ingo Berensmeyer, Gert Buelens, and Marysa Demoor. Cambridge: Cambridge University Press, 2019.

Stillinger, Jack. *Multiple Authorship and the Myth of Solitary Genius*. Oxford: Oxford University Press, 1991.

Tolkien, J. R. R. *The Hobbit, or There and Back Again*. London: George Allen & Unwin, 1937.

Tomashevsky, Boris. "Literature and Biography." Pages 83–90 in *Biography in Theory*. Edited by Wilhelm Hemecker and Edward Saunders. Berlin: De Gruyter, 2017.

Wolf, Friedrich August. *Prolegomena to Homer, 1795*. Translated and edited by Anthony Grafton, Glenn W. Most, and James E. G. Zetzel. Princeton: Princeton University Press, 1985.

Contributors

NICHOLAS BAKER-BRIAN is a Reader in New Testament and Early Christian Studies at Cardiff University, as well as Deputy Head of Ancient History and Religion.

CHANCE E. BONAR is a postdoctoral fellow in the Center for the Humanities at Tufts University and a Lecturer of Advanced Greek at Harvard Divinity School.

JEREMIAH COOGAN is an Assistant Professor of New Testament at the Jesuit School of Theology, Santa Clara University.

ELENA DUGAN is an Instructor of Philosophy and Religious Studies at Phillips Academy Andover and an associate of the Department of Classics at Harvard University.

SOPHUS HELLE is a postdoctoral fellow at Freie Universität Berlin.

CLAIRE RACHEL JACKSON is a postdoctoral researcher in the Department of Literary Studies at Universiteit Gent.

JULIA D. LINDENLAUB is an independent researcher and Content Manager for Academic Journals at Cambridge University Press.

EMILY C. MITCHELL is a PhD candidate in Classical Philology at Harvard University.

ROBYN FAITH WALSH is an Associate Professor of Religious Studies at the University of Miami.

REBECCA SCHARBACH WOLLENBERG is an Assistant Professor of Judaic Studies at the University of Michigan.

Index of Ancient Sources

Old Testament

Genesis
1:27 — 76
9:25 — 79
25:6 — 80
25:12 — 80
25:19 — 80

Exodus
12:36 — 79
12:40 — 79

Numbers
34:2 — 79

Joshua
22:22 — 76

Amos
3:2 — 75

New Testament

Matthew
5:25 — 144n61
7:17–19 — 122
23 — 162
23:12 — 141

Luke
1:1 — 211
1:2–3 — 214
11 — 162
12:58 — 144n61
18:3 — 144n61

John
1:1 — 215

Acts
15:40 — 133
16:1 — 133
16:19–40 — 133
17:14 — 133
18:5 — 133

Romans
1:7 — 34
2:7 — 34–35
5:21 — 35
6:22 — 35
6:23 — 35
8:7–8 — 143n57

1 Corinthians
1:2 — 34
1:8 — 34
2:16 — 35
3 — 143
4:16 — 138n37
9:1 — 115
9:24–25 — 145
11:1 — 138
16 — 132
16:9 — 14n61

2 Corinthians
1:2 — 34
1:19 — 130n11
12:1 — 114

244 Index of Ancient Sources

12:2–4	113	1:6	138
12:2–5	114	2:4	140
		2:11–12	138
Galatians		2:14	138n38
1:1	34, 113	2:19	145
1:3	34	3:2	131, 131n17
1:11–12	114	3:5	131n17
1:11	34	4:1	140
2:5	34	4:11	141
2:14	34	4:12	11
2:20	35	5:4–8	142
6:18	35	5:26	35
Ephesians		*2 Thessalonians*	
2:10	34	1:1	135
		2	128, 143
Philippians		2:2	134
1:2	34	2:3–12	144
1:3–4	34	2:3	143, 143n57, 144
1:6	34	2:4	144
1:7	35	2:5	130, 133
1:10	34	2:15	133
1:12	34	2:18	130
1:13	34	3:17	130
1:18–20	35		
1:20–21	35	*1 Timothy*	
1:21	35	6:12	145n63
1:28	144n61		
2:2	35	*2 Timothy*	
2:5	35	4:7–8	145n63
2:12	35		
2:13	35	*Titus*	
2:14	35	3:5	35
3:1–2	35		
3:1	22	*James*	
3:2	27	4:10	141
4:6	35		
4:7–8	35	*1 Peter*	
4:8–9	35	2:5	140, 143
4:22	35	5	141
4:23	35	5:1–4	145
		5:3	145
Colossians		5:4	145
2:4	34	5:6	141
4:16	16–17, 35	5:7	142
		5:8	142, 144
1 Thessalonians		5:12	132, 135–36, 145
1:1	135		

Index of Ancient Sources

245

2 Peter		Jude	
2:9	34	5	171
3:4	34	6	171
3:7	34	7	171
		11	171
1 John		16	171
5:7–8	33n101		

Old Testament Pseudepigrapha

1 Enoch		98.2	165
91–108	156–57	98.3	164–65
91	156	98.4	156
91.1	156n18	98.5	164
91.3–4	156n18	99.5	165
91.11–17	156n18	99.9	162
92.1	156n18	99.11	161
92.5	156n18	99.15	161, 164
93	156	100.1	165
93.1–10	156n18	100.6	160
93.12–13	156n18	104.2	158
94–105	156, 167	106–7	156, 166
94.1	161	106.13–17	166
94.7	156n18	106.17	158, 166
97–105	166	107.3	158
97.6–107.3	156		
97.8–10	157	Sibylline Oracles	
98.1–3	157	3.809–29	54

Rabbinic Texts

Babylonian Talmud		Jerusalem Talmud	
b. Avodah Zarah		y. Berakhot	
4a	75		
		Pesikta Rabbati	
b. Sanhedrin		5.14b	78n26
90b–91a	74		
91a	79		

246   *Index of Ancient Sources*

Early Christian Authors & Texts

Ambrose, *Comm. Luc.*
1.2	212n30

Apocryphon of James (NHC I,2)
1.1–2.7	92
1.1–35	208
1.8–18	94
1.18–25	95
1.23–25	210
1.30–31	93
2.1–7	92n29
2.8–15	92, 95, 209
2.33–15.33	92
2.38–39	210
15.34–16.2	92
16.12–30	92, 208
16.12–16	97

Athanasius, *On the Incarncation*
54.3	139n40

Augustine, *Contra Faustum*
14.1	116

Bardaisan, *Book of the Law of Countries*
46	120

Clement, *Paedagogus*
I.(9.)84.2–4	155

Clement, *Stromata*
1.28.177.2	213n32

Epiphanius of Salamis, *Anac.*
13.1.5	216n40
46	216n40
50.6	216n40

Epiphanius of Salamis, *Hom. In fest. Palm.*
43:432.8	216n40

Epiphanius of Salamis, *Mens.*
35	216n40

Epiphanius of Salamis, *Panarion*
28.5.1–3	216n40

29.9.1	216n40
39.3.7	216n40
30.6.7–9	216n40
30.11.5	216n40
30.13.1	216n40
30.13.6–8	216n40
30.14.2–3	216n40
30.14.5	216n40
30.16.4–5	216n40
30.22.4	216n40
42	216n40
42.9.4	8
42.12.3	18
46.1.1–5	216n40
51	215
51.3.1	215n38
51.3.2	215n38
51.4.5	216
51.4.11	216
51.5.9	216
51.6.5	217
51.15.14	217
51.17.3	217
64.8.5–9.1	216n40
66.2.9	216n40
66.35.6	216n40
66.40.1	216n40
66.78.1	216n40

Epistle to the Laodiceans
1	25, 34
2	34
3	34
4	25–26, 34
5	34
6	26, 34
7	35
8	35
9	35
10	35
11	35
12	35
13	35
14	35
15	35

Index of Ancient Sources 247

16	35
17	35
18	35
19	35
20	26, 35

Eusebius, *Ecclesiastical History*

2.25.6–7	215n39
3.28.2	215n39
3.39.3–4	209
6.20.3	215n39

Gospel of Truth (NHC I,3)

28.23–30.23	142n50

(Pseudo-)Hippolytus, *Refutations*

9.15.3	117

Irenaeus, *Haer.*

3.11.9	215n39

Jerome, *Comm. Matt.*

praef. 1	212n30

Jerome, *De vir. ill.*

5	18

Justin, *1 Apology*

66.3	209n21

Lactantius, *Divine Institutes*

7.18.2	121

Melito, *On the Passover*

48–52	164
49–56	154–55
49	154, 164
50	164
51	165
52	165
53	165
57	155
59	155
83–85	166

Origen, *Hom. Luc.*

1.1–2	212–13
1.3	214
1.4	214
1.6	214

Teachings of Silvanus (NHC VII,4)

85.7	141
85.30	137n34
86.24	137n34
87.4–12	137n34
87.11	144
87.19–20	137n34
88.12	144n61
88.22–23	137n34
88.24–27	142
89.16–17	142
89.21–31	144
91.20–21	137n34
91.20	144
95.1	144
98.14–15	141
98.18–20	140
98.19–20	141
103.34–104.14	139
104.16–18	140
104.20	140
106.1	144
108.26–32	138
108.32–35	140
109.15–25	143
110.35–111.13	141
111.8–13	139
112.19–22	144
114.6	144
114.24–25	143

Tertullian, *Adv. Marc.*

5.17.1	18

Theodore of Mopsuestia, *Reb. Maur. Op.*

6	18

248   *Index of Ancient Sources*

Medieval Christian Authors & Texts

Iohannes Georgides, *Sententiae*
240   63n102

Lives of Saint Galaction and Episteme
(*BHG* 665)
1   57
2   60
3   61

Michael Psellus, *Corpus Parisinum*
3.276   63n102

Michael Psellus, *de Heliodoro
et Achille Tatio iudicium*
4–5   63n102

Photius, *Bibliotheca*
137b27–138a15   48

Symeon Metaphrastes, *Menologion*
(*BHG* 666)
1   59, 61
6   61
11   62
24   60
41   60

Manichaean Texts

Al-Nadīm, *Fihrist*
69.16–72.8   109

Bīrūnī, *Āthār*
207   105
208   107

Book of Mysteries
1   118
12   118
13   118

Cologne Mani Codex (Life of Mani)
48.16–62.9   106
62.9–63.1   114
64.8–65.22   112
66.18–68.5   113
70.10–72.4   115

Kephalaia
342   107–8, 122

424.4–6   108
424.7–11   107
424.7–10   108
424.11–12   108

M49   108

M98I   111

M99I   111

M464a   108

M805a   108

M3414   108

M7980   111

M7984   111

Index of Ancient Sources

Greek And Roman Authors & Texts

Achilles Tatius, *Leucippe and Clitophon*
Praef. 3	44
1.1.1–1.3.1	43
1.1.1–1.1.2	45
1.1.2	43n18, 46, 49
1.1.3–4	49
1.1.3	49
1.1.6	50
1.1.10–12	49
1.2.1	43n18, 49
1.2.2	58
1.2.3	50, 58n81
1.3.1	46, 52, 61
1.4.3	43n16
2.2.1	46n33
2.11.4–8	43n15
2.26.1	62
5.1	40n8
5.17.6	62
8.19.3	43

Chariton, *Callirhoe*
1.1.1	41n10

Cicero, *Att.*
11.5.1	131n14

Cicero, *Fam.*
14.14.1	131n13
14.18.2	131n13
16.1	131n13
16.3	131n13
16.4	131n13

16.6	131n13
16.11	131n13

Heliodorus, *Aithiopika*
10.41.4	41n10

Herodotus, *Histories*
1.2.1–1.5.3	48
1.4.1–1.5.3	48
2.59	49n39
4.147	49n39
5.59.1	52

Homer, *Iliad*
21.257–262	50

Nonnus, *Dionysiaca*
1.45	47

Plato, *Phaedrus*
229a1–230c5	51
275b3–4	52
275d9–e5	63n103

Strabo, *Geography*
16.2.22	46n31

Suda
α 4695	41n9

Xenophon, *Ephesiaca*
1.1.1	41n10

Inscriptions

AE 1946, 208
2–4	184n21
2	184
3–6	184n21
3	184
4	184

5–6	184
6	184

AE 1997, 362 + *AE* 1998, 374
1	185
2	185
5	186

Index of Ancient Sources

6   186

CLE 78 (= *CIL* XII 912)
4–8   189
4–7   189

CLE 959 (= *CIL* I 1221, *CIL* VI 9499)
2–3   195–96
3   196
4–6   196
4   196
7   195
8–12   196
8–10   196
10   196
14–15   196

CLE 963 (= *CIL* VI 17130)
5–6   188
7–10   187
7–8   187
11–14   188

CLE 987 (= *CIL* VI 19747)
1   198
2   198
5–6   198

CLE 990 (= *CIL* XIV 2298)
     179–80
2–3   181
5–6   182
7–8   181
8–9   183, 196

10–12   183
13–15   181, 184n21
13   181
14   181

CLE 995 (= *CIL* VI 12652)
1–8   193
1–5   193
3   192
4–6   193
6–14   193
9–11   193
12–26   193
13–14   193
15–18   193
18–26   193
19–22   193
23–25   193
23   193

CLE 1175 (= *CIL* VI 29896)
     180

CLE 1310 (= *CIL* III 6475, III 10762)
1–2   199
3–4   199
5–6   199

Kartīr inscription
15   110
22   109–10
22–36   109
34   109
36   109–10, 114

Index of Modern Authors

Achtemeier, Paul J. 133n22, 140n45
Aland, Kurt 3n4
Alexander, Loveday 211n29
Allen, Garrick V. 160n27
Alwis, A. P. 41n11, 53n58, 54n62, 56n73, 57n80, 58n83, 60n91, 60n92, 61n96
Aringer, Nina 47n38
Arnal, William E. 16n17, 32n99, 33
Askwith, E. H. 132n18
Auwers, Jean-Marie 19n29
Ayres, Lewis 86n2

Backus, Irena 16n16, 19n30, 20n33
Bahr, Gordon J. 130n11
Bakker, Egbert 4n8
Barns, J. W. B. 127n1
Barthes, Roland 3, 39n1, 40n6, 228, 230, 234–35
Bartsch, Shadi 49n44
Batey, Richard 18n23
Bauckham, Richard 21
Baum, Armin D. 209n21
Bazzana, Giovanni 213n32
Becker, Adam H. 172n51
BeDuhn, Jason 107n11, 108n16
Beecroft, Alexander 225, 227, 235
Beet, Joseph Agar 2n1
Behemenberg, Lena 49n44
Bennett, Andrew 40n6, 51n51, 63, 227, 237
Berardi, Roberta 4n8
Biriotti, Maurice 39n1
Blackwell, Ben C. 139n40
Blumell, Lincoln H. 89n18
Bodel, John 194n33
Boex, Allison 178n4, 180, 189
Bond, Sarah 146n69
Bonner, Campbell 154n10, 155, 156n18, 164n33
Bonner, Stanley Frederick 146n65

Boring, M. Eugene 138n39
Bourdieu, Pierre 14n5
Boustan, Ra'anan 73n16
Bovon, François 5, 15–16, 17n19, 21n40, 22–24, 27, 31, 33
Bowersock, Glen 87n4
Boyarin, Daniel 75n21
Boyce, Mary 108n18
Brakke, David 2, 143, 208n17, 208n19, 210n22, 210n23
Braund, David 87n4
Bregman, Marc 77n25
Brent, Allen 215n39
Breu, Clarissa 4n10, 5n11
Briquel-Chatonnet, Françoise 47n34
Broek, Roelof van den 127n2, 129n6, 136, 142n52
Brown, Jonathan 33n96
Browne, G. M. 127n1
Bruce, F. F. 131n17
Buitenwerf, Rieuwerd 55n67
Buonocore, Marco 185n22
Burke, Séan 29n86, 30n88, 39n1
Burke, Tony 4n9
Burns, Dylan 106

Cabaniss, Allen 169n40
Canfield, C. E. B. 131, 132n18
Carroll, Maureen 187n24
Castle, Terry 54
Cerquiglini, Bernard 233n20
Chadwick, Henry 18n25
Chartier, Roger 205n7
Cirafesi, Wally V. 209n21
Clackson, James 93n33
Cohn, Dorrit 45
Collatz, Christian-Friedrich 215n37
Collins, Adela Yarbro 206n13
Collins, John J. 105, 111
Comstock, Susan 169n40
Constantinou, Stavroula 56n74

Index of Modern Authors

Coogan, Jeremiah 88n11, 91n22, 93n34, 95, 96n41, 97n45, 205n8, 205n10, 206n12, 208n17, 211n26, 213n32, 214n36, 217n45
Cooley, Alison E. 177n1
Courtney, Edward 193n31
Coyle, John Kevin 122n95
Crawford, Matthew R. 88n11
Cribiore, Raffaella 146n65
Crouzel, Henri 212n30, 213n33
Cueva, Edmund P. 4n9
Cullmann, Oscar 213n31

Davis, Kipp 4n9
Delehaye, Hippolyte 41n12
De Temmerman, Koen 47n34, 51n50, 52n57
Dietler, Michael 32n96
Dilley, Paul 106–8, 110, 113, 122
Dodge, Bayard 112n44
Doering, Lutz 160n29
Drawnel, Henryk 169n39
Drijvers, H. J. W. 118n76, 119n79, 119n80, 120n84, 121n89
Dugan, Elena 168n38
Durkin-Meisterernst, Desmond 108n19

Edmondson, Jonathan 177n1
Edwards, Ruth B. 47n36
Ehrman, Bart D. 4n9, 130n10
Eliot, Thomas Stearns 228n11
Erho, Ted M. 156n15
Eshleman, Kendra 86n1, 87, 97n45
Eyl, Jennifer 23n57

Falkenberg, René 207n14, 207n16
Felski, Rita 227
Fewster, Gregory P. 93n30, 97n46, 209n21
Fish, Stanley 3n5
Fitzgerald, John T. 139n42
Fitzgerald, William 205n8
Fletcher, Richard 40n5
Foreman, Gabrielle P. 178n5
Formisano, Marco 39n3
Foucault, Michel 3, 29–31, 39n1, 55, 71, 88n12, 179, 205, 227, 230
Fournier, François 212n30
Fraade, Steven D. 77n25

Franco, Laura 57n78, 60n89
Frey, Jörg 4n9
Funk, Wolf Peter 134n23

Gamble, Harry Y. 89n18, 90n21, 206n13
Gardner, Iain 105n3, 106n5, 107n11, 108n16, 109n22, 112n45, 119n78, 122
Garnaud, Jean-Philippe 45n29
Gathercole, Simon J. 206n13, 206n14
Genette, Gerard 55n69, 205n9, 205n11
Gerson, Lloyd P. 106n7
Geue, Tom 5n12, 39n3, 40n4, 94n36, 204n6, 205n10
Giatromanolakes, Giorges 54n62, 61n94, 62n100
Given, J. Gregory 99n51, 208n18
Goldhill, Simon 43n15, 54, 56n71
Grant, Robert M. 204n4
Graziosi, Barbara 225n2, 227
Greensmith, Emma 55n67
Griffin, Robert J. 205n7
Gruen, Erich 46n32, 47n36, 48n40

Hadjittofi, Fotini 47n38
Hafner, Markus 54n66, 63n103
Haines-Eitzen, Kim 170, 171n48
Hall, Stuart George 154n10, 166n36
Hanink, Johanna 40n5
Hansen, William 94n36
Harl Sellew, Melissa 17n21, 19, 21–23, 27n74, 34n105
Harnack, Adolf von 18n27, 19n30, 21, 23, 131n17
Hartenstein, Judith 92n26
Hathaway, Ronald F. 136n31
Hayes, Christine 74
Head, Peter 133n20
Heath, Jane M. F. 88n16, 89n18
Heilmann, Jan 90n21
Heine, Ronald 211n26
Helle, Sophus 227n8, 229n14
Hengel, Martin 204n4, 206n13
Hermann, Leon 18n23
Hill, Charles E. 4n7, 162n30, 215n39
Hill, Jonathan 4n10
Hinterberger, Martin 56n72
Hobsbawm, Eric 14n8, 16n17, 32
Høgel, Christian 56n74, 58n78, 59, 60n89

Index of Modern Authors

Holder, R. Ward 20n38
Holl, Karl 215n37, 216n41, 217n42
Holloway, Paul A. 19n32, 26n73, 27n76
Hope, Charles 231n17
Hopkins, John North 4n9
Horbury, William 75n21
Horner, George W. 138n36, 140n44, 142n54, 144, 145n64
Horrell, David G. 171
Hoskote, Ranjit 229, 231
Howley, Joseph A. 87n4, 95n38, 97n45, 205n8, 205n10, 210n22
Hurst, André 146n67
Hutter, Manfred 110, 111n39

Jacobs, Andrew 214n36, 215n38
Jaffee, Martin S. 75n21, 77n25
James, M. R. 21
Jansen, Laura 205n9
Janssens, Yvonne 135–36, 143, 145n63
Jenott, Lance 98n49, 99n51, 127n1, 207n17
Johnson, Samuel B. 211n26
Johnson, William A. 72, 73n12, 87n7, 90, 91n23, 95, 210n22
Jones, Brice C. 169n40, 170
Jonge, H.J. de 19n29
Jonge, Martinus de 159n21

Kalmin, Richard 75n21, 76n22
Kanavou, Nikoletta 41n11, 42n14, 54n62, 59n86, 60n91
Keith, Chris 96n43, 208, 208n19, 209n21, 211n26
Kenyon, Frederic G. 152, 154n6
Kessler, Konrad 117n64
King, Karen 4n10, 27n76, 29n81, 88, 94n35, 95n39, 97n45, 128–29, 179, 214n34
Kiperwasser, Reuven 73n16
Klimkeit, Hans-Joachim 111, 116n57
Kloppenborg, John S. 210n22
Knox, John 18n23
Koenen, Ludwig 112n45
Kraft, Robert A. 151, 159n21
Kreps, Anne 99n53
Kruchió, Benedek 41n11, 42n14, 53n61, 54n64, 60n91

Krueger, Derek 55n70, 56n73, 58
Kühr, Angela 47n36

Lambert, David 72n9
Larsen, Matthew D. C. 206n13, 209n21
Last, Richard 87n4
Latour, Bruno 129, 229
Lea, Thomas 132n20
Letteney, Mark 4n8, 206n13
Lied, Liv Ingeborg 159n21, 172n50
Lienhard, Joseph T. 212n30, 213n33
Lieu, Samuel N. C. 112n45, 113n48, 114, 115n52
Lightfoot, J. B. 18, 19n30, 20–21, 27n74, 28
Lindenlaub, Julia D. 96n43, 208n17, 209n20, 210n23
Lofthouse, W. G. 132n18
Löhr, Winrich A. 89n18
Luijendijk, AnneMarie 89n18
Lundhaug, Hugo 93n31, 94n36, 96n40, 99n49, 127n1
Luttikhuizen, Gerard P. 112n46, 117n62

Macalister, Suzanne 42n13, 53n61, 54n64
Maciver, Calum 44n25
MacKenzie, D. N. 109n23, 110, 114n49, 116n58
MaGee, Gregory S. 23n55
Mailer, Norman 30
Malherbe, Abraham J. 139n42
Malina, Bruce J. 130n11
Malinine, Michel 207n16
Mal-Maeder, Danielle van 51n53
Marinčič, Marko 44n19, 45n27, 51n53
Markschies, Christoph 86n2, 215n37
Marmodoro, Anna 4n10
Martin, R. P. 50n45
Martin, Richard C. 117n67
Martin, Victor 170
Martínez, Javier 4n9
Martínez, Victor M. 146n68
Matera, Robert 180
McGann, Jerome 233n20
McGill, Scott 4n9
McRae, Duncan 81n28
Merell, Jean 206n14
Messis, Charis 53n60, 58n82

254 Index of Modern Authors

Metzger, Bruce 18n22
Mheallaigh, Karen ní 44n22, 51, 52n54, 94n36, 98n47
Milik, J.T. 157n18
Miller, Nancy K. 40n6
Miller, Nicole 39n1
Miller, Patricia Cox 56n71
Moessner, David P. 211n29
Moi, Toril 40n6
Möllendorf, Peter von 49n44
Montanari, Franco 233
Moore, Stephen D. 72n9
Morales, Helen 43n16
Morgan, J.R. 43n15, 44n19, 44n25, 45n30, 62n99
Morgan, Jonathan 139n40
Morris, Leon 132n19
Moss, Candida R. 97n45, 130n11, 205n8, 205n10, 218n46
Most, G.W. 44n20
Mouritsen, Henrik 194n33
Mroczek, Eva 5n12, 24n62, 31–32, 71n5, 72n7, 81n29, 206n12
Muehlberger, Ellen 2
Mueller, James R. 155n12, 156n14
Mullett, Margaret 39, 53n61
Muro, Ernest A. 168n39
Murphy-O'Connor, Jerome 130n11, 131
Myllykoski, Matti 92n28

Najman, Hindi 4n9, 40n4, 47n35, 71n1, 128, 146
Nakatani, Saiichiro 43n17
Nasrallah, Laura Salah 87n6
Nautin, Pierre 211n27
Nebe, Gerhard-Wilhelm 168n39
Nickelsburg, George W.E. 156, 158–59, 168n39
Nicklas, Tobias 88n14, 94n34, 170, 171n48
Niehoff, Maren R. 145n66
Nilsson, Ingela 53n61
Nongbri, Brent 152n2, 154n6, 169n41

O'Callaghan, José 168n39
O'Connor, John J. 30n91
Oltermann, Philip 30n90

Pagels, Elaine 96n43, 99n51, 99n54, 207n16
Papaioannou, Stratis 53n58, 55n70, 56n73, 57n78, 58n82, 59n87, 60n89, 64n105
Parkhouse, Sarah 92n27
Patterson, Orlando 181–83, 200
Pearson, Birger A. 134–35
Peel, Malcolm 134–35, 141, 142n51, 143n57
Peirano Garrison, Irene 4n9, 14, 16, 17n18, 24–25, 26n70, 28, 30, 33n98, 40n4, 71n1, 88n12, 128, 146, 205n10
Penland, Elizabeth C. 98n50
Penny, Donald N. 22n49, 24n61
Périchon, Pierre 212n30
Perkins, Pheme 208n17
Petersen, Silke 206n13
Picus, Daniel 81n27
Pietersma, Albert 156n18, 169n40
Pizzone, Aglae 56n73
Plepelits, Karl 40n7, 42n13
Plisch, Uwe-Karsten 92n26
Porter, Stanley E. 163
Possekel, Ute 119–20
Pratsch, Thomas 58n85, 61n96
Preuschen, Erwin 210n26
Prior, Michael 129n7, 130n9, 132n18
Puech, Émile 168n39
Puksar, Jason 230n15

Quinn, Josephine Crawley 46n32, 48n40

Ramelli, Ilaria L.E. 119n82, 120n83, 121n88
Rapp, Claudia 56n72, 58n82
Rattmann, Arnd 215n37
Rauer, Max 212n30
Reardon, B.P. 44n19
Reay, Brendon 217n45
Reck, Christiane 107n13, 110n32, 111n37
Reece, Steve 130n10, 132n30
Reed, Annette Yoshiko 71n3, 172n51
Reeves, John C. 105–6, 107n12, 108n14, 109n20, 112n44, 117n64, 118, 122n94
Repath, I.D. 43n17
Richards, E. Randolph 129, 130n11, 131, 132n20

Index of Modern Authors

Richardson, John 13n2, 32n96
Ries, Julien 106n5
Robiano, Patrick 54n64, 55n68
Robinson, James M. 207n16
Robinson, Stephen E. 155n12
Rocchi, Maria 52n56
Rodriguez, Jacob A. 208n17, 209n21
Roller, Otto 132n19
Römer, Cornelia 106n4, 112n45
Rouleau, Donald 207n16
Roy, Louise 207n16
Rudhardt, Jean 146n67
Rüpke, Jörg 146n68
Russell, Norman 139n40
Ruzer, Serge 74n20

Saller, Richard P. 182n17
Sandnes, Karl Olav 23n57
Sanzo, Joseph E. 73n16
Sargent, Benjamin 133
Savoie, Alice 204n5
Schedtler, Justin P. Jeffcoat 146n66
Schermann, Theodor 216n40
Schneemelcher, Wilhelm 18n24, 19n29, 19n30, 21, 34n103
Schoedel, W. R. 127n2, 137n33, 140n43
Schremer, Adiel 74n18, 75n21
Secord, Jared 86n1, 87, 93n33, 95n38
Selden, Daniel L. 48
Senseney, Megan Finn 146n68
Shaked, Shaul 111n41
Shaw, Brent D. 183n19
Shelton, J. C. 127n1
Siegal, Michal Bar Asher 74n19
Simonis, Marcel 199n37
Sivan, Hagith 77n25
Skjærvø, Prods Oktor 109, 118n75
Small, Jocelyn Penny 147
Smith, Mitzi J. 142n51
Snyder, H. Gregory 96n41
Sogno, Christiana 39n3
Spittler, Janet E. 211n29
Spottorno, Maria Victoria 168n39
Stachon, Markus 2n1
Stang, Charles 113n47, 116n59
Starling, Drew 203, 204n3, 204n6, 207
Stefaniw, Blossom 134, 137, 139n42, 140n46, 141n47, 145, 147

Stewart, Eric C. 139n42
Stillinger, Jack 228–29
Stock, Brian 88n16, 210n22
Stowers, Stanley K. 30n89
Stroumsa, Guy G. 72n8, 116–17, 121n89
Stuckenbruck, Loren T. 156n15, 156n18, 158n19, 159n21, 160n25, 165n34, 166, 168n38
Sundermann, Werner 108, 109n21, 112

Tardieu, Michel 117n68, 118n70, 119n77, 121n89
Teppler, Yaakov 75n21
Thomas, Samuel Isaac 77n25
Thomas, Todne 182
Tigchelaar, Eibert 106n8, 108n15, 115, 156n18
Tite, Philip L. 19n29, 19n32, 21n39, 21n48, 22n50, 23n56, 24n60, 27
Tolkien, J. R. R. 236n25
Tomashevsky, Boris 227n4
Towers, Susanna 111n38
Trapp, M. B. 51n48
Trebay, Guy 13n1
Tregelles, Samuel Prideaeux 2
Trzaskoma, S. M. 53n59
Tubach, Jürgen 114n50, 115n53
Turner, Eric Gardner 152n4, 154n7

Ullucci, Daniel 206n13

Vaught, Curtis 132n20
Vayntrub, Jacqueline 4n10
Vilborg, Ebbe 46n33
Visotzsky, Burton 77n24

Walsh, Robyn Faith 5n12, 28n80, 29n85, 34n102, 86–87
Ward III, H. Clifton 86n2
Wasserman, Tommy 169n41, 170, 171n48
Wasserstrom, Steven M. 117n65
Watson, Francis 96n43, 208n17, 209n20, 210n23, 211n26, 213n32, 215n38, 217n42
Watson, Steven 13n2
Wendt, Heidi 86n3
White, Peter 90n21

Whitmarsh, Tim 40n7, 41n9, 42n13, 43n15, 44n19, 45n28, 46n31, 48, 50n45, 51n49, 63n101
Wilkins, John 87n4
Williams, Francis E. 92n29
Wilson, Stephen G. 154n9
Winkler, J. J. 44n19
Wolf, Friedrich August 226
Wollenberg, Rebecca Scharbach 74n20, 81n29

Wright, Benjamin 5n12, 72n6, 155n12, 156n14
Wyrick, Jed 4n10

Yadin-Israel, Azzan 89n17
Yunis, Harvey 51n51, 52n55

Zandee, Jan 127n2, 134–35, 137n34, 141, 142n51, 144n57

Index of Subjects

anonymity 3, 5, 40–41, 43, 45, 49, 53, 55–56, 58–59, 64, 203–4, 206, 225
anonymous 2, 5, 13, 25, 32, 40, 44–46, 56, 206, 225
Apocalypse of Adam 123
Apocalypse of Enoch 123
Apocalypse of Enosh 123
Apocalypse of Sethel 123
Apocalypse of Shem 123
apocrypha 18, 33, 135
apocryphal 17, 22, 24n60, 64, 93, 112, 135
Apocryphon of Ezekiel 7, 151–52, 154–56, 158, 159n22
attribution 1–2, 4–5, 7–9, 13n1, 20, 22, 25–26, 30–31, 55, 64, 71, 98, 127–28, 134–37, 145–47, 151, 172, 177, 179, 181, 186, 189, 203–7, 209, 212n30, 214n35, 219, 225–26, 228–34, 237–38
authentic 5, 13, 16–17, 94, 115–16, 177, 186
authenticity 4n8, 8, 17, 24, 26n72, 30–31, 59, 72, 94, 115, 130n10, 136n31, 182, 204n4
author-function 1, 3, 29, 63, 71, 88, 92n28, 97–98, 128, 179–81, 183–86, 189–90, 194, 197n35, 198, 200, 205, 214n35
authorial fiction 1, 6, 39, 41, 53, 64, 85, 88–89, 91–92, 96–99, 177, 180, 186, 188, 190, 200, 226, 234–37
authority 4, 7, 16, 23, 24n59, 27, 40, 42–43, 47–52, 54–61, 63–64, 73n17, 80, 87, 89n17, 105, 107, 109–10, 113–14, 121–23, 128, 136, 182, 210, 213n32, 230, 232

Book of Elchasai 117

Donation of Constantine 226

Exaltation of Inana 8, 227

fictional 24n60, 46, 50, 63, 74n20, 75, 93, 97–98
fictive 6–7, 26–27, 85, 88, 93, 96–99, 178, 180–83, 186n23, 189–90, 193–94, 196–97, 199–200, 205
Filastrius of Brescia, *Diversarum haereseon liber* 18
forgery 16–17, 18n27, 19n32, 20n35, 24–25, 73n13, 128, 146, 214n35, 226, 234

genre 6, 22–23, 25–26, 29, 53, 71, 75, 111, 113, 120, 127, 137, 160, 205
Gilgamesh 8, 26–27
Gregory the Great, *Moralia* 20n37

Haimo of Auxerre, *In Epistolam ad Colossenses* 20
Homer 23, 29, 31, 55, 146, 168n39, 225–28, 233
Homer, *Iliad* 50, 225, 227
Homer, *Odyssey* 225, 227

John of Salisbury, *Epistulae* 20

Letter to Edessa 123
literary culture 52n54, 94n36, 211n29
Living Gospel 122
Longus, *Daphnis and Chloe* 44

Martial, *Epigrams* 187n24
Muratorian Fragment 18

narrator 41–46, 49–52, 55–60, 63, 145

Oracles of Hystaspes 118
Ovid 2, 47

Paraphrase of Shem 127
Plato, *Symposium* 44n22
Pliny the Younger, *Epistles* 187n24
Prayer of the Apostle Paul (NHC I,1) 99

258   Index of Subjects

pseudepigrapha 8, 14–16, 24–30, 32–33, 106, 108, 112, 114, 151, 159, 172
pseudepigraphal 151
pseudepigraphic 6, 15, 17, 24–28, 31, 40, 71–72, 74–75, 79, 81, 105, 121, 128, 130, 133, 147, 207, 218–19, 230, 232–34, 237
pseudepigraphy 4–5, 71–73, 97n45, 128, 146, 152, 226, 233–34, 236, 238
(Pseudo-)Augustine, *Speculum* 19n31
pseudonymity 3, 25
pseudonymous 2, 24n60, 129, 135, 203

reader 3, 6–7, 9, 21, 23n57, 24n61, 25, 28, 30, 42, 54–55, 71–81, 85–87, 91–92, 94–99, 128, 130, 132–33, 138–43, 158–59, 166, 171, 186, 203–7, 212, 215n36, 218–19, 225–26, 228–30, 232, 235–36

readership 21, 85, 88, 89, 95, 99
reading culture 72–73, 81, 85–86, 87n7, 89n18, 90–91, 98–99
reception 6–7, 16–17, 20, 25–26, 28, 32, 39–42, 53, 64, 107, 204n6, 205n9, 206n13, 213n32, 225–27, 229

Second Treatise of Great Seth 127
Sentences of Sextus 134
Shābuhragān 7, 105, 107–13, 116–17, 120, 122

Tacitus, *Annals* 197n34
Theodoret 17n19, 18
Three Steles of Seth 127

Vergil 2, 14n6, 23, 26n69, 26n71